OMNIBUS

A LONG TIME AGO. . . .

VOLUME TWO

DARK HORSE BOOKS®

cover illustration Al Williamson
publisher Mike Richardson
series editors Danny Fingeroth, Archie Goodwin, Louise Jones, and Jim Shooter
collection editor Randy Stradley
assistant editor Freddye Lins
collection designer Stephen Reichert

special thanks to Jann Moorhead, David Anderman, Troy Alders, Leland Chee, Sue Rostoni, and Carol Roeder at Lucas Licensing

Star Wars® Omnibus: A Long Time Ago. . . . Volume Two

This volume collects Marvel Star Wars issues #28–#49 and Star Wars King Size Annual #1.

Published by Dark Horse Books
A division of Dark Horse Comics, Inc.
10956 SE Main Street
Milwaukie, OR 97222

darkhorse.com | starwars.com

To find a comics shop in your area, call the Comic Shop Locator Service toll-free at 1-888-266-4226

publisher Mike Richardson • executive vice president Neil Hankerson • chief financial officer Tom Weddle • vice president of publishing Randy Stradley • vice president of business development Michael Martens • vice president of marketing, sales, and licensing Anita Nelson • vice president of product development David Scroggy • vice president of information technology Dale LaFountain • director of purchasing Darlene Vogel • general counsel Ken Lizzi • editorial director Davey Estrada • senior managing editor Scott Allie • senior books editor Chris Warner • executive editor Diana Schutz • director of design and production Cary Grazzini • art director Lia Ribacchi • director of scheduling Cara Niece

Library of Congress Cataloging-in-Publication Data

Star Wars omnibus. A long time ago / writers, Archie Goodwin ... [et al.] ; artists, Howard Chaykin ... [et al.] ; colorists, Janice Cohen ... [et al.]. -- 1st ed.
    v. cm.
ISBN 978-1-59582-486-8 (v. 1)
1. Comic books, strips, etc. I. Goodwin, Archie. II. Dark Horse Comics. III. Title: Long time ago.
PN6728.S73S7336 2010
741.5'973--dc22
                        2010000142

Printed at Midas Printing International, Ltd., Huizhou, China

First edition: October 2010
ISBN 978-1-59582-554-4

10 9 8 7 6 5 4 3 2 1

CONTENTS

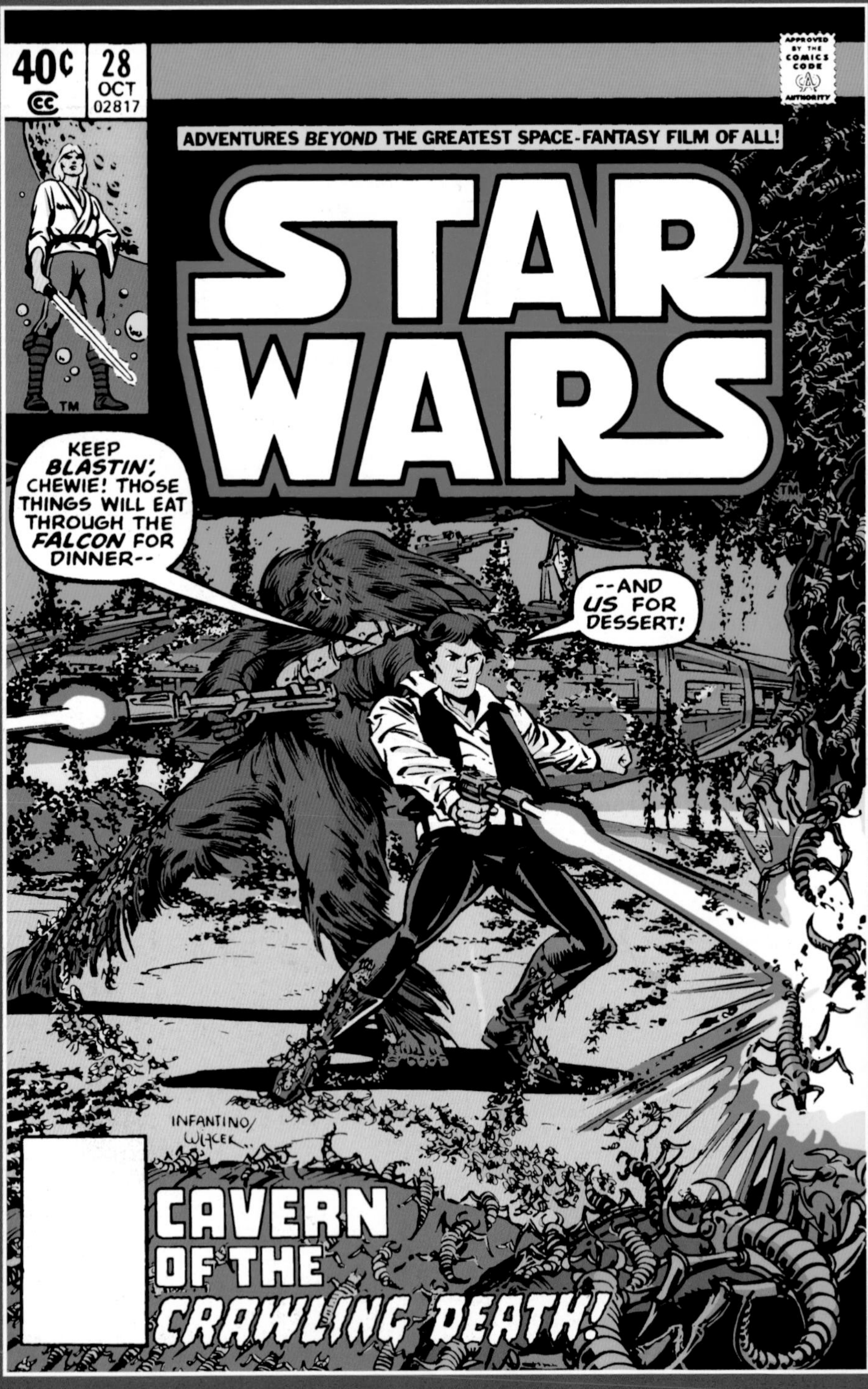
40¢
28
OCT
02817
APPROVED BY THE COMICS CODE AUTHORITY
ADVENTURES BEYOND THE GREATEST SPACE-FANTASY FILM OF ALL!
STAR WARS
KEEP BLASTIN', CHEWIE! THOSE THINGS WILL EAT THROUGH THE FALCON FOR DINNER--
--AND US FOR DESSERT!
INFANTINO/ WIACEK
CAVERN OF THE CRAWLING DEATH!

Long ago in a galaxy far, far away. . .there exists a state of cosmic *civil war*. A brave alliance of *underground freedom fighters* has challenged the tyranny and oppression of the awesome *Galactic Empire*. This is their story!

LucasFilm PRESENTS: STAR WARS™ THE GREATEST SPACE FANTASY OF ALL!

CONTINUING THE SAGA BEGUN IN THE FILM BY GEORGE LUCAS RELEASED BY TWENTIETH CENTURY-FOX

ARCHIE GOODWIN WRITER/EDITOR • CARMINE INFANTINO & GENE DAY ARTISTS • JOHN COSTANZA LETTERER • GLYNIS WEIN COLORIST • JIM SHOOTER CONSULTING EDITOR

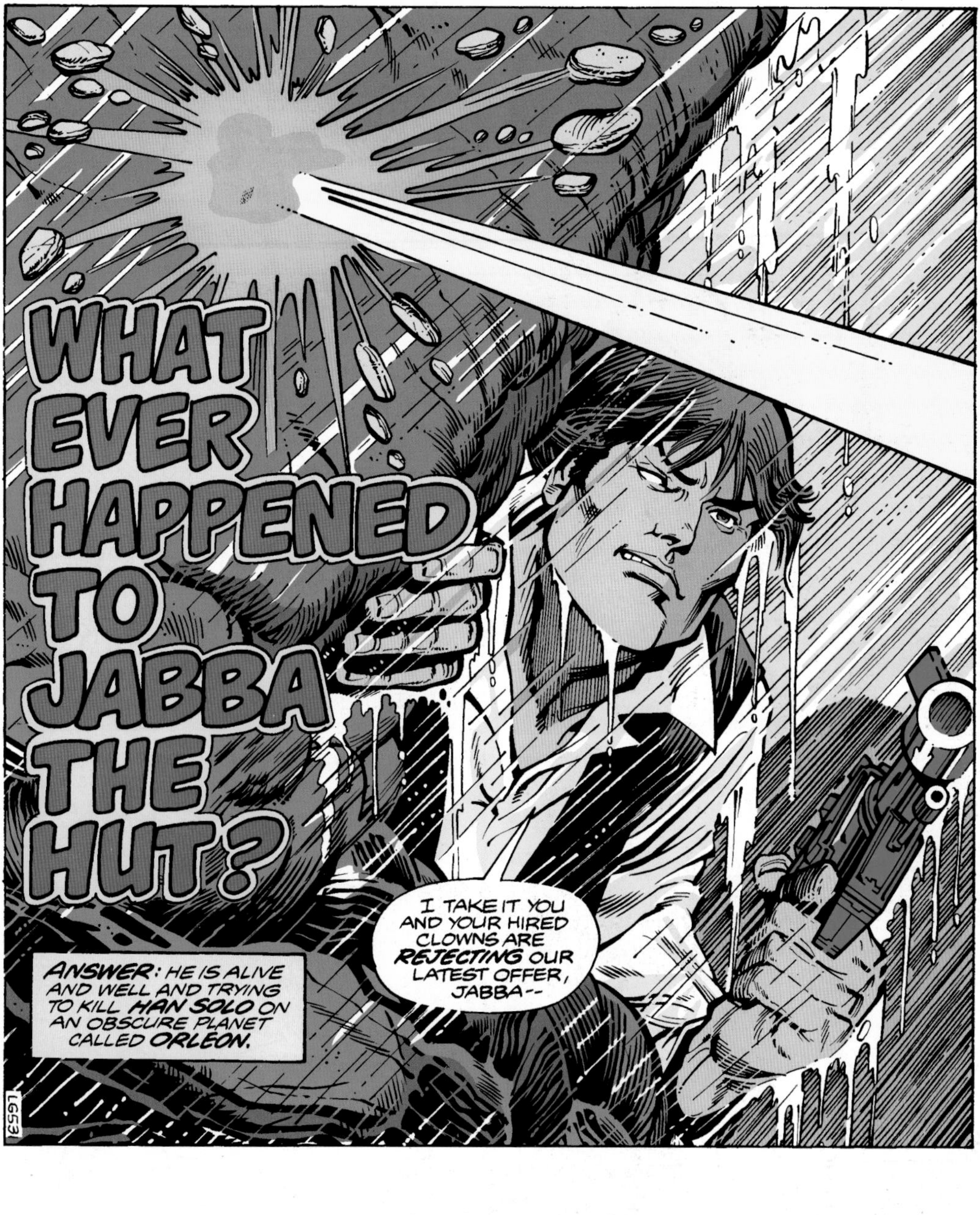
WHAT EVER HAPPENED TO JABBA THE HUT?
ANSWER: HE IS ALIVE AND WELL AND TRYING TO KILL HAN SOLO ON AN OBSCURE PLANET CALLED ORLEON.
I TAKE IT YOU AND YOUR HIRED CLOWNS ARE REJECTING OUR LATEST OFFER, JABBA--

--NEXT TIME JUST A SIMPLE 'NO' WILL DO!

VA-WUM

A WEEK IN THE RAIN HASN'T DONE A *THING* FOR JABBA'S *DISPOSITION.*

WAIT'LL HE FINDS OUT THIS IS ORLEON'S *DRY SEASON!*

FORGET THE REPAIRS AND GRAB YOUR *BLASTER,* CHEWIE! NEGOTIATIONS JUST *BROKE DOWN* AGAIN!

YOU'RE GETTING TIRED OF THIS--?

BORRKK!

THINK OF THE WAY *I* FEEL! THE BLASTED CAVE HAS SPRUNG A LOT OF *LEAKS* SINCE WE LAST USED IT AS A *HIDE-OUT*--

AND DO YOU KNOW HOW *BAD* WET WOOKIEE FUR *SMELLS?*

ABOUT *HALF* AS BAD AS WET *HUMAN* HAIR AND CLOTHING...?

OAAARRRK!

WELL, MAYBE I *DID* SPEAK OUT OF TURN. LIVING IN THIS *ROCKPILE* HASN'T DONE MUCH FOR MY *NERVES.*

BUT RIGHT NOW--

6

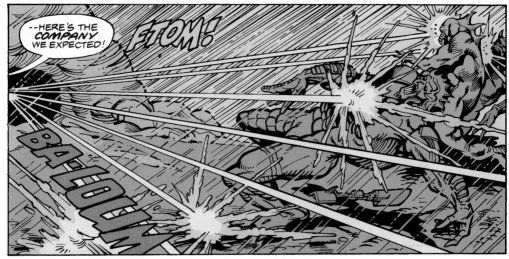

--HERE'S THE *COMPANY* WE EXPECTED!

FTOM!

BALOOM

HOW MANY DID WE LOSE *THIS* TIME?

ONLY *SKUD*, JABBA. BUT IF YOU'D JUST LET US ATTACK *FULL FORCE* WITH *PROTON GRENADES,* WE COULD--

DESTROY THE *MILLENNIUM FALCON* ALONG WITH HAN SOLO AND CHEWBACCA!

CAN'T ANY OF YOU *THUGS* UNDERSTAND THAT I'M A *BUSINESS MAN...?*

HAN HAS FAILED TO REPAY A VERY *LARGE DEBT* RUN UP WHILE SMUGGLING *SPICE* IN MY SERVICE--*

THAT JUSTIFIES HIS *DEATH,* BUT THERE'S NO *PROFIT* IN DESTROYING THE BEST *SPICE FREIGHTER--*

--TO EVER MAKE THE *KESSEL RUN!* NOT WHEN TIME-- AND THE *ODDS*-- ARE ON *OUR* SIDE!

*A BIT OF ANCIENT HISTORY FROM *STAR WARS #2.* -- ARCHIVIST ARCHIE.

7

NUTRIENT PASTE--! FOR A MAN USED TO PRIME SAND LIZARD STEAK AND FIVE YEAR OLD SPICE WINE!

IF WE'RE DOWN TO THIS STUFF... OUR SITUATION'S WORSE THAN I THOUGHT!

BLAST IT! A FEW MORE ROTATIONS OF THIS MUD BALL AND WE'LL BE BEGGING JABBA TO BLAST US SO WE DON'T HAVE TO STARVE!

HOW'D I MANAGE TO GET US INTO SUCH A DUMB SPOT...?!

IT BEGAN WITH AN ESCAPE... FROM THE GREAT GALACTIC GAMBLING CENTER KNOWN AS THE WHEEL, AND FROM THE DARK LORD OF THE SITH, DARTH VADER!

THAT MONSTER'S GOT US DEAD IN ITS SIGHTS... BUT IT'S NOT FIRIN'! *

I NEVER LOOK A GIFT MIRACLE IN THE MOUTH, CHEWIE--

--WE'RE MAKIN' THE JUMP TO HYPER-SPACE BEFORE SOMEONE COMES TO THEIR SENSES!

* DUE TO LORD VADER SUDDENLY EXPERIENCING FEEDBACK OF THE FORCE. SEE STAR WARS #23 FOR THE FULL STORY. --ARCHIE.

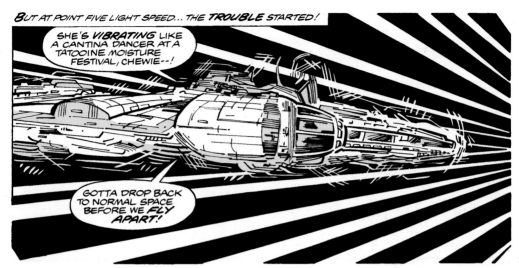

SHE'S *VIBRATING* LIKE A CANTINA DANCER AT A TATOOINE MOISTURE FESTIVAL, CHEWIE--!

GOTTA DROP BACK TO NORMAL SPACE BEFORE WE *FLY APART!*

HRONK!

YEAH, I WAS THINKIN' THE *SAME* THING.

WHEN THOSE WHEEL TECHNOS THREW THE FALCON BACK TOGETHER AFTER *STRIPPING* AND *SEARCHING* IT--*

* SHOWN IN SW *#19.*--ARCH.

--THEY MUST HAVE LEFT SOMETHING *OUT!* BUT NO PROBLEM, BIG BUDDY--

CHECK THE NAVIGATIONAL COMPUTER *READ OUT--*

--WE'RE NOT *THAT* FAR FROM *ORLEON!*

AND BY A CAREFULLY ORCHESTRATED SERIES OF SHORT HOPS IN AND OUT OF *WARP,* THE AILING SPICE FREIGHTER IS COAXED TO ITS *DESTINATION...*

AH! JUST AS MISERABLE AND *UNINVITING* AS EVER! ONE OF THE FEW PLACES IN THE MID-SYSTEMS *NO ONE* CAN STAND--

--WHICH MAKES IT THE *PERFECT PLACE* FOR A COUPLE OF SHREWD SPICE SMUGGLERS TO HAVE AN *EMERGENCY STATION,* EH, CHEWIE?

BUT AS THE FALCON TOUCHED DOWN AND TAXIED INTO THE MOUNTAIN CAVERN THAT WAS THEIR OLD HIDEAWAY...

...NEITHER OF THE 'SHREWD SPICE SMUGGLERS' NOTICED AN ADDITION TO THE EQUIPMENT STORED INSIDE.

UNTIL...

VISITORS ARRIVING ON THE MUD PLAIN, CHEWIE! WHY WOULD ANYBODY--

WARRK!

BLAST IT... YOU'RE RIGHT! THAT'S THE VOIDRAKER...JABBA THE HUT'S PERSONAL FREIGHTER!

WELL, HAN, MY BOY...! THIS MOMENT HAS BEEN DREADFULLY LONG COMING.

I DIDN'T TRULY EXPECT YOU'D DARE VISIT THIS OLD HAUNT... BUT I INSTALLED A BUG TO ALERT ME JUST IN CASE!

SINCE THIS SAVES ME THE PRICE OF THE BOUNTY I'VE POSTED...I'VE ORDERED MY LADS TO GIVE YOU A SWIFT, DIGNIFIED DEATH.

THE CORELLIAN SKIPPER AND HIS MATE COUNTERED WITH A LONG, DESPERATE SIEGE!

VORRP!

YEAH, YEAH! WE'VE HELD OUT LONG ENOUGH TO HAVE THE FALCON BACK IN SOMETHING LIKE FLYING SHAPE.

BUT THE VOIDRAKER'S GUNS CAN NAIL US BEFORE WE EVEN--

CHEWIE--! BACK HERE... FAST!

FTOOM! FTOOM! VOW!

WURGUH!

NO, I HAVEN'T GONE *CAVE HAPPY.*

BUT IT'D BE *BETTER* IF I *WERE* IMAGINING THINGS!

I SPOTTED *THIS* CRAWLING ON THAT *FOOD TIN* I THREW AWAY EARLIER, PAL--

--IT'S A *STONE MITE!* THEY'RE THE *ULTIMATE SCAVENGERS!*

AN OLD TIMER TOLD ME ABOUT 'EM... THEY'RE A *BIOLOGICAL WEAPON* DEVELOPED DURING THE CLONE WARS.

THEIR BODIES MANUFACTURE AN *ACID* THAT ENABLES 'EM TO EAT THROUGH *ANYTHING!*

LOOK WHAT THIS *ONE* DID TO THAT TIN--

--AND THEY USUALLY MOVE IN *SWARMS!* THOUSANDS...MAYBE MILLIONS... SPECIALLY CREATED TO DEVOUR A PLANET'S *MINERAL RESOURCES.*

THEY MOSTLY TRAVEL THROUGH *SHEER ROCK*...FEEDING ON ANY VEINS OF *ORE!*

NARRLL!

RIGHT! THAT SCARES *ME,* TOO! IF OUR OLD HIDEOUT HAS SUDDENLY SPRUNG SOME *LEAKS*...IT MIGHT JUST BE *INFESTED* WITH THOSE LITTLE MONSTERS!

GET TO THE *FALCON*...! BEFORE IT BECOMES A *MAIN COURSE*... AND YOU AN' ME THE *DESSERT!*

11

BUT, AS THE PAIR *NEAR* THEIR SHIP...!

JABBA'S *GOONS* ARE HITTING THE *ENTRANCE* AGAIN--!

PA-VOOM! BA-DOW!

AND THEY'RE *NOT SPARING* THE PROTON GRENADES!

ROOWRP!

I *SEE* IT, CHEWIE...! THE *FORCE* OF THOSE *BLASTS* HAS STARTED A *CRACK* IN THE CAVERN CEILING--

IT'S TRAVELING *BACK...* TOWARD THE *FALCON!*

MOVE! BEFORE THE WHOLE *WORKS* COLLAPSES!

MEANWHILE...

LOOKS LIKE WE WERE *RIGHT* TO DISOBEY JABBA AND USE THOSE *GRENADES.* THE CAVE'S STILL STANDING--

--AND CHEWBACCA AND SOLO WOULDN'T LET US GET THIS *CLOSE* UNLESS THEY WERE *DEAD!*

NO! THERE'D BE *SOME* TRACES OF THEIR BODIES.

THEY'VE RETREATED BACK INTO THE *CAVERN*--

STAY CLOSE TO THE *WALLS* AND MOVE *IN* ON THEM!

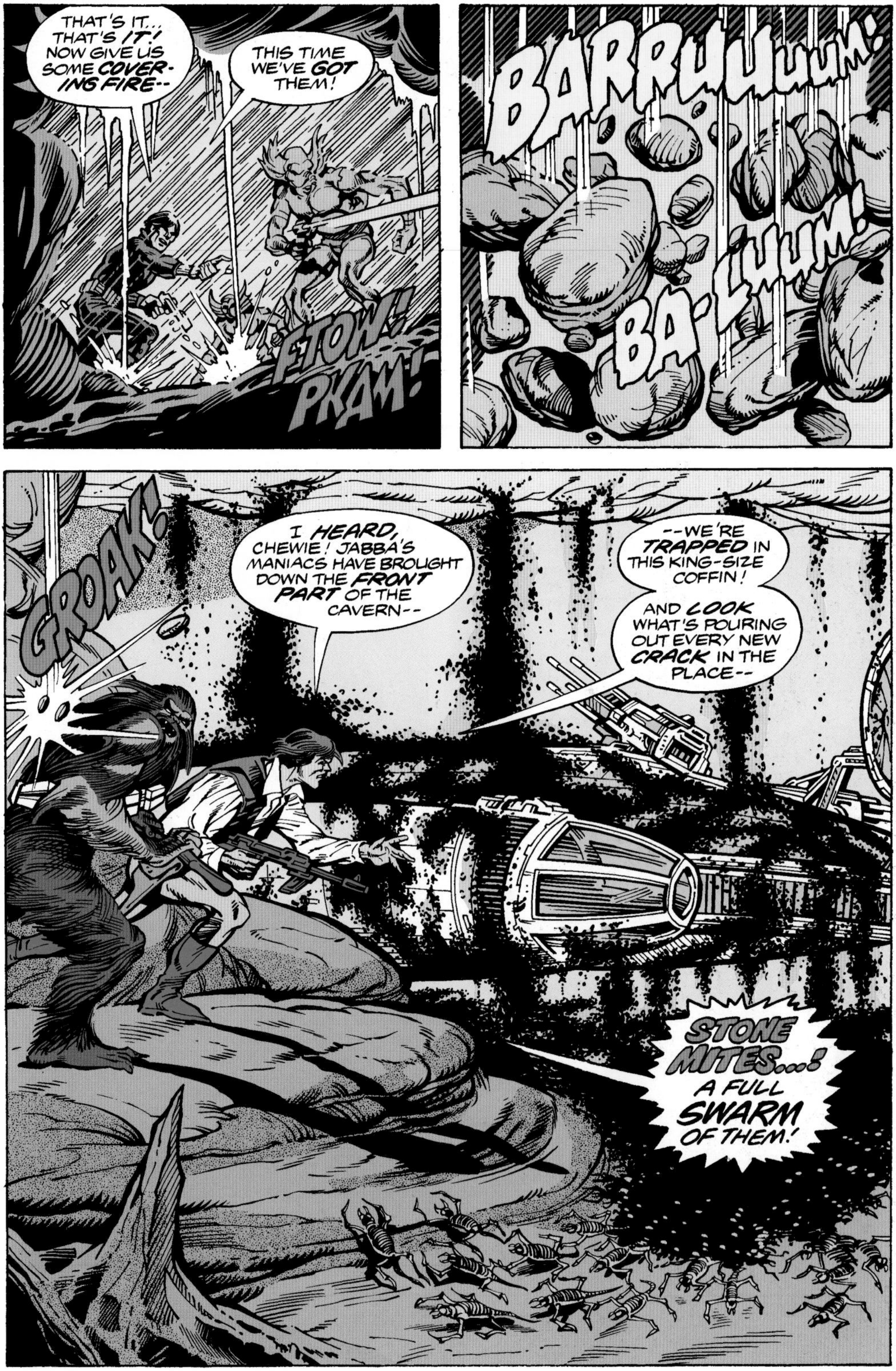
THAT'S IT.. THAT'S IT! NOW GIVE US SOME COVERING FIRE--
THIS TIME WE'VE GOT THEM!
FTOW! PKAM!
BARRUUUUM!
BA-LUUM!
GROAK!
I HEARD, CHEWIE! JABBA'S MANIACS HAVE BROUGHT DOWN THE FRONT PART OF THE CAVERN--
--WE'RE TRAPPED IN THIS KING-SIZE COFFIN!
AND LOOK WHAT'S POURING OUT EVERY NEW CRACK IN THE PLACE--
STONE MITES...! A FULL SWARM OF THEM!

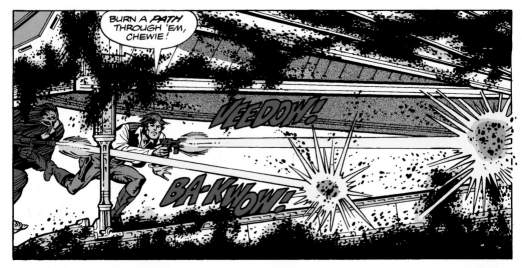

BURN A *PATH* THROUGH 'EM, CHEWIE!

VEEDOW!

BA-KWOW!

ROWRP!

JUST MOVE UP THE *RAMP* SO WE CAN *SEAL OFF* THE SHIP!

THERE'LL BE TIME *LATER* TO COMPLAIN ABOUT HOW MUCH TINY CRAWLING THINGS GIVE YOU THE *CREEPS*... AT LEAST, I *HOPE* THERE WILL!

OKAY, BIG BUDDY...! MAKE SURE WE DIDN'T CARRY ANY OF 'EM *ABOARD*... THEN START THE *ENGINES*!

LET 'EM RUN *ROUGH*... BUT HOLD TO A DEAD *HOVER*.

WITH *LUCK*, YOU CAN SHAKE *OFF* SOME OF THOSE LITTLE DEVILS WITHOUT BRINGING THE *MOUNTAIN* DOWN ON TOP OF US!

MEANWHILE, I'M GOING TO TRY TO DO SOME FAST *CONVERSION* WORK... BEFORE THEY EAT THROUGH THE *HULL*!

FRRRROOOMM!

14

WHILE ON ORLEON'S RAIN-LASHED MUD PLAIN... THE *VOIDRAKER* PREPARES TO DEPART. WHEN...

JABBA, I'M *GETTING* SOMETHING ON THE SCANNER... THE *FALCON'S* ENGINES, I BELIEVE.

THEN SOLO STILL *SURVIVES* WITHIN THAT GREAT STONE RUBBLE--

--THOSE FOOLS ONLY BURIED *THEMSELVES,* NOT HIM AND THE WOOKIEE! WHAT'S *WRONG* WITH THIS GALAXY THAT A SMUGGLING LORD CAN'T BUY COMPETENT *HELP?!*

AND WHAT'S THAT CRAZY *CORELLIAN* UP TO...? THERE'S *NO WAY* HIS SHIP CAN BLAST OUT OF THAT MOUNTAIN--

--NOT THROUGH *SOLID ROCK* THICK ENOUGH TO WITHSTAND AN *IMPERIAL BOMBARDMENT!*

ORDER OUT EVERY *HAND*... I MEAN TO SETTLE *ACCOUNTS* WITH SOLO ONCE AND FOREVER!

AND SOON...

MOSTLY *LOOSE ROCK* BLOCKING THE ENTRANCE, JABBA... THE *LASER-BORER* WILL BE THROUGH IT IN SECONDS!

THERE'S SOMETHING ON THE *SCOPE* ALREADY...!

I-IT'S... ONE OF *OURS*...! BUT *WHAT...?*

STONE MITES! BACK TO THE SHIP... BACK!

AND BACK AT THE MILLENNIUM FALCON...

NARRRGH

YOU DON'T HAVE TO CONVINCE *ME*, PAL... I CAN TELL BY THE HULL *SENSORS!*

THOSE LITTLE DEMONS ARE HANGIN' ON LIKE SARGONIAN *BEHEMOTH TICKS!*

WHICH MEANS IT'S *CAST RESORT* TIME....!

IF I DID EVERYTHING *RIGHT*, OUR *DE-ICING SYSTEM* SHOULD NOW BE DRAWING POWER FROM THE *MAIN REACTOR*--

KLIK!

FULL HOVER POWER, CHEWIE! LET'S SEE HOW OUR UNWANTED *GUESTS* FEEL ABOUT HAVING THEIR *FOOD* FRY *THEM!*

HSSSSSST!

IT'S *WORKING...!* WE'RE GENERATING ENOUGH *HEAT* THROUGH THE HULL PLATING TO *SCORCH* 'EM OFF!

ALL WE HAVE TO *DO* IS KEEP IT *UP!*

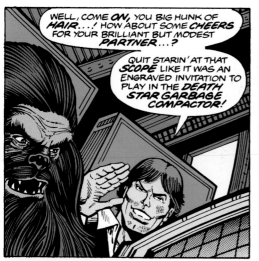

WELL, COME *ON*, YOU BIG HUNK OF *HAIR*...! HOW ABOUT SOME *CHEERS* FOR YOUR BRILLIANT BUT MODEST *PARTNER*...?

QUIT STARIN' AT THAT *SCOPE* LIKE IT WAS AN ENGRAVED INVITATION TO PLAY IN THE *DEATH STAR GARBAGE COMPACTOR*!

HEY! LEMME *SEE* THAT! W-WHAT...?

THE ENTIRE *MOUNTAIN* MUST BE *HONEY-COMBED* BY THOSE MISERABLE, EVER-MULTIPLYIN' *STONE MITES*! THEY'RE DROPPING *ON* US FASTER THAN WE'RE BURNIN' 'EM *OFF*!

MORE *POWER*, CHEWIE...! WE GOTTA FEED THE *DE-ICERS* MORE--

PA-KWOM!

THE SYSTEMS CAN'T *TAKE* IT... ALL MY CONVERSION MODULES ARE *BLOWING*!

BLADDX!

SHUT 'ER *DOWN*, CHEWIE...! BEFORE THE WHOLE *CABIN* GOES!

BLAST IT...! WE MADE DARTH VADER AND THE WHOLE EMPIRE LOOK *SILLY* WITH THIS SHIP!

HOW CAN A BUNCH OF MINDLESS, MUNCHIN' *INSECTS* BE THE ONES TO *DESTROY* IT?!

WAIT A MINUTE! BUMP US UP TO A BROADER BAND ON THIS SCANNER, CHEWIE--

I WANNA DO SOME PROBIN' *BEYOND* THE FALCON.

MAYBE... *MAYBE*...

FIRE 'ER *UP* AGAIN, CHEWIE...! ONLY *THIS* TIME WE WON'T USE THE *DE-ICING* SYSTEM.

OKAY! I'M AT THE MAIN GUNS, PAL. WHEN I START *SHOOTING*--

ARRK!

--TAKE OFF!

PTOM! PTOM! BVOM!

AND IN THE SHATTERING EXPLOSION OF FLYING STONE... *THE MILLENNIUM FALCON BURSTS* FREE *OF ITS SEEMINGLY* INES- CAPABLE *MOUNTAIN PRISON!*

WE *DID* IT, BIG BUDDY... WE *DID* IT!

OUR TINY *FRIENDS* MAY HAVE CAUSED US A LOT OF *GRIEF*... BUT WE COULDN'T HAVE *BUSTED LOOSE* WITHOUT 'EM! INSTEAD OF A ROOF OF *SOLID ROCK* ABOVE US--

THE STONE MITES HAD REDUCED THAT SECTION I BLASTED TO A *HOLLOW SHELL!*

VROWWK!!

WATTA YA *MEAN*, WHY DIDN'T I CHECK THE SCANNER *EARLIER* TO FIND THAT OUT...?

WHY DIDN'T *YOU?*

JUST BE GLAD THE HEAT OF HITTING *ESCAPE VELOCITY* IS TAKING THOSE NASTY LITTLE BUGGERS OFF *PERMANENTLY!*

FROM NOW ON THERE'S NOTHING AHEAD OF US BUT *CLEAR SAILIN'* AND--

JABBA'S *VOIDRAKER!!*

ACTIVATE ALL *SHIELDS*, CHEWIE... FAST!

THAT GREEDY BLOODSUCKER HAS CAUGHT US *FLAT-FOOTED!*

HARSH *WORDS*, HAN--

-- PARTICULARLY SINCE I'VE ALMOST *FATHERLY FEELINGS* ABOUT YOU, MY BOY.

TRUE... I *SUBDUED* THEM SOMEWHAT DOWN ON ORLEON.

BUT AWAY FROM *THAT* PLACE'S DREARY ATMOSPHERE... I FEEL MORE *FORGIVING*. AS PROOF--

--YOU WILL NOTE THAT DESPITE A SUPERIOR *POSITION*, I HAVEN'T *OPENED FIRE* ON YOU.

I NOTE YOU'VE OPENED FIRE ON *SOMETHING*, JABBA...THAT'S A *BLASTER* I HEAR.

AIRLOCK

YOU'RE NOT HAVING A *PROBLEM*, ARE YOU?

LET'S *SEE*...IT *COULDN'T* BE MUTINY. YOUR BRAND OF HIRED HELP ISN'T THAT *INTELLIGENT*.

NOW WHAT WOULD BE *BAD* ENOUGH TO DRIVE YOU OFF ORLEON WITHOUT EVEN MAKING CERTAIN CHEWIE AND ME WERE *DEAD*...?

STONE MITES, YOU CORELLIAN CONNIVER! ONE OF MY DOLTISH CREW LET THEM GET INTO A *LASER-BORER* HE BROUGHT BACK TO THE SHIP!

NOW THEY'RE *EVERYWHERE*... DESTROYING *EVERYTHING*!

I'M THE ONLY ONE *LEFT*, HAN... YOU'VE GOT TO TAKE ME *ABOARD*!

IF YOU'RE ALL DONE BLUFFING...MY *PLEASURE*, JABBA! JET ON OVER TO THE FALCON!

THAT'S WHAT I *ALWAYS* LIKED ABOUT YOU, HAN, MY BOY... THERE ISN'T A *VINDIC-TIVE BONE* IN YOUR BODY.

RIGHT, JABBA. CHEWIE AN' ME DON'T *BELIEVE* IN GETTING EVEN--

ROART!

-- WE LIKE TO COME OUT *AHEAD!*

SO ALONG *WITH* THE GENEROUS OFFER YOU NO DOUBT PLAN TO MAKE CANCELING MY *DEBT* AND THE *PRICE* ON OUR HEADS--

-- I'M SURE YOU'LL INCLUDE A *BONUS* FOR OUR TIME AND TROUBLE. YOU KNOW...LIKE OPENING *AIRLOCKS* AN' THE LIKE.

BUT NO NEED TO *RUSH*, JABBA...YOU MUST HAVE AT *LEAST* TWO HOURS BREATHING TIME IN THAT ARMOR.

UNLESS A FEW *STONE MITES* GOT TO IT BEFORE YOU ABANDONED SHIP!

JABBA THE HUT STARTS TO *CURSE*... THEN SHRUGS AND RELUC-TANTLY *SMILES.*

MENTALLY HE CALCULATES A LIKELY *OFFER*, AUTOMATICALLY CUTS IT IN *HALF*, ELECTS TO WAIT AN HOUR TO MAKE IT LOOK *GOOD...*

...AND BEGINS PLANNING FOR *ANOTHER* DAY, WHEN *HE'LL* HAVE THE UPPER-HAND.

BUT MEANTIME, *DARTH VADER* IS ALSO PLANNING, AS WILL BE SHOWN *NEXT ISSUE* IN...

DARK ENCOUNTER

40¢
CC
29
NOV
02817

ADVENTURES *BEYOND* THE GREATEST SPACE-FANTASY FILM OF ALL!

STAR WARS

™

INFANTINO/
WACEK

DARK
ENCOUNTER!

Long ago in a galaxy far, far away. . .there exists a state of cosmic *civil war*. A brave alliance of *underground freedom fighters* has challenged the tyranny and oppression of the awesome *Galactic Empire*. This is their story!

LucasFilm PRESENTS: **STAR WARS**™ THE GREATEST SPACE FANTASY OF ALL!

CONTINUING THE SAGA BEGUN IN THE FILM *BY* **GEORGE LUCAS** *RELEASED BY* **TWENTIETH CENTURY-FOX**

ARCHIE GOODWIN WRITER/EDITOR * **CARMINE INFANTINO** & **BOB WIACEK** ARTISTS * **JOHN COSTANZA** LETTERER * **GLYNIS WEIN** COLORIST * **JIM SHOOTER** CONSULTING ED.

DARK ENCOUNTER

...DARTH VADER, LORD OF THE SITH.

THE ABILITY TO *RESIST* IS ALWAYS *FASCINATING,* EH, WERMIS?

IT VARIES *ENDLESSLY* FROM INDIVIDUAL TO INDIVIDUAL.

THIS *SPY* WAS BETTER AT IT THAN *AVERAGE,* WOULDN'T YOU SAY?

I--I WONDER...IF I MIGHT BE *EXCUSED,* LORD VADER...? I SEEM TO HAVE A TOUCH OF...*INDIGESTION.*

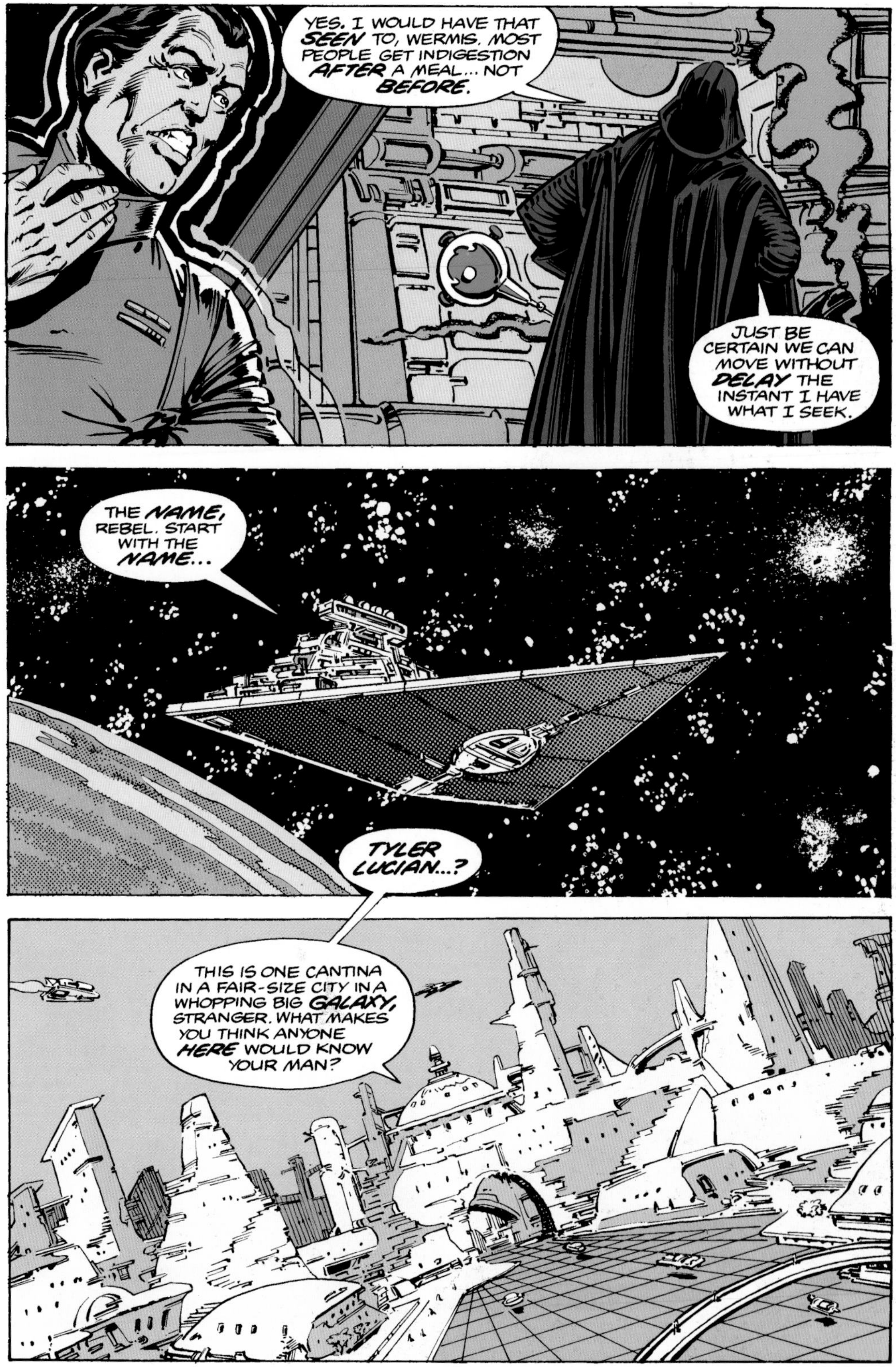
YES. I WOULD HAVE THAT SEEN TO, WERMIS. MOST PEOPLE GET INDIGESTION AFTER A MEAL... NOT BEFORE.
JUST BE CERTAIN WE CAN MOVE WITHOUT DELAY THE INSTANT I HAVE WHAT I SEEK.
THE NAME, REBEL. START WITH THE NAME...
TYLER LUCIAN...?
THIS IS ONE CANTINA IN A FAIR-SIZE CITY IN A WHOPPING BIG GALAXY, STRANGER. WHAT MAKES YOU THINK ANYONE HERE WOULD KNOW YOUR MAN?

BECAUSE IN ADDITION TO RUNNING *THIS* DINGY ESTABLISHMENT, YOU *HIDE* PEOPLE, MERL... FOR A *PRICE*.

AND TYLER LUCIAN HAS *GOOD REASON* TO HIDE... HE'S A *DESERTER* FROM THE REBEL ALLIANCE.

STRANGER, IF *ANY* OF WHAT YOU SAY IS TRUE... AIN'T IT A BIT *FOOLISH* TO GO BLURTIN' IT OUT?

THERE ISN'T *TIME* TO BE *SUBTLE*, MERL--

--AND ON YOUR TYPE IT WOULD BE *WASTED* ANYWAY!

MY *HAND!*

WRAAK!

Y-YOU... SMASHED RIGHT *THROUGH* THE BAR...! THAT'S NOT POS--

:*AAGGHHHH!*: URI... GLOCKEN...! *MOVE!* HE'S *CRUSHING* MY HAND...!

FA-KOWM!

26

ZA-DAAP!

BWOW!

NOW, *MERL*, YOU WERE ABOUT TO *TELL* ME SOMETHING.

WEREN'T YOU?

YOU... YOU'RE NOTHING *SENTIENT...!* YOU...*CAN'T...* BE...*EEEEEEEEE!*

SWIFTLY, THE CANTINA OWNER BEGINS TO TALK. A SHORT TIME LATER, THE CLOAKED FIGURE **DEPARTS,** *STEPPING OUT ONTO THE MAIN THOROUGHFARE OF CENTARES SPACE PORT'S INFAMOUS* **OLD TOWN** *SECTION. BUT AS HE STARTS ANXIOUSLY* **AWAY...**

ONE *MOMENT,* CITIZEN.

WE'VE HAD REPORTS OF A *DISTURBANCE* AT MERL'S... WHICH YOU SEEM IN A *HURRY* TO LEAVE.

TURN AROUND AND TELL US *WHY...* BUT BE *SLOW* AND *CAREFUL* ABOUT IT.

NATURALLY. THE *LAST* THING I WANT IS TROUBLE WITH *IMPERIAL TROOPERS.*

27

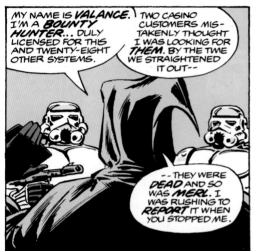

MY NAME IS *VALANCE.* I'M A *BOUNTY HUNTER...* DULY LICENSED FOR THIS AND TWENTY-EIGHT OTHER SYSTEMS.

TWO CASINO CUSTOMERS MIS-TAKENLY THOUGHT I WAS LOOKING FOR *THEM.* BY THE TIME WE STRAIGHTENED IT OUT--

--THEY WERE *DEAD* AND SO WAS *MERL.* I WAS RUSHING TO *REPORT* IT WHEN YOU STOPPED ME.

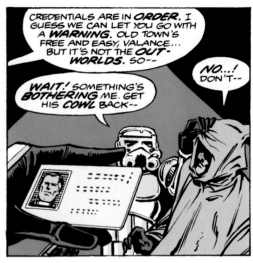

CREDENTIALS ARE IN *ORDER.* I GUESS WE CAN LET YOU GO WITH A *WARNING.* OLD TOWN'S FREE AND EASY, VALANCE... BUT IT'S NOT THE *OUT-WORLDS.* SO--

WAIT! SOMETHING'S *BOTHERING* ME. GET HIS *COWL* BACK--

NO...! DON'T--

I *THOUGHT* I SAW A GLINT OF *METAL!* HE'S--

A BORG! MISERABLE *CYBORG...* TRYING TO *PASS!*

WE CAN'T LET SOMETHING LIKE *HIM* GET AWAY WITH KILLING *NORMAL ORGANICS!*

THANK YOU, *TROOPER!* UNTIL *NOW* I DON'T THINK I WAS *CERTAIN* ABOUT MY COURSE OF ACTION--

FRAZAK!

NOW I'M *COMMITTED.* I'M IN A RACE AGAINST *DARTH VADER--*

--AND *TYLER LUCIAN* IS THE PRIZE!

IN THE DAYS OF THE OLD REPUBLIC, RUBYFLAME LAKE WAS A SPLENDID, POPULAR **RESORT**, ATTRACTING VISITORS BY THE THOUSANDS TO CENTARES FROM THROUGHOUT THE MID-SYSTEMS.

UNDER THE HAND OF THE **EMPIRE**, DEEPLY BURIED LAVA BEDS WHICH WARMED THE LAKE WERE TAPPED FOR INTENSE **INDUSTRIAL PURPOSE**...

WITHIN A DECADE, THE LAVA BEDS WERE **EXHAUSTED**. THE ONCE SPARKLING, GEM-LIKE WATERS WERE OPAQUE, CLOUDED FOREVER BY **WASTE**...

...AND ONCE ELEGANT **GUEST TOWERS** WERE FALLEN INTO RUIN AND DISUSE.

YET...THE AREA STILL ATTRACTS **SOME**. IF THEY ARE **DESPERATE**...OR WITHOUT **HOPE**.

TYLER LUCIAN IS **BOTH**...AND NO MORE SO THAN DURING THE LONG MELANCHOLY MOMENTS OF **SUNSET**.

THE POLLUTANTS IN THERE CAN DISSOLVE **METAL** IN HOURS... **FLESH** WOULD SURELY ONLY TAKE MINUTES.

ONE MORE **STEP** IS ALL IT WOULD TAKE... AN EASY **PLUNGE** INTO THOSE BLOOD RED WATERS.

BUT IF I HAD *THAT* KIND OF NERVE... I WOULDN'T HAVE FLED *YAVIN BASE* AS THE *DEATH STAR* WAS APPROACHING!

ANNIHILATION SEEMED SO *CERTAIN.* IF THERE'D BEEN A *SHRED* OF HOPE... I MIGHT HAVE HELD ON.

ONLY *AFTER* I'D STOLEN THE SUPPLY SHIP... RACED AWAY... *THEN* I HEARD ON THE TRANSCEIVER... ABOUT *HIM!*

THE T-65 PILOT WHO SHUT DOWN HIS *COMPUTER*... AND PUT A TORPEDO INTO THE DEATH STAR EXHAUST PORT *UNASSISTED!*

A MERE *FARM BOY* FROM TATOOINE... *LUKE SKYWALKER!*

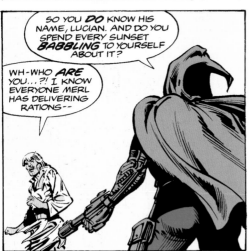

SO YOU *DO* KNOW HIS NAME, LUCIAN. AND DO YOU SPEND EVERY SUNSET *BABBLING* TO YOURSELF ABOUT IT?

WH-WHO *ARE* YOU...?! I KNOW EVERYONE MERL HAS DELIVERING RATIONS--

MERL WON'T BE *PROVIDING* ANYMORE SERVICES, LUCIAN.

AND YOU WON'T BE *NEEDING* ANY.

M-MERL *SAID* ALLIANCE SPIES WERE SEARCHING FOR ME. ARE *YOU*--?

UP 'TIL NOW, IF I FAVORED ANYONE... IT WAS THE *EMPIRE.* AFTER ALL, I USE TO *SERVE* THEM--

--UNTIL A REBEL BOMBARDMENT TURNED ME INTO SOMETHING I HATED... A *MACHINE!*

THEN... WHY ARE YOU *DOING* THIS...?!

I'VE... *VALUE* TO THE EMPIRE... WITH WHAT I *KNOW.* I'D HOPED TO JUST BE LEFT *ALONE*... BUT IF IT WILL SAVE MY *LIFE*...

YOU'RE *PITIFUL,* TYLER LUCIAN.

UNFORTUNATELY... I'M NOT *KNOWN* FOR MY PITY.

THE *TIE* FIGHTER APPEARS SUDDENLY, SCREAMING LOW OVER THE LAKE OUT OF THE SETTING SUN.

AND ITS BENT-WING SILHOUETTE, ITS SLEEK STRUCTURE, MAKE IT PLAIN IT IS NOT JUST *ANY* TIE SHIP.

DARTH VADER!

*IT IS ONLY A **MOMENT'S** DISTRACTION...*

HERE *THIS* SOON...!

*BUT A MOMENT IS FAR MORE THAN TYLER LUCIAN **THOUGHT** HE HAD...*

*HE GRASPS IT DESPERATELY, USING IT TO **RACE** FOR SANCTUARY!*

V-DOOM!

TOO *LATE*... HE'S INSIDE THE TOWER! YOU'RE A *FOOL,* VALANCE.

AND NOW YOU'RE GOING TO *DIE* FOR IT.

BUT THEN YOU'VE SUSPECTED *THAT* FOR SOME TIME... EVER SINCE YOU LET *LUKE SKYWALKER* AND *C-3PO* GET AWAY *ALIVE* BACK ON THE JUNCTION. ✳

THE HUNTER TURNS HIS BACK ON HIS PREY. AND FLINGING OFF HIS CLOAK, HE CHARGES TOWARD THE WALKWAY LEADING TO SHORE...

*...THE WAY **DARTH VADER** WILL COME.*

✳ *STAR WARS* #27--ARCHIE.

INTERLUDE: THE MAIN REBEL BASE ON THE FOURTH MOON OF THE GAS GIANT, YAVIN.

HERE, WITHIN THE GREAT STONE WALLS OF THE MASSASI RUINS... A *VIGIL* IS IN PROGRESS.

THIS IS UNFAIR... TOTALLY *UNFAIR!* A PROTOCOL DROID ISN'T EQUIPPED TO SUFFER AN EXPERIENCE LIKE THIS *ONCE*... MUCH LESS *TWICE!*

WHAT CAN BE TAKING SO *LONG...?* MASTER LUKE AND I BROUGHT BACK ALL THE *MATERIALS* THEY NEEDED.

SUPPOSE SOME OF THE PARTS WE GOT ON JUNCTION ARE *FAULTY!?*

WITH THE IMPERIAL BLOCKADE... THEY CAN'T BE EASILY *REPLACED!* MAYBE ARTOO DEETOO *CAN'T* BE REPAIRED* AS HE WAS AFTER THE BATTLE OF THE *DEATH STAR!*

*HE WAS ALMOST *FATALLY* DISABLED IN *STAR WARS #26.*--ARCH.

NO, *NO...!* I MUSTN'T *THINK* THAT! WHY, IF THEY CAN MAKE THAT LITTLE DROID *FUNCTIONAL* ONCE MORE... I'LL *NEVER* SAY A HARSH WORD TO HIM! I'LL--

BEEP-A-DEEP!

SURPRISE...?! WHY YOU UNREASONING LITTLE MOUND OF MISPLACED CIRCUITRY!

DO YOU SUPPOSE I HAVE NOTHING *BETTER* TO DO THAN IDLE ABOUT WAITING FOR *YOU* TO PLAY PRACTICAL JOKES?!

FWEE-BOOP!

JUST LIKE *OLD TIMES* AGAIN...? WHAT DO YOU *MEAN*, TWERP...?

AND AS A PERPETUAL ARGUMENT IS RESUMED OUTSIDE THE SUPPLY AND MAINTENANCE AREA...

...*OTHERS* ARE HAVING WORDS AS WELL.

HOW COULD YOU *DO* IT, GENERAL DODONNA... LET THE PRINCESS RUN OFF ON A MISSION *ALONE?!*

32

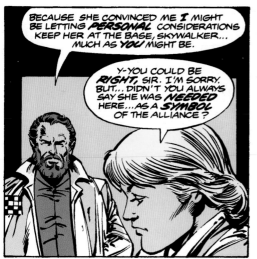

BECAUSE SHE CONVINCED ME *I* MIGHT BE LETTING *PERSONAL* CONSIDERATIONS KEEP HER AT THE BASE, SKYWALKER... MUCH AS *YOU* MIGHT BE.

Y-YOU COULD BE *RIGHT,* SIR. I'M SORRY. BUT... DIDN'T YOU ALWAYS SAY SHE WAS *NEEDED* HERE... AS A *SYMBOL* OF THE ALLIANCE?

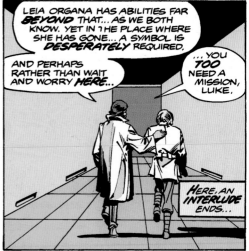

LEIA ORGANA HAS ABILITIES FAR *BEYOND* THAT... AS WE BOTH KNOW. YET IN THE PLACE WHERE SHE HAS GONE... A SYMBOL IS *DESPERATELY* REQUIRED.

AND PERHAPS RATHER THAN WAIT AND WORRY *HERE*...

...YOU *TOO* NEED A MISSION, LUKE.

HERE, AN *INTERLUDE* ENDS...

...AS LIGHT YEARS AWAY, ABOVE THE *POISONED* WATERS OF *RUBYFLAME LAKE* ON *CENTARES*...

...A *CONFRONTATION* BEGINS.

THE MAN IN THE TOWER HAS A *NAME* I REQUIRE, BOUNTY CHASER--

--THE ONLY PROFIT FOR *YOU* WILL BE IN LETTING ME PASS TO *GET* IT.

TODAY, LORD OF THE SITH... I'M NOT *AFTER* PROFIT.

YOU MAY HAVE WRUNG *TYLER LUCIAN'S* NAME FROM SOME REBEL SPY--

--BUT I'M READY TO *FIGHT* TO SEE YOU DON'T GET THE DEATH STAR DESTROYER'S NAME FROM *HIM.*

I *BELIEVE* YOU, VALANCE--

--BUT THE *WHY* OF IT INTRIGUES ME. WHEN I FIRST *HEARD* OF YOU... * WE SEEMED *RIVALS* FOR THE SAME PREY.

DON'T *TALK,* VADER,... *DEFEND* YOURSELF.

SURELY YOU'VE NOTICED... I ALREADY *AM.*

* *SW* #21.--AG

WHY *ELSE* HAVEN'T YOU BEEN ABLE TO *FIRE* YET--?

WHY ELSE HAS YOUR WEAPON BECOME SO *HEAVY*--

--IT IS *IMPOSSIBLE* FOR YOU TO HOLD?

HOW CAN YOU *FIGHT*... AGAINST THE POWER OF THE *FORCE*?

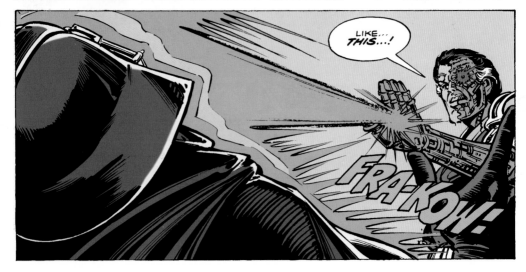

LIKE....! *THIS....!*

FRA-KOW!

34

IT'S NO *SMALL THING* TO BRING DARTH VADER TO HIS KNEE. ON SOME WORLDS, IT MIGHT BE THE STUFF OF *LEGEND...*

BUT IT'S *NOT* *ENOUGH.*

SLAYING YOU WILL BE A *WASTE.* A BOUNTY HUNTER... WITH YOUR PARTICULAR *ABILITIES...* COULD SERVE ME *WELL.*

A USEFUL *FREAK--*

--NOT UNLIKE YOUR *OWN* POSITION WITH THE EMPIRE.

VRAMP!

HIGH IN THE DECAYING TOWER BEYOND THE WALKWAY, TYLER LUCIAN WATCHES WITH HORRIBLE FASCINATION...AND *LISTENS.*

THAT *BOY* YOU'RE SEEKING...AND HIS *DROID...* HELD OUT HOPE OF SOMETHING *BETTER,* VADER.

A TIME, A LIFE, WHEN EVEN SOMEONE LIKE ME MIGHT NOT *BE* A FREAK.

A FOOLISH *DREAM,* NO DOUBT... BUT SO WAS DESTROYING THE *DEATH STAR!*

FRRAK!

THE CHASM TORN BY THE BLAST IS **WIDE**... WIDER THAN MOST MEN MIGHT LEAP.

BUT THE LORD OF THE SITH IS **NOT** MOST MEN!

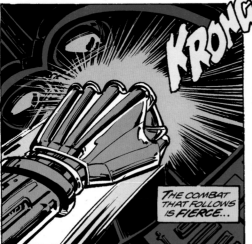

KRONG!

THE COMBAT THAT FOLLOWS IS **FIERCE**...

...AND **BRIEF**.

SHRAAAK!

AND DARTH VADER TURNS TO THE BUSINESS THAT **BROUGHT** HIM...

TYLER LUCIAN!

N-NO...!

THE CYBERNETIC HAND CLAMPS LIKE A **VISE**...

...SQUEEZING, TIGHTENING.

STILL *ALIVE*...! STILL FIGHTING...! I COULD ALMOST *ADMIRE* YOU, VALANCE.

GIVE THIS UP, *JOIN* ME... THE MEDICS ON MY CRUISER CAN PROBABLY STILL *SAVE* YOU.

N-*NO!*

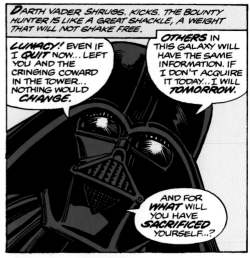

DARTH VADER SHRUGS, KICKS. THE BOUNTY HUNTER IS LIKE A GREAT SHACKLE, A WEIGHT THAT WILL NOT SHAKE FREE.

LUNACY! EVEN IF I *QUIT* NOW... LEFT YOU AND THE CRINGING COWARD IN THE TOWER... NOTHING WOULD *CHANGE*.

OTHERS IN THIS GALAXY WILL HAVE THE SAME INFORMATION. IF I DON'T ACQUIRE IT TODAY... I WILL *TOMORROW*.

AND FOR *WHAT* WILL YOU HAVE *SACRIFICED* YOURSELF...?

TIME, FORCE MASTER. THE BOY YOU SEEK... THE ONE WITH THE DROIDS... IS *GOOD*. AND HE'S GROWING...

SOMEDAY HE'LL BE YOUR *EQUAL*... OR YOUR *BETTER*.

ANY *DELAY* WORKS IN HIS *FAVOR*... INCREASES HIS *CHANCES*.

ANY...

DELAY...

THEN, VALANCE... THERE CAN *BE* NO MORE!

BUT AS THE LIGHT SABER FLASHES... THE DOOMED MAN *ROLLS*...

HURTLING HIMSELF TOWARD THE CORROSIVE WATERS *BELOW*...

WHHAAMM

...HAULING THE SITH LORD *WITH* HIM!

AND DARTH VADER BEGINS TO FEEL JUST HOW *HEAVY*...

...A DYING MAN, HALF-HUMAN, HALF-*MACHINE*, CAN BE.

THE MOMENTS THAT FOLLOW ARE *LONG*...

BUT...

SKRAAK!

...THEY *END*.

ENDING WITH THEM...

...*VALANCE*, THE HUNTER.

BUT HIS LAST WORDS STILL ECHO IN THE MIND OF TYLER LUCIAN.

AND THE MAN WHO COULD NOT FACE THE *DEATH STAR*...

38

...FINDS THE COURAGE THAT HAS SO LONG DESERTED HIM.

FOR A TIME, THE ONLY SOUND ON RUBYFLAME LAKE IS THE STEADY, LABORED RASP OF THE DARK LORD'S BREATH MASK.

THEN, HE TURNS...

...AND MAKES HIS WAY BACK TO THE ORBITTING CRUISER.

FINALLY OFF-DUTY. I HATE THESE DOUBLE-SHIFTS.

RIGHT! CAN'T WAIT TO SHED THIS ARMOR. BEEN IN IT SO LONG I FEEL LIKE A BLASTED BORG--

--OR WORSE.

GET UNDER WAY AT ONCE, WERMIS. I'LL SUPPLY YOU WITH COORDINATES.

AND UNTIL I DECREE OTHERWISE--

-- WE ARE ON ALERT STATUS. EVEN OFF-DUTY PERSONNEL WILL REMAIN IN FULL ARMOR!

AND A LONG SEARCH...

...BEGINS AGAIN.

NEXT ISSUE: A PRINCESS ALONE!

40¢ CC 30 DEC 02817

APPROVED BY THE COMICS CODE AUTHORITY

ADVENTURES *BEYOND* THE GREATEST SPACE-FANTASY FILM OF ALL!

STAR WARS

TRAPPED IN AN IMPERIAL STRONGHOLD!

INFANTINO/WIACEK

A PRINCESS ALONE!

Long ago in a galaxy far, far away. . .there exists a state of cosmic *civil war*. A brave alliance of *underground freedom fighters* has challenged the tyranny and oppression of the awesome *Galactic Empire*. This is their story!

LucasFilm PRESENTS: **STAR WARS** THE GREATEST SPACE FANTASY OF ALL'

CONTINUING THE SAGA BEGUN IN THE FILM BY GEORGE LUCAS RELEASED BY TWENTIETH-CENTURY-FOX

ARCHIE GOODWIN
WRITER/EDITOR

CARMINE INFANTINO & GENE DAY
ARTISTS

JOE ROSEN
LETTERER

PETRA GOLDBERG
COLORIST

JIM SHOOTER
CONSULTING EDITOR

A PRINCESS ALONE!

THAT'S *IT*, YOUR HIGHNESS... *METALORN!*

JUST *ONE* IN HUNDREDS OF IMPERIAL *FACTORY PLANETS.*

HARDLY SEEMS THE *KIND* OF PLACE THE ALLIANCE SHOULD BE SENDING ITS BEST KNOWN *LEADER.*

PERHAPS, CAPTAIN, THAT'S THE *REASON* THEY DECIDED TO *SEND* ME.

LG590

41

WELL, *STRATEGY'S* NOT MY DEPARTMENT, PRINCESS LEIA, LONG AS THIS OLD CARGO ORBITTER'S *CLEARANCES* DON'T GET CHECKED TOO CLOSELY--

--GETTING IN AND OUT SHOULDN'T BE A *PROBLEM.*

CAPTAIN--

--IS THAT A SUBTLE WAY OF HINTING THAT THE PROBLEM WILL BE WHILE I'M *THERE?*

DON'T YOU THINK I CAN *PASS* AS PART OF THE LOCAL *LABOR FORCE?*

THE SURFACE OF METALORN IS *CHAOS.* SHIFTING GREY ASH, BARREN ROCK, GREAT FIERY PITS OF MOLTEN SLAG. BUT BELOW THAT SURFACE IS *ORDER.* CLEAN, GLEAMING METAL, FILTERED AIR, UNENDING ARTIFICIAL LIGHT, AND THE DISCIPLINED HAND OF THE *EMPIRE.*

SHIFT 114E IS NOW DISEMBARK-ING AT JUNCTION 206-994!

MAINTAIN YOUR RANK AND FILE ON THE *SLIDEWAY...* YOU'LL BE MOVING AGAIN *SHORTLY.*

YOU DOWN THERE! *WOMAN!* YOU'RE VIOLATING THE *WORK FORMATION!*

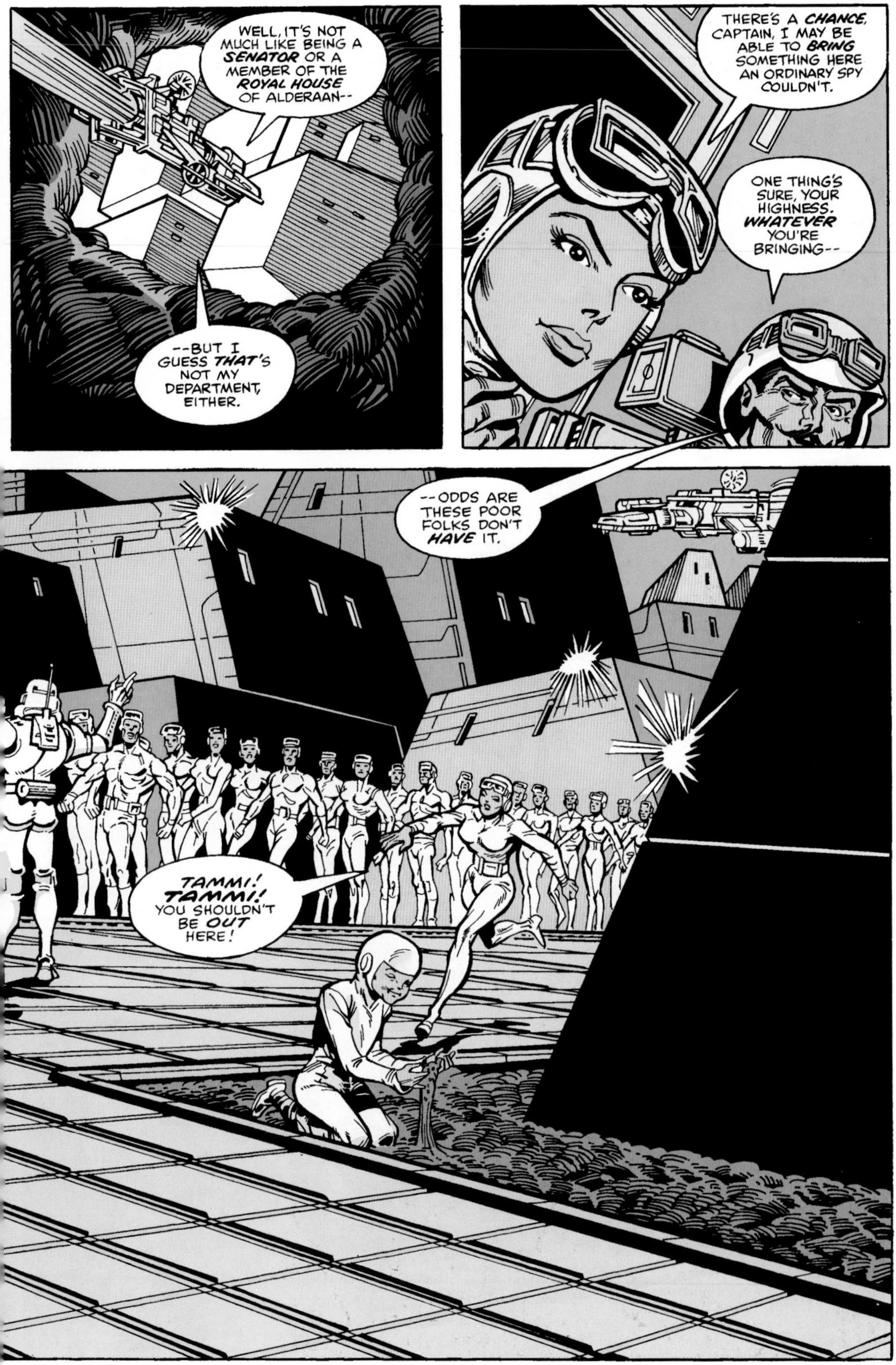
WELL, IT'S NOT MUCH LIKE BEING A SENATOR OR A MEMBER OF THE ROYAL HOUSE OF ALDERAAN--
--BUT I GUESS THAT'S NOT MY DEPARTMENT, EITHER.
THERE'S A CHANCE, CAPTAIN, I MAY BE ABLE TO BRING SOMETHING HERE AN ORDINARY SPY COULDN'T.
ONE THING'S SURE, YOUR HIGHNESS. WHATEVER YOU'RE BRINGING--
--ODDS ARE THESE POOR FOLKS DON'T HAVE IT.
TAMMI! TAMMI! YOU SHOULDN'T BE OUT HERE!

LOOK, MOMMY... THEY LEFT SOME *GROUND* UNCOVERED. I SAVED *SEEDS* FROM THE BREAKFAST FRUIT... GONNA *PLANT* THEM.

TAMMI, YOU'RE SUPPOSED TO BE IN THE *LEARNING CENTER.*

IT'S ONLY UNTIL NEXT *WEEK.* THEN, WHEN MY WORK SHIFT IS OVER... WE'LL HAVE A WHOLE *DAY* TOGETHER.

SO GO BACK *INSIDE* BEFORE--

I *WILL,* MOMMY... SOON AS MY *GARDEN'S* PLANTED.

DARLING, *NOTHING* CAN GROW ON METALORN... IT'S A FACTORY PLANET. ALL ITS *RESOURCES* ARE DRAINED FOR INDUSTRY. WHEN IT'S *ALL* USED UP... THE EMPIRE WILL MOVE US TO *ANOTHER* WORLD.

BUT MAYBE NOTHING GROWS 'CAUSE NOBODY *TRIES,* MOMMY!

I'M GONNA GIVE MY SEEDS SPECIAL *CARE* AND--

THIS IS *NOT* AN APPROVED VISITATION PERIOD, WOMAN... BACK TO THE *SLIDEWAY.*

MOVE *FAST!* IF I HAVE TO *REPORT* YOU... YOU'LL LOSE YOUR FREE TIME CREDITS.

NOW *YOU*...GET TO YOUR *INSTRUCTION UNIT!*

AND NO *MORE* OF THIS! GARBAGE BELONGS IN DISPOSALS... NOT *BURIED* ON A PUBLIC THOROUGHFARE!

IF YOU WANT TO *GROW* SOMETHING, REQUEST TRANSFER TO AN *AGRI-PLANET* WHEN YOU'RE OF AGE!

MEANWHILE, IN ONE OF THE *HIGHEST* OF THE UNDERGROUND CITY'S MONOLITHIC TOWERS...

BARON TAGGE! THE HEAD OF THE GALAXY'S MOST *RENOWNED* INDUSTRIAL CONCERN VISITING *MY* HUMBLE FACTORY WORLD... WHAT AN UNEXPECTED *PLEASURE!*

PLEASURE DOESN'T ENTER INTO IT, GOVERNOR CORWYTH--

MY PRESENCE ON METALORN AMOUNTS TO *PENANCE.*

THE FAILURE OF *ONE* TAGGE PROJECT AGAINST THE REBEL ALLIANCE* LEFT THE EMPEROR DOUBTING *ALL* OF THEM. TO *REASSURE* HIM... I'M FORCED TO *PERSONALLY* CHECK EACH ONE.

YOU'LL GAIN AN EASY ENDORSEMENT *HERE,* DEAR FELLOW.

*SCUTTLED BY *LUKE* IN *SW 25 & 26.* --ACCOUNTABLE ARCH.

THANKS TO YOUR *TAGGE WEAPONS DETECTION SYSTEM,* AND MY OWN *INFORMATION CONTROL PROGRAM*--

--THE REBELLION DOESN'T *EXIST* ON METALORN. NOT EVEN AS A *RUMOR.*

MY SYSTEM CAN DETECT UNAUTHORIZED *ARMS* OR *EXPLOSIVES* BROUGHT ONTO YOUR PLANET, GOVERNOR--

--THAT DOESN'T PRECLUDE *UNARMED SPIES* SLIPPING PAST NORMAL SECURITY.

AND SO AN OCCASIONAL ONE *MIGHT,* MY DEAR BARON! BUT *THEN* WHAT...? *SABOTAGE...?*

TO DO ANY *REAL* DAMAGE... THEY'D HAVE TO *STEAL* A STORM-TROOPER'S WEAPON. *DIFFICULT,* AT BEST--

--SINCE YOUR EXCELLENT SYSTEM *ALSO* MONITORS THOSE! SO, IN OUR REGIMENTED SOCIETY, IT IS ALMOST *IMPOSSIBLE* TO--

SIR! WE'VE A *CONDITION RED* AT POST 994-203!

PULSE BEAT SENSORS INDICATE MONITORED WEAPON IS *NO LONGER* IN AUTHORIZED HANDS!

SOMEONE SEEMS TO HAVE *DONE* THE DIFFICULT, CORWYTH... THE *IMPOSSIBLE* MAY NOT BE FAR BEHIND.

POST 994-203...

WE'VE *FOUND* THE *TROOPER,* MONITOR CONTROL.

PLAYBACK OF HIS *RECORDING UNIT* INDICATES HE STOPPED A LONE *FEMALE* COMING FROM THE DOCKING AREA FOR *ROUTINE QUESTIONING.*

HE WAS ABOUT TO CHECK AN *IRREGULARITY* ON HER PAPERS... WHEN SHE *ATTACKED!*

THE ASSAILANT WAS *CLEVER*...USED *ADHESIVE SPRAY* FROM A FIRST AID PACK TO CLOG THE *VENTILATION SYSTEM* OF OUR MAN'S ARMOR.

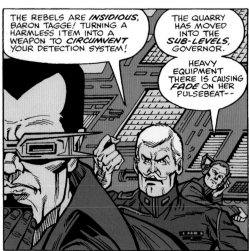

THE REBELS ARE *INSIDIOUS,* BARON TAGGE! TURNING A HARMLESS ITEM INTO A WEAPON TO *CIRCUMVENT* YOUR DETECTION SYSTEM!

THE QUARRY HAS MOVED INTO THE *SUB-LEVELS,* GOVERNOR.

HEAVY EQUIPMENT THERE IS CAUSING *FADE* ON HER PULSEBEAT--

--BUT WE STILL HAVE A STRONG *MONITOR FIX* ON THE BLASTER ITSELF, SIR!

ALERT ALL THE MEN IT *TAKES*... *FOLLOW* THAT SIGNAL! INSTEAD OF *ARMING* HERSELF, OUR LITTLE SPY WILL FIND SHE'S TIED A *NOOSE* TO HER NECK!

"AND THE FURTHER AND FASTER SHE *RUNS*...

"...THE *TIGHTER* IT'S GOING TO GET!"

THOSE SLEEP-IMPRINTING SESSIONS ON THE JOURNEY HERE SEEM TO HAVE *WORKED*...! I'VE ENOUGH INFORMATION ABOUT METALORN TO KEEP *ONE STEP* AHEAD OF PURSUIT.

AT LEAST UNTIL I CAN--

HALT! THIS IS *NOT* AN AUTHORIZED PASSAGEWAY! GET *OVER* HERE BEFORE--

A *BLASTER!* HOW DID YOU--?

BY *ACTING* WHILE YOU STORM-TROOPER TYPES ARE STILL *TALKING!*

BDOW!

VA-ZAK!

JUST WHAT I *FEARED*...! THE MORE I *SHOOT*--

--THE *QUICKER* I DRAW THEM *TO* ME!

AND HERE COMES THE BUNCH THAT WAS *ALREADY* FOLLOWING ME!

WELL, I *WANTED* TO GO FORWARD--

FTOOM! FTOOM!

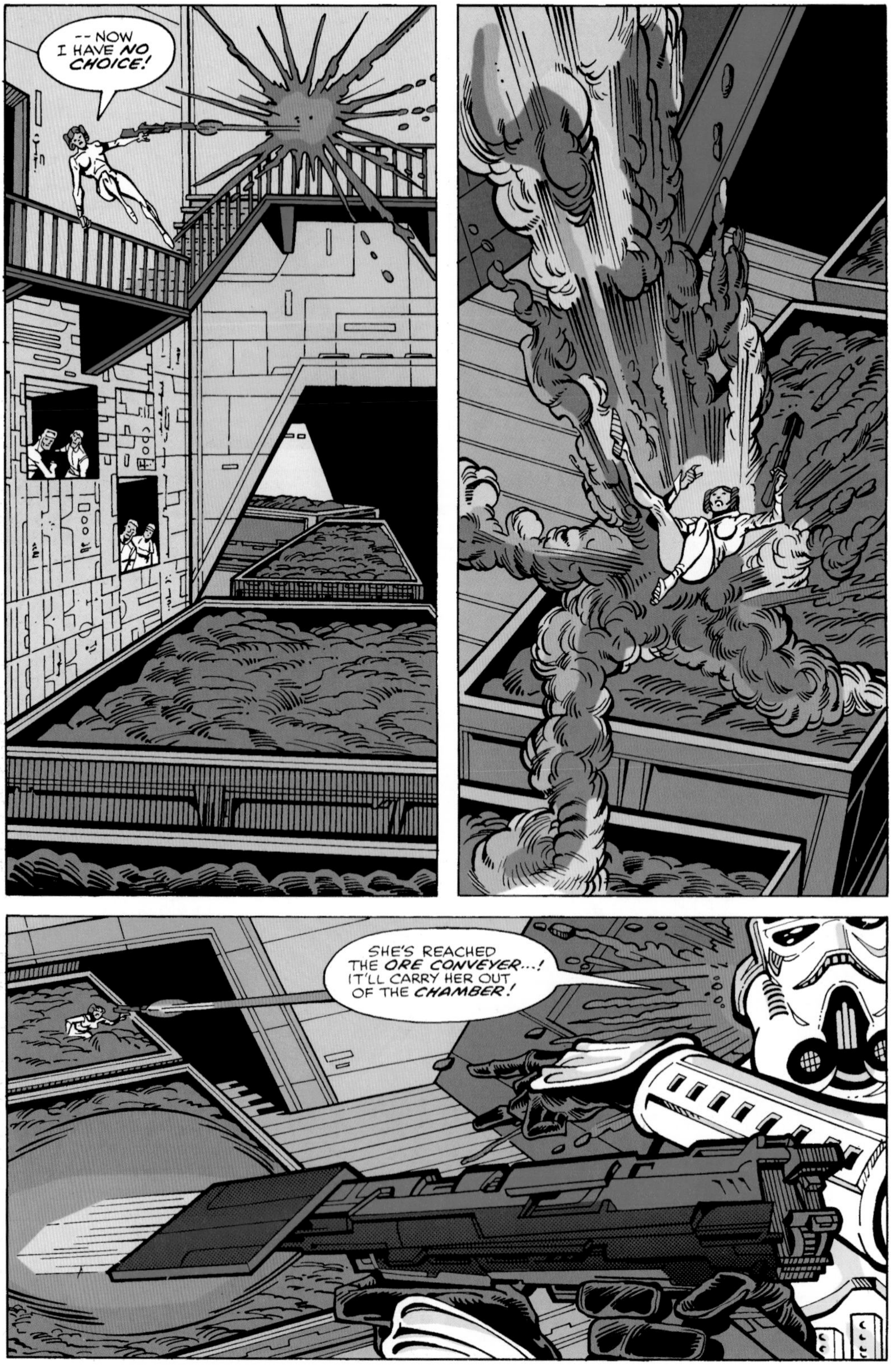
-- NOW I HAVE NO CHOICE!
SHE'S REACHED THE ORE CONVEYER...! IT'LL CARRY HER OUT OF THE CHAMBER!

THE REBEL SPY HAS ELUDED THE *PURSUIT SQUADS*, GOVERNOR CORWYTH... SHALL I HAVE THE CONVEYER *HALTED*?

AND CUT OFF THE *ORE FLOW* TO THE PLANET'S *FURNACES*...? CAUSE A TEMPORARY *SHUT DOWN*?!

THAT WOULD BE DOING THE ALLIANCE'S WORK *FOR* THEM, YOU FOOL! EVEN *MY* INFORMATION CONTROL COULDN'T HIDE SOMETHING LIKE *THAT*!

AS LONG AS WE'RE MONITORING THE *WEAPON*... SHE CAN'T *ESCAPE*! ORDER OUT *MORE UNITS*...HAVE THEM *CONVERGE* ON THE SIGNAL!

"NATURALLY, ALL THIS ACTIVITY WON'T GO *UNNOTICED* BY OUR WORKER-CITIZENS. SEE THAT THEY HAVE A REASONABLE-- AND *FALSE*-- EXPLANATION."

DO NOT BE *ALARMED*. THIS IS MERELY A *SECURITY TEST* FOR YOUR PROTECTION.

MAINTAIN YOUR *WORK STATIONS*. THIS IS--I REPEAT-- A *TEST*.

MONITOR INDICATES SHE'S STAYING *WITH* THE ORE CONVEYER, SIR.

SHE MUST INTEND *SABOTAGE* TO ONE OF THE FURNACES.

BUT WE'LL HAVE EVERY AVAILABLE UNIT WAITING TO *CUT HER OFF* AT SMELTER BAY FIVE!

EXCELLENT! YOU HEAR THAT, TAGGE--

--THIS WHOLE NASTY EPISODE IS JUST GOING TO WIND UP *PROVING* THAT THE SYSTEM STILL *WORKS*!

UH... *BARON*...?

HE RUSHED OUT *EARLIER*, GOVERNOR--

--WHEN THE *TROUBLE* STARTED.

49

ODD! HE NEVER HAD THE *REPUTATION* OF A MAN WHO SHIED AWAY FROM TROUBLE.

PERHAPS THAT WAS *BEFORE* HIS RUN-IN WITH *DARTH VADER!**

BEING BLINDED BY A *LIGHT SABER*...FORCED TO RELY ON *CYBER-VISION*... WOULD MAKE *ANYONE*...UH... CAUTIOUS.

* A TALE YET TO BE *CHRONICLED.* -- ARCHIE.

AH WELL....!

WE HAVE BETTER THINGS TO DO THAN PONDER THE ARISTOCRATIC *PSYCHE*...HOW DOES THE *HUNT* PROGRESS?

THE *LAST UNIT* IS NOW IN POSITION IN SMELTER BAY FIVE, GOVERNOR CORWYTH. AND THE *MONITOR* SHOWS...

"...THE ORE CONVEYER IS SPEEDING THE REBEL SPY STRAIGHT *INTO* THEIR WAITING GUNS!"

5

THE NEXT CAR WILL BE THE *ONE!* SET ALL BLASTERS AT LOW LEVEL INTENSITY--

--WE WANT TO DESTROY THE *WOMAN*, NOT THE CONVEYER! AT MY *COMMAND*--

50

--FIRE!

SH-TUM! BA-KOW! VDOW!

THE *REBEL'S* NOT IN THE CAR... ONLY THE STOLEN *WEAPON!*

NOW IT'S CLEAR WHY THE GOOD *BARON* FLED! HE MUST HAVE *KNOWN* HIS WEAPON DETECTION SYSTEM WOULD *FAIL US!*

IN ALL *FAIRNESS,* GOVERNOR... THE SYSTEM *WORKED.*

WHO COULD ANTICIPATE THE ALLIANCE AGENT *USING* IT TO DECOY US AFTER THE BLASTER INSTEAD OF *HER?*

IS THAT SUPPOSED TO *COMFORT* ME? THE WOMAN'S *DEADLY...* AND THERE ARE *MILES* OF ENDLESS CORRIDORS AND BYWAYS SHE COULD HAVE *VANISHED* INTO WHILE *WE* CHASED THE SIGNAL FROM THAT GUN!

FIND HER! IF IT TAKES EVERY *STORM-TROOPER* ON METALORN... *FIND* THAT REBEL *WITCH!*

...AND GOVERNOR CORWYTH *HIMSELF* WILL GIVE THE *FULL DETAILS* ON THIS SPECTACULAR SECURITY TEST IN A LATER TRANSMISSION.

NOW A LOCAL REMINDER: SHIFTS 114E AND 111B... YOU HAVE *NINE MINUTES* LEFT ON YOUR MEAL PERIOD.

ARN HORADA...?

DO... DO I *KNOW* YOU, YOUNG WOMAN? YOU'RE NOT ON MY SHIFT...

NO, I'M FROM YOUR *PAST.* WHEN YOU TRAVELED FROM HERE TO *ALDERAAN* TO INSTRUCT A LITTLE GIRL IN GALACTIC HISTORY--

--*LEIA*, PROFESSOR HORADA, PRINCESS LEIA ORGANA.

N-NO...! ARE YOU TRYING TO GET ME IN *TROUBLE*...? ALDERAAN IS *DESTROYED*... OBLITERATED BY A *METEOR STORM*...!

CENTRAL INFORMATION TOLD US THAT *LONG AGO*...! NONE OF THE ROYAL HOUSE SURVIVED... *NONE!*

THEY *LIED* TO YOU, PROFESSOR... I'M HERE TO TELL YOU THE *TRUTH.*

AND TO *ENLIST* HIM IN BRINGING THE *REBELLION* TO METALORN, PRINCESS...?

YOU'RE... BARON TAGGE.

YES! SINCE YOU HAVE MOST OF THE AREA'S TROOPERS ON A WILD GOOSE CHASE IN THE SUB-LEVELS--

--I THOUGHT SOMEONE SHOULD BE WAITING WHEN YOU CONTACTED YOUR OLD INSTRUCTOR!

HOW COULD YOU KNOW...?

WHILE IMPERIAL GOVERNOR CORWYTH WAS DELIGHTING IN METALORN'S WEAPONS DETECTION SYSTEM... I DECIDED TO GET A VOICE PRINT FROM THE RECORDING UNIT OF THAT STORMTROOPER YOU DISPATCHED.

ONCE THAT WAS IDENTIFIED FROM THE KNOWN ENEMIES FILE, IT WAS JUST A MATTER OF FINDING WHICH CITIZEN HERE--

--MIGHT HAVE A PREVIOUS CONNECTION TO YOU.

WHY THE ALLIANCE WOULD LET ITS MOST RENOWNED LEADER RISK HER LIFE ATTEMPTING TO RECRUIT SOME BROKEN, USELESS FORMER HISTORIAN ELUDES ME...

I'LL LET YOU EXPLAIN THAT TO THE EMPEROR... WHEN I DELIVER YOU PERSONALLY!

SINCE HE WOULDN'T UNDERSTAND ANY MORE THAN YOU DO--

--LET'S NOT BOTHER WITH THE TRIP!

BLAST YOU, WOMAN! FOR **THAT**--

SHRAAAAK!

--YOU'LL VISIT THE **EMPEROR** AS A **CORPSE!**

BUT WITH HIS CYBER-VISION **BLOCKED**, THE THREAT IS EASIER MADE THAN CARRIED OUT...

AND EVEN AS TAGGE STRUGGLES TO CLEAR HIS LENSES OF FOOD PASTE... UNSEEN **OBSTACLES** APPEAR!

PROFESSOR **HORADA** KICKED THE CHAIR INTO HIS PATH...!

GIVEN THE OPPORTUNITY, THE PRINCESS MOVES SWIFTLY TO **CAPITALIZE** ON IT...

...USING THE **ENERGY SHACKLES** MEANT FOR HER!

KLIK!

DON'T STAND LIKE UNPROGRAMMED **DROIDS!** AN ENEMY OF THE **EMPEROR** IS ESCAPING!

B-BUT... THE EMPEROR **HAS** NO ENEMIES...! THE DAILY **INFORMATION BROAD-CASTS** ASSURE US OF THIS...!

AND MATTERS OF DIS-OBEDIENCE ARE ONLY TO BE SETTLED BY IMPERIAL TROOPERS...!

YES! WHERE ARE THE STORM-TROOPERS...?!

ALREADY CHASING THAT WITCH.... DOWN A FALSE TRAIL!

VRAM!!

MOVE, YOU MISINFORMED DOLTS! CLEAR MY WAY TO THE NEAREST EXIT... THAT'S WHERE SHE WAS HEADED!

THE BARON PLUNGES ON... THE EXCITEMENT FADES... THE CROWD DISPERSES...

THANKS FOR THE COVER, YOUNG LADY. YOU'RE VERY BRAVE TO HELP ME.

IT WAS FUN! I UNDERSTAND 'CAUSE SOMETIMES I GET IN TROUBLE, TOO!

ONLY... AREN'T YOU SCARED WITH STORMTROOPERS AND EVERYBODY CHASING YOU?

VERY. BUT SOMETIMES-- WHEN YOU BELIEVE IN SOMETHING ENOUGH-- YOU DO IT ANYWAY.

E-EVEN IF EVERYONE ELSE SAYS YOU CAN'T...? THAT IT'S IMPOSSIBLE...?

MAYBE ESPECIALLY THEN.

NOW I CAN'T STAY ANY LONGER, SWEETHEART.

MAY THE FORCE BE WITH YOU.

THE F-FORCE...?

AND AS THE REST OF SHIFT 114 AND INSTRUCTION UNIT 51 RUSH THROUGH WHAT'S LEFT OF THEIR MEAL PERIOD, LEIA ORGANA VANISHES INTO THE LABYRINTH CORRIDORS OF METALORN...

...WATCHED ONLY BY A GIRL NAMED TAMMI.

PRINCESS *LEIA ORGANA* RIGHT HERE ON *MY* PLANET... AND SHE SLIPS THROUGH OUR *FINGERS!*

I BLAME *YOU* FOR THIS, TAGGE! KEEPING HER PRESENCE *SECRET*... SO YOU COULD REGAIN THE EMPEROR'S *FAVOR* BY CAPTURING HER *YOURSELF!*

AND *I* BLAME YOUR *GOVERNING POLICIES* AND STUPID *HANDLING* OF THE WHOLE AFFAIR.

NEITHER STANCE WILL *UNDO* WHAT'S HAPPENED.

I CAN AT LEAST REASSURE THE EMPEROR BY *EXECUTING* THAT OLD MAN... *ARN HORADA!*

ANY RETALIATION TO HIM IS LIKE AN *ADMISSION* THAT YOU'VE *LIED* ABOUT THE REBELLION... AND THAT THE EMPIRE QUAKES IN *FEAR* OF IT.

BUT I'M THE *GOVERNOR*...! THERE MUST BE *SOMETHING* I CAN DO!

YES, YOU CAN KEEP *QUIET*... NOT TROUBLE THE EMPEROR OR METALORN'S CITIZENS ANY MORE THAN THEY ALREADY *ARE.*

THAT'S *MY* ADVICE. AND EVEN IF IT'S WRONG, THE NICE THING ABOUT IT IS--

--YOU WON'T BE ANY *WORSE* OFF THAN YOU ARE *NOW.*

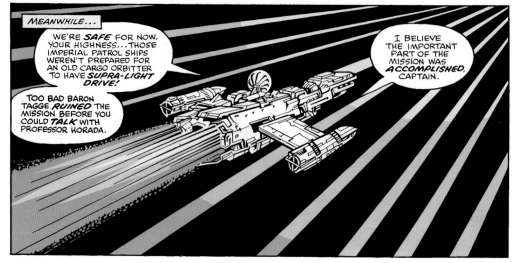

MEANWHILE...

WE'RE *SAFE* FOR NOW, YOUR HIGHNESS...THOSE IMPERIAL PATROL SHIPS WEREN'T PREPARED FOR AN OLD CARGO ORBITTER TO HAVE *SUPRA-LIGHT DRIVE!*

TOO BAD BARON TAGGE *RUINED* THE MISSION BEFORE YOU COULD *TALK* WITH PROFESSOR HORADA.

I BELIEVE THE IMPORTANT PART OF THE MISSION WAS *ACCOMPLISHED*, CAPTAIN.

56

WITH ALL RESPECT, PRINCESS LEIA...*HOW?* NOTHING WAS SABOTAGED... NO RESISTANCE FORCE ESTABLISHED.

WHAT'S DIFFERENT ABOUT METALORN *NOW* THAN *BEFORE* WE ARRIVED?

YOU'RE MAKING THE SAME MISTAKE THE *EMPIRE* DOES, CAPTAIN. THERE'S *MORE* TO THE REBELLION THAN GUERILLA WARFARE.

A TEACHER, A HISTORIAN, LIKE *ARN HORADA* CAN EVENTUALLY LEAD A RESISTANCE WHEN IT'S SAFE. NOT TO *FIGHT*... BUT TO POUR *SAND* IN THE IMPERIAL WAR MACHINE.

A *BLASTER* ISN'T CONSTRUCTED RIGHT...*TRANSCEIVER SETS* GET FAULTY PARTS.

BUT *FIRST*... HE AND OTHERS THERE NEEDED TO BE SHOWN THERE *WAS* A REBELLION... TO SEE THAT ITS LEADERS *SURVIVE* AND CONTINUE THE *FIGHT*...

TO *GIVE* METALORN WHAT IT'S BEEN LACKING BEFORE--

--HOPE.

AND ON THE IMPERIAL CONTROLLED FACTORY PLANET LEFT BEHIND...A YOUNG *GIRL* SNEAKS AWAY FROM HER INSTRUCTION UNIT DURING PLAY PERIOD.

A YOUNG GIRL NAMED *TAMMI*...

TASK ACCOMPLISHED, SHE SITS DOWN AND WAITS. WAITS FOR HER *SEEDS* TO GROW...

PATIENTLY. HOPEFULLY.

NEXT: *RETURN TO TATOOINE!*

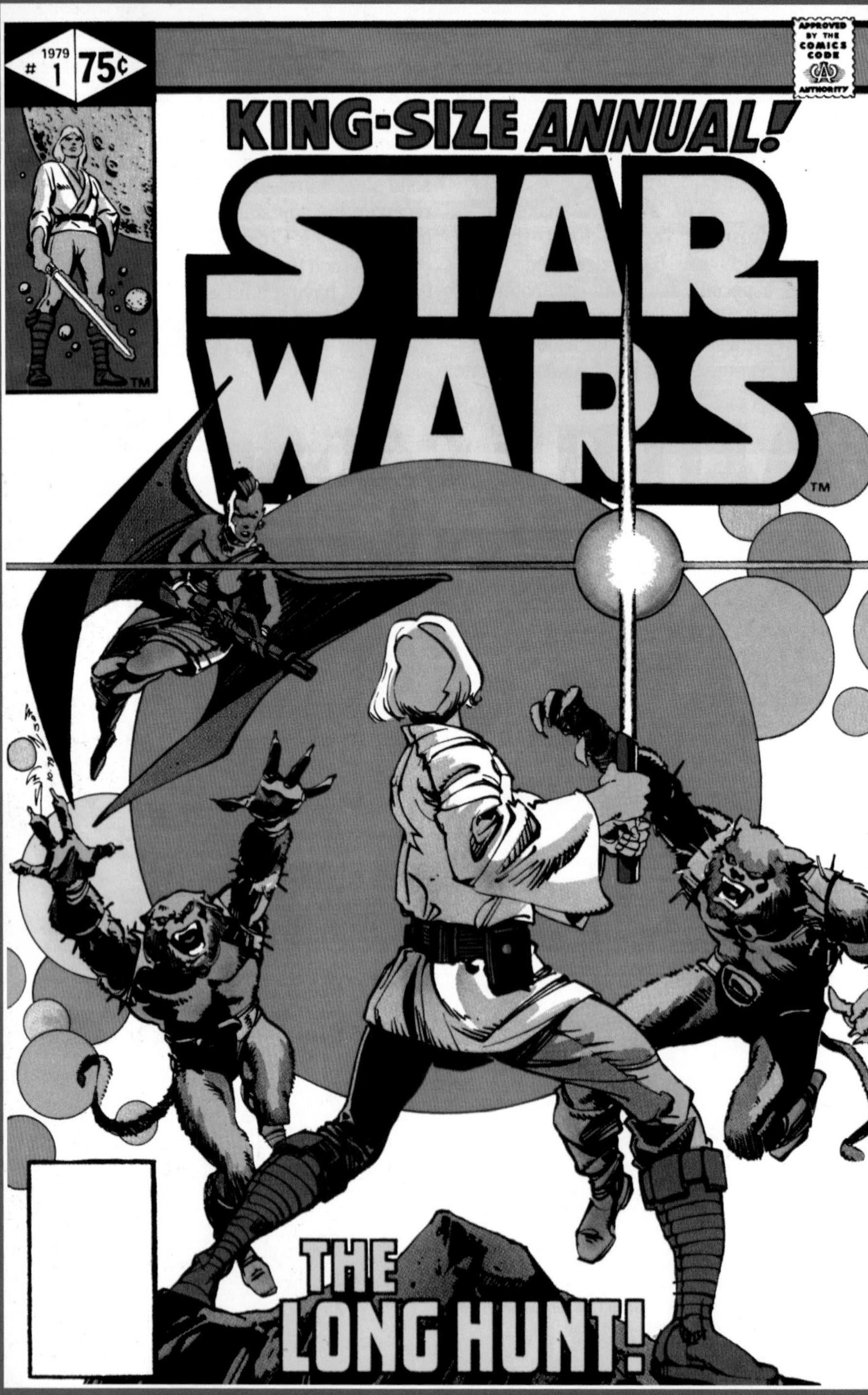
1979
1
75¢
APPROVED BY THE COMICS CODE AUTHORITY
KING-SIZE ANNUAL!
STAR WARS
TM
THE
LONG HUNT!

Long ago in a galaxy far, far away. . .there exists a state of cosmic *civil war*. A brave alliance of *underground freedom fighters* has challenged the tyranny and oppression of the awesome *Galactic Empire*. This is their story!

LucasFilm PRESENTS: **STAR WARS** THE *GREATEST* SPACE FANTASY OF ALL!

CONTINUING THE SAGA BEGUN IN THE FILM BY *GEORGE LUCAS* RELEASED BY *TWENTIETH CENTURY-FOX*

CHRIS CLAREMONT • **MIKE VOSBURG** & **STEVE LEIALOHA** • **JOHN COSTANZA** • **BOB SHAREN** • **ARCHIE GOODWIN** • **JIM SHOOTER**
guest writer   guest artists   letterer   colorist   editor   consulting ed.

THE LONG HUNT

AS THE SAYING GOES, IT'S A **BIG** EMPIRE-- STRETCHING FROM ONE SPIRAL ARM OF THE GALAXY TO THE OTHER, ENCOMPASSING MILLIONS OF STAR SYSTEMS, THOUSANDS OF INHABITED WORLDS.

IN ALL THAT VAST AMOUNT OF SPACE, AMONG ALL THOSE COUNTLESS BILLIONS OF SAPIENT BEINGS, IT'S EASY TO UNDERSTAND HOW A MERE **FOUR** MIGHT OCCASIONALLY GO UNNOTICED.

Y'KNOW, PRINCESS, I'M GLAD HAN HAD TO PUT THE **MILLENNIUM FALCON** IN HERE FOR SUPPLIES. I'VE BEEN COOPED UP TOO LONG ON STARSHIPS. I WAS STARTING TO GO BATTY!

EVEN WHEN TWO OF THOSE FOUR ARE **PRINCESS LEIA ORGANA**-- FORMER IMPERIAL SENATOR FROM ALDERAAN, NOW A LEADER OF THE REBEL ALLIANCE--

--AND **LUKE SKYWALKER**, TATOOINE MOISTURE FARMER TURNED STARFIGHTER PILOT.

THEY'RE RUNNING A CALCULATED RISK BY VISITING TIRAHNN THAT-- AMONG THE CROWDS THRONGING THIS ANCIENT, LEGENDARY BAZAAR-- NO ONE WILL RECOGNIZE THEM. THE ODDS ARE IN THEIR FAVOR.

BUT SOMETIMES, EVEN WHEN YOU PLAY THE ODDS, YOU LOSE.

BY THE SEVEN MOONS OF SKÄRTIS-- IT'S THEM!

"TWO OF THOSE THE TYRANT SEEKS! AND IF THE FEMALE AND THE YOUTH ARE HERE--

"--HAN SOLO CANNOT BE FAR AWAY! I MUST NOTIFY THE TYRANT-- AT ONCE!"

UNAWARE THAT THEY'VE BEEN SPOTTED...

...LUKE AND LEIA CONTINUE THEIR STROLL THROUGH THE BAZAAR.

ALL MY LIFE, I'VE HEARD TALES OF THE GREAT TIRAHNN FAIR, BUT I NEVER THOUGHT I'D GET TO VISIT IT.

LIKE WHAT YOU SEE?

WELLL-- THAT OUTFIT LOOKS A LITTLE DARING TO ME. ON TATOOINE, SHE'D BE ASKING FOR A BAD CASE OF SUNBURN OR WIND SCAR.

BUT THIS ISN'T TATOOINE, LUKE, ACTUALLY, THE GOWN'S A LITTLE... DEMURE FOR MY TASTES.

WHAAAT--???

PRINCESS...

...YOU'RE... JOKING, AREN'T YOU?

I WAS WONDERING HOW LONG IT WOULD TAKE YOU TO NOTICE.

FOR THE FIRST TIME IN QUITE A WHILE...

TWO YOUNG PEOPLE WHO'VE SEEN MORE THAN THEIR SHARE OF TRAGEDY REVEL IN THE JOY OF SIMPLY BEING ALIVE.

THE MOOD DOESN'T LAST LONG.

HUH--?! PRINCESS, THE CROWD--!

STAND THOU ASIDE, GRUBBERS!

MAKE WAY FOR THE *MAJESTRIX OF SKYE!*

THE WOMAN'S RACE IS UNKNOWN, AS IS HER TITLE, BUT ALL HASTEN TO OBEY THE SNARLED COMMANDS OF HER ESCORT--

--*CATUMAN WARRIORS!* BORN AND BRED TO THE ARTS OF WAR... FELINE MERCENARIES SAID TO BE FURY INCARNATE, AMONG THE DEADLIEST KILLERS IN EXISTENCE.

LIKE EVERYONE ELSE, LEIA MOVES ASIDE-- BUT NOT QUITE FAST ENOUGH.

:OH!!:

THAT WINGED WOMAN SLAMMED INTO YOU *DELIBERATELY!* WHO THE HECK DOES SHE THINK SHE IS--?!

HUSH, LUKE. I'M ALL RIGHT.

LET IT PASS.

THE LAST THING WE NEED IS TO MAKE TROUBLE AND DRAW ATTENTION TO OURSELVES.

I SUPPOSE, I'LL ADMIT THOSE CATUMEN SURE LOOKED DANGEROUS.

IT'S SAID EVEN WOOKIEES GIVE THEM A WIDE BERTH, WHAT'S THAT?

A MONEY POUCH-- ISN'T IT YOURS?

THIEF!!

YOU DARE PRACTICE YOUR *PICK-POCKET'S* TRADE ON ME?!

THAT'S CRAZY. YOU MUST HAVE DROPPED THIS...

LIAR!

THESE HUMANS HAVE OFFENDED ME, MY PETS-- --*SLAY THEM!!*

LUKE'S REACTION IS INSTINCTIVE...

...AND FAR FASTER THAN HE WOULD HAVE BELIEVED POSSIBLE NOT SO LONG AGO. IN ONE SMOOTH, FLUID MOTION, HIS *LIGHTSABER* IS IN HIS HAND, ITS SEARING ENERGY BLADE SENDING THE LEAD CATUMAN TO A WELL-DESERVED REWARD.

AARRRGH!!

THE OTHER WARRIORS PAUSE, SUDDENLY RESPECTFUL OF THEIR FOE'S WEAPON AND HIS OBVIOUS ABILITY.

FOR THE MOMENT, THE ADVANTAGE IS LUKE'S. HE DOESN'T INTEND TO THROW IT AWAY.

PRINCESS-- *RUN!* HEAD FOR THE FALCON. I'LL BE RIGHT BEHIND YOU!

BUT, LUKE-- WHAT ABOUT THE CATUMEN?!

"DON'T WORRY. I THINK I'VE GOT A WAY TO SLOW 'EM DOWN."

LUKE FEINTS LEFT, THEN SLASHES RIGHT WITH HIS LIGHTSABER, CUTTING THROUGH A THICK TANGLE OF HALYARDS...

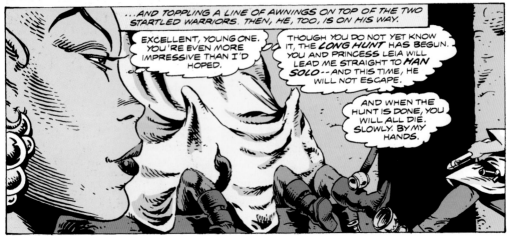

...AND TOPPLING A LINE OF AWNINGS ON TOP OF THE TWO STARTLED WARRIORS. THEN, HE, TOO, IS ON HIS WAY.

EXCELLENT, YOUNG ONE. YOU'RE EVEN MORE IMPRESSIVE THAN I'D HOPED.

THOUGH YOU DO NOT YET KNOW IT, THE *LONG HUNT* HAS BEGUN. YOU AND PRINCESS LEIA WILL LEAD ME STRAIGHT TO *HAN SOLO* -- AND THIS TIME, HE WILL NOT ESCAPE.

AND WHEN THE HUNT IS DONE, YOU WILL ALL DIE. SLOWLY. BY MY HANDS.

TIRAHNN-- TRADING NEXUS OF AN ENTIRE STELLAR CLUSTER, A CITY LARGER THAN SOME COUNTRIES, ITS ARCHITECTURE RANGING FROM THE STREET LEVEL HURLY-BURLY OF THE BAZAAR TO MILE-HIGH CORPORATE SKYSCRAPERS AND LUXURY PALACES.

IT'S AN EASY PLACE TO LOSE SOMEONE IN. SOMETIMES, ALL YOU HAVE TO DO IS TURN A CORNER, OR LOOK THE WRONG WAY AT THE WRONG MOMENT.

BUT, TRY AS THEY MIGHT, LUKE AND LEIA CAN'T SHAKE THE TWO CATUMEN RELENTLESSLY DOGGING THEIR TRAIL.

LUKE TRIES EVERY TRICK HE'D EVER LEARNED ON TATOOINE-- HE EVEN INVENTS SOME BRAND NEW ONES ON THE SPOT-- TO NO AVAIL. EVERY TIME HE SPARES A QUICK GLANCE OVER HIS SHOULDER, THE CATUMEN ARE THERE.

SEEMS LIKE WE'VE BEEN RUNNING FOR-EVER. DON'T KNOW ABOUT THE PRINCESS, BUT I'M ALMOST *WINDED.* WE CAN'T KEEP UP THIS PACE MUCH LONGER.

SUDDENLY...

LUKE!

OH, *NO!* ONE OF THEM CUT AHEAD OF US! WE'RE TRAPPED IN THIS ALLEY!

NO CHOICE-- WE HAVE TO MAKE A STAND.

HE DOES HIS BEST, BUT HE'S TIRED, SLOW, AND THIS TIME THE CATUMAN IS READY FOR HIM.

BEFORE LUKE QUITE KNOWS WHAT HAPPENED, THE WARRIOR'S FIST RAKES HIS CHEST, KNUCKLE-SPIKES DRAWING *BLOOD.*

LUKE GOES DOWN, STUNNED, SLIPPING INTO SHOCK AS THE SECOND CATUMAN RUSHES TO HELP ITS BROTHER FINISH THEM OFF.

THE WARRIOR'S HASTE MAKES HIM CARELESS. THE CATUMAN NEVER SEES THE MASSIVE ARM THAT BRINGS HIM DOWN.

NOR DOES HIS BROTHER SEE THE BLASTER BOLT THAT STOPS HIM IN HIS TRACKS.

KRAK

THE FORCE BE PRAISED...!

VDOW

HAN SOLO! CHEWBACCA!

HRONNK!

YEAH, CHEWIE, I CAN SEE THE KID'S HURT. AFTER GOING ONE ON ONE WITH A "CAT," HE'S LUCKY TO BE ALIVE.

C'MON, YOUR WORSHIP, LET'S GET OUTTA HERE BEFORE THE LOCAL PRE-FECTS WORK UP ENOUGH COURAGE TO COME SEE WHO'S STILL BREATHING.

LATER, ABOARD THE STAR-SHIP *MILLENNIUM FALCON*, DOCKED AT TIRAHNN'S CENTRAL STARPORT...

HOW DID YOU FIND US, HAN? HOW DID YOU KNOW WE WERE EVEN IN TROUBLE?

I WISH I COULD TAKE THE BOWS, PRINCESS...

...BUT THE CREDIT BELONGS TO YOUR *DROID BUDDIES. ARTOO* HEARD THE ORIGINAL RADIO ALARM TO SECURITY HEADQUARTERS, THEN PATCHED INTO ONE OF SECURITY'S AIRBORNE "SPY-EYES" TO TRACK YOU DOWN.

PRINCESS-- WILL MASTER LUKE RECOVER?

BOIP BOIP.. BOEEP?

THANKS TO YOU TWO, THREEPIO, I THINK HE'LL BE JUST FINE.

KID, IF YOU FEEL UP TO TALKING... WHAT EXACTLY HAPPENED IN THE BAZAAR? THE REPORTS ARTOO PICKED UP WERE PRETTY CON-FUSED.

UH-OH... I HEAR SOMEONE OUTSIDE THE MAIN HATCH. I'D BETTER ANSWER-- COULD BE PREFECTS.

COVER ME, CHEWIE, IN CASE IT'S BROOD MATES OF THOSE CATUMEN WE ZAPPED--

SAME OLD SOLO-- SAYIN' "HI" TO AN OLD FRIEND BY STICKING A BLASTER IN HER FACE.

WHA--?! MOONS OF YAVIN-- KATYA!!

IT'S BEEN YEARS, WOMAN! HOW'VE YOU BEEN?!

LIVIN', SOLO. WORKIN'. LAUGHIN'. NOTHIN' SPECTACULAR-- BUT NO COM-PLAINTS, EITHER.

LUKE, PRINCESS-- MEET KATYA M'BUELE.

WE CREWED TOGETHER ON A CORELLIAN RIM-RUNNER-- YOU NAME IT, WE'D SMUGGLE IT. THEY WERE GOOD TIMES, MOSTLY.

WELL, WELL, WELL-- THIS IS A SIDE TO CAPTAIN SOLO WE'VE NEVER SEEN BEFORE.

SHE'S A NICE-LOOKING LADY. PRINCESS, ARE YOU JEALOUS?

LEIA DOESN'T REPLY, AND FOR THE UMPTEENTH TIME, LUKE SKYWALKER THINKS OF HIS ATTRACTION TO SHE, AND WONDERS HOW SHE TRULY FEELS ABOUT HIM.

BACK TO BUSINESS, KID. I STILL WANT TO HEAR YOUR STORY.

THERE ISN'T MUCH TO TELL. WE WERE IN THE BAZAAR, WHEN THIS WINGED WOMAN ACCUSED US OF...

WINGED WOMAN?! DESCRIBE HER, LUKE!

UH, TALLER THAN YOU, REAL SLIM, BEAUTIFUL. HER BODY AND WINGS WERE GREEN, SHE WAS BALD, TOO, EXCEPT FOR A SILVER CREST...

HAN-- IT'S HER!

HAN-- WHAT IS IT?! DO YOU KNOW THE WOMAN?!?

IT'S OLD BUSINESS, KID. NOTHIN' FOR YOU TO WORRY ABOUT. AN' NOTHIN' YOU CAN HELP WITH.

HAN, WHAT ARE YOU GOING TO DO?

SEE A MAN, ASK SOME QUESTIONS. CALL IN SOME OLD DEBTS.

I'M COMING WITH YOU.

YOU'RE STAYING.

I KNOW YOU'RE SCARED, KATYA; I'M SCARED, TOO. BUT WHAT I HAVE TO DO, I CAN DO BEST ALONE. YOU'LL BE SAFER HERE, ANYWAY.

IF I'M NOT BACK BY DAWN, TAKE THE FALCON AND RUN. WHEN YOU'RE SPACEBORNE, TELL CHEWIE AND THE OTHERS WHO THE TYRANT IS, WHY SHE'S AFTER US. DO WHAT I ASK, KATYA--PLEASE?

YOU KNOW I COULD NEVER REFUSE YOU ANYTHING, YOU HANDSOME LUG.

TAKE CARE, SOLO. I'LL BE HERE WAITING FOR YOU.

THE HEIGHTS.

THESE ARE HOMES OF TIRAHNN'S ELITE-- THE MERCHANT PRINCES WHO RULE THIS WORLD--HUGE, FANTASTIC PALACES SPRAWLING ACROSS MILES OF GROUND, OR REACHING IMPOSSIBLY HIGH INTO THE EMERALD SKY.

IN ONE SUCH TOWER LIVES A MAN ONCE KNOWN AS LASKAR. HE USED TO BE A SNEAK THIEF AND SMALL-TIME FENCE, BUT OVER THE YEARS HE'S AMASSED A CONSIDERABLE FORTUNE...

...UNTIL NOW, HE RANKS AS ONE OF THE MOST POWERFUL MEN ON TIRAHNN. HE THINKS HE BURIED HIS PAST LONG AGO, THAT HE HAS NOTHING--AND NO ONE--TO FEAR FROM THE OLD DAYS.

HE'S IN FOR A SURPRISE.

THE ONE AND ONLY, LASKAR.

EVENIN', LASKAR.

WHA--?! WHO--?!? HOW DARE YOU-- BY THE STARS!

HAN SOLO!

SOLO, DON'T GET HASTY, MAN! I CAN PAY-- I ALWAYS MEANT TO PAY!

GLAD TO HEAR IT, OL' BUDDY. BUT FIRST, LET'S TALK ABOUT A MUTUAL ACQUAINTANCE--

--THE GREAT TYRANT OF SKYE.

THE MILLENNIUM FALCON'S CARGO HOLD. AN UNUSUALLY DISGRUNTLED WOOKIEE DOES A LATE GUARD TOUR. CHEWBACCA AND SOLO ARE AS CLOSE AS TWO BEINGS CAN GET; THEY'VE SAVED EACH OTHER'S LIVES MORE TIMES THAN EITHER CARES TO COUNT.

YET, THIS EVENING, FOR THE FIRST TIME, HAN REFUSED TO CONFIDE IN HIS FIRST MATE. AND, THOUGH CHEWBACCA WOULD DIE BEFORE ADMITTING IT, HAN'S ACTIONS *HURT.*

THE WOOKIEE IS SO WRAPPED UP IN HIS OWN TROUBLED THOUGHTS THAT HE FAILS TO NOTICE A SPARKLING SPIRAL OF SMOKE...

...MATERIALIZING IN THE MAIN AREA BEHIND HIM.

SILENT AS DEATH, THE SHIFTING CLOUD SLITHERS ACROSS THE DECK, ITS SHAPE BECOMING MORE DEFINITE, MORE OMINOUS...

...AS IT PAUSES BEFORE EACH OF THE TEMPORARY CABINS HAN HAD PARTITIONED OFF FOR THIS TRIP...

...UNTIL IT FINDS THE ONE IT WANTS.

INSIDE, KATYA M'BUELE LIES ASLEEP...

...A RIFLE BLASTER CRADLED IN HER ARMS...

...SECURE IN THE KNOWLEDGE THAT THE SLIGHTEST SOUND, THE MEREST HINT OF DANGER, WILL WAKE HER.

BUT THIS TIME, HER SENSES FAIL HER. SHE AWAKENS TO THE SMOKE DEMON'S TOUCH.

TOO LATE. WITH SOME WARNING, HER MIND, HER NERVES, MIGHT HAVE RESISTED. BUT NOW...

EH--?!?

NO--OH, *NO!!*

ITS TOUCH PARALYZES HER COMPLETELY...

...LEAVING HER CONSCIOUS, BUT HELP-LESS.

THEN, THE DEMON'S SMOKY SUBSTANCE FLOWS INTO HER BODY, ENTERING THROUGH HER VERY PORES.

KATYA'S SKIN TURNS TRANS-LUCENT, TRANSPARENT, AND FINALLY FADES AWAY...

...AS HER ENTIRE BODY IS TURNED TO SMOKE AND ABSORBED BY THE DEMON.

IN A FEW SECONDS, IT'S ALL OVER. THERE ARE MANY SLOWER WAYS TO DIE, BUT FEW MORE TERRIBLE. IT DOES NOT GO UNNOTICED.

I HEARD--FELT--A DISRUPTION IN THE FORCE-- LIKE A SCREAM OF ANGUISH INSIDE MY MIND!

KATYA--!?!

THE DEMON REACTS WITH THE SPEED OF THOUGHT, AND THE RAW, IRRESISTABLE POWER OF AN ENRAGED BANTHA.

WH-WHAT IS THIS THING?! HOW DID IT GET ABOARD WITHOUT TRIGGERING THE ALARMS?!

I-IT SEEMS SOLID...BUT I FEEL IT... IN MY MIND...

WEAK...! BUT... MUST... KEEP FIGHTING...

WITHOUT WARNING, A BLUR OF DARK-BROWN FUR FLASHES BEFORE YOUNG SKYWALKER'S EYES, SMASHING THE DEMON OFF HIM...

CHEWBACCA!

BOY, I WAS NEVER SO GLAD TO SEE SOMEONE IN MY LIFE!

LUKE'S JOY IS SHORT-LIVED, HOWEVER, AS THE DEMON SHRUGS OFF THE GIANT WOOKIEE'S ATTACK WITH CONTEMPT-UOUS EASE.

LUKE, CHEWBACCA, GET AWAY FROM THERE! I'LL COVER YOU!

LEIA'S INTENTIONS ARE ADMIRABLE, HER AIM PERFECT...

NICE IDEA, PRINCESS!

:OH!!:

UNFORTUNATELY, ALL HER BLASTER BOLTS SEEM TO DO IS MAKE THE DEMON *MADDER* THAN EVER.

TOO BAD IT DIDN'T WORK.

BUT WHAT NOW?! OUR WEAPONS WON'T STOP THE CREATURE--

--AND I'VE A NASTY FEELING THESE WALLS WON'T KEEP IT OUT. *UH-OH!*

LUKE!

AS THE DEMON TOUCHES LUKE, ITS SMOKY ESSENSE BEGINS...

...TO PENETRATE HIS BODY AS IT DID KATYA'S.

LUKE FEELS HIS LIMBS STIFFEN-- HIS MIND AND SOUL BEGIN TO COLLAPSE UNDER THE HELLISH PSYCHIC AND PHYSICAL ONSLAUGHT. HE GROPES DESPERATELY FOR *SALVATION...*

...AND FINDS IT!

WITH A CRACK OF THUNDER, HIS *LIGHT-SABER* KEYS TO LIFE IN HIS HAND, THE PURE LIGHT OF ITS *ENERGY BLADE...*

...SWEEPING UP IN A CLASSIC KILLING STROKE THAT IMPALES THE SMOKE DEMON! THE CREATURE DIES WITHOUT AUDIBLE SOUND, YET THE PSYCHIC SCREAM THAT ECHOS AND RE-ECHOS IN LUKE'S MIND WILL STAY WITH HIM TILL HE DIES.

AS THE SMOKE CLEARS, LUKE ISN'T ALL THAT SURPRISED TO FIND HIMSELF SHAKING, TO FIND HIS FACE STAINED WITH UNACCUSTOMED TEARS.

IS--IS IT...DEAD?

IT'S DEAD.

AND ALL THE SOULS OF ITS VICTIMS--TRAPPED WITHIN THAT MONSTER --ARE FINALLY FREE.

I'VE BEEN SCARED BEFORE--I'VE FACED DEATH BEFORE, LOTS OF TIMES-- BUT I'VE NEVER FELT ANYTHING LIKE THIS.

THAT DEMON WAS...A CREATION OF THE FORCE-- GIVEN LIFE BY SOMEONE WHOSE POWER RIVALS DARTH VADER'S.

CHEWBACCA--MEDICINE AND HOT SOUP, QUICKLY! AND BLANKETS, TOO! LUKE'S SLIPPING INTO SHOCK!

I DON'T LIKE IT. HE'S SO PALE. HE LOOKS ALMOST AS BAD AS HE DID THAT TIME HIS MIND ACCIDENTALLY TOUCHED DARTH VADER'S. *

THAT SOUND-- IT'S THE ENTRY ALARM!

BREEP BREEP BREEP

* WAAAAY BACK IN STAR WARS #18--ARCHIE.

CAUTIOUSLY, CHEWBACCA ADMITS THE VISITOR, AND...

WHAT THE BLAZES IS GOIN' ON HERE?! I'VE BEEN POUNDIN' ON THAT BLASTED HATCH FOR FIVE MINUTES!

HAN! THANK THE FORCE IT'S YOU.

LEIA QUICKLY TELLS THE CORRELLIAN STAR-PILOT WHAT'S HAPPENED...

KATYA--LAUGHIN' KATYA...DEAD...?

I'M SORRY, HAN, I KNOW SHE WAS YOUR FRIEND.

SHE WAS THAT, PRINCESS-- AND A LOT MORE.

SHOW ME.

IT'S MY FAULT. I SHOULDN'T HAVE LEFT HER. I THOUGHT SHE'D BE SAFE HERE--THAT I'D BE TAKING ALL THE RISKS.

YOU DID ALL YOU COULD, HAN.

YEAH? I COULD HAVE RUN, LADY. I SURE WANTED TO.

SOMEHOW, THAT DOESN'T SEEM YOUR STYLE.

YOUR *ROYALNESS*, WHAT YOU DON'T KNOW ABOUT ME-- OR MY '*STYLE*'--WOULD FILL THE *IMPERIAL LIBRARY!*

--WE'RE GETTIN' OUTTA HERE.

STRAP LUKE IN, CHEWIE--AN' THE PRINCESS AS WELL--

AND, A FEW MINUTES LATER...

WHAT IN THE NINE MOONS--?!?

HAN LIFTS THE *MILLENNIUM FALCON* OUT OF THE PLANETARY ATMOSPHERE AT *FULL THROTTLE*--

UNIDENTIFIED FREIGHTER, FROM TIRAHNN PORT CONTROL-- ABORT LIFT-OFF AT ONCE! *ABORT--!*

OH, WHAT'S THE USE?

--BARELY MISSING A HOUSE OF *TAGGE* STARLINER ON FINAL APPROACH--

--AND HE MAKES THE JUMP INTO *HYPERSPACE* AS SOON AS IT'S *FEASIBLE*, SHAVING THE TOLERANCES AS *CLOSE* AS ANYONE HAS EVER DARED AND LIVED TO TELL THE TALE.

HE'S A *DRIVEN* MAN THIS NIGHT...

...AND HE REMAINS ONE FOR THE NEXT FEW DAYS, AS THE FALCON 'JUMPS' TOWARD THE *RIM.*

THEN...

WELL, WE'RE ALMOST THERE.

THAT'S NICE, WHERE'S '*THERE*'?

MARAT V-- KNOWN TO ITS INHABITANTS AS *SKYE.*

"NOT MANY PEOPLE IN THE EMPIRE HAVE HEARD OF IT; IT'S A *RESTRICTED* WORLD.

"*KATYA* AND I WERE PART OF A *SMUGGLING* CREW THAT SNEAKED IN THERE YEARS AGO, ON THE PROD FOR SOME FAST, EASY TAKINGS. WE WERE CAPTURED BY *KHARYS*, THE MAJESTRIX--THE WINGED FEMALE YOU AND LUKE RAN INTO IN THE BAZAAR.

"SHE AND HER PEOPLE...*HUNTED* US. TWENTY MEN AND WOMEN--*CORRELLIANS* ALL, AS TOUGH AND DANGEROUS A CREW AS EVER RAISED SHIP TOGETHER. ONLY KATYA AND I *ESCAPED.*

IN A WAY, I GUESS I'VE BEEN RUNNING EVER SINCE. I DON'T THINK A *DAY* HAS PASSED WHEN I HAVEN'T LOOKED OVER MY SHOULDER, EXPECTING KHARYS TO BE THERE.

WELL, I'VE *HAD IT* WITH RUNNING, WITH PLAYING THIS GAME BY *HER* RULES. WE'RE HEADING FOR SKYE, PRINCESS. I'M GONNA DO WHAT THE LADY LEAST EXPECTS, CONFRONT HER ON HER OWN TURF-- *HUH?!?*

HRRRAK!

OH, SOLO, MY POOR SOLO-- YOUR BIGGEST PROBLEM...

A HOLOGRAM IMAGE-- *OH.!!*

BLASTER FIRE!

YOU AND YOUR FRIENDS ARE VERY RESOURCEFUL, SOLO, VERY *LUCKY...*

...BUT I'M AFRAID YOUR STRING HAS JUST ABOUT *RUN OUT.*

"*FAREWELL. FOR NOW. WE WILL MEET AGAIN,*"

NOT IF *I* CAN HELP IT.

HAN-- WHAT ARE WE UP AGAINST?!

OH, BROTHER!

TIE FIGHTERS-- A WHOLE SQUADRON...

...WAITING TO HIT US THE INSTANT WE DROPPED OUT OF HYPERSPACE.

TAKE THE TOP TURRET, PRINCESS...

...WHILE *I* TRY TO *LOSE 'EM!*

...IS THAT YOU'RE SO TOTALLY *PREDICTABLE.* FAR FROM OUTSMARTING ME, YOU'VE PLAYED RIGHT INTO MY HANDS.

HOLD THE *FALCON* STEADY FOR A MOMENT LONGER, HAN. I'M LOCKED ON SOME TARGETS.

THREE SHOTS. THREE DIRECT HITS. THREE *LESS* TIE FIGHTERS TO WORRY ABOUT

THREE DEAD IMPERIALS TO WEIGH IN THE BALANCE AGAINST THE *MILLIONS* SLAUGHTERED WITHOUT MERCY WHEN THE EMPEROR'S *DEATH STAR* DESTROYED LEIA'S HOMEWORLD, *ALDERAAN.* ✳

NICE SHOOTING, PRINCESS!

I DO MY HUMBLE BEST.

✳ *STAR WARS* #3 --ARCHIE.

TROUBLE IS...

...THERE'S A LOT *MORE* WHERE THOSE CAME FROM. THEY'RE HITTING US FROM *ALL* SIDES!

AS A *STAR-PILOT,* HAN SOLO IS IN A CLASS BY HIMSELF--

--AND SO IS HIS SHIP--

--BUT THERE ARE TIMES WHEN ALL THE SKILL AND DARING IN CREATION WON'T DO YOU A BIT OF GOOD.

THIS IS *ONE OF THEM.*

STOP *BLEEP-ING,* ARTOO!

YOU RUST-CHOKED GEAR-BOX-- I CAN *SEE* WE'RE FLOATING!

THE ARTIFICIAL GRAVITY'S GONE!

VRP-BEEP!

CHEWIE-- AUXILIARY SYSTEMS! *FAST!*

I'M SORRY, SIR, BUT THOSE ARE ALSO COM-PLETELY *DIS-FUNCTIONAL.*

IN ADDITION, WE SEEM TO HAVE LOST MOST OF OUR SHIELDS.

FOR ALL INTENTS AND PURPOSES, SIR, WE ARE *DEFENSELESS.*

TUMBLING END OVER END...

...AND TRAILING A TAIL OF FIRE *KILOMETERS* LONG, THE MILLEN-IUM FALCON PLUNGES INTO SKYE'S ATMOSPHERE.

A TIE FIGHTER FOLLOWS HER DOWN, UNTIL SHE FINALLY *DISAPPEARS* INTO THE MASSIVE CLOUD FORMATIONS THAT SHROUD SKYE'S MAJESTIC MOUNTAIN PEAKS.

IN SECONDS, THE IMPERIAL WARCRAFT IS ONCE MORE IN SPACE, AND REPORTING TO ITS BASE...

...ATMOSPHERIC TURBULENCE PRECLUDED CONTINUED CLOSE PURSUIT. WILL CONTINUE TRACKING WITH SURFACE-SCANNING RADAR.

SOLO CAN'T STAY DOWN THERE FOREVER, AND WHEN HE RISES...

...HE'S OURS!

MEANWHILE...

INTO THE LIFEPOD, YOU TWO.

HAN--N-NO...! WE CAN...HELP YOU.

MISTRESS, MASTER LUKE'S LIFE-READINGS...!

I KNOW, THREEPIO. LUKE...

PRINCESS--! HE'S PASSED OUT. HE'S RUNNING A FEVER.

HELP ME WITH HIM, THREEPIO.

A MOMENT LATER, SOLO POINTS HIS STAR-SHIP SPACEWARD IN A LAST, DESPERATE BID TO ESCAPE.

AS THE FALCON SKIMS A HIGH MOUNTAIN PASS, THE LIFEPOD IS EJECTED.

HE DOESN'T GET VERY FAR.

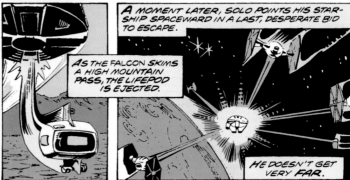

MISTRESS, WHY DID MASTER SOLO ABANDON US? ARE YOU AND MASTER LUKE NOT HIS FRIENDS?

HE DID IT TO SAVE US, THREEPIO. HE KNEW THE FALCON HAD NO CHANCE--IT'S TOO BIG A TARGET TO MISS.

BUT THE IMPERIALS MIGHT OVERLOOK A LIFEPOD.

"THERE HAS TO BE A STARPORT ON SKYE--OTHERWISE, HOW COULD THE MAJESTRIX TRAVEL TO TIRAHNN? WE MIGHT BE ABLE TO BUY OR STEAL A SHIP. IT'S A SLIM HOPE, BUT IT'S STILL A HOPE. THAT'S A LOT MORE THAN HAN OR CHEWBACCA HAVE."

BOLD WORDS. THEY HAUNT LEIA NOW...

...AS SHE SITS IN THE DARK, SHIVERING--DESPITE THE THICK FUR CLOAK GATHERED TIGHT AROUND HER SHOULDERS.

OOOOOHHH...

WHERE...AM I? WHY...SO COLD...?

LUKE! YOU'RE ALL RIGHT!!

I'M...ALIVE. BEYOND THAT, I WOULDN'T TAKE ANY BETS. WHAT...HAPPENED?! WHERE'S HAN AND THE FALCON?! WHERE ARE WE?!?

SLOW DOWN! IT FEELS LIKE YOUR FEVER'S BROKEN, BUT YOU'RE STILL WEAK AS A BABY. SAVE YOUR STRENGTH; YOU'LL NEED IT.

HAN, CHEWBACCA--THE FALCON--ARE GONE. THEY SACRIFICED THEMSELVES TO GIVE US A CHANCE FOR FREEDOM. AND THEY DIED FOR NOTHING. WE WERE CAPTURED THE MINUTE OUR LIFE-POD LANDED. YOU AND I HAVE BEEN IN THIS CELL EVER SINCE.

OUTWORLDERS, I AM ARAGH, LORD OF THE HIGHLANDS, PATRIARCH OF THE S'KYTRI-- THE WINDBORN.

IN THE NAME OF THE COUNCIL, I GREET YOU, AND SUMMON YOU TO TRIAL!

HAN...CHEWIE-- DEAD?! I DON'T BELIEVE IT-- LEIA!

OH!!

LUKE, THIS IS WHAT I STARTED TO TELL YOU. THESE BEINGS WHO CAPTURED US ARE THE SAME RACE AS THE MAJESTRIX WHO WANTED US DEAD!

TRIAL?! ON WHAT CHARGE?!

WE'RE STRANGERS TO YOUR WORLD, PATRIARCH. WE CAME IN PEACE. WE'VE COMMITTED NO CRIME.

YOU ARE WALKERS. THAT IS CRIME ENOUGH. YOUR PRESENCE HAS PROFANED OUR SACRED AERIES. THAT, TOO, IS A CRIME.

ARISE AND FOLLOW ME--AT ONCE! AND SPEAK NO MORE TO ME. IT IS FOR THE COUNCIL TO DECIDE YOUR FATE--

--LIFE... OR DEATH!

PART 2 A DUEL OF EAGLES!

UNDER GUARD, LUKE AND LEIA ARE LED OUT OF THEIR MAKESHIFT PRISON. THE SIGHT, AS THEY EMERGE INTO THE BRILLIANT MORNING SUNLIGHT, TAKES THEIR BREATH AWAY.

FOR AS FAR AS THE EYE CAN SEE IN EVERY DIRECTION, HUGE, MAJESTIC MOUNTAINS REACH TOWARDS THE HEAVENS. THEY'RE THE BIGGEST, MOST IMPRESSIVE PEAKS LEIA HAS EVER SEEN, AND THEY DWARF THE ONES LUKE KNEW ON TATOOINE.

THE CITY OF THE WINGED PEOPLE IS FORMED FROM THE LIVING ROCK ITSELF, HALFWAY UP THE SLOPE OF ONE OF THE MORE MASSIVE PEAKS. TO REACH THE COUNCIL TOWER, LUKE AND LEIA MUST FIRST CROSS AN OPEN-AIR CAUSEWAY. FOR THEIR WINGED ESCORT, THAT IS NO PROBLEM.

FOR THE TWO YOUNG PEOPLE, IT IS AN ACT OF COURAGE.

YOU STAND BEFORE THE **SUPREME COUNCIL** OF THE HIGHLAND CLANS.

IF YOU HAVE GODS, OUTWORLDERS, I SUGGEST YOU **PRAY** TO THEM.

I AM DEVERÉN.

I SPEAK FOR THE COUNCIL.

YOU HAVE VIOLATED S'KYTRI SPACE. YOU COME TO OUR WORLD UNINVITED, BEARING WEAPONS, AND WITH THE STENCH OF BATTLE ABOUT YOU.

WE ALSO CAME WITH FRIENDS! WHERE ARE THEY? WHAT HAVE YOU DONE WITH OUR DROIDS?!

DO NOT RAISE YOUR VOICE TO ME, YOUNG MALE. YOUR LIVES HANG BY A THIN ENOUGH THREAD AS IT IS.

YOUR..."FRIENDS"... ARE HERE—AND, LIKE YOU, THEY ARE UN-HARMED, FOR THE MOMENT.

MASTER LUKE! OH, THANK THE MAKER—IT'S SO GOOD TO SEE YOU AGAIN!

SEE-THREEPIO! ARTOO-DETOO!

LUKE, WHAT ARE YOU DOING?!

THEY'RE BEING HELD IN SOME KIND OF STASIS LOCK. I'M GOING TO SEE IF THEY'RE ALL RIGHT!

WHREET! DEEDLE-BOOP!

ON SECOND THOUGHT, MAYBE I'LL JUST STAY RIGHT WHERE I AM.

AS HE BACKS AWAY FROM THE DROIDS, LUKE THINKS OF HAN SOLO...

WE SHOULD HAVE STAYED WITH YOU, HAN. WE'D BE NO WORSE OFF THAN WE ARE NOW.

...AND OF THE *SACRIFICE* THE DASHING SMUGGLER MADE TO SEE HIS FRIENDS SAFELY AWAY IN THE LIFEBOAT...

EVEN IF I GOT MY LIGHTSABER—AND LEIA HER BLASTER—WE COULDN'T ESCAPE FROM THIS CITY WITHOUT A SHIP, OR ANTI-GRAVITY BELTS, OR *WINGS*.

PATRIARCH, COUNCILLORS, WE KNOW YOUR WORLD IS RESTRICTED. BUT BEFORE WE COULD MAKE PROPER DIPLO-MATIC APPROACH...OUR SPACE-CRAFT WAS ATTACKED. OUR VIOLATIONS ARE UNINTENTIONAL.

ALL WE ASK IS SAFE TRANSPORT TO YOUR PLANETARY STARPORT. WE'LL BE OFF-PLANET AS SOON AS WE CAN BOOK PASS-AGE.

AN ELOQUENT APPEAL— *PRINCESS LEIA ORGANA OF ALDERAAN!*

BUT THIS IMPERIAL WARRANT SPEAKS JUST AS *ELOQUENTLY,* DOES IT NOT?

LEIA ORGANA, PRINCESS-SENATOR OF ALDERRAN

WANTED:

OR TREASON AGAIN THE EMPIRE

YOU ARE A LEADER OF THE *REBEL ALLIANCE*. YOU CRASHED BECAUSE IMPERIAL FORCES STATIONED IN THIS SYS-TEM ATTACKED IN PERFOR-MANCE OF THEIR DUTY.

I SEE. WHAT WILL YOU DO WITH US, THEN?

YOU ARE ENEMIES OF THE IMPERIUM THE WINDBORN ARE SWORN TO *SERVE*. *OUR* DUTY REQUIRES THAT WE *SURRENDER* YOU IMMEDIATELY TO THE IMPERIAL LEGATE HERE.

THAT'S IT, THEN. WE'RE AS GOOD AS *DEAD*.

YOUNG MALE, THIS WEAPON IS *YOURS*?

IT IS.

I WOULD KNOW YOUR NAME.

LUKE SKYWALKER.

‹BY THE DAWN WIND, I THOUGHT THAT WEAPON LOOKED *FAMILIAR.*›

‹IS HE THE *ONE?*›

‹HIS NAME IS THE *SAME* AS OUR *WINGLESS BLOOD BROTHER'S.*›

‹BUT HE IS SO YOUNG --AND VIRTUALLY *ALONE!* THE MAJESTRIX IS POWERFUL, WITH AN *ARMY* AT HER BACK!›

‹YET, IF HE IS THE ONE, WE OWE HIM A DEBT THAT CAN NEVER BE REPAID. I WILL PUT FOR-WARD ONE FINAL TEST-- ONE OF *HONOR.*›

‹THEN WE WILL *DECIDE.*›

WHAT ARE THEY SAYING, LUKE?

I WISH I KNEW. I DON'T LIKE IT, THOUGH.

YOUR STARSHIP WAS ATTACKED AS IT NEARED OUR WORLD.

AND DESTROYED. AFTER WE... ABANDONED HER.

NOT SO. THE VESSEL WAS *CAPTURED* AND TAKEN INTACT TO THE MAJESTRIX' FORTRESS.

"*INTACT?!*" THEN-- THAT MEANS HAN AND CHEWBACCA COULD STILL BE *ALIVE!*

WE DON'T KNOW THAT FOR SURE.

I DON'T CARE. IF THERE'S THE *SLIGHTEST* CHANCE THEY'RE ALIVE, WE'VE GOT TO TRY TO *RESCUE* THEM.

LUKE-- YOU'RE *CRAZY!* YOU'RE GOING TO BREAK INTO AN *IMPERIAL* STRONGHOLD, TAKE ON LORD KNOWS *HOW* MANY STORM-TROOPERS, TO SAVE TWO PEOPLE WHO ARE PROBABLY ALREADY DEAD?!

YES.

THEN *I* MUST BE CRAZY, TOO--

--BECAUSE I'M GOING WITH YOU.

‹PRAISE THE *SACRED WINDS*-- HE *IS THE ONE!*›

‹AS THE PROPHECY FORETOLD-- WITH HIS HELP, THE S'KYTRI MAY ONCE MORE FLY *FREE!*›

HEAR AND HEED THE WORDS OF THE COUNCIL! WE PROCLAIM LUKE SKYWALKER AND LEIA ORGANA-- *FRIENDS* OF THE S'KYTRI.

WHAT AID WE CAN GIVE IS THEIRS FOR THE ASKING.

ELSEWHERE...

...ATOP THE HIGHEST PEAK IN THIS MOST AWESOME OF MOUNTAIN RANGES...

...STANDS THE FORTRESS-KEEP OF *KHARYS*, MATRIARCH OF THE *S'KYTRI*-- SELF-PROCLAIMED *MAJESTRIX OF SKYE.*

UNDER HER DIRECT COMMAND IS A FORCE OF STARSHIPS AND STORM-TROOPERS THAT MANY SECTOR GOVERNORS WOULD ENVY. EVEN SO, SHE CARES NOT A WHIT FOR THE EMPIRE SHE IS PLEDGED TO SERVE; SHE IS BOUND BY AN OLDER, DEEPER OBLIGATION, TO A MAN THAT MOST OF THE GALAXY HAS REASON TO FEAR-- *DARTH VADER.*

THAT FURRY MISANTHROPE MAKES TOO MUCH NOISE, CAPTAIN, IT DISTURBS ME. *SILENCE* THE BEAST-- WITHOUT HARMING IT-- OR YOU WILL TAKE ITS PLACE.

UH...YES, MAJESTRIX.

HRRAWR!

CHEWIE, SHUT UP! YOU BOTHER THE NICE LADY!

AND, AS EVER, YOUR MOUTH KEEPS GETTING YOU INTO *TROUBLE.*

WHAT'S THE POINT OF BEING NICE, KHARYS? YOU'RE GOING TO *KILL* ME ANYWAY, RIGHT?

OF COURSE, BUT THERE ARE *MYRIAD* WAYS TO DIE, SOLO.

SOME WOULD MAKE MY "SMOKE DEMON" SEEM QUITE *PLEASANT* BY COMPARISON.

AS *GALLANT* AS EVER, HAN SOLO.

IT'S BEEN A LONG TIME SINCE WE LAST PARTED.

NOT LONG ENOUGH--

UNNNGNH!

YOU AND YOUR FELLOW CORRELLIANS PROVIDED ME A RARE, FINE HUNT, SOLO, BUT NOW THE HUNT IS *ENDED.*

BEFORE I TAKE YOUR LIFE, HOWEVER...

THERE ARE SOME THINGS I WOULD KNOW ABOUT YOUR TRAVELLING COMPANIONS, PRINCESS LEIA AND, MORE IMPORTANTLY, THE BOY WHO DESTROYED THE DEATH STAR, THE ONE YOU CALL *LUKE*.

WHAT ARE THEY TO YOU?

TO ME-- NOTHING. TO THE DARK LORD OF SITH, WHOM I SERVE, PERHAPS *EVERY-THING*.

NO ANSWER? WHAT A...PITY.

YOU FORCE ME TO RESORT TO THE TENDER MERCIES OF AN IMPERIAL *INTERROGATOR*.

HAN'S FACE PALES SLIGHTLY UNDER HIS SPACER'S TAN AS THE HUMMING, GLEAMING ORB MOVES TOWARDS HIM.

DARTH VADER USED A SIMILAR MACHINE ON LEIA WHEN SHE WAS HIS PRISONER ABOARD THE DEATH STAR.

SHE STILL REFUSES TO SPEAK OF WHAT HAPPENED, AND THE MEMORIES STILL GIVE HER *NIGHTMARES*.

MEANWHILE, UP ON THE FORTRESS' BATTLEMENTS...

CAPTAIN OF THE GUARD!

FLIERS, SIR-- SCORES OF 'EM! I'VE NEVER SEEN SO MANY!

HM-- THEY'RE HIGHLAND CLANS, BY THEIR MARKINGS. LED BY *ARAGH* HIMSELF, TOO. PROBABLY TAKING SOME HATCHLINGS OUT FOR THEIR INITIATION HUNT.

BUT ALERT THE GARRISON-- AND THE *MAJESTRIX*-- JUST IN CASE.

YOU KNOW, LUKE, IF I WEREN'T SO SCARED, I'D BE HAVING THE TIME OF MY LIFE RIGHT NOW.

I KNOW WHAT YOU MEAN.

OUR *ANTI-GRAV* BELT PACKS KEEP US ALOFT, BUT THESE WINGS GET US WHERE WE WANT TO GO, JUST LIKE THE S'KYTRI, WE HAVE TO FOLLOW THE WINDS, RIDE THE AIR CURRENTS AND THERMALS, WATCH OUT FOR DOWNDRAFTS.

THE DIFFERENCE IS, THEY'VE HAD A WHOLE *LIFETIME* TO PRACTICE. WE'VE ONLY HAD A *DAY*.

THESE BODY-SUITS SHOULD *DISGUISE* US UNTIL WE'RE RIGHT ON TOP OF THE CASTLE.

THE CLANS HAVE COME AS FAR AS WE CAN, GIVEN WHAT ASSISTANCE WE CAN. I AM SORRY, SKYWALKER, BUT YOU TWO MUST WIN OR LOSE YOUR FIGHT... *ALONE*.

GREAT.

READY, LEIA?

NOT REALLY -- BUT DO I HAVE A CHOICE?

MAY THE *FORCE* BE WITH YOU.

SHE SCREAMS, HER WINGS FOLDING IN ON THEM-SELVES...

...AND THEN, SHE *FALLS*.

WHAT IS IT, CAPTAIN?

ONE OF 'EM'S HIT A DOWN-DRAFT, HER MATE'S TRYING TO SAVE HER.

A KILOBUCK SAYS HE DOESN'T MAKE IT.

YOU'RE ON. ANYONE ELSE WANT TO *BET*?

BY THE ETERNAL-- SHE'S NO FLIER!

SHE'S *HUMAN!*

CORRECT, BUTCHER-- AND A *PRINCESS OF ALDERAAN!*

VORP!

VOOW

SOUND THE ALARM! IT'S AN *AMB-- AARRRGH!!*

THEIR INITIAL STRAFING RUN CUTS DOWN EVERY STORMTROOPER IN SIGHT, AND, AS THEY WHEEL FOR A SECOND PASS...

...LEIA *DISENGAGES* FROM HER WINGS AND DROPS LIGHTLY TO THE PARAPET.

I'M DOWN-- AND STILL IN ONE PIECE!

UH-OH! MORE TROOPERS!

BLAST! I'M PINNED DOWN!

IF LUKE DOESN'T GET THESE KILLERS OFF MY BACK, OUR GREAT ESCAPE WILL BE *OVER* BEFORE IT'S EVEN BEGUN!

AND, ALMOST ON CUE...

WHA--?! *BLASTER FIRE!*

YEAAGKH!

TAKE COVER, MEN! WE'RE *SITTING DUCKS* OUT HERE IN THE OPEN!

I DIDN'T WANT LEIA GOING INTO THE CASTLE BY HERSELF, BUT I COULDN'T THINK OF ANY OTHER VIABLE PLAN.

I FLEW *GLIDERS* ON TATOOINE LONG BEFORE I BUILT MY T-16. I'M A LOT *BETTER* WITH THESE WINGS THAN SHE IS-- IT'S UP TO ME TO KEEP THE STORM-TROOPERS OCCUPIED...

...WHILE SHE LOOKS FOR HAN AND CHEWBACCA.

SOUNDS LIKE LUKE'S GIVING KHARYS' STORMTROOPERS A RUN FOR THEIR MONEY-- *GOOD.* I'LL BET HE'S MORE WORRIED ABOUT *ME* THAN THEM!

I CAN TAKE CARE OF MYSELF, MR. SKYWALKER, THANK YOU VERY MUCH.

STILL, IT'S NICE TO KNOW HE *CARES.*

THESE CATACOMBS SEEM TO GO ON *FOREVER.*

I WONDER HOW DEEP INSIDE THE MOUNTAIN I AM?

WAIT-- THAT MUFFLED CRY!

HER ENTRANCE IS DRAMATIC-- AND VERY EFFECTIVE-- SHE *KICKS* THE DOOR IN.

EVERYONE-- *FREEZE!!*

HAN! HE'S HOOKED UP TO AN IMPERIAL INTERROGATOR...

...JUST AS *I* WAS.

THE MAJESTRIX IS TRYING TO *PSYCHO-PROBE* HIM!

WHO DARES--?!

...UNLESS YOU WANT TO TEST WHETHER THOSE *WINGS* CAN OUT-FLY MY *BLASTER FIRE!*

I DARE! *LEIA ORGANA!*

RELEASE HAN SOLO AND CHEWBACCA-- *NOW!* AND NO FALSE MOVES...

YOU SEEM TO HAVE ME AT A *DISADVAN-TAGE*, PRINCESS. BUT SURELY YOU KNOW YOU HAVEN'T A PRAYER OF LEAVING HERE ALIVE.

WE'LL TAKE OUR CHANCES.

BEHIND ME-- A *NOISE!?*

SEIZE HER!

CATUMAN WARRIORS!

AAYIIII--!!

TWO OF THEM!

LOST MY RIFLE! CAN'T TRY FOR IT-- OUT OF REACH!

GOT TO KEEP MOVING, STAY AWAY FROM THEM--BUT THEY'RE SO FAST!

MY *SHOULDER!*

SPIKES BIT DEEP--HOPE THEY WEREN'T *POISONED.* THEY EXPECT ME TO KEEP RUNNING. INSTEAD, I'LL MAKE A STAND...

...AND HOPE MY *HAND BLASTER* IS ENOUGH TO STOP THEM!

WITH BLINDING, UNEXPECTED SPEED, LEIA DRAWS HER SIDEARM...

...BUT QUICK AS SHE IS, THE CATUMAN IS EVEN *QUICKER.*

NO!!

THE WARRIOR'S ARM HITS LEIA'S LIKE A STEEL BAR, AND HER LIMB GOES *NUMB* FROM HAND TO SHOULDER...

THE STUNNING IMPACT SENDS THE HAND-GUN FLYING. AGAIN, LEIA DOES THE *UNEXPECTED*, RAKING HER NAILS DOWN THE CATUMAN'S FACE...

BOK!

...BEFORE KICKING *AWAY* FROM HIM WITH ALL HER STRENGTH.

THE "CATS" ARE *OFF-BALANCE.* THEY UNDERESTIMATED ME, THOUGHT I'D BE AN EASY KILL.

NOT A BIG ADVANTAGE. BUT IN COMBAT... EVEN A *SMALL* ONE CAN MAKE THE DIFFERENCE. SHE FIRES AS SHE ROLLS...

...THE THIN, SCARLET BEAM CUTTING A DEADLY SWATHE ACROSS THE VAST CHAMBER. ONE CATUMAN DUCKS HER SHOT. HIS BROODMATE ISN'T SO LUCKY.

YAHHRRR

HRRR

ZRAKT

AS HE DIES, HE TWIST-FALLS BACKWARDS INTO THE *FORCE FIELD* HOLDING CHEWBACCA--A COMPLEMENT TO THE *MANACLES* CLAMPED TIGHT AROUND THE WOOKIEE'S WRISTS. THE FIELD SHORTS OUT.

THE SUPPOSEDLY *"UNBREAKABLE"* MANACLES RESTRAIN CHEWIE FOR ALL OF A SECOND LONGER.

AS THE SURVIVING CATUMAN LUNGES TOWARDS LEIA, THE *MILLENNIUM FALCON'S* FIRST MATE DIVES FOR HIM.

THE FIGHT IS *NO CONTEST.*

SHOULDER SLASH IS MESSY, BUT I DON'T THINK IT'S SERIOUS. I CAN STILL MOVE MY ARM FAIRLY EASILY.

NO SIGN OF KHARYS-- TOO BAD. WE HAVEN'T TIME TO *SEARCH* FOR HER, EITHER.

HEY, BEAUTIFUL... REMEMBER ME...?

HAN!

ARE YOU ALL RIGHT?!

NEVER FELT... BETTER... YOUR REGALNESS.

CAN YOU *WALK?*

SHOW ME SOME *PROFIT* IN IT AND I'LL RUN A *MARATHON.*

CHEWBACCA, CARRY HIM. AND FOLLOW ME.

SURE YOU WILL.

FUNNY. DON'T UNDER-STAND... WHY... LEGS FOLDED UP LIKE THAT.

THEY WORKED... FINE... THIS MORNING.

HEAR THOSE EXPLOSIONS, OL' BUDDY? SOUNDS LIKE THIS PLACE IS COMING APART AT THE SEAMS.

MY COMPLIMENTS, PRINCESS. THIS ESCAPE PLAN'S GOING SO WELL, YOU'D THINK IT WAS ONE OF *MINE.*

OH? ALL OF A SUDDEN, I'M *WORRIED.*

AM I DELIRIOUS, OR HAVE I JUST BEEN *INSULTED?*

DON'T *SAY* ANYTHING, CHEWIE... I THINK I *KNOW* THE ANSWER!

RARP

LEIA, WE'VE GOT TO GO WAY *DEEPER* TO REACH THE *FALCON.*

GOOD, THE FARTHER I AM FROM THOSE BLASTS, THE BETTER I LIKE IT.

MEANWHILE, ABOVE THE FORTRESS...

WHERE ARE THESE STORM-TROOPERS COMING FROM?!

SEEMS LIKE MORE IMPERIALS IN THIS CASTLE THAN WERE ON THE *DEATH STAR!*

ONE *BOY?!* MY AERIE GUTTED AND RUINED BY *ONE--WINGLESS--BOY?!?*

I *CURSE* THE DAY I ALLIED MYSELF WITH THOSE ARMORED IDIOTS. SCORES OF THEM ARE *DEAD,* WHILE THE YOUTH REMAINS *UN-TOUCHED!*

THE *FORCE* IS STRONG IN HIM.

IT REMINDS ME OF-- BY THE GREAT WIND, THE *PROPHECY!* CAN HE BE-- THE *ONE?!* IF SO, IT IS EVEN MORE IMPERATIVE--FOR VADER'S SAKE AS WELL AS MY OWN--THAT HE *DIE!*

FORMIDABLE THOUGH HE SEEMS TO BE--

--THIS BOY WILL MEET HIS MATCH, AND MORE, IN *KHARYS!*

YOW!

KTANG

SHK!

THROWING STARS! BARELY DODGED 'EM! BUT *WHO--?!*

UH-OH!

KHARYS!

STAND YOU BACK, STORM-TROOPERS!

THE BOY'S LIFE IS *MINE!*

SHE'S CARRYING A *LIGHT-SABER!* AND I HAVE A NASTY FEELING...

...SHE *KNOWS* HOW TO USE IT!

SO, THE HATCHLING HAS *FANGS* OF HIS OWN.

THAT LIGHTSABER WILL NOT *SAVE* YOU, BOY.

YOU COULD BE THE FINEST WARRIOR IN CREATION -- ON THE *GROUND* --

-- BUT NOW, YOU ARE IN *MY* ELEMENT!

SHE'S -- *GOOD!*

AND, WORSE, I'VE GOT TO WORRY ABOUT HER WING AND FOOT CLAWS, AS WELL AS THAT SABER.

ARAGH AND THE CLAN ELDERS -- THEY'RE WATCHING! THEN THEY, TOO, MUST BELIEVE HE IS -- THE *ONE.*

THE ONE WHOSE COMING TO SKYE WILL MEAN *MY* DEATH, AND MY PEOPLES' *LIBERATION.*

BEN KENOBI HARDLY HAD ANY TIME TO TRAIN ME HOW TO USE THIS THING...

...BEFORE DARTH VADER KILLED HIM.

BUT IT'S OBVIOUS KHARYS HAS BEEN USING LIGHTSABERS ALL HER LIFE!

I NEED... BREATHING SPACE...

HIT *FULL-RISE* ON MY *ANTI-GRAV* BELT. IT'LL TAKE ME OUT OF HER REACH, BUY ME SOME TIME.

BUT, WHAT NOW?! I'M ONLY DELAYING THE INEVITABLE. KHARYS IS *TOO GOOD* FOR ME. I CAN'T-- CAN'T... BEAT HER.

NO! WHAT... AM I THINKING?! SO... *HARD* TO THINK-- *WHY?!*

"IT'S THE *FORCE!*

"SHE'S USING IT TO DULL MY WITS, MAKE ME AN EASY, *HELPLESS* TARGET. AND HERE SHE COMES TO *FINISH THE JOB!*

NO MORE FANCY MOVES-- MY HEAD'S STILL PRETTY *MUDDLED.*

I CAN'T AFFORD TO SPLIT MY CONCENTRATION.

GRIMLY, ALMOST DESPERATELY-- LUKE SKYWALKER FOCUSES ALL THE POWER OF HIS WILL.

BY THE DARK LORD!

HE'S TRYING TO SHAKE OFF MY PSYCHIC ATTACK!

HE WANTS ONLY ONE THING-- TO MOVE. HE TRIES. HE FAILS.

WITH THE BATTLE CRY OF HER ANCIENT, AVIAN RACE...

...KHARYS DIVES FOR THE KILL.

BUT AT THE LAST INSTANT-- IMPOSSIBLY-- THAT ATTACK IS CHECKED!

HER SABER GLANCES OFF LUKE'S AND BEFORE HER STARTLED MIND IS EVEN AWARE OF WHAT'S HAPPENING, THE MATRIARCH IS DEAD.

IT TOOK *EVERYTHING* I HAD TO PRETEND I WAS STILL FROZEN-- BUT I HAD TO DECOY HER IN CLOSE.

I HAD TO BE SURE I WOULDN'T *MISS.*

FUNNY-- I THOUGHT I'D FEEL GOOD ABOUT WINNING THIS FIGHT. BUT I DON'T. I FEEL.... SOMEHOW SAD.

LATER, AFTER THE WINGED CLANS OF S'KYTRI HAVE MADE SHORT WORK OF THE AERIE'S IMPERIAL GARRISON, AND THE MILLENNIUM FALCON IS ONCE MORE READIED FOR SPACE...

WE ARE NO LONGER BOUND BY OUR OATH-- THANKS TO SKYWALKER. IF ANY IMPERIALS COME SEEKING VENGEANCE FOR THEIR SLAIN COMRADES, THEY WILL FIND THE WINDBORN WAITING FOR THEM.

ARAGH, I'VE HEARD YOUR PEOPLE REFER TO LUKE AS *"THE ONE."* ONE WHAT? WHAT DO THEY *MEAN* BY THAT?

"*YEARS AGO, MY FRIEND, DURING WHAT YOU HUMANS CALLED THE 'CLONE WARS,' THREE JEDI KNIGHTS SAVED SKYE FROM DESTRUCTION. ONE WAS OBI-WAN KENOBI; THE OTHERS, HIS PUPILS. IN GRATITUDE, WE SWORE ETERNAL FRIENDSHIP AND FEALTY TO THEM.*

"*MUCH LATER, ONE OF THE PUPILS RETURNED. HE TOLD US THAT OBI-WAN AND THE JEDI WERE DESTROYED-- BY HIS HAND-- THEN, HE INVOKED OUR OATH AND MADE SKYE AN IMPERIAL SATRAPY, TO BE RULED IN HIS NAME BY KHARYS, TO WHOM HE GAVE A PORTION OF HIS KNOWLEDGE AND POWERS. THAT... MAN WAS DARTH VADER.*"

AND OBI-WAN'S *OTHER* PUPIL, WHO WAS HE?

YOUNG ONE...

YOU WEAR HIS SABER.

LUKE, IS ANYTHING THE MATTER?

I'M FINE, PRINCESS. HONEST. I'VE JUST GOT SOME THINGS TO THINK ABOUT...

....SOME... MEMORIES TO *CHERISH.*

YOU LOOK SO...*STRANGE.*

"*I NEVER KNEW MY FATHER, BUT I KNOW NOW... THAT HE WAS A MAN TO BE PROUD OF.*

"*I HOPE I CAN BE HALF AS GOOD.*"

FIN.

40¢ 31
JAN
02817

CC

ADVENTURES *BEYOND* THE GREATEST SPACE-FANTASY FILM OF ALL!

STAR WARS

™

LUKE
DEFIES
THE
EMPIRE
ON HIS
HOMEWORLD!

RETURN
TO
TATOOINE!

INFANTINO/
WIACEK...

Long ago in a galaxy far, far away. . .there exists a state of cosmic *civil war*. A brave alliance of *underground freedom fighters* has challenged the tyranny and oppression of the awesome *Galactic Empire*. This is their story!

LucasFilm PRESENTS: STAR WARS™ THE GREATEST SPACE FANTASY OF ALL!

CONTINUING THE STORY BEGUN IN THE FILM BY *GEORGE LUCAS* RELEASED BY *TWENTIETH CENTURY FOX*

ARCHIE GOODWIN | **CARMINE INFANTINO & BOB WIACEK** | **JIM NOVAK** | **CARL GAFFORD** | **JIM SHOOTER**
WRITER/EDITOR | ARTISTS | LETTERER | COLORIST | CONSULTING EDITOR

PROLOGUE:
DEEP SPACE! HERE, A MEETING IS IN PROGRESS. A *RENDEZVOUS* BETWEEN A HOUSE OF TAGGE MINING EXPLORER AND AN IMPERIAL BATTLE CRUISER...

LF619

...AND BETWEEN TWO *BROTHERS!*

...NOT *ANOTHER* PLAN, ORMAN! THE *LAST* WAS NEARLY AS GREAT A FIASCO AS THE *DEATH STAR!*

BECAUSE OF ONE YOUNG REBEL WHO DID THE IMPOSSIBLE... *LUKE SKYWALKER.* *

*STAR WARS #26. --ARCHIE.

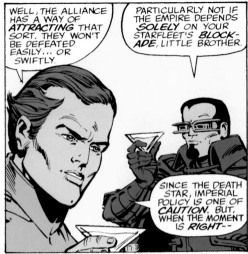

WELL, THE ALLIANCE HAS A WAY OF *ATTRACTING* THAT SORT. THEY WON'T BE DEFEATED EASILY... OR SWIFTLY.

PARTICULARLY NOT IF THE EMPIRE DEPENDS *SOLELY* ON YOUR STARFLEET'S *BLOCK-ADE,* LITTLE BROTHER.

SINCE THE DEATH STAR, IMPERIAL POLICY IS ONE OF *CAUTION.* BUT, WHEN THE MOMENT IS *RIGHT*--

--THE EMPIRE WILL *STRIKE BACK!*

LED NO DOUBT BY *DARTH VADER!* WHY SHOULD YOUR CAREER-- AND OUR FAMILY'S *PRES-TIGE*--TAKE HIND POSITION IN THE EMPER-OR'S FAVOR TO THAT BLASTED *WIZARD?!*

A SUCCESS *NOW* COULD *ECLIPSE* THE SITH LORD!

HE'S *DANGEROUS* TO OPPOSE OPENLY, ORMAN. BUT...YOU ALREADY *KNOW* THAT.

I'M MOVING IN *SECRET,* ULRIC...USING THE HOUSE OF TAGGE'S GREAT SCIEN-TIFIC AND COMMERCIAL RESOURCES. WITH *YOU* TO ASSURE CONTINUED MILI-TARY COOPERATION--

WE'LL HAVE *REVENGE*... AND *MORE!*

IT'S ALL COMING TO *FRUITION*-- LITTLE BROTHER--

--ON A QUIET, UNSUSPECTING BACKWATER WORLD CALLED *TATOOINE!*

"IF THERE'S A BRIGHT **CENTER** TO THIS UNIVERSE, YOU'RE ON THE WORLD **FARTHEST** FROM IT." TO LUKE SKYWALKER, IT SEEMS **AGES** AGO THAT HE SPOKE THOSE WORDS ABOUT HIS HOME PLANET. IT FEELS AS IF HE WERE A DIFFERENT **PERSON** THAN THAT RESTLESS, INEXPERIENCED FARM BOY. NOW HE IS A **HERO**... AND A WARRIOR'S MISSION HAS BROUGHT HIM **BACK.**

RETURN TO TATOOINE!

ARTOO AND I HAVE UNLOADED THE **LANDSPEEDER,** SIR.

GREAT, THREEPIO! GET THE CAMOUFLAGE COVER OVER THE **FREIGHTER!**

EVEN THE **SAND PEOPLE** DON'T SPEND MUCH TIME IN **THIS** PART OF THE DUNE SEA, BUT THERE'S NO POINT IN TAKING--

MOVE WITH THAT **COVERING! FAST!**

OH, DEAR! IT'S PROBABLY WILD *BANTHAS*...OR PERHAPS EVEN THOSE REPULSIVE LITTLE *JAWAS*!

I *KNEW* IT WAS A MISTAKE COMING BACK TO THIS FORSAKEN PLACE!

WHAT DO YOU *MEAN* IF I FEEL THAT WAY I SHOULDN'T HAVE *VOLUNTEERED*...?!

I COULDN'T TRUST A NON-LOGICAL *RUST-POT* LIKE *YOU* TO LOOK AFTER MASTER *LUKE*!

FREEPA BRIIT!

THREEPIO! THE *COVER*--!!

"-- THERE'S AN *IMPERIAL PATROL* OUT ON THE FAR RIDGE!

"ONE OF THEM IS CARRYING A *SCANNER PACK!*"

KEEP YOUR MIND ON THE *JOB*. YOU DIDN'T SCAN THE SECTOR OFF ON OUR *LEFT*.

MY MIND IS ON THE FACT THAT ONE *TIE FIGHTER* COULD DO THE WORK OF *TEN* OF THESE PATROLS.

AND ATTRACTS TEN TIMES THE *ATTENTION*. ORDERS ARE TO *AVOID* THAT.

ARE THEY AFRAID WE'LL UPSET THE LOCAL *SAND LICE?* THAT'S ABOUT ALL WE EVER--

WAIT! I'VE *GOT* SOMETHING--!

RELAX--! IT'S ONLY A *LAND-SPEEDER.* SOME LOCAL FARMER OUT HUNTING *WOMP RATS,* NO DOUBT.

ATMOSPHERIC DISTORTION MADE IT SEEM *BIGGER* FOR AN INSTANT... NOTHING WORTH INVESTIGATING.

ALL RIGHT THEN. QUIT WASTING OUR TIME... WE'VE GOT A LOT OF *TERRITORY* TO COVER.

DON'T COMPLAIN ...*WE'RE* THE ONES WHO ARE *WALKING.* TOMORROW *I* GET THE DEWBACK.

ALL *CLEAR*, THREEPIO. YOU AND ARTOO GOT THE FREIGHTER COVERED JUST IN *TIME.*

THAT *ELECTRONICALLY-CHARGED FABRIC* WILL KEEP ANY SCANNER FROM PICKING UP WHAT'S *UNDER* IT.

BUT THAT *PATROL* WORRIES ME. EXCEPT FOR A SMALL GARRISON AT MOS EISLEY... YOU USED TO *NEVER* SEE A STORMTROOPER ON TATOOINE.

NO *OFFENSE* TO A NATIVE, SIR... BUT IT DOESN'T *COMPUTE* THAT THIS GRITTY SAND PILE SUDDENLY HAS *STRATEGIC VALUE.*

WELL, OUR MISSION IS TO RECRUIT *BLOCKADE RUNNERS.*

SINCE SOME OF THE BEST *SMUGGLER PILOTS* IN THE GALAXY HANG OUT AT MOS EISLEY... *THAT'S* WHERE WE'RE HEADED.

AND IF ANYTHING *ELSE* IS GOING ON ... THERE'S SURE TO BE *GOSSIP* ABOUT IT!

BUT AS THE TRIO MOVE ALONG A CIRCUITOUS ROUTE TO THE DESERT WORLD'S *SPACE-PORT...*

THREEPIO! *STOP* THE SPEEDER!

MASTER LUKE! THIS SURELY CAN'T BE *WISE.* IF SOMETHING *STRANGE* IS GOING ON, WE SHOULDN'T--

BRR-KLIK VADOOT!

HOW *DARE* YOU SAY MY *MEMORY CIR-CUITS* HAVE WARPED, ARTOO! I--OH! OF *COURSE!*

WHAT HAS DRAWN LUKE IS A *RUIN...* A RUIN ONCE THE MAIN BUILDING OF A *MOISTURE FARM.* AND FOR MOST OF HIS TWENTY YEARS... THAT FARM WAS LUKE SKYWALKER'S *HOME.*

AUNT BERU....! UNCLE OWEN....! MUCH AS I ALWAYS COMPLAINED ABOUT BEING *STUCK* HERE...

...MUCH AS I GLORY IN SOME OF THE THINGS I'VE DONE SINCE *LEAVING*... I STILL *MISS* YOU BOTH VERY MUCH!

THEN... A *SOUND* MAKES LUKE TURN HIS MISTY EYES BEYOND THE LONG-CHARRED RUBBLE.

THAT *VAPORATOR...!* IT'S WORKING... ACTIVE...!

B-BUT... THAT SHOULDN'T *BE!*

HOLD IT RIGHT *THERE!*

DO *EXACTLY* WHAT I SAY... OR START SPENDING THE REST OF YOUR LIFE *DEAD!*

EASE YOUR *BLASTER* FROM ITS HOLSTER... JUST USE TWO FINGERS... *THAT'S* IT....!

NOW TOSS IT *BACK* TO ME.

LUKE *OBEYS.* BUT HE MAKES THE TOSS TOO *HIGH...*

...SO HIS CAPTOR'S *EYES* INADVERTANTLY FOLLOW IT, ONLY FOR AN INSTANT...

...BUT *IN* THAT INSTANT, HE SWIFTLY *WHIRLS!*

HAN SOLO TAUGHT ME ABOUT *DISTRACTING* A FOE--

SHRAAAAK

--AND THE FAST *LIGHT SABER* WORK I LEARNED FROM *OBI-WAN KENOBI!* THAT'S TWO REASONS YOU'RE SUDDENLY ON THE *WRONG END* OF THIS FRACAS!

SUPPOSE *YOU* COME UP WITH ONE FOR *WHY* IT STARTED IN THE *FIRST PLACE!*

S-SKY-WALKER...?

FIXER! WHY AREN'T YOU AT TOSHI STATION REPAIRING EQUIPMENT INSTEAD OF OUT HERE *AMBUSHING* INNOCENT TRAVELLERS?!

I-I DON'T *WORK* AT THE STATION ANYMORE, LUKE. GOT A BETTER JOB... MORE FUTURE.

AT LEAST... THAT'S WHAT I *THOUGHT.*

E-EVERYONE ASSUMED YOU *DIED*, LUKE... ALONG WITH YOUR AUNT AND UNCLE WHEN THE *TUSKEN RAIDERS* HIT THIS PLACE.*

I'VE BEEN MAKING IT *OPERATIONAL* FOR THE NEW OWNER.

WHAT?!

*FIXER DOESN'T KNOW IT WAS THE *EMPIRE'S* DOING. SEE SW #2.--A.G.

THE HOUSE OF *TAGGE* HAS BOUGHT UP A LOT OF LOCAL MOISTURE FARMS... THOUGH *YOUR* SHOWING UP COULD FOUL THEIR *CLAIM.*

BUT THAT LEGAL STUFF CAN *WAIT.* COME OVER *HERE*, LUKE!

HOLD IT, FIXER! I WANT--

HEY, SWEETHEART! YOU CAN EASE UP GUARDING THE *SKY HOPPER!* INSTEAD OF A THIEVING *PARTS SCAVENGER* LIKE I EXPECTED TO CATCH--

--IT'S *SKYWALKER...* BACK FROM THE DEAD!

NOT LITTLE *WORMIE...?!*

HELLO, CAMIE...I HAVEN'T HEARD THAT NICKNAME FOR A *LONG* TIME.

NOT SINCE THAT DAY I CAME RACING INTO ANCHORHEAD TO TELL EVERYONE ABOUT THE BIG *SPACE BATTLE...*

AND IF THE LOVE OF MY LIFE HAD SEEN YOU IN *ACTION* A MINUTE AGO... SHE'D NEVER HAVE *DARED* TO USE IT.

*ANCIENT HISTORY FROM *STAR WARS* #1.-- A.G.

I DON'T KNOW WHAT LUKE BOY'S BEEN *DOING* ALL THIS TIME.... BUT HE'S SURE *CHANGED.*

YES, I CAN *SEE* THAT NOW. HE LOOKS.... *TALLER* SOMEHOW.

WE'VE CHANGED TOO. RIGHT, CAMIE...? *MARRIED.* THE TAGGE OUTFIT'S SET US UP IN THE OLD *DARKLIGHTER* PLACE.

THEIR PEOPLE ARE CONCENTRATING ON *EXPANSION WORK* OUT IN THE DUNE SEA AND JUNDLAND WASTES--

--SO THEY TOOK ME ON AS A SORT OF *CARE-TAKER* OF THEIR OTHER PROPERTIES. DOESN'T *SOUND* TOO EXCITING...

BUT YOU DON'T *GET* MANY BIG OPPORTUNITIES ON A PLACE LIKE *TATOOINE.*

AND ANY KIND OF *TROUBLE* COULD *RUIN* IT.

LIKE *ME* TRYING TO RECLAIM MY UNCLE'S PLACE, CAMIE? I'VE BEEN OFF WORLD TOO LONG TO GO BACK TO *MOISTURE FARMING.* MY ONLY BUSINESS IS IN *MOS EISLEY.*

I JUST DON'T LIKE THE *TAGGE* FAMILY GETTING IT... WITH THEIR CONNECTIONS, IT'S PRACTICALLY LIKE GIVING IT TO THE *EMPIRE!*

FIXER AND I DON'T HAVE MUCH TIME FOR *POLITICS*... WE'RE KEPT BUSY JUST TRYING TO MAKE OUR *LIVES* A LITTLE BIT BETTER!

I *UNDERSTAND,* CAMIE, IT'S ONLY THAT--

MASTER LUKE--!

"ARTOO'S SENSORS HAVE PICKED UP A *VEHICLE* IN THE AREA, SIR. *LARGER* THAN A LAND SPEEDER... *SMALLER* THAN A JAWA SAND-CRAWLER.

"THAT SOUNDS DISTRESSINGLY LIKE AN IMPERIAL *TROOP CARRIER* TO ME, SIR!"

THIS IS *TAGGE COMMAND,* UNIT THREE. ANY *SUCCESS* YET?

NEGATIVE, COMMAND. WE ARE STILL *SEARCHING.*

I'M SORRY TO HAVE RUSHED YOU AWAY FROM YOUR OLD **FRIENDS**, SIR. IT SEEMED **BEST** UNDER THE CIRCUMSTANCES.

IT'S **OKAY**, THREEPIO, WE DON'T SEEM TO HAVE MUCH IN **COMMON** NOW ANYWAY.

FUNNY. ONCE I WOULD'VE GIVEN **ANYTHING** TO BE IN FIXER'S PLACE...TO HAVE A GIRL LIKE **CAMIE**. BUT NOW I--

MASTER **LUKE!** LOOK OUT--!

HOLY--! HOLD **TIGHT!** IT'S GONNA BE **CLOSE!**

VROOO!

EVERYONE ALL **RIGHT...?** WE STOPPED SHY OF THE CANYON WALL BY AT LEAST AN **INCH!**

THREEPIO...? **THREEPIO?!**

W-WHAT...? OH... **EXCUSE** ME, SIR, I THINK I **SHUT DOWN** FOR A MOMENT.

IS THAT AWFUL **BEAST** STILL--

STANDING THERE LIKE A **STATUE!** I'VE NEVER HEARD OF A **BANTHA** BEHAVING LIKE THAT!

I'M GOING TO TAKE A **LOOK,** THREEPIO.

AND LUKE'S STEADY, CAUTIOUS MOVEMENT FORWARD *ALSO* PRODUCES NO REACTION...

THIS CAN'T *BE*...! I-IT'S *DEAD*--

BUT...IT FEELS *COLD!* FROZEN *STIFF*--

--RIGHT HERE UNDER TATOOINE'S *TWIN SUNS!*

MASTER LUKE! ARTOO'S AUDIO RECEPTORS HAVE CAUGHT THE *SOUND* OF THAT *TRANSPORT*--

IT'S COMING *THIS* WAY...WE'VE GOT TO *RUN* OR *HIDE!*

BUDDA-DEEP.

NO SOONER DO THE TRIO GET THE LANDSPEEDER TO COVER, THAN...

AT *LAST*, COMMANDER! STUPID CREATURE MUST HAVE WANDERED INTO THE CANYON BEFORE THE *EFFECT* TOOK!

THAT EXPLAINS WHY OUR *SCANNER* HAD TROUBLE PICKING IT UP!

NOW THAT WE'VE *FOUND* IT...YOU *KNOW* WHAT TO DO.

SUDDENLY, THE CANYON IS *ALIVE* WITH THE ECHOING THUNDER OF LASER BOLTS AND PROTON GRENADES...

FOLLOWED BY...*SILENCE.*

THEY'RE *GONE*... AND SO IS ANY *TRACE* OF THAT BANTHA.

THE SAME MIGHT BE TRUE OF *US*, SIR...IF WE HADN'T BACKED AROUND THIS *BEND* IN THE CANYON.

THE WHOLE *INCIDENT* SEEMS QUITE SINISTER AND IRRATIONAL.... WHY *VAPORIZE* SOMETHING ALREADY DEAD?

MAYBE SO NO ONE CAN LEARN *HOW* IT DIED, THREEPIO.

WHATEVER THE TAGGE INTERESTS ARE DEVELOPING OUT IN THE WASTELANDS,... IT SURE ISN'T NEW METHODS FOR *MOISTURE FARMING!*

OUR FIRST DUTY IS TO DIG UP SOME *BLOCKADE RUNNERS* LIKE GENERAL DODONNA ASSIGNED US TO DO.

BUT THAT TAGGE BUNCH IS OBVIOUSLY WORKING ON *SOMETHING* FOR THE *EMPIRE* --

-- AND I'M NOT LEAVING *TATOOINE* UNTIL I FIND OUT *WHAT!*

THE *JUNDLAND WASTES.* ONCE ONLY WILD BEASTS AND TUSKEN RAIDERS DARED ROAM HERE. RECENTLY HOWEVER, THERE ARE *OTHERS.* OTHERS FAR MORE *CIVILIZED.*

AND PERHAPS... FAR MORE *DANGEROUS.*

YOU TOOK THE ESCAPE OF THE *BANTHA* VERY WELL, ORMAN. I EXPECTED YOU TO GO *RAGING* ABOUT... SLASHING THINGS WITH THAT OUTMODED *WEAPON* YOU CARRY.

I HAD THIS LIGHT SABER CONSTRUCTED IN *IMITATION* OF THOSE CARRIED ONCE BY JEDI KNIGHTS.

I'M *SAVING* IT FOR THE DAY WHEN I CAN PAY DARTH VADER BACK IN *KIND* FOR WHAT HE DID TO ME.

AND *YOU'RE* CLOSE ENOUGH TO SUCCESS THAT A *SLIGHT* SECURITY BREACH-- SWIFTLY REPAIRED-- SHOULDN'T MATTER.

IN *FACT*, SILAS, ONE REASON I *PICKED* THIS ABOMINABLE LITTLE WORLD AS A SPOT FOR YOU TO CONDUCT YOUR *EXPERIMENTS*--

--WAS THE HOPE THAT *WORD* OF IT MIGHT REACH A CERTAIN PARTY. A YOUNG *REBEL.*

ANOTHER VENDETTA? DOESN'T BEING *BARON* AND RUNNING OUR *FAMILY* KEEP YOU *BUSY* ENOUGH?

GETTING *EVEN* IS ONE OF THE GREAT FOSSIL FUELS OF *LIFE,* BROTHER SILAS. AND THE HAND OF *FATE* IN THIS MATTER SEEMED TOO *STRONG* TO RESIST.

THERE WERE SEVERAL ARID PLANETS THAT FIT *YOUR* CONDITIONS... BUT A NAME IN THE IMPERIAL CENSUS RECORDS DREW ME TO *THIS* ONE. *LUKE SKYWALKER.*

PERHAPS HE'LL COME. PERHAPS HE WON'T. BUT IF HE *SHOULD*... I'LL BE READY.

EMOTIONAL, ORMAN. BUT TO BE EXPECTED FROM A MAN WHO STILL PREFERS *REAL MEAT*--

-- WHEN SCIENCE PROVIDES SOMETHING AS EFFICIENT AS *FOOD PASTE.*

LIGHTS AHEAD, MASTER LUKE...WE'RE APPROACHING MOS EISLEY.

EVENING'S A GOOD TIME. COMING OUT OF THE DESERT LIKE THIS, I'LL SEEM LIKE ANY FARM BOY LOOKING FOR A WILD NIGHT IN THE WICKED CITY.

HOPEFULLY, THAT'S NOT WHAT WE'LL FIND, SIR.

Y'KNOW, THREEPIO, MAYBE AFTER THIS MISSION, YOU'LL FINALLY JUST START CALLING ME LUKE... INSTEAD OF 'SIR' AND 'MASTER' ALL THE TIME.

YOU, ARTOO, AND I HAVE BEEN THROUGH TOO MUCH TOGETHER FOR THAT.

OLD PROGRAMMING DIES HARD, BUT I'LL CERTAINLY TRY, SI-- ER...MAS--UH...LUKE!

NONE OF YOUR COMPLAINING, ARTOO DETOO! YOUR BALANCE INTENSIFIER IS PERFECTLY CAPABLE OF HANDLING YOUR BEING ON YOUR SIDE THIS LONG.

YOU BOTH CAN RELAX IN A MOMENT...THE CANTINA IS JUST AHEAD.

WEEE-RRT-WOOO

I DON'T REALLY HAVE FOND RECOLLECTIONS OF THAT PLACE. ARE YOU SURE YOU'LL BE ALL RIGHT?

WELL, NOTHING'S CERTAIN IN THIS GALAXY. BUT I KNOW MY WAY AROUND A BIT BETTER THAN MY FIRST VISIT THERE.

OF COURSE... I DON'T HAVE BEN KENOBI TO BAIL ME OUT OF TROUBLE.

PULL AROUND TO THE REAR...AND KEEP THE SPEEDER READY TO MOVE. JUST IN CASE.

OH, BROTHER...! THE PLACE HASN'T **CHANGED** A BIT!

GENERAL DODONNA GAVE ME THIS ASSIGNMENT SO I'D HAVE **SOMETHING** TO DO INSTEAD OF WORRYING ABOUT THE **PRINCESS**--*

WRAK!

*LEIA HAS HER **OWN** MISSION. SEE **LAST ISSUE.**-- ARCH AGAIN.*

TRYING TO SELECT A FEW REASONABLY TRUSTWORTHY **STAR HOPPERS** FROM THIS MOTLEY COLLECTION OUGHT TO **MORE** THAN DO THE TRICK!

I'D GIVE **ANYTHING** JUST TO SEE A **FRIENDLY FACE** RIGHT NO--

UNGHHH!

HAN!

HEY, KID! HAVEN'T YOU LEARNED TO **STAY OUT** OF LOW CLASS DIVES... YOU DON'T KNOW **WHO** YOU'LL BUMP INTO!

WRAP UP THE **FIGHT,** CHEWIE! WE'VE GOT SOME **SERIOUS** CELEBRATING TO DO!

THOK!

...SO AFTER RESOLVING OUR DIFFERENCES WITH *JABBA THE HUT,** CHEWIE AN' ME DELIVERED HIM BACK *HERE* AND DECIDED TO HANG OUT FOR A WHILE.

WANTED TO LET *YOU* ENJOY A FEW MOMENTS WITH HER *ROYALNESS* BEFORE *I* SHOWED UP TO SWEEP HER OFF HER FEET.

*CHRONICLED IN *STAR WARS #28.* --ARCHIE.*

BESIDES...YOU NEEDED SOME TIME TO SPEND THAT EXTRA *BONUS* YOU FORCED OUT OF JABBA.

CAN YOU BEAT THAT, CHEWIE...? KID DOES A LITTLE STAR-ROVING AND HE BECOMES A *CYNIC!*

WELL, IF *YOU'RE* FEELING IDEALISTIC, HAN, I'M ON A MISSION THAT YOU TWO WOULD BE *PERFECT* FOR AND--

WAIT A SECOND!

FIXER! WHAT ARE *YOU* DOING IN THIS PLACE?

CAMIE AN' ME... DID SOMETHING *BAD.* I... CAME TO *WARN* YOU.

LUKE...? I-I'VE BEEN TRYING TO *FIND* YOU!

TRY TO *UNDERSTAND,* SKYWALKER... YOU MADE IT *OFF* THIS SANDPILE. BUT CAMIE AN' ME ARE *STUCK* HERE... WE'VE GOT TO GET BY AS *BEST* WE CAN!

FROM STUFF SAID THIS AFTERNOON... IT SOUNDS LIKE YOU'RE A *REBEL,* LUKE! TO PROTECT MY *JOB* CAMIE AN' ME DECIDED THERE WAS NO *CHOICE* BUT TO--

YOU *REPORTED* ME, FIXER! I OUGHT TO--

FORGET ANY *THREATS,* KID...YOU GOT NO TIME TO CARRY 'EM *OUT!* YOU'RE *FINGERED*... AND CHEWIE AND ME ARE *GUILTY* BY ASSO- CIATION!

OUT THE *REAR!* WE GOT *IMPERIAL VISITORS* COMIN' IN THE FRONT DOOR!

YOU THREE... *HALT!*

SECONDS LATER...A MOS EISLEY ALLEYWAY BECOMES A **BATTLEGROUND**...

PILE ONTO THE **LAND-SPEEDER**!

THREEPIO, GET US **OUT** OF HERE!

STREETS ARE CRAWLING WITH **STORMTROOPERS!** NO CHANCE OF REACHING THE **FALCON**, KID!

HEAD FOR THE **OPEN DESERT**, THREEPIO!

SWERVING WILDLY BETWEEN TWO OUTLYING BUILDINGS... THE ONE-TIME PROTOCOL DROID DOES JUST **THAT!**

NOT **BAD**, BRONZE BRITCHES, WE'RE MOVING OUT OF THEIR **RANGE**.

IF THIS BABY DOESN'T COLLAPSE FROM THE **LOAD** IT'S CARRYING... I THINK WE'LL BE **OKAY!**

BUT BACK AT THE EDGE OF TOWN...

I'VE CALLED OUT A **TROOP CARRIER**... BUT THOSE REBELS HAVE A **BIG LEAD**.

NO MATTER! ONE OF OUR BLASTS **SCORED**. THAT SPEEDER IS LEAKING COOLANT...IT'LL BE **BURNT OUT** BY MORNING!

IF ONE OF OUR **DESERT PATROLS** DOESN'T GET THEM OUT THERE... THE **TWIN SUNS** WILL!

NEXT ISSUE: **THE JAWA EXPRESS!**

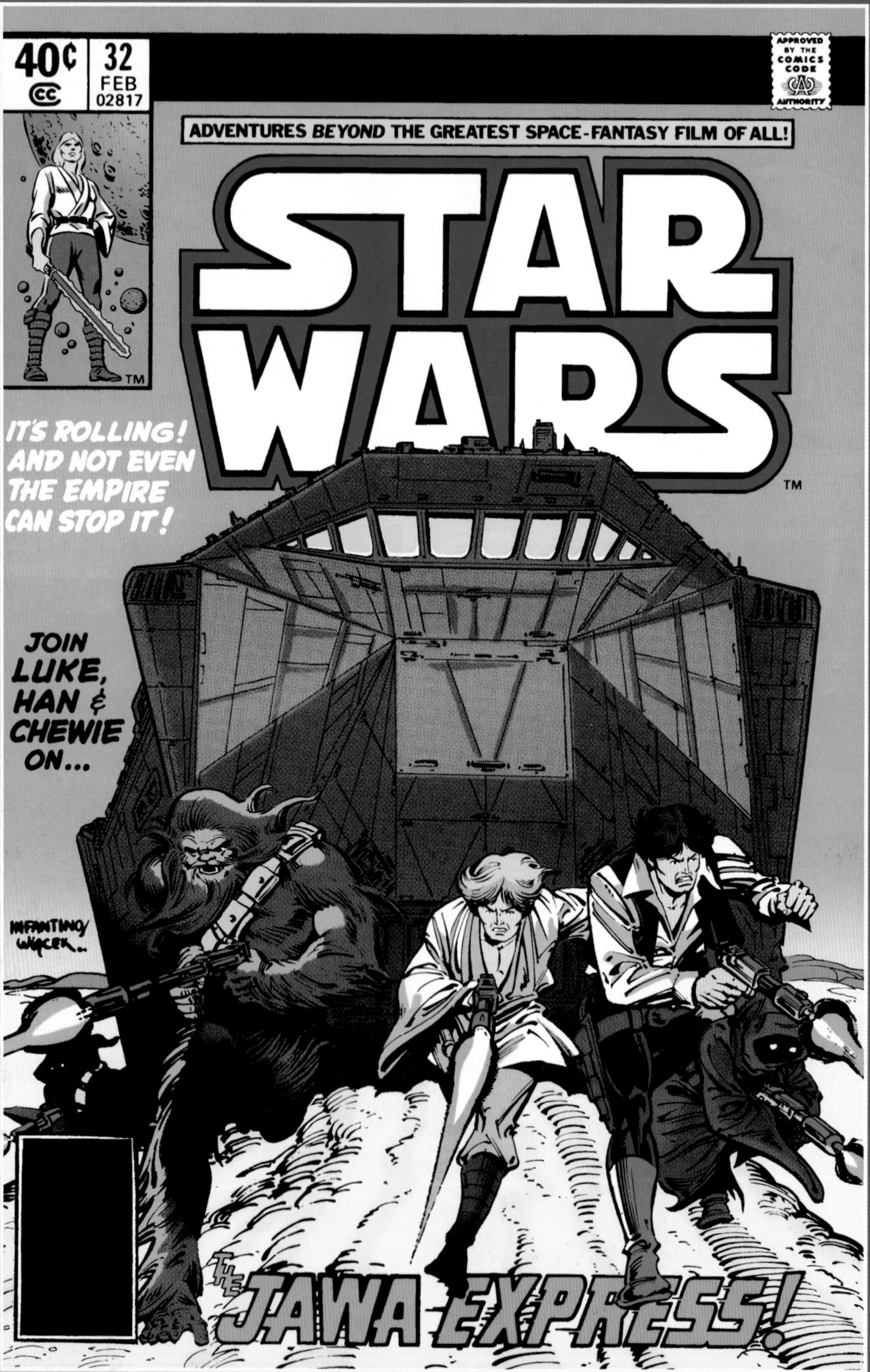
40¢
32
FEB
02817
APPROVED BY THE COMICS CODE AUTHORITY
ADVENTURES BEYOND THE GREATEST SPACE-FANTASY FILM OF ALL!
STAR WARS
IT'S ROLLING! AND NOT EVEN THE EMPIRE CAN STOP IT!
JOIN LUKE, HAN & CHEWIE ON...
THE JAWA EXPRESS!

Long ago in a galaxy far, far away. . .there exists a state of cosmic *civil war*. A brave alliance of *underground freedom fighters* has challenged the tyranny and oppression of the awesome *Galactic Empire*. This is their story!

LucasFilm PRESENTS: STAR WARS™ — THE GREATEST SPACE FANTASY OF ALL!

CONTINUING THE SAGA BEGUN IN THE FILM BY *GEORGE LUCAS* RELEASED BY *TWENTIETH CENTURY-FOX*

ARCHIE GOODWIN · CARMINE INFANTINO & BOB WIACEK · JOHN COSTANZA · PETRA GOLDBERG · JIM SHOOTER
WRITER/EDITOR — ARTISTS — LETTERER — COLORIST — CONSULTING EDITOR

YOU DON'T HAVE TO TELL AN *EX-MOISTURE FARMER* WHAT THE MIDDAY HEAT HERE CAN *DO*, HAN.

BUT WITH A LITTLE MORE *WORK*, I THINK WE CAN *BYPASS* THESE FUSED PARTS.

IT'S *COOLANT* WE NEED, LUKE... TO REPLACE WHAT LEAKED AWAY. WITHOUT IT, ANY *REPAIRS* WILL MELT JUST LIKE THE *ORIGINAL* PARTS.

YEAH. I THOUGHT WE *ESCAPED* THOSE STORMTROOPERS IN MOS EISLEY FREE AND CLEAR,... BUT *ONE* OF THEIR PARTING SHOTS FIXED US *GOOD!* *

* *LAST ISSUE.*--ARCHIE G.

AS *LUKE* AND *HAN SOLO* GRIMLY DISCUSS THEIR SITUATION... *CHEWBACCA* SUDDENLY COMES ALERT. NOSE TWITCHING...

NORRF?

...HE *RISES*.

AND MOVES SWIFTLY TO A NEARBY *RIDGE*...

WHAT HE SEES IN THE DISTANCE, THROUGH SHIMMERING HEAT, IS NOTHING TO *GLADDEN* A WOOKIEE'S HEART.

IT'S A **BIG** PATROL. I GUESS WE SHOULD BE **FLATTERED**, KID.

I'M **SORRY**, HAN. I SEEM TO HAVE A **KNACK** FOR GETTING YOU TWO **INTO** MESSES LIKE THIS AND--

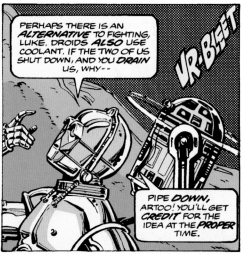

PERHAPS THERE IS AN **ALTERNATIVE** TO FIGHTING, LUKE. DROIDS **ALSO** USE COOLANT. IF THE TWO OF US SHUT DOWN, AND YOU **DRAIN** US, WHY--

VR-BEEP

PIPE **DOWN**, ARTOO! YOU'LL GET **CREDIT** FOR THE IDEA AT THE **PROPER** TIME.

SOON...

THANKS TO THREEPIO AND ARTOO-DETOO WE'RE **MOBILE**, KID... BUT I DUNNO FOR HOW **LONG**.

BEST WE CAN HOPE FOR IS TO GET A LITTLE **DISTANCE** BETWEEN US AND THOSE TROOPERS--

--BEFORE THIS THING DIES OF **STRAIN!**

WE CAN DO BETTER THAN **THAT.** THE DROIDS AND I DIDN'T **WALK** HERE FROM YAVIN, HAN.

WE'VE GOT A **SHIP** HIDDEN FURTHER OUT IN THE DUNES. EVEN **MY** REPAIRS SHOULD HOLD UP TILL WE **GET** THERE.

THEY **DO.** BUT AT THEIR DESTINATION... **MORE** BAD NEWS.

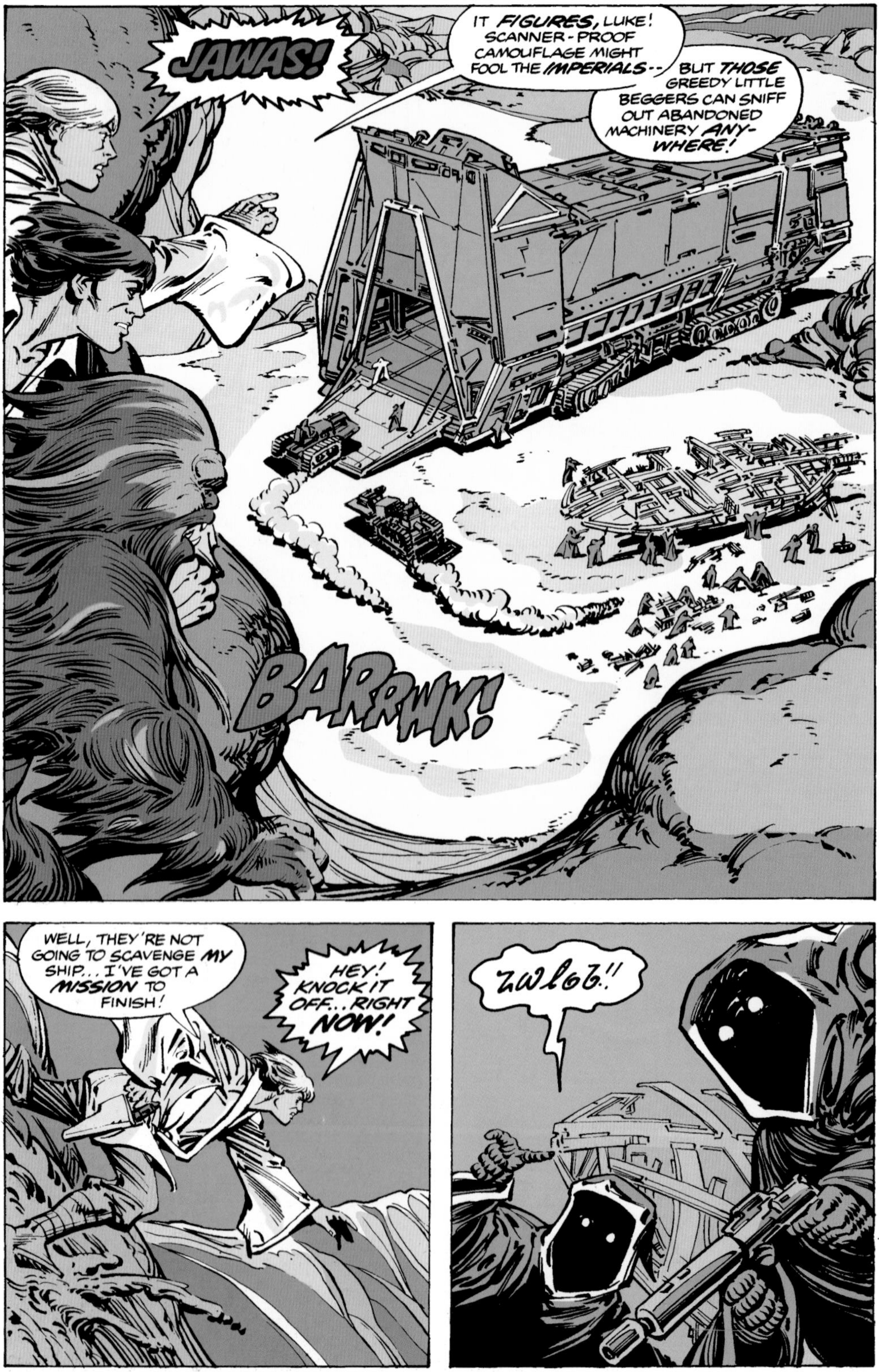
JAWAS!
IT FIGURES, LUKE! SCANNER-PROOF CAMOUFLAGE MIGHT FOOL THE IMPERIALS--
BUT THOSE GREEDY LITTLE BEGGERS CAN SNIFF OUT ABANDONED MACHINERY ANY-WHERE!
BARRWK!
WELL, THEY'RE NOT GOING TO SCAVENGE MY SHIP... I'VE GOT A MISSION TO FINISH!
HEY! KNOCK IT OFF... RIGHT NOW!

EASY, KID! WE'VE ALREADY GOT ENEMIES... RIGHT NOW WE COULD USE SOME FRIENDS. YOUR SHIP'S TOO FAR GONE TO HELP US NOW.

BUT, HAN--

FACE IT, LUKE... FINDERS KEEPERS IS ALL THESE GUYS KNOW. WITH THE LANDSPEEDER WHEEZIN' ITS LAST... IT'S TIME TO BE CHARMING.

SMILE! WE NEED A LIFT IN THEIR SANDCRAWLER...

AND THAT INVOLVES CHALLENGING THE JAWAS AT WHAT THEY DO BEST... HAGGLING.

THEY'RE NOT GOING FOR JUST THE 'SPEEDER, HAN... THEY WANT THE DROIDS TOO!

PROMISE 'EM ANYTHING, KID... LONG AS THEY AGREE TO GET US BACK TO MOS EISLEY.

THREEPIO AND ARTOO AREN'T JUST ROBOTS TO ME... THEY'RE FRIENDS! I'D FEEL LIKE A SLAVER!

CHEWIE AN' I STASHED PART OF OUR BONUS * FROM JABBA THE HUT * ABOARD THE MILLENNIUM FALCON... WE CAN USE IT TO BUY BACK THE DROIDS!

MAKE A FAST DEAL AND GET US OUT OF HERE!

* SEE SW #28.--AG.

BUT THERE CAN BE DANGER IN FAST DEALS...

MOVIN' AT LAST, KID! NOT EXACTLY WARP SPEED... BUT MOVIN'.

BY THE TIME WE HIT MOS EISLEY, THE HEAT SHOULD BE OFF AND--

ONE PROBLEM, HAN... THIS ISN'T THE WAY TO MOS EISLEY.

HEY! WHAT *IS* THIS, GUYS? WE HAVE A *BARGAIN!*

OW!

HAN, IF I *UNDERSTAND* RIGHT... THEY'RE *KEEPING* THE BARGAIN. BUT THEY'RE GOING TO *FINISH* THEIR SCAVENGER RUN *FIRST!*

NICE! HOW MANY *DAYS* OUT OF OUR WAY IS *THAT?*

NOT DAYS, HAN... *MONTHS. THREE* OF 'EM!

THREE MONTHS?! WE'LL DIE OF CONCUSSIONS BANGIN' AROUND IN THESE *JAWA*-SIZED COMPARTMENTS! KID, YOU GOTTA--

VEEDOW!

HALT THAT VEHICLE! MY MEN ON THE *RIDGE* WILL STOP IT WITH *PROTON GRENADES* IF YOU FAIL TO *OBEY!*

SUSPECTED *REBELS* ARE IN THE AREA... WE'RE COMING ABOARD TO *SEARCH!*

UH...HAN, I BELIEVE THEY FEEL WE WEREN'T TOTALLY *HONEST* WITH THEM AND--

AND UNLESS WE DO SOMETHING *FAST*...OUR BARGAIN IS *OFF!* TELL 'EM TO *RELAX,* KID.

GOOD *NEWS,* CHEWIE! I THINK THERE'S A WAY WE CAN FINALLY *STAND UP* IN THIS ROLLING TORTURE CHAMBER.

MOMENTS LATER... TWO HATCHES ON THE SAND-CRAWLER ROOF ARE EASED SLOWLY OPEN.

YEAH. IF WE MISS EVEN *ONE* TROOPER ON THE RIDGE...HE CAN BLOW US *AWAY.*

WOWRK!

FA-DOW!

VDAM!

THAT'S WHY YOU GOTTA FOLLOW MY *LEAD*--

DON'T SHOOT AT THE *TROOPERS*--

--BLAST THE *RIDGE* OUT FROM *UNDER* THEM!

RESULT: INSTANT AVALANCHE...

...THAT SWEEPS THE STORMTROOPERS *ABOVE* INTO THEIR COMPANIONS *BELOW*...

BA-WOM!

...CARRYING THEIR *ARMED* PROTON GRENADES *WITH* THEM!

BETTER HAVE OUR LITTLE PALS *BACK UP*, LUKE... THIS ISN'T MUCH OF A *THOROUGHFARE* ANYMORE.

THEY'RE *DOING* IT, HAN... BUT I GET THE FEELING THEY'RE NOT TOO *HAPPY* ABOUT IT.

APPARENTLY THEY'D HOPED TO *AVOID* THE JUNDLAND WASTES... NOW THEY *CAN'T*.

WHAT'S THE *PROBLEM?* ARE THEY AFRAID OF *SAND PEOPLE?*

NO. SOMETHING *ELSE*... BUT I THINK I CAN GUESS *WHAT*, HAN.

THE HOUSE OF *TAGGE* IS UP TO SOMETHING OUT HERE... AND THEY'RE DOING IT FOR THE *EMPIRE*.

THREEPIO, ARTOO, AND I *SAW* ENOUGH TO BE CERTAIN OF THAT *YESTERDAY* WHILE WE WERE MAKING OUR WAY INTO *MOS EISLEY*.*

LAST ISSUE. --ARCHIE.

MY MISSION FOR THE ALLIANCE IS TO RECRUIT *PILOTS* TO BECOME *BLOCKADE RUNNERS* FOR US, SO I COULDN'T TAKE TIME TO *INVESTIGATE,* BUT--

HEY! WE'RE *STOPPING* AGAIN!

THAT SEEMS TO BE WHAT THIS THING DOES *BEST*.

WHAT'S GOING *ON,* LUKE...? EVERYONE ABANDONING *SHIP* OR WHAT IT--

:OW!:

THE *ANSWER* LIES OUTSIDE...

MACHINERY, HAN...! LOOKS LIKE A GIANT *VAPORATOR!*

NO WONDER OUR SHORT FRIENDS ARE *EXCITED,* KID... THERE'S ANOTHER *SAND-CRAWLER.* THEY'VE GOT *COMPETITION* FOR THE LOOT.

WAIT, HAN. WHATEVER THIS *IS...* IT *ISN'T* A VAPORATOR. I'VE SEEN *TOO MANY* TO THINK THAT AND--

A CHILLING *TINGLE* GOES THROUGH LUKE...

HAN! CHEWBACCA!

WE'VE GOT TO GET THE JAWAS AND OURSELVES *AWAY* FROM THIS THING... *FAST!*

HUSTLE IT, HALF-PINTS! THE KID'S NOT GIVEN TO *PRACTICAL JOKES.*

AWRK!

?...WWL?!

THEN, WITH THE SUDDENESS OF LIGHTNING STRIKING...
SOMETHING SWEEPS THE DESERT PLAIN BEFORE THE TOWER. SOMETHING *IMPOSSIBLE.*

AND ON THE *OPPOSITE* SIDE, BELOW THE RISE...

LUKE...! THE *WIND*... THE *SAND*...

I *KNOW,* HAN... THEY FEEL *COLD.*

MOMENTS PASS... NOTHING HAPPENS. CAUTIOUSLY, THE GROUP MOVES *FORWARD.*

YOU *SAID* IT, BIG BUDDY! BETWEEN HERE AN' THAT DISTANT TOWER... THE WHOLE PLAIN'S *FROZEN!*

WRAAG!

NOT *JUST* THE PLAIN... *LOOK!*

"THE OTHER *SANDCRAWLER*...! I--IT'S *COLLAPSING*...! THE COLD IS SO *GREAT*... EVEN THE *METAL* IS SHATTERING!"

SSHHRAAAAAAAAAKKK!!!

THAT COULD'VE BEEN *US*, KID...IF YOU HADN'T *YELLED*. WAS THAT THE *FORCE* IN ACTION...?

NOT *THIS* TIME, HAN... I *FELT* THE TOWER STARTING TO GET *COLD*. IT REMINDED ME OF *YESTERDAY*--

--AND A FROZEN *BANTHA* THE DROIDS AND I DISCOVERED!*

*ALSO *LAST ISSUE*.--ARCH.

I THINK WE'VE FOUND--

ЗЗ-ЛЧЬ.?

DON'T BOTHER *TRANSLATING*, LUKE! THE *TONE* SOUNDS LIKE: EVERYBODY *DOWN*!

AND FOR GOOD REASON. THERE ARE *NEW* ARRIVALS ON THE SCENE...

EXCELLENT, SILAS... *EXCELLENT!* UNDER THE MERCILESS TWIN SUNS OF THIS HELLHOLE PLANET... YOU'VE ACHIEVED *THIS!*

IF YOU'LL EXAMINE THE *BODIES* OF THOSE LITTLE CREATURES WHO WERE *IN* THE MACHINE--

--YOU'LL FIND *THEY* WERE FROZEN AS WELL, ORMAN.

I BELIEVE IT'S SAFE TO SAY THAT *NOTHING* CAUGHT BETWEEN THE CONDUCTOR TOWERS CAN *SURVIVE*--

--NOT WHEN WE GENERATE THE *OMEGA FROST*, MY DEAR BROTHER.

YOU'LL BE ABLE TO *DUPLICATE* THIS SUCCESS ANYWHERE... IN ANY *ENVIRONMENT?*

PERHAPS NOT IN THE HEART OF A *NOVA*. BUT IF IT WORKS UNDER *THESE* ARID CONDITIONS... I'M CONFIDENT I CAN ADJUST IT FOR *WHATEVER* YOU REQUIRE.

THE *OMEGA FROST!* BRILLIANT, SILAS ....! IT'S GOING TO BE THE *CLUB* WITH WHICH WE BEAT *DARTH VADER* FROM THE EMPEROR'S FAVOR.

BARON TAGGE? WHAT ABOUT THE *REBELS*, SIR? THEY'RE STILL *OBSERVING* US.

GOOD, THEY HAVEN'T *GUESSED* THAT THE CONDUCTOR TOWER HAS A *SENSOR SYSTEM* THAT DETECTED THEM AND *ALERTED* US.

IF UNITS TWO AND THREE ARE IN *POSITION*... LET'S BEGIN HERDING THEM WHERE WE *WANT* THEM.

AND WITH TAGGE *ABOARD*, THE IMPERIAL TROOP CARRIER SUDDENLY, SWIFTLY *MOVES*...

...OPENING FIRE WITH ITS *LASER CANNON!*

NOT *TOO* CLOSE TO THEIR POSITION--

--ONE OF THEM IS *LUKE SKYWALKER.*

I WANT HIM *ALIVE*... TO DEAL WITH *PERSONALLY!*

WHILE AHEAD...

HAN, SOMETHING'S *ROTTEN* ABOUT THIS.

YEAH. WE COULD GET *KILLED*--

--THAT *ALWAYS* DEPRESSES ME.

VWOOM!

NO, HAN. IF THEY *SUSPECTED* WE WERE SPYING ON THEM... WHY SUCH A *SLOPPY* ATTACK?

EVEN *IMPERIALS* KNOW TO CUT OFF OUR LINE OF *RETREAT* BEFORE MOVING IN!

SOUNDS LIKE YOU'VE BEEN SITTING IN ON SOME OF THOSE REBEL *STRATEGY* MEETINGS, KID.

HOW DO *YOU* FIGURE IT?

THEY'RE DRIVING US *INTO* SOMETHING. WE'VE GOT TO GET THE JAWAS TO *RESIST.*

NOW YOU'RE FLYING *BLIND*, LUKE. *SCROUNGING* AND *SCAVAGING* ARE THESE LITTLE CHARACTERS' SPECIALTIES.

BEFORE THEY *FIGHT*... THEY'LL TURN US OVER TO TAGGE AND COMPANY *THEMSELVES.*

ยย·ววืฟฒฒฃ·ลฅฃฅฎ::

THAT *MAY* HAVE BEEN THE CASE, HAN--

BUT *THIS* GUY IS GRATEFUL BECAUSE WE *SAVED* THEM,...AND WANTS TO KNOW HOW *THEY* CAN HELP!

THUS, MOMENTS LATER, WHEN THE IMPERIAL TROOP CARRIER **TOPS** THE RISE...

...A **RUDE SURPRISE** IS WAITING!

BARON! THEY DIDN'T **FLEE**...THE MADMEN ARE **CHARGING US!**

WE'RE TOO **CLOSE** TO BLAST THEM, FOOL!

TURN BEFORE WE CRASH **HEAD ON**... **TURN!**

BUT EVEN **THAT** ALTERNATIVE LEAVES MUCH TO BE DESIRED! AND...

TAGGE BASE...THIS IS THE **BARON!** MY BROTHER AND I NEED **ASSISTANCE.**

UNITS TWO AND THREE... ABANDON **AMBUSH** POSITIONS AND GIVE **CHASE** TO FUGITIVE SAND-CRAWLER!

TELL OUR HOSTS... **GREAT WORK**, LUKE! THE **JAWA EXPRESS** IS ON THE MOVE!

NEXT STOP... **MOS EISLEY!**

WE'RE PICKING UP TAGGE'S **TRANSMISSION BAND**, HAN--

--WE MAY HIT A COUPLE OF **OBSTACLES!**

YOU *CALLED* IT, KID! THE LANDSCAPE IS SUDDENLY FURNISHED WITH HOT AND COLD RUNNING *TROOP CARRIERS!*

HOT TO *CATCH* US... AND COLD *CERTAIN* TO DO IT AT THE SPEED *THEY* CAN TRAVEL!

HAN, HE SAYS THAT ALONG WITH THEIR *OTHER* PICKINGS... THEY HAVE SOME LOOSE DRUMS OF *SKYHOPPER* PROPELLANT. GIVE YOU ANY *IDEAS?*

THAT'S IT, CHEWIE! HEAVE 'EM *OUT!*

NOT *TOO CLOSE* TOGETHER... WE WANT 'EM *SPREAD* ACROSS THE PLAIN.

LUKE'S ON THE *ROOF* TO TAKE CARE OF THE *REST.*

BLAST THE WAY THIS LUMBERING *MONSTROSITY RATTLES* AND *SHAKES!*

STILL... THIS SHOULDN'T BE ANY TOUGHER THAN POTTING *WOMP RATS* FROM A LAND-SPEEDER WITH UNCLE OWEN'S OUTMODED OLD *ENERGY RIFLE.*

COME TO *THINK* OF IT... THAT WAS PRETTY *TOUGH!*

FTOOM! FTOOM! FTOOM!

*BUT DESPITE CONCERN...LUKE'S SHOTS ARE **TRUE**. PROPELLANT DRUMS **EXPLODE** IN A FIERY SPRAY...*

*...PRODUCING A **CHAIN REACTION** THAT TOUCHES **ALL** THE DRUMS SPREAD ACROSS THE PLAIN...*

*...UNTIL A MASSIVE WALL OF **FLAME** RISES BEFORE THE PURSUING CARRIERS OF THE EMPIRE'S TROOPS! THE WARRIORS ARE LEFT BUT ONE CHOICE. **HALT**...*

*...OR BE **DESTROYED!***

KA-VWOOM!

THAT SAVED US, LUKE...FOR THE *MOMENT*. BUT THEY'RE *BOUND* TO HAVE SIGNALLED AHEAD TO *MOS EISLEY*--

-- AND WE CAN'T EXACTLY *SNEAK* INTO THERE WITH A *SANDCRAWLER!*

BUT, HAN, IT'S MORE IMPORTANT THAN *EVER* THAT WE REACH THE MILLENNIUM FALCON AND *GET OFF* TATOOINE!

THE ALLIANCE *HAS* TO KNOW WHAT THE HOUSE OF TAGGE HAS *CREATED* HERE!

MAY *WE* MAKE A SUGGESTION, SIR?

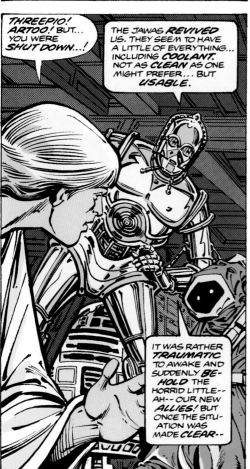

THREEPIO! ARTOO! BUT... YOU WERE *SHUT DOWN*...!

THE JAWAS *REVIVED* US. THEY SEEM TO HAVE A LITTLE OF EVERYTHING... INCLUDING *COOLANT*. NOT AS *CLEAN* AS ONE MIGHT PREFER... BUT *USABLE*.

IT WAS RATHER *TRAUMATIC* TO AWAKE AND SUDDENLY *BE-HOLD* THE HORRID LITTLE-- AH-- OUR NEW *ALLIES!* BUT ONCE THE SITUATION WAS MADE *CLEAR*--

--I REASONED THAT IF THEIR COOLANT WORKS IN *US*... IT WILL REVIVE OUR AILING *LAND-SPEEDER* TOO!

VREET!

OH, VERY WELL, ARTOO... *YOU* REASONED IT! THE MAIN THING IS WE *CAN* REACH MOS EISLEY.

AND...

SINCE THE IMPERIALS ARE AFTER A *SANDCRAWLER*... THIS SHOULD DO THE TRICK, KID.

RIGHT, HAN! AND OUR FRIENDS, THE *JAWAS*, CAN *LOSE* THEMSELVES IN THE DUNE SEA.

TAGGE'S *SCHEME* MAY NOT BE *FINISHED*...BUT NEITHER ARE *WE!*

NEXT ISSUE! IN THE DEPTHS OF SPACE...LUKE SKYWALKER VS. BARON TAGGE!

SABER CLASH!

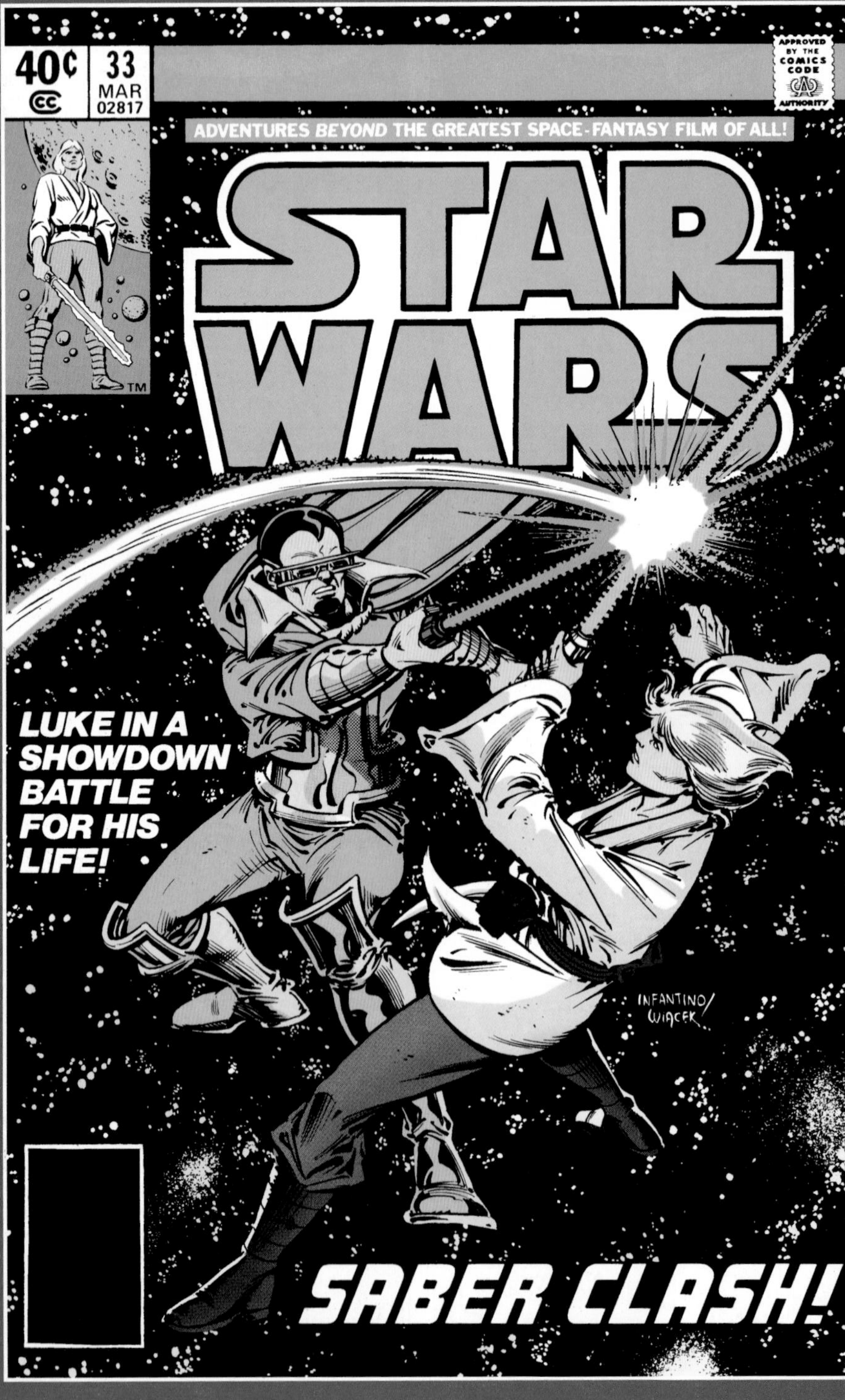

40¢
33
MAR
02817
APPROVED BY THE COMICS CODE AUTHORITY
ADVENTURES BEYOND THE GREATEST SPACE-FANTASY FILM OF ALL!
STAR WARS
TM
LUKE IN A SHOWDOWN BATTLE FOR HIS LIFE!
INFANTINO/ WIACEK
SABER CLASH!

Long ago in a galaxy far, far away. . .there exists a state of cosmic *civil war*. A brave alliance of *underground freedom fighters* has challenged the tyranny and oppression of the awesome *Galactic Empire*. This is their story!

LucasFilm PRESENTS: STAR WARS

THE GREATEST SPACE FANTASY OF ALL!

CONTINUING THE SAGA BEGUN IN THE FILM BY GEORGE LUCAS RELEASED BY TWENTIETH CENTURY-FOX

ARCHIE GOODWIN
WRITER/EDITOR

CARMINE INFANTINO and GENE DAY
ARTISTS

JOHN COSTANZA
LETTERER

PETRA GOLDBERG
COLORIST

JIM SHOOTER
CONSULTING EDITOR

OUTWARD BOUND! THE MILLENNIUM FALCON SOARS AWAY FROM THE LOOMING BULK OF TATOOINE... PUTTING LUKE, HAN, CHEWIE, AND THE DROIDS A SIGH OF RELIEF REMOVED FROM WHAT BEN KENOBI ONCE REFERRED TO AS 'IMPERIAL ENTANGLEMENTS.'

MAKE THAT A SHORT SIGH OF RELIEF.

HAN! THAT MINING EXPLORER...! I RECOGNIZE IT!

SABER CLASH!

IT'S THE SAME *HOUSE OF TAGGE* SHIP THAT WAS FERRYING *TIE FIGHTERS* TO YAVIN TO ATTACK THE *REBEL BASE* THERE!*

NOT *SURPRISING*, KID... CONSIDERING THAT *BARON TAGGE* WAS BEHIND ALL THE *TROUBLE* WE HAD BACK ON TATOOINE.

*BACK IN *STAR WARS #25*--ARCHIE G.

WOWRK!

YEAH, I SEE THE *SCOPE* TOO, CHEWIE! CHECK IT *OUT*, LUKE--

"-- THERE'S A *SHUTTLE CRAFT* APPROACHING THAT LUMBERING *SPICE SNIFFER*.

"*NOT A CARGO ORBITTER*... THEY MUST BE TAKING ON *PASSENGERS*, GETTING READY TO *EMBARK*."

HAN, IT *HAS* TO BE THE BARON! WHO *ELSE* WOULD THEY BE TAKING ABOARD?

EVERYTHING SEEMS TO BE WORKING TO TAKE ME FURTHER AWAY FROM MY *ORIGINAL* MISSION FOR THE ALLIANCE, BUT--

WE'VE *GOT* TO FOLLOW HIM!

WHAT WE WITNESSED OUT IN THE *JUNDLAND WASTES** MAKES IT TOO *IMPORTANT* FOR US NOT TO!

*LAST ISSUE -- ARCH AGAIN.

IT IS CALLED THE *OMEGA FROST.* IT IS GENERATED FROM TWO *CONDUCTOR TOWERS.* ANYTHING CAUGHT IN ITS PATH CONTAINING EVEN MINUTE QUANTITIES OF *MOISTURE...* FREEZES AND SHATTERS.

SINCE MOST THINGS IN THIS GALAXY CONTAIN *SOME* MOISTURE... IT IS *AWESOME.*

WHAT WE SAW WAS OBVIOUSLY ONLY AN *EXPERIMENT.* NOW BARON TAGGE'S PROBABLY MOVING TO *REALLY* USE IT!

IT'S UP TO US TO *STOP* HIM!

KID, YOU'RE A *BAD INFLUENCE...*

...EVERY TIME I'M AROUND YOU, I GET TURNED INTO A *HERO* IN SPITE OF MYSELF.

OKAY, CHEWIE. CUT OUR *ACCELERATION.* WE'LL MANEUVER SO THAT *ASTEROID CLUSTER* IS BETWEEN US AND THE *TAGGE* SHIP...

WE'LL WAIT 'EM OUT AND SEE WHERE THEY'RE *HEADED.*

MEANTIME, IN THE DOCKING BAY OF THE SPICE EXPLORER...

REALLY, ORMAN... THIS EMOTIONAL *OUTBURST* IS UNWARRANTED.

WE WERE REMARKABLY *SUCCESSFUL* ON TATOOINE.

SKRAAAAAAAAK

SUCCESSFUL WITH THE *OMEGA FROST*, SILAS... BUT *NOT* IN CAPTURING *LUKE SKYWALKER!*

HE TURNED ONE OF OUR *TRIUMPHS* INTO *HUMILIATION!* I WON'T LET HIM GO *UNPUNISHED!*

* SHOWN IN *STAR WARS* #26 --ARCHIE.

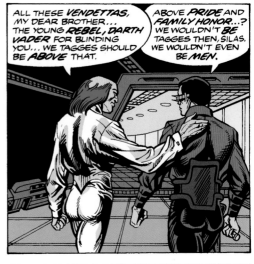

ALL THESE *VENDETTAS*, MY DEAR BROTHER... THE YOUNG *REBEL*, DARTH *VADER* FOR BLINDING YOU... WE TAGGES SHOULD BE *ABOVE* THAT.

ABOVE *PRIDE* AND *FAMILY HONOR...?* WE WOULDN'T *BE* TAGGES THEN, SILAS, WE WOULDN'T EVEN BE *MEN.*

ROMANTIC, ORMAN... BUT SOMEWHAT LACKING IN *LOGIC.* I SUPPOSE THAT'S WHY *YOU* HAVE THE TITLE AND I'M CONTENT TO BE A MERE *SCIENTIST.*

CHIEF SCIENTIST... OF ALL THE TAGGE INDUSTRIES.

SHANKS, CONTACT MY *YOUNGER* BROTHER. TELL THE GENERAL WE'RE READY TO *RENDEZVOUS* WITH HIM.

A VERITABLE *FAMILY REUNION*, ORMAN. PITY OUR DEAR LITTLE *SISTER* DOESN'T HAVE A *ROLE* IN OUR SCHEME.

SILAS, YOUR *BANTER* IS NOT TO EXTEND TO HER. *EVER.*

BE CONTENT THAT THIS MEETING SHOULD SPELL *DOOM* FOR THE REBEL ALLIANCE.

THERE THEY *GO!* NOT MUCH HOPE OF FOLLOWING THEM THROUGH HYPERSPACE--

--UNLESS YOU AND YOUR *STUBBY FRIEND* HAD SOME LUCK, THREEPIO.

NATURALLY IT WAS A *DIFFICULT* TASK, CAPTAIN SOLO... EVEN WITH ARTOO AUGMENTING YOUR *BROADCAST MONITER.*

OF COURSE, HE HAD *ME* DIRECTING HIM, SO--

THE *BOTTOM LINE*, BRIGHT EYES, DID YOU *PICK UP* ANYTHING?

THE FRAGMENT OF A *TRANCEIVER COMMUNICATION.* THEIR DESTINATION IS APPARENTLY *JUNCTION.*

JUNCTION...?! *WE* KNOW THAT PLACE! SINCE THE *IMPERIAL BLOCK-ADE*... IT'S ONE OF YAVIN BASE'S CHIEF SOURCE OF *SUPPLIES.*

WHAT COULD *TAGGE* BE PLANNING *THERE?*

GUESS WE WON'T KNOW UNTIL WE *REACH* THE PLACE, LUKE--

--BUT I'LL BET ALL THE *SAND* ON TATOOINE IT'S *NOTHING* THAT WE'LL LIKE!

THE *MILLENNIUM FALCON* LEAPS INTO HYPERSPACE... AND A LONG *JOURNEY* BEGINS.

WORD-ARRK!

IT'S *AMAZING*, ARTOO, YOU'D THINK HE'D GROW *TIRED* OF CONSTANTLY WINNING.

TRY ONE MORE *GAME.* AN EVEN *TWENTY* VICTORIES WILL SURELY PUT HIM IN A MOOD TO LET SOMEONE *ELSE* PLAY.

KID, YOU'RE A LOT *BETTER* AT THAT THAN THE *FIRST TIME* I SAW YOU DO IT.

I'VE HAD A LOT MORE *PRACTICE*, HAN, WITH THE SABER.... *AND* THE FORCE!

AND THE LONG JOURNEY *CONTINUES* UNTIL...

JUNCTION, LUKE!

AND LOOK WHAT OUR *QUARRY* IS CUDDLING *UP* TO!

HAN, YOU SAID ONCE THAT *ONE* OF THE TAGGE BROTHERS WAS AN *IMPERIAL FLEET COMMANDER...* THAT *CRUISER* MUST BE HIS!

WE'VE *GOT* TO FIND OUT WHAT'S GOING *ON* HERE!

NOT *LIKELY*, KID... UNLESS THEY INVITE US *ABOARD.*

WAIT! LOOK WHAT THEY'RE STARTING TO *DO*, HAN!

THAT'S *IT!* I *CAN* GET ABOARD!

A SHIP TO SHIP *TRANSFER* IS UNDERWAY. CARGO HANDLERS FROM THE TAGGE MINING EXPLORER GUIDE *MODULE PACKS* TOWARD THE IMPERIAL STAR DESTROYER BELOW...

IT IS AN *OLD FASHIONED* OPERATION, SOMETIMES STILL NECESSARY WHEN ONE SHIP CANNOT FIT IN ANOTHER'S DOCKING BAY...

...AND MATERIALS ARE TOO DELICATE-- OR *DANGEROUS*-- TO TRUST TO *TRACTOR BEAMS.*

I'M NOT SURE I *LIKE* THIS, ORMAN. THERE'S TOO MUCH *TRAFFIC* AROUND JUNCTION.

THIS OPERATION IS STIRRING UP *CURIOSITY*...MAKING THE LOCALS HOVER AROUND US LIKE *TOURISTS.*

AND NO DOUBT SOME OF THEM ARE *SPIES*... REBELS, SURELY. PERHAPS EVEN SOME FROM OUR FRIEND, THE *SITH LORD.*

IT'S TO BE *EXPECTED,* LITTLE BROTHER. INDEED, ULRIC... JUST ONE MORE PART OF OUR *PLAN.*

A GOOD PLAN SHOULDN'T BE *COMPLICATED--*

"--SOMETHING *UNEXPECTED* IS LIKELY TO HAPPEN."

NO ONE SEEMS TO HAVE PICKED UP MY *APPROACH*... THEIR MONITORS MUST BE CONCENTRATED ON THE *TRANSFER.*

TIME TO JOIN THE *WORK FORCE...* AND TUNE IN ON THE *INTERCOM GOSSIP.*

--ASTED *STORMTROOPERS* OUGHT TO BE *HELPING!* THEY'RE THE ONES WHO'LL BE *USING* THIS STUFF.

QUIT *GRIPING.* THE BARON'LL DUMP YOU ON *JUNCTION.* YOU WOULDN'T WANT TO BE *THERE* WHEN THIS IS ASSEMBLED AND WORKING.

YOU *SAID* IT! SAW ONE OF THE *DEMON-STRATIONS* ON THAT DESERT PLANET.

OMEGA FROST. I DON'T EVEN LIKE THE *NAME...* MUCH LESS THINKING ABOUT WHAT IT'D DO TO AN *ENTIRE WORLD.*

NO TIME TO BE *SUBTLE!* GOT TO GET BACK TO THE *FALCON...* ALERT THE *ALLIANCE* AT ALL COSTS!

HEY! NO ONE CALLED A *BREAK!*

AND LUKE *GETS* NONE...

STORMTROOPERS! THEY WEREN'T THERE *BEFORE--!*

HAN! CHEWIE! I'M *CAUGHT!* THE EMPIRE'S GOING TO *USE* THAT THING WE SAW ON *TATOOINE--*

--USE IT ON *JUNCTION!* GET *HELP!* GET-- :UNGHHHH!:

AW... *NO*, KID!

WHY DIDN'T YOU LET ME TALK YOU *OUT* OF THIS CRAZY STUNT LIKE I *TRIED* TO DO?

YEAH, YEAH, YOU'RE *RIGHT*, CHEWIE. MAYBE THEY ONLY *STUN-BLASTED* HIM.

WHATEVER'S HAPPENED, I GOTTA GET *HOLD* OF MYSELF... GET US *AWAY* FROM HERE.

WE'LL BRING WORD TO THE *REBELS* LIKE LUKE WANTED IF WE HAVE TO WARP STRAIGHT *THROUGH* HALF THE BATTLE WAGONS IN THE *IMPERIAL BLOCKADE!*

BUT THERE'S ONE *PARTICULAR* REBEL I DON'T RELISH BREAKING THE *NEWS* TO.

I CAN'T *BELIEVE* IT, HAN SOLO! LUKE HAS THE EXCUSE OF BEING *YOUNG* AND *EAGER*... BUT *YOU* SHOULD HAVE KNOWN BETTER!

HOW DID I EVER BECOME INVOLVED WITH TWO MEN SO *BRAVE*... AND SO *STUPID?!*

I DON'T THINK YOU *MEAN* THAT, YOUR ROYALNESS. BUT IF BEING ANGRY *HELPS*... LAY IT ON.

PERHAPS IT SHOULD BE DIRECTED AT *ME*, PRINCESS LEIA--

IT WAS *MY* DECISION TO SEND HIM OUT TO RECRUIT *BLOCKADE RUNNERS*... RATHER THAN HAVE HIM MOON AROUND THE BASE WAITING FOR *YOU* TO COMPLETE YOUR MISSION ON *METALORN*. *

I THINK *HAN* DIFFUSED MY NEED TO *ATTACK*, GENERAL DODONNA--

* CHRONICLED IN SW #30 -- ARCHIE.

--BUT IT SEEMS LIKE AN ASSIGNMENT *ANYONE* MIGHT HAVE HANDLED, WITH LUKE'S WAY OF STUMBLING INTO *TROUBLE*...

I *CONSIDERED* THAT, YOUR HIGHNESS. BUT *DOES* HE STUMBLE... OR IS HE *GUIDED*?

WE ALL *SPEAK* OF THE FORCE... BUT SKYWALKER SEEMS TRULY *TOUCHED* BY IT. PERHAPS IN MORE WAYS THAN WE *KNOW*.

WELL, *I* KNOW WHILE WE STAND HERE *TALKIN*... A LOT OF FOLKS ON *JUNCTION* ARE THAT MUCH NEARER THE *BIG FREEZE*.

BESIDES BEING A VALUABLE SOURCE OF *SUPPLIES*... THAT OUTPOST WORLD ATTRACTS A LOT OF HOT-SHOT *STAR HOPPERS*.

GOOD POTENTIAL *BLOCKADE RUNNERS*... ESPECIALLY ONCE THEY LEARN WE'RE SAVING THEIR *TAILS*!

VA-BLEET! DA-TOOT!

FOR A CHANGE, I COULDN'T *AGREE* MORE, ARTOO. *WHATEVER* ACTION THEY DECIDE UPON... I HOPE IT REVEALS *SOON* WHETHER POOR LUKE IS *ALIVE* OR *DEAD*!

WE'VE REACHED THE *ASTEROID CORRIDOR*, BARON TAGGE.

PROCEED ACCORDING TO *PLAN*, MY BROTHER, *SILAS*, WILL DIRECT THE OPERATION.

I WISH TO CHAT WITH OUR YOUNG *GUEST* NOW THAT HE'S AWAKE.

YOU'RE *AUDACIOUS*, REBEL. IF I HADN'T BEEN FAMILIAR-IZING MYSELF WITH YOUR *FACE* FROM OFFICIAL RECORDS... I MIGHT HAVE *MISSED* YOU ON THE MONITORS DURING THE *TRANSFER* AT JUNCTION.

INTERESTING. YOU DRESS LIKE A *FARM BOY*... YET YOU CARRY *THIS*. THE WEAPON OF A *JEDI KNIGHT*.

I HOPE YOU'RE AS *SKILLFUL* WITH IT AS YOU WERE WITH AN *X-WING FIGHTER* DURING MY OPERATION ON YAVIN...* BECAUSE I HAVE IN MIND A LITTLE *GAME* AS MY WAY OF *AVENGING* THAT BUSINESS.

*ISSUE #26 -- ARCHIE.

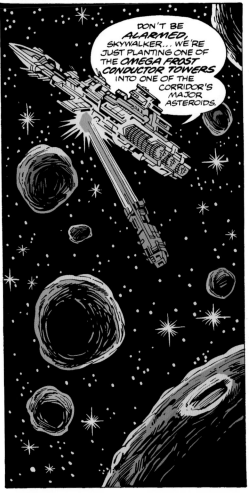

BEFORE LUKE CAN RESPOND IN ANY WAY... A GREAT VIBRATION SHAKES THE TAGGE MINING EXPLORER!

DON'T BE *ALARMED*, SKYWALKER... WE'RE JUST PLANTING ONE OF THE *OMEGA FROST CONDUCTOR TOWERS* INTO ONE OF THE CORRIDOR'S MAJOR ASTEROIDS.

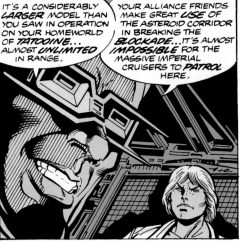

IT'S A CONSIDERABLY *LARGER* MODEL THAN YOU SAW IN OPERATION ON YOUR HOMEWORLD OF *TATOOINE*... ALMOST *UNLIMITED* IN RANGE.

YOUR ALLIANCE FRIENDS MAKE GREAT *USE* OF THE ASTEROID CORRIDOR IN BREAKING THE *BLOCKADE*...IT'S ALMOST *IMPOSSIBLE* FOR THE MASSIVE IMPERIAL CRUISERS TO *PATROL* HERE.

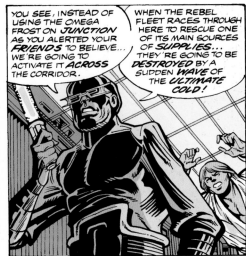

YOU *SEE*, INSTEAD OF USING THE OMEGA FROST ON *JUNCTION* AS YOU ALERTED YOUR *FRIENDS* TO BELIEVE... WE'RE GOING TO ACTIVATE IT *ACROSS* THE CORRIDOR.

WHEN THE REBEL FLEET RACES THROUGH HERE TO RESCUE ONE OF ITS MAIN SOURCES OF *SUPPLIES*... THEY'RE GOING TO BE *DESTROYED* BY A SUDDEN *WAVE* OF THE *ULTIMATE COLD!*

NO!

IT IS A *RASH ACT* OF ANGER AND DESPERATION. AGAINST A MAN OF THE SKILL AND EXPERIENCE OF *BARON TAGGE*, IT SHOULDN'T SUCCEED...

...YET, SOMEHOW, IT *DOES.*

PERHAPS.

MY PRISONER HAS *ESCAPED*... AS I *PLANNED.* ALERT ALL PERSONNEL TO STAY OUT OF HIS WAY AND MAKE NO ATTEMPT TO *INTERFERE.*

MEANTIME, TELL MY *CREW* TO PROCEED TO THE FAR SIDE OF THE *ASTEROID CORRIDOR*... MY LITTLE *GAME* SHOULDN'T INTERRUPT GETTING THE *FINAL* CONDUCTOR TOWER INTO POSITION.

LIGHTSABER OPPONENTS ARE DIFFICULT TO *FIND* IN THIS AGE OF BLASTERS, LUKE SKYWALKER... I HOPE YOU CAN PROVIDE ME WITH VALUABLE *PRACTICAL EXPERIENCE.*

WHEN THE DAY COMES THAT I CHALLENGE *DARTH VADER* WITH THE VERY SAME WEAPON HE USED TO *BLIND* ME --

-- IT WILL BE MOST USEFUL TO KNOW THAT MY *KILLING TECHNIQUES* WORK --

-- BECAUSE I HAVE *PROVEN* THEM ON *YOU!*

LUKE HAS MOVED AS QUICKLY AS HE CAN THROUGH THE STRANGE SHIP, USING ACCESS CORRIDORS AND REPAIR TUBES, AT LAST FINDING HIS WAY TO...

THE *DOCKING BAY...!* GOT TO GRAB A SHIP AND GET OUT OF HERE TO WARN THE *ALLIANCE.*

THAT *TIE FIGHTER* LOOKS LIKE MY BEST BET!

UNFORTUNATELY, SKYWALKER...THERE IS AN *OBSTACLE* IN REACHING IT. *ME.*

SO FAR, I FIND YOU A BIT *PREDICTABLE*, MY YOUNG REBEL FRIEND, I HOPE THAT DOESN'T EXTEND TO WIELDING THE *LIGHTSABER--*

--FOR YOUR SAKE!

YOUR *REFLEXES* ARE EXCELLENT...YOU SHOW SOME *SKILL*...BUT YOUR *TECHNIQUE* IS PRIMITIVE. ALMOST *NONEXISTENT.*

A TALENTED *AMATEUR*...WITH THE BENEFIT OF ONLY A *FEW* LESSONS.

THAT'S JUST *NOT GOOD ENOUGH*, YOUNGSTER.

NOT *NEARLY!*

141

PICK UP YOUR *LIGHT-SABER*, SKYWALKER. I'LL END THIS *SWIFTLY*.

EVEN FOR *VENGEANCE*... THERE'S NO SPORT IN TORMENTING A *NOVICE*.

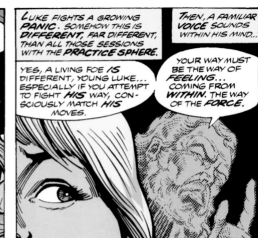

LUKE FIGHTS A GROWING *PANIC*. SOMEHOW THIS IS *DIFFERENT*, FAR DIFFERENT, THAN ALL THOSE SESSIONS WITH THE *PRACTICE SPHERE*.

YES, A LIVING FOE *IS* DIFFERENT, YOUNG LUKE... ESPECIALLY IF YOU ATTEMPT TO FIGHT *HIS* WAY, CON-SCIOUSLY MATCH *HIS* MOVES.

THEN, A FAMILIAR VOICE SOUNDS WITHIN HIS MIND...

YOUR WAY MUST BE THE WAY OF *FEELING*... COMING FROM *WITHIN*. THE WAY OF THE *FORCE*.

NOT EVEN RAISING YOUR BLADE IN *DEFENSE*...? PERHAPS THAT'S JUST AS *WELL*.

AND *TAGGE* LUNGES... A SURE *KILLING* LUNGE...

...THAT SOMEHOW IS *NOT*.

ZRAAAK!

W-WHAT--?

VRAAAMP!

REACTIONS HONED IN COUNTLESS HOURS OF PRACTICE AND TRAINING *SAVE* THE BARON...

BUT SUDDENLY HE REALIZES A MUCH *DIFFERENT BATTLE* IS BEING FOUGHT THAN THE ONE HE BEGAN...

...AND TO *WIN* THAT BATTLE, EVEN WITH *ALL* HIS CONSIDERABLE SKILL...

...HE MUST FIGHT FOR HIS *LIFE!*

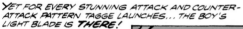

YET FOR EVERY STUNNING ATTACK AND COUNTER-ATTACK PATTERN TAGGE LAUNCHES... THE BOY'S LIGHT BLADE IS *THERE!*

LUKE'S STROKES ARE AWKWARD... *UNORTHODOX...* COMING FROM NO TRAINING PRINCIPLES OR FIGHTING SYSTEMS THE BARON HAS EVER ENCOUNTERED...

...AND HIS *MIND* SEEMS FOCUSED ON SOMETHING *BEYOND* THE COMBAT.

FOR THE FIRST TIME SINCE HE ACHIEVED *MASTERY* OF THE LIGHTSABER... BARON TAGGE FEELS THE NEED TO GIVE *GROUND!*

THERE'S MORE TO YOU THAN MEETS THE *EYE*, SKYWALKER... YOU'VE THE TOUCH OF THE *WIZARD* ABOUT YOU, LIKE THAT BLASTED *DARTH VADER!*

TIME FOR A *NEW* STRATEGY--

VER-RAAAN!

--THE *FINAL* STRATEGY I WAS SAVING TO DISPATCH THE *DARK LORD* HIMSELF!

WITH THE SUDDEN FLARE OF SHORTED CIRCUITRY...THE DOCKING BAY PLUNGES INTO *DARKNESS.*

DARKNESS PIERCED ONLY BY THE GLOW OF A SOLITARY LIGHT-SABER.

THAT... AND THE *CYBER-VISION* OF BARON TAGGE.

MECHANIZED SIGHT HAS *SOME* ADVANTAGES, MY YOUNG FRIEND...

...BUT I WON'T UNDERESTIMATE YOU *TWICE.* TO FIGHT AS YOU HAVE SO FAR, *ALL* YOUR SENSES MUST BE EXCEPTIONAL.

AND SINCE YOU'RE SO *INTENT--*

--I'M *GIVING* THOSE SENSES SOMETHING TO *DETECT!*

THE WHISPER OF CLOTH. SLIGHT. BUT ENOUGH. ENOUGH TO MAKE LUKE REACT...

...ENOUGH TO GIVE TAGGE THE UNPROTECTED TARGET HE HAS BEEN WAITING FOR!

LIGHTSABER CLICKED ON... THE BARON LUNGES FOR THE KILL!

BUT HIS BLADE STRIKES *THIN AIR!* HIS TARGET HAS MOVED, NOT *STOPPING* WITH THE CUT OF THE CLOTH AS EXPECTED, BUT *CONTINUING* THE SWING...

VRAAAAMMP!

...*CONTINUING* IN A PERFECT ARC THAT *ENDS* AT THE FACE OF BARON TAGGE!

MOMENTS LATER, A *TIE FIGHTER* BLASTS OUT OF THE DOCKING BAY...

IT IS PILOTED BY A BOY WHO HAS LEARNED ONCE AGAIN *HOW MUCH* HE CAN DO WITH THE *FORCE* AWAKENED IN HIM BY OBI-WAN KENOBI...

...AND HAS ALSO DISCOVERED AT WHAT POINT HE *PREFERS* TO STOP.

...H-HE DIDN'T *KILL* ME...! DIDN'T... *NEED* TO...! CONTROLLED STROKE SO *PERFECTLY...* DESTROYED MY *CYBER-VISION*... WITHOUT HARMING *ME*...!

HE... WAS *THAT* GOOD...! TH-THAT... *GOOD*...!

THE BARON'S IN *SICK BAY,* SILAS... BEING TREATED FOR *SHOCK.* I'M ORDERING OUT A FLIGHT TO *PURSUE* THE REBEL SO--

IT'S *UNNECESSARY,* SHANKS. WHEN I LEARNED OF THE *'GAME'* MY BROTHER PLANNED... I ORDERED SOME *PRECAUTIONS* TAKEN.

SKYWALKER'S SHIP HAS *NO ARMAMENT, NO COMMUNICATIONS...* AND JUST ENOUGH *FUEL* TO CARRY HIM TO *DISASTER.*

ORMAN IS THE *ROMANTIC.* I AM *NOT.*

NEXT ISSUE: THUNDER IN THE STARS

40¢ CC

34 APR 02817

ADVENTURES *BEYOND* THE GREATEST SPACE-FANTASY FILM OF ALL!

STAR WARS

NO! HAN'S LEADING THE REBEL FLEET INTO A *TRAP*--

--AND STUCK ON THIS ASTEROID, I CAN'T *WARN* HIM!

INFANTINO / WIACEK

THUNDER IN THE STARS!

Long ago in a galaxy far, far away. . .there exists a state of cosmic *civil war*. A brave alliance of *underground freedom fighters* has challenged the tyranny and oppression of the awesome *Galactic Empire*. This is their story!

LucasFilm PRESENTS: **STAR WARS** THE GREATEST SPACE FANTASY OF ALL!

CONTINUING THE SAGA BEGUN IN THE FILM BY **GEORGE LUCAS** RELEASED BY **TWENTIETH CENTURY-FOX**

ARCHIE GOODWIN
WRITER / EDITOR

CARMINE INFANTINO & BOB WIACEK
ARTISTS

JOE ROSEN
LETTERER

PETRA GOLDBERG
COLORIST

JIM SHOOTER
CONSULTING EDITOR

HAN SOLO, IS THIS THE *BEST* YOU CAN DO? I THOUGHT THIS SHIP WAS *FAST!*

A *WORLD* IS AT STAKE... ONE OF THE ALLIANCE'S *PRIME SOURCES* OF SUPPLIES!

AND *LUKE SKYWALKER* HAS HIS LIFE ON THE LINE! I *UNDERSTAND* ALL THAT, YOUR WORSHIPFULNESS--

BUT THIS IS A BIT *TRICKIER* THAN MY RUN OF THE MILL SPICE-SMUGGLING RAZZLE DAZZLE--

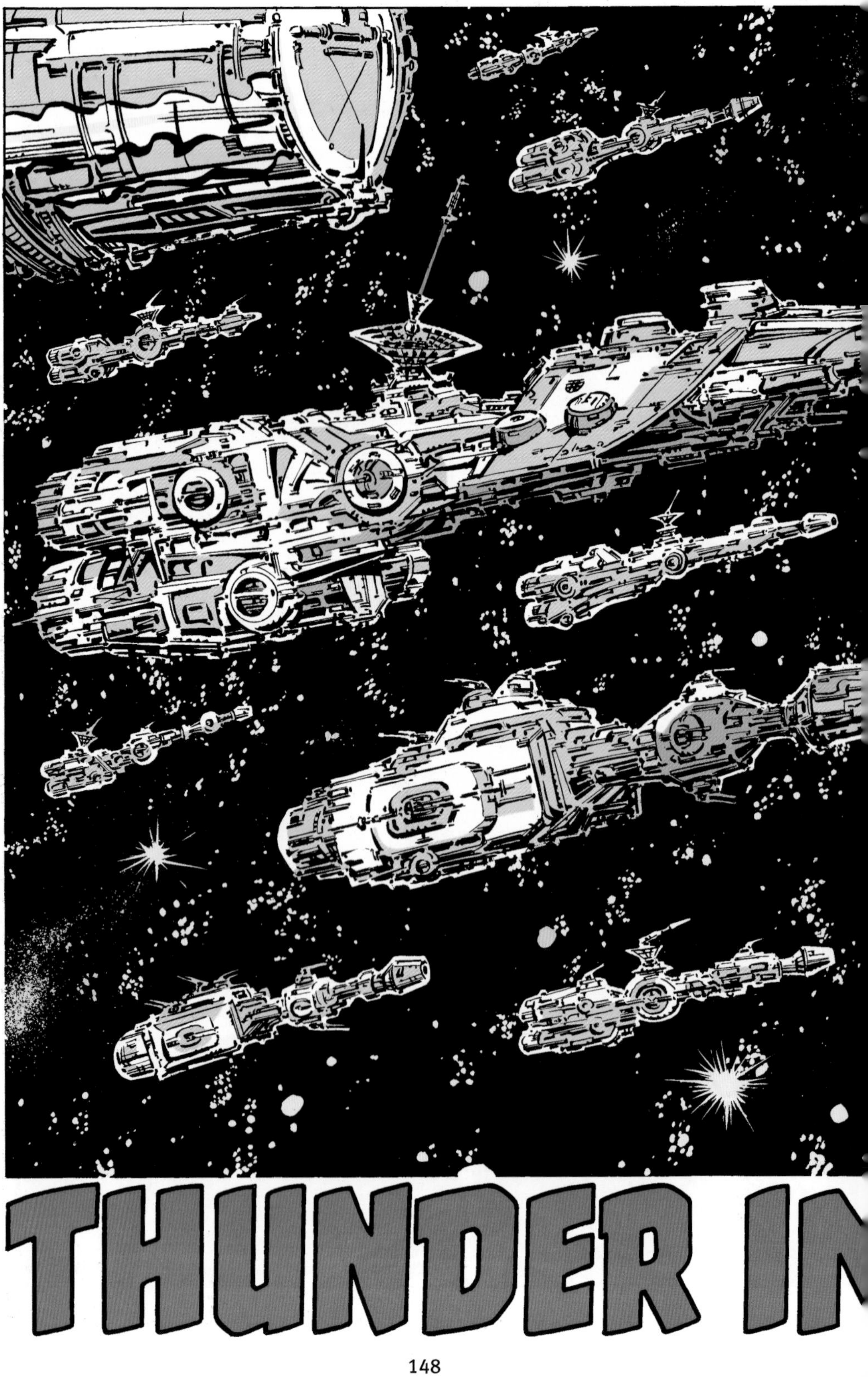
THUNDER IN

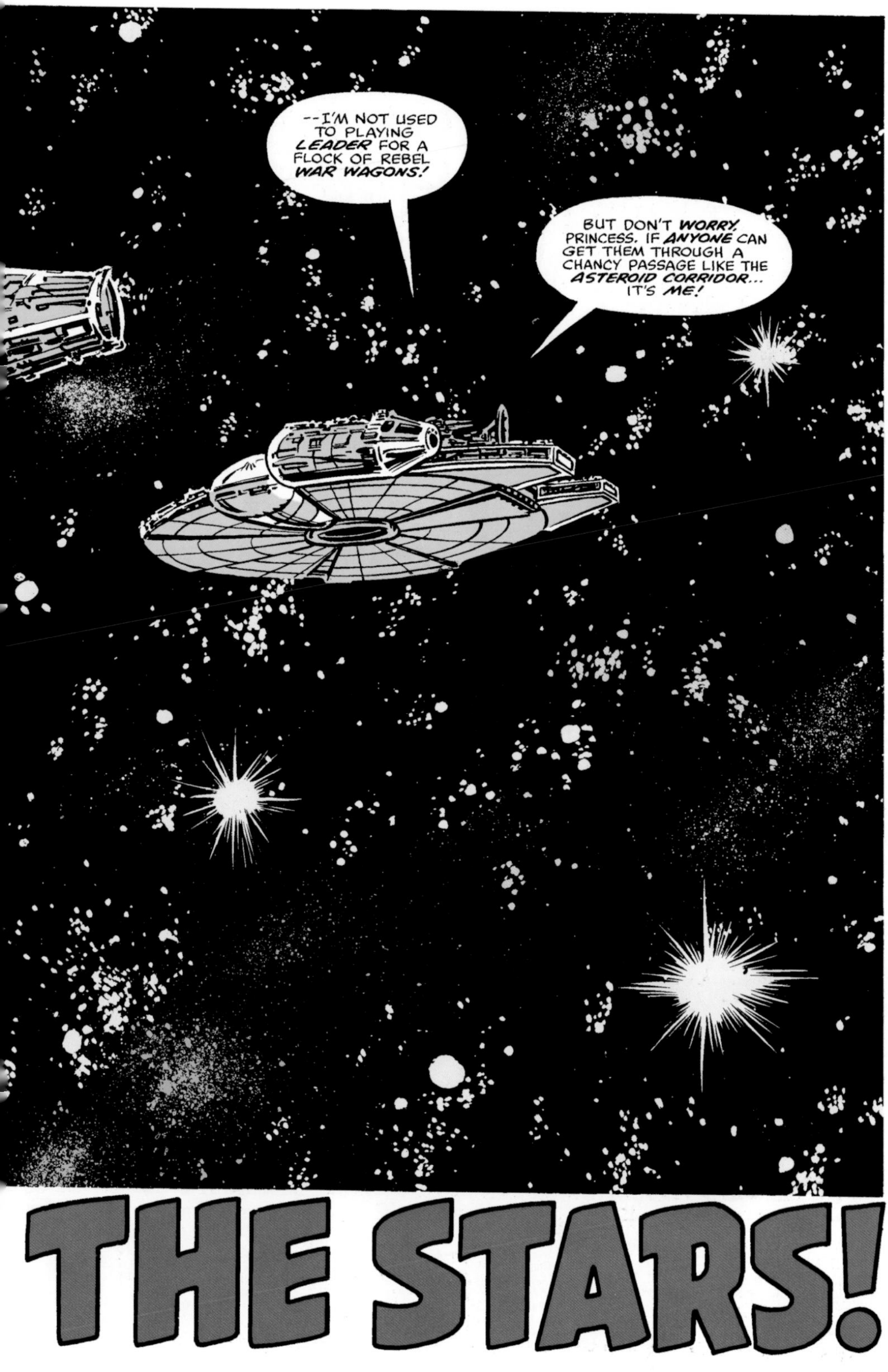
--I'M NOT USED TO PLAYING LEADER FOR A FLOCK OF REBEL WAR WAGONS!
BUT DON'T WORRY, PRINCESS. IF ANYONE CAN GET THEM THROUGH A CHANCY PASSAGE LIKE THE ASTEROID CORRIDOR... IT'S ME!
THE STARS!

I *HOPE* SO, MR. SOLO. THE REBEL ALLIANCE DOESN'T HAVE SHIPS TO *SPARE*.

LADY, I DON'T HAVE ANY *LIVES* TO SPARE. I'M NOT ABOUT TO *WASTE* THE ONE I'VE GOT BUTTING HEADS WITH AN *ASTEROID*.

TENSION HAS TEMPERS RUNNING HIGH IN THE COCKPIT, ARTOO, AT TIMES LIKE *THESE* I'M GRATEFUL TO HAVE THE MECHANICAL CALM AND LOGIC OF--

VREEE-DLIT!

CHECKMATE?! HOW DARE YOU, YOU ROLLING SCRAP BIN! YOU *KNOW* I'M TOO CONCERNED OVER MASTER LUKE'S FATE TO *CONCENTRATE*!

WHAT DO YOU *MEAN* I PLAYED *BETTER* THAN WHEN I *DO* CONCENTRATE?

IF YOU'RE GOING TO BE *INSOLENT* PERHAPS YOU SHOULD HAVE A MORE *WORTHY* OPPONENT! LET ME CALL *CHEWBACCA* AND--

YOU DROIDS BETTER GET *SET*... WE'RE APPROACHING *WARP TIME*.

PRINCESS, LET'S BREAK *COMMUNICATIONS SILENCE* LONG ENOUGH TO CLUE IN THE REST OF THE *FLEET*--

NEXT STOP: THE *ASTEROID CORRIDOR*!

BUT *AHEAD*, IN THAT VERY SECTOR OF SPACE...

TARGET IN *SIGHT*--

--LAUNCH!

" UNFORTUNATELY FOR THEM, OUR CONDUCTOR TOWERS NOW *BRACKET* THE CORRIDOR. ONCE THEY ARE *MIDWAY*, I SHALL *ACTIVATE* THE TOWERS...

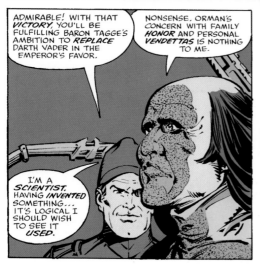

ANYONE WHO DEFEATED BARON TAGGE IN A *LIGHTSABER DUEL* * SHOULDN'T BE UNDERESTIMATED.

I *HAVEN'T*, SHANKS. REMEMBER, I WAS THE ONLY ONE ON THE SHIP TO EVEN *CONSIDER* THAT THE BOY MIGHT *WIN*... AND TAKE *PRECAUTIONS*.

*SHOWN *LAST ISSUE*-- ARCHIE.

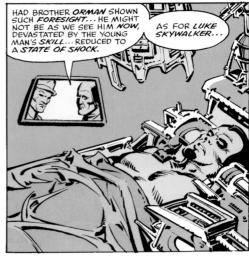

HAD BROTHER *ORMAN* SHOWN SUCH *FORESIGHT*... HE MIGHT NOT BE AS WE SEE HIM *NOW*, DEVASTATED BY THE YOUNG MAN'S *SKILL*... REDUCED TO A *STATE OF SHOCK*.

AS FOR *LUKE SKYWALKER*...

"...HE CAN'T BE *ENJOYING* HIS VICTORY. NOT SINCE HE'S UNDOUBTEDLY DISCOVERED THE *ADJUSTMENTS* I HAD MADE IN HIS *ESCAPE CRAFT!*"

THE GUNS AREN'T *ENERGIZED*... THE COMMUNICATIONS SYSTEM IS *OUT*... AND I JUST HAD TO *EXHAUST* WHAT LITTLE *FUEL* THIS CRATE HAS--

--TO GET IT ON THE *COURSE* I WANT!

SOMEBODY FIXED IT SO THERE'S NO WAY I CAN *WARN* THE ALLIANCE OR TURN THIS FIGHTER AGAINST THAT *TAGGE* SHIP!

HAVE TO ACT *MYSELF*...! CRAFT WON'T LOSE ITS *THRUST* OUT HERE IN SPACE... BUT WITHOUT FUEL, I CAN'T *MANEUVER*.

WHICH MAKES *FLYING* IT A GREAT WAY TO COMMIT *SUICIDE*...! 'CAUSE IN A PLACE LIKE THE *ASTEROID CORRIDOR*--

--SOMETHING'S *BOUND* TO GET IN THE WAY!

AND AS ROCKY *DEATH* LOOMS BEFORE THE ONRUSHING *TIE* FIGHTER...LUKE HITS THE *EJECTION BUTTON!*

P-VOW!

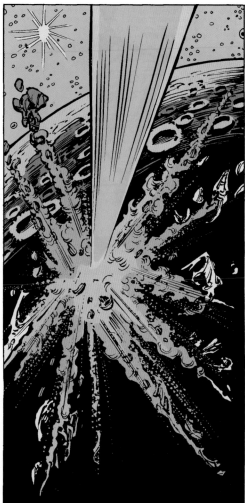

THIS IS CARRYING ME FARTHER AND *FARTHER* FROM THE WAY I *WANT* TO GO...!

GOT TO GET OUT OF THIS *SEAT...* *FAST!*

MY FIRST *BREAK...!* THE *TAMPERING* DIDN'T EXTEND TO THE SURVIVAL ARMOR'S *JET PACK.*

MUST'VE FIGURED ONE *EX-FARM BOY* FLOATING AMONG THE ASTEROIDS COULDN'T *HURT* THEM MUCH...AND THEY MAY BE *RIGHT!*

153

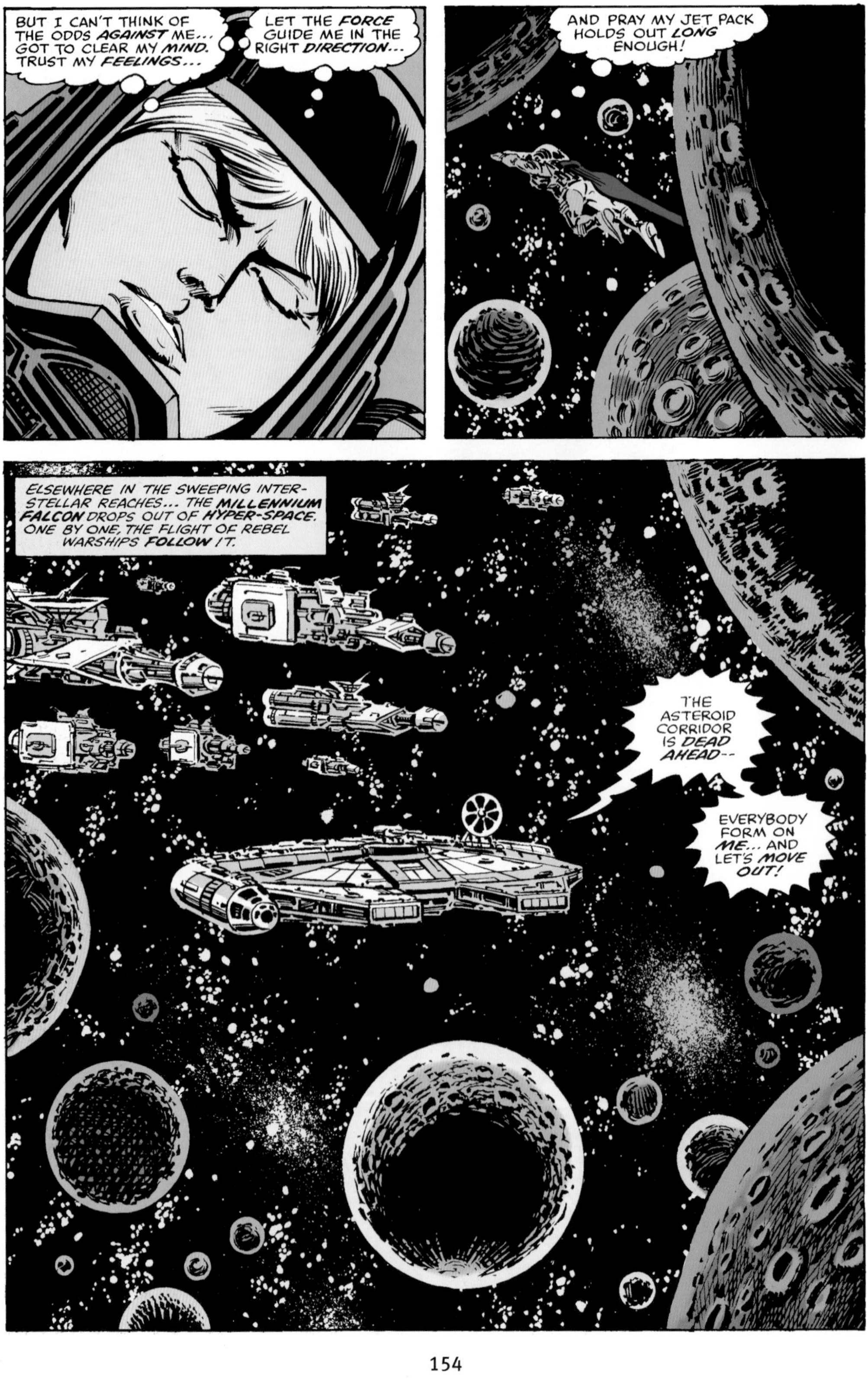
BUT I CAN'T THINK OF THE ODDS AGAINST ME... GOT TO CLEAR MY MIND. TRUST MY FEELINGS...
LET THE FORCE GUIDE ME IN THE RIGHT DIRECTION...
AND PRAY MY JET PACK HOLDS OUT LONG ENOUGH!
ELSEWHERE IN THE SWEEPING INTER-STELLAR REACHES... THE MILLENNIUM FALCON DROPS OUT OF HYPER-SPACE. ONE BY ONE, THE FLIGHT OF REBEL WARSHIPS FOLLOW IT.
THE ASTEROID CORRIDOR IS DEAD AHEAD--
EVERYBODY FORM ON ME... AND LET'S MOVE OUT!

YEAH, THIS *IS* GONNA BE A LOT *DIFFERENT* THAN DODGING AROUND THOSE KING-SIZE BOULDERS ON OUR *LONESOME*, CHEWIE. BUT LOOK AT THE *BRIGHT* SIDE--

--SO FAR THIS TIME, NOBODY'S *CHASIN'* US! PRINCESS, BETTER GO BACK AND *STRAP IN*...JUST IN CASE WE *SCRAPE* SOMETHING.

WAARGH!

IF YOU'RE AS GOOD AS YOU ALWAYS *SAY* YOU ARE, YOU SHOULDN'T *NEED* THIS, FLYBOY--

--BUT *GOOD LUCK* ANYWAY.

DR. TAGGE, THE LONG RANGE SCANNERS HAVE PICKED UP A GROUP OF *REBEL SHIPS*--

DESPITE AN ATTEMPT AT *JAMMING*...IT'S DEFINITE THEY'RE MOVING INTO THE *CORRIDOR*.

UH...*SILAS*? ARE WE FAR ENOUGH *REMOVED* FROM THE ASTEROIDS NOT TO BE AFFECTED BY THE *OMEGA FROST*...?

A MILITARY MAN SHOULDN'T ALLOW *NERVES* TO SHOW, SHANKS. AND IF I WERE A LESS *LOGICAL* MAN... I MIGHT BE *DISTURBED* BY YOUR LACK OF FAITH.

THERE'S NO *FALLOUT* FROM MY *CREATION*. SO LONG AS YOU AREN'T CAUGHT *BETWEEN* THE CONDUCTOR TOWERS... IT'S PERFECTLY *SAFE*.

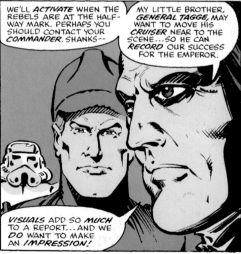

WE'LL *ACTIVATE* WHEN THE REBELS ARE AT THE HALF-WAY MARK. PERHAPS YOU SHOULD CONTACT YOUR *COMMANDER*, SHANKS--

MY LITTLE BROTHER, *GENERAL TAGGE*, MAY WANT TO MOVE HIS *CRUISER* NEAR TO THE SCENE...SO HE CAN *RECORD* OUR SUCCESS FOR THE EMPEROR.

VISUALS ADD SO *MUCH* TO A *REPORT*...AND WE *DO* WANT TO MAKE AN *IMPRESSION!*

THAT'S *IT...!* THE EDGE OF THE CORRIDOR... AND THE *FIRST* TOWER SET UP BY TAGGE'S PEOPLE!

I'VE GOTTEN *WHERE* I WANTED... BUT I'VE *EXHAUSTED* MY JET PACK *DOING* IT.

WHICH LEAVES ME WITH LOADS OF *MOMENTUM*...AND NO WAY OF *BRAKING!* I COULD WIND UP SMEARED INTO *THIS* ASTEROID JUST LIKE THAT *TIE FIGHTER* I ABANDONED HIT THE *OTHER* ONE!

UNLESS...

ZAMP!

AND AS HE PLUNGES TOWARD THE AIRLESS SURFACE SPREAD BEFORE HIM, LUKE BRINGS UP HIS *LIGHTSABER*...LETTING THE POWER OF ITS BLADE BECOME A *COUNTER-FORCE* TO HIS OWN FORWARD THRUST!

CLICKING THE BLADE ON AND OFF.... HE MAKES A ROUGH, BUT MORE OR LESS *CON-TROLLED,* DESCENT.

UNTIL...

THE *TOWER*...! IT'S A LOT *BIGGER* THAN THE EXPERIMENTAL ONES HAN, CHEWIE, AND I SAW *TESTED* BACK ON TATOOINE! *

BUT THEN, TO GENERATE THE *OMEGA FROST* ACROSS THE ASTEROID CORRIDOR... IT'D *HAVE* TO BE.

* STAR WARS #32-- ARCH.

ONLY IT'S *NOT GOING TO!* NOT WHEN THE REBEL ALLIANCE PROBABLY ALREADY HAS A *RESCUE FORCE* MOVING THROUGH THE CORRIDOR--

NOT WHEN MY *FRIENDS* MAY VERY WELL BE *LEADING* IT!

BARON TAGGE *TRICKED* ME INTO BROADCASTING THE INFORMATION THAT WOULD *BRING* THEM HERE-- *

VRAAMP!

BUT NOW I'M GOING TO *MAKE UP* FOR THAT! NOW I'M--

*LAST ISSUE--ARCH AGAIN.

SHRA-DAAAAAAK!

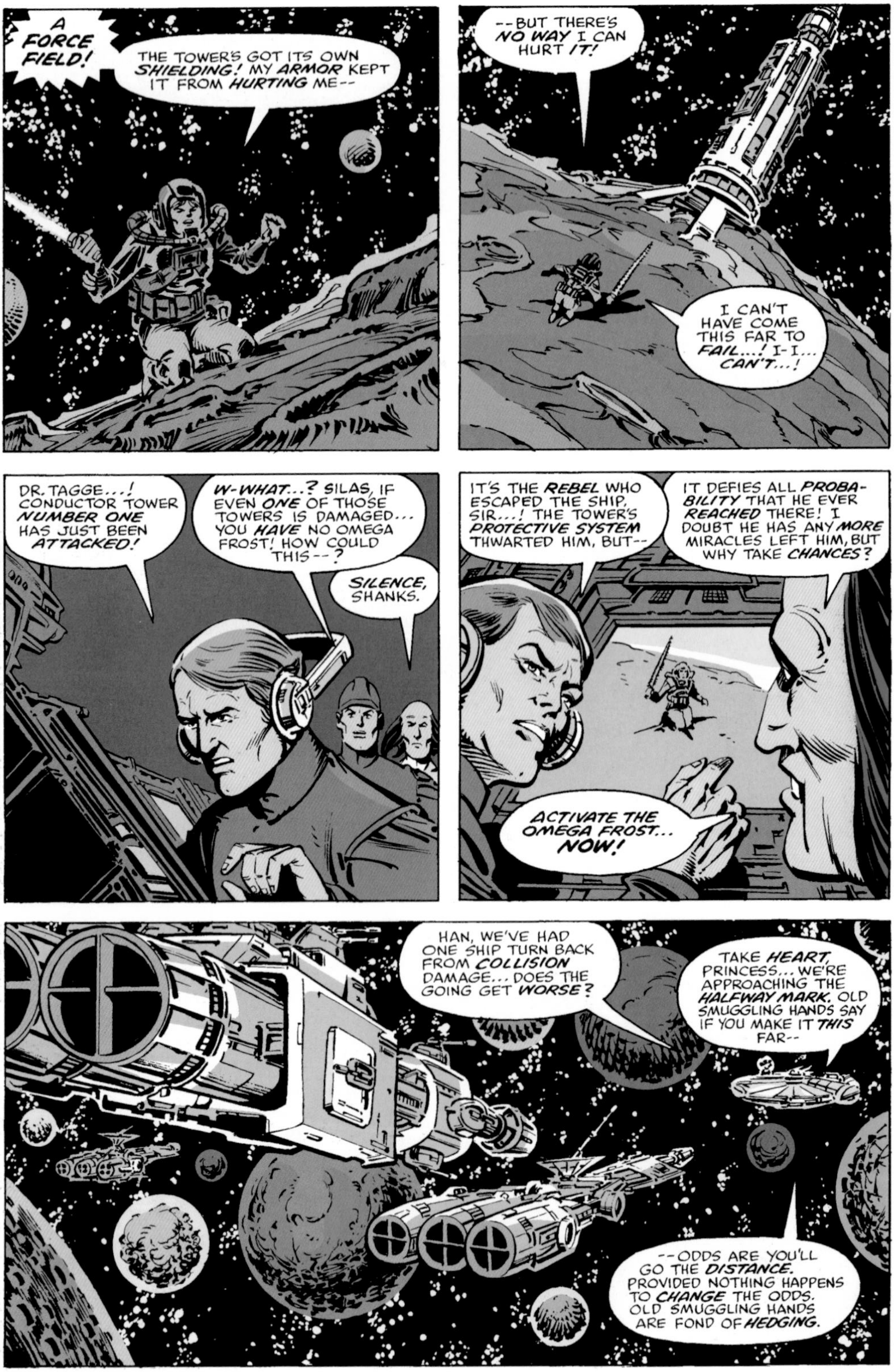
A FORCE FIELD!
THE TOWER'S GOT ITS OWN SHIELDING! MY ARMOR KEPT IT FROM HURTING ME--
--BUT THERE'S NO WAY I CAN HURT IT!
I CAN'T HAVE COME THIS FAR TO FAIL...! I-I... CAN'T...!
DR. TAGGE...! CONDUCTOR TOWER NUMBER ONE HAS JUST BEEN ATTACKED!
W-WHAT...? SILAS, IF EVEN ONE OF THOSE TOWERS IS DAMAGED... YOU HAVE NO OMEGA FROST! HOW COULD THIS--?
SILENCE, SHANKS.
IT'S THE REBEL WHO ESCAPED THE SHIP, SIR...! THE TOWER'S PROTECTIVE SYSTEM THWARTED HIM, BUT--
IT DEFIES ALL PROBABILITY THAT HE EVER REACHED THERE! I DOUBT HE HAS ANY MORE MIRACLES LEFT HIM, BUT WHY TAKE CHANCES?
ACTIVATE THE OMEGA FROST... NOW!
HAN, WE'VE HAD ONE SHIP TURN BACK FROM COLLISION DAMAGE... DOES THE GOING GET WORSE?
TAKE HEART, PRINCESS... WE'RE APPROACHING THE HALFWAY MARK. OLD SMUGGLING HANDS SAY IF YOU MAKE IT THIS FAR--
--ODDS ARE YOU'LL GO THE DISTANCE. PROVIDED NOTHING HAPPENS TO CHANGE THE ODDS. OLD SMUGGLING HANDS ARE FOND OF HEDGING.

THE BLINK OF AN EYE. SUDDENLY, THE *MILLENNIUM FALCON'S* FORWARD SCANNERS GO *WILD* AS...

THE ASTEROIDS *AHEAD* OF US HAVE TURNED TO *ICE*, HAN...! AS IF THEY'D BEEN SWEPT BY SOME KIND OF... *IMPOSSIBLE COLD!*

IT'S A TRAP! THAT TAGGE DEVICE LUKE THOUGHT WAS GOING TO BE USED ON *JUNCTION* HAS BEEN SET UP FOR US *HERE*, PRINCESS --

-- AND WE'LL BE IN ITS *RANGE* IN SECONDS!

WHILE ON THE BRIDGE OF THE TAGGE MINING EXPLORER...

WE'VE ACTIVATED *MOMENTS* TOO EARLY... THE ALLIANCE SHIPS ARE JUST *SHY* OF THE OMEGA FROST'S EFFECTIVE BAND, DOCTOR!

MAINTAIN THE *POWER.* EVEN WITH THEIR MUCH VAUNTED *MANEUVERABILITY,* THE REBEL CRAFT CAN'T DO A *FULL REVERSE* AMID THOSE ASTEROIDS --

-- NOT WITHOUT COLLISION AND *DISASTER.* EITHER WAY, WE *WIN.*

YOU SEE THE VALUE OF THE *SCIENTIFIC MIND,* SHANKS? I'VE CONSIDERED ALL CONTINGENCIES SO --

YOU'VE FORGOTTEN *SKYWALKER!* LOOK AT THE *MONITOR...* HE *HASN'T* GIVEN UP!

IT IS HIS LAST CHANCE. HIS ARMOR'S *AIR RESERVES* ARE NEARLY SPENT. EACH DRIVING SWING OF THE LIGHTSABER IS TORTUROUS *EFFORT...*

...BUT HE HAS *MEDITATED,* AND THIS WAY SEEMS *RIGHT.*

THERE...! THE *BASE* OF THE TOWER...! NOW WE *TEST* MY THEORY --

-- THAT THEY WOULDN'T EXTEND THE TOWER'S PROTECTIVE FORCE FIELD *BELOW* THE ASTEROID'S SURFACE!

ZDAK!

AND THE ANSWER *LUKE* SEEKS... IS LEARNED ABOARD THE *MILLENNIUM FALCON* AS WELL!

THAT'S *RIGHT,* CHEWIE! WE SHOULD BE *ICICLES...* BUT WE'RE *NOT!* SOMETHING'S *SPOILED* THE HOUSE OF TAGGE'S *COLD WAVE!*

VROWRRK!

LONG AS WE'VE GOTTEN OUR *LIVES* HANDED BACK TO US...LET'S KEEP ON *PRESERVING* THEM.

SINCE THE JUNCTION BUSINESS WAS A *SET UP,* WE DON'T HAVE TO CONTINUE ON IN THE *CORRIDOR.* I'LL TELL THE OTHER SHIPS TO *SCATTER* OUT OF IT AND--

NO, HAN. WE'LL BE *MISSING* AN OPPORTUNITY...

THE CONDUCTOR TOWER HAS BEEN *SHORTED OUT,* DOCTOR TAGGE! THE *OMEGA FROST* CAN NO LONGER BE GENERATED. WHAT DO WE DO *NOW?*

THAT BOY...THAT BOY *SKYWALKER...!* THIS IS *ALL* HIS FAULT! CONTACT MY YOUNGER BROTHER...HAVE HIM SEND A *TIE FIGHTER* FROM HIS CRUISER TO *DESTROY* SKYWALKER AND...AND...

NONE OF MY PLANS *INCLUDED* THIS...! I-IT'S...SO *CONFUSING.* NOT LIKE DOING *EXPERIMENTS* IN THE *LABORATORY...!* I-I--

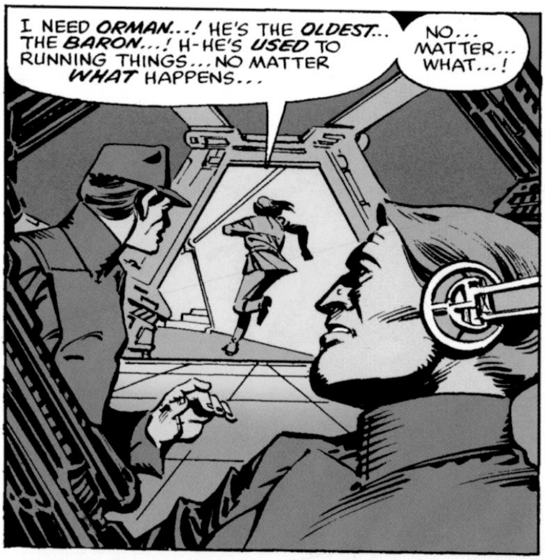
I NEED ORMAN...! HE'S THE OLDEST... THE BARON...! H-HE'S USED TO RUNNING THINGS... NO MATTER WHAT HAPPENS...
NO... MATTER... WHAT...!

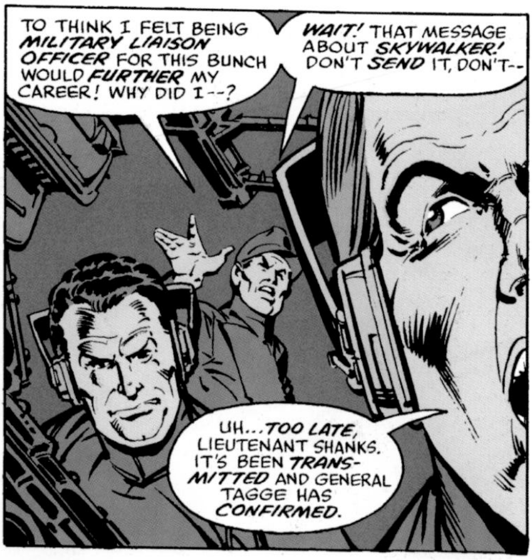
TO THINK I FELT BEING MILITARY LIAISON OFFICER FOR THIS BUNCH WOULD FURTHER MY CAREER! WHY DID I--?
WAIT! THAT MESSAGE ABOUT SKYWALKER! DON'T SEND IT, DON'T--
UH... TOO LATE, LIEUTENANT SHANKS. IT'S BEEN TRANSMITTED AND GENERAL TAGGE HAS CONFIRMED.

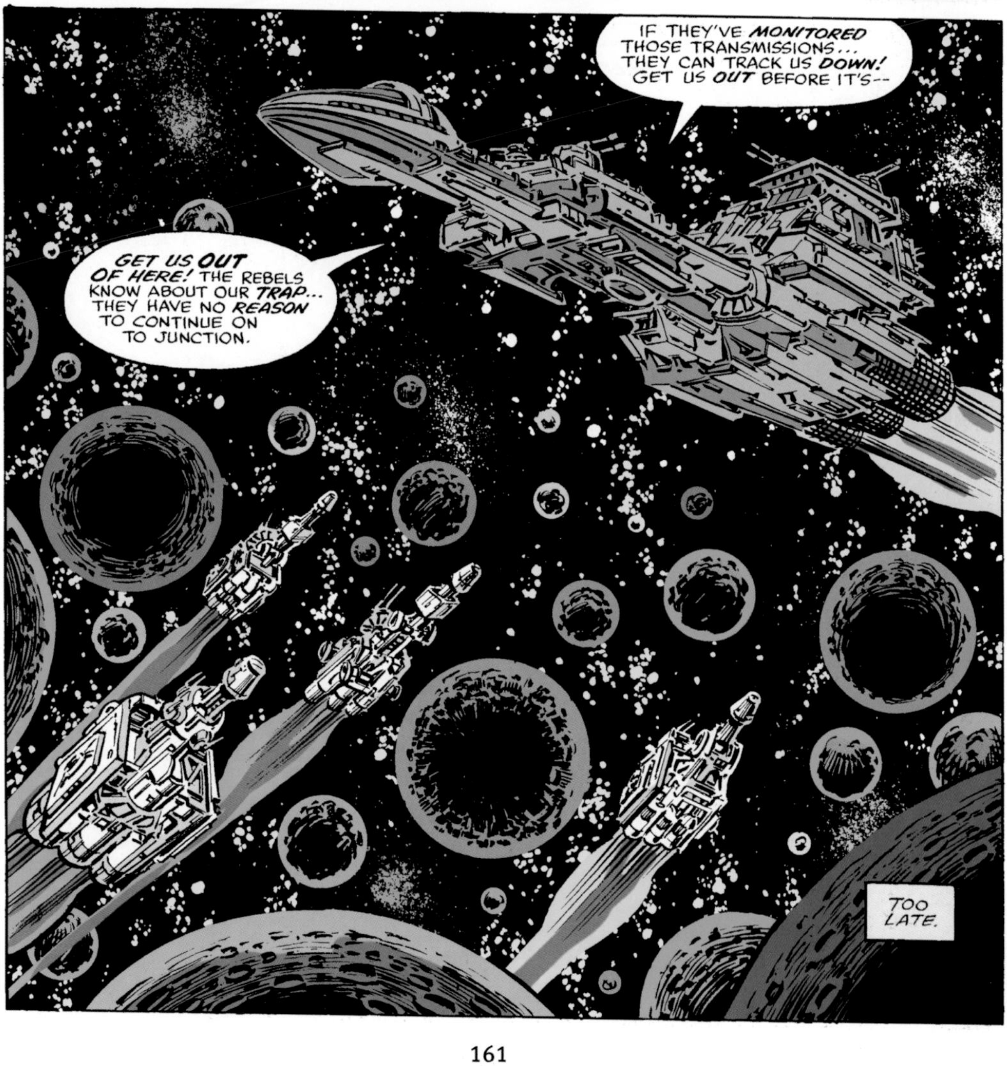
IF THEY'VE MONITORED THOSE TRANSMISSIONS... THEY CAN TRACK US DOWN! GET US OUT BEFORE IT'S--
GET US OUT OF HERE! THE REBELS KNOW ABOUT OUR TRAP... THEY HAVE NO REASON TO CONTINUE ON TO JUNCTION.
TOO LATE.

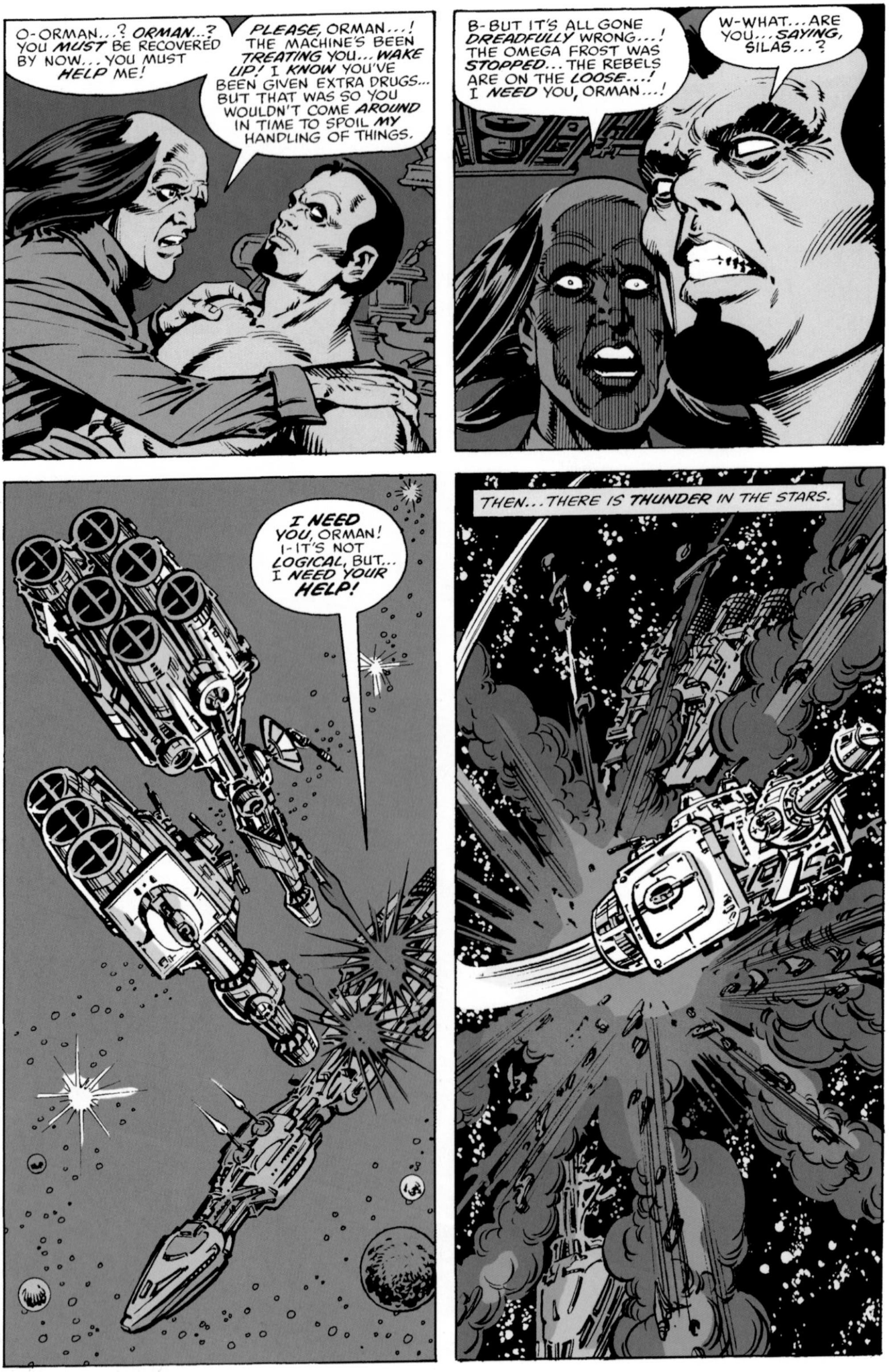
O-ORMAN...? ORMAN...? YOU MUST BE RECOVERED BY NOW... YOU MUST HELP ME!
PLEASE, ORMAN...! THE MACHINE'S BEEN TREATING YOU... WAKE UP! I KNOW YOU'VE BEEN GIVEN EXTRA DRUGS... BUT THAT WAS SO YOU WOULDN'T COME AROUND IN TIME TO SPOIL MY HANDLING OF THINGS.
B-BUT IT'S ALL GONE DREADFULLY WRONG...! THE OMEGA FROST WAS STOPPED... THE REBELS ARE ON THE LOOSE...! I NEED YOU, ORMAN...!
W-WHAT... ARE YOU... SAYING, SILAS...?
I NEED YOU, ORMAN! I-IT'S NOT LOGICAL, BUT... I NEED YOUR HELP!
THEN... THERE IS THUNDER IN THE STARS.

THE THUNDER IS *ECHOED* IN A *TIE* FIGHTER'S APPROACH ON A HUMAN TARGET. A TARGET THROWN TO THE GROUND BY THE AFTERSHOCK OF DISRUPTING THE *OMEGA FROST*...

...A TARGET RENDERED TOTALLY *HELPLESS* AS HE FIGHTS FOR THE LAST BITS OF *AIR* HIS SUIT PROVIDES.

HELPLESS... BUT NOT WITHOUT *HELP*.

NO *SCORE* TODAY, IMPERIAL. THE SAME TRANSMISSION THAT BROUGHT *YOU* HERE... BROUGHT *US* TOO!

HAN, SENSORS INDICATE LUKE'S STILL *ALIVE* DOWN THERE BUT--

UNFURROW YOUR *BROW*, PRINCESS... I'VE NEVER MISSED A LAST MINUTE *RESCUE* YET. CHEWIE WILL TAKE OVER WHILE I PICK UP THE KID.

DESPITE MY CYNICAL SOUL, EVEN *I* ENJOY AN OCCASIONAL *HAPPY* ENDING.

NEXT. ISSUE: DARK LORD'S GAMBIT!

40¢ 35 MAY 02817

APPROVED BY THE COMICS CODE AUTHORITY

ADVENTURES *BEYOND* THE GREATEST SPACE-FANTASY FILM OF ALL!

STAR WARS

™

DARTH VADER PLAYS A GAME OF DEATH AGAINST THE STAR WARRIORS!

™

DARK LORD'S GAMBIT!

INFANTINO/WIACEK

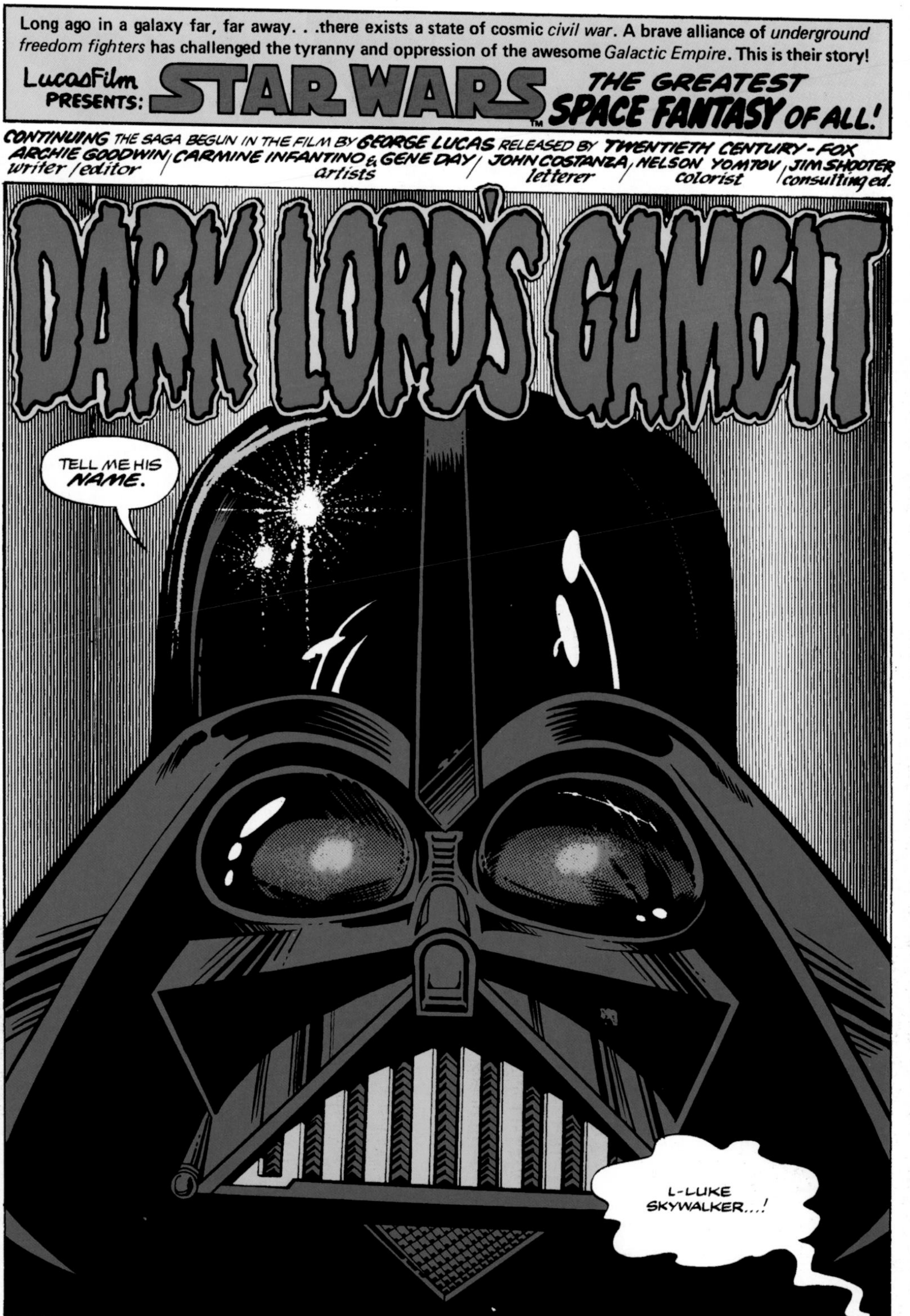
Long ago in a galaxy far, far away. . .there exists a state of cosmic civil war. A brave alliance of underground freedom fighters has challenged the tyranny and oppression of the awesome Galactic Empire. This is their story!
LucasFilm PRESENTS: STAR WARS™ THE GREATEST SPACE FANTASY OF ALL!
CONTINUING THE SAGA BEGUN IN THE FILM BY GEORGE LUCAS RELEASED BY TWENTIETH CENTURY-FOX
ARCHIE GOODWIN writer/editor / CARMINE INFANTINO & GENE DAY artists / JOHN COSTANZA letterer / NELSON YOMTOV colorist / JIM SHOOTER consulting ed.
DARK LORD'S GAMBIT
TELL ME HIS NAME.
L-LUKE SKYWALKER...!

LUKE SKYWALKER. A LONG BREATH RASPS FROM THE SITH LORD'S MASK. IN SOMEONE LESS AWESOME, IT MIGHT ALMOST HAVE BEEN A *SIGH.* TWO WORDS; ONE NAME. ALMOST *ANTICLIMACTIC* CONSIDERING THE LONG TIME IT HAS TAKEN HIM TO LEARN IT.

STILL, THE IMPORTANT THING IS THAT HE HAS IT AT LAST.

CAPTAIN WERMIS, WE ARE RETURNING TO THE *CRUISER*... MAKE READY TO *DEPART.* THE REBELS NO LONGER HAVE A *REFUELING STATION* HERE --

-- AND THE NAME OF THE T-65 PILOT WHO DESTROYED THE *DEATH STAR* IS NO LONGER A *SECRET.*

AND HAVING ACQUIRED THAT INFORMATION... WE SHALL NOW TAKE *ACTION.*

SOON, ABOARD THE ORBITING CRUISER...

WHAT ARE YOUR *ORDERS*, LORD VADER?

ARRANGE AN IMMEDIATE *RENDEZVOUS* WITH THE FLEET COMMANDER MAINTAINING THE IMPERIAL BLOCKADE... *GENERAL TAGGE.*

SURELY YOU'RE NOT GOING TO ENLIST *HIM* IN YOUR PLAN...? HASN'T THERE BEEN *TROUBLE* BETWEEN YOU AND THE HOUSE OF TAGGE?

DON'T *ANTICIPATE* WHAT I WILL OR WON'T DO, WERMIS. YOUR TALENT IS FOR *SUBSERVIENCE*... NOT *STRATEGY*.

AND IN A GALAXY WHERE *LIGHT YEARS* ARE CROSSED MORE EASILY THAN *MILES*... THE RENDEZVOUS IS SWIFTLY KEPT.

WELCOME, GENERAL. OR SHOULD I SAY *BARON?* I UNDERSTAND THE FAMILY *TITLE* HAS RECENTLY FALLEN TO YOU.

MY *CONGRATULATIONS* ON *THAT*--

-- AND ON YOUR NARROW *ESCAPE* FROM THE *REBELS.* EVEN IF IT *DID* COST THE EMPIRE A *CRUISER.*

IS *THIS* WHY YOU CALLED ME FROM DUTY, VADER...TO *TAUNT* ME?

I CALLED YOU BECAUSE IT SUITS MY *PURPOSES,* MY INSOLENT, AMBITIOUS YOUNG FRIEND!

YOUR OFFICIAL REPORT INDICATED THE *DEFEAT* GREW OUT OF A STANDARD *BLOCKADE* ACTION. MY *SPIES* TELL ME IT WAS *MORE.* I WANT THE *TRUTH!*

Y-YES... YES...!

M-MY OLDER BROTHERS-- ORMAN, THE *BARON*, AND SILAS, *CHIEF SCIENTIST* OF THE FAMILY INDUSTRIES-- CONVINCED ME TO TRY AN *INVENTION* OF THEIRS AGAINST THE REBELS. *

WE SET A *TRAP* THAT, IF SUCCESS- FUL, WOULD HAVE WON THE EMPEROR'S *FAVOR* AWAY FROM *YOU*.

*SEE *STAR WARS* # 31-34 --ARCHIE

BUT... SOMETHING WENT *WRONG!* THE INVENTION *FAILED*... AND THE ALLIANCE FLEET IT WAS INTENDED TO *CRUSH* TURNED THE TRAP AGAINST US!

MY BROTHER'S VESSEL WAS SWIFTLY *DESTROYED*. AND BEFORE MY CRUISER COULD *RETREAT* FROM THE SECTOR--

"-- THE REBELS CAME SWEEPING *IN* ON US! STILL, I GOT MY DEFENSIVE FIGHTERS INTO ACTION AND WE WERE HOLDING OUR OWN--

"-- WHEN *ANOTHER* SHIP SURGED INTO THE FRAY!

"IT LOOKED LIKE A FREIGHTER, BUT ITS *SPEED* AND *MANEUVER- ABILITY* EQUALLED ANY CRAFT IN THE BATTLE... AND *THEN* SOME!

THE ACCURACY OF ITS FIRE PIERCED ONE OF OUR *SHIELDS*...A RESERVE *REACTOR* EXPLODED!

MY STAFF AND I WERE FORCED TO *FLEE* IN AN ESCAPE CRAFT... EVERYTHING ELSE WAS *LOST*.

OUR MONITORS PICKED UP SOME OF THE REBELS' SHIP-TO-SHIP *COMMUNICATION*.

IT LEFT NO DOUBT THAT PRINCESS *LEIA ORGANA* WAS ABOARD THAT FREIGHTER...AND THAT ITS DEADLY WORK WITH THE *LASER CANNON* WAS BY INDIVIDUALS NAMED *SOLO* AND *SKYWALKER*.

YOU HAD *ALL* THAT...! THE ONE I'VE BEEN *SEEKING*... THE SHIP THAT *RUINED* MY DEFENSE OF THE DEATH STAR... AND YOU *COST* IT!

I'M *WEARY* OF YOUR FAMILY WORKING AT *CROSS PURPOSES* TO ME, TAGGE!

WE'RE PUTTING AN *END* TO IT! *RIGHT NOW!*

BEHOLD!

IT CAN'T BE...! M-MY *BROTHERS*...! ORMAN... SILAS...! BUT... THEY'RE *DEAD*... SLAIN BY THE *REBELS*...DESTROYED WITH THEIR SHIP!

NO, EVIDENTLY THEIR *COMPARTMENT* SUFFERED NO DAMAGE... THE EMERGENCY SEALS KEPT IT *AIRTIGHT.*

STILL, THEY HAD NEARLY *SUFFOCATED* WHEN MY SPIES INVESTIGATED THE WRECKAGE AND *FOUND* THEM... BUT, IN TIME, THESE MACHINES CAN RESTORE THEIR LIFE FUNCTIONS TO *NORMAL.*

YOU MEAN TO *REVIVE* THEM...?

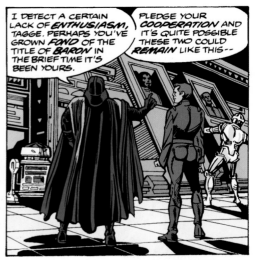

I DETECT A CERTAIN LACK OF *ENTHUSIASM,* TAGGE. PERHAPS YOU'VE GROWN *FOND* OF THE TITLE OF *BARON* IN THE BRIEF TIME IT'S BEEN YOURS.

PLEDGE YOUR *COOPERATION* AND IT'S QUITE POSSIBLE THESE TWO COULD *REMAIN* LIKE THIS--

--CONTINUE TO OPPOSE ME AND I'LL HAVE THE *THREE* OF YOU BROUGHT BEFORE THE *EMPEROR* WITH A FULL ACCOUNT OF YOUR *FIASCO* AGAINST THE REBELS!

I MEAN TO GO FORWARD WITH PLANS OF MY *OWN,* GENERAL TAGGE...AND I WANT *NO SCHEMING* BEHIND MY BACK WHEN I DO!

I...I WAS *NEVER* ENTHUSIASTIC ABOUT THE BARON-- ER... *ORMAN'S* PLAN, LORD VADER.

IF *I* DON'T RETAIN THE TITLE...ONLY MY *SISTER* REMAINS, A GIRL LIKE HER JUST ISN'T *READY* TO ASSUME LEADERSHIP OF THE HOUSE OF TAGGE'S VAST HOLDINGS...

YES. I *THOUGHT* DUTY WOULD DEMAND THAT YOU *ACCEPT* MY TERMS.

THEN I WILL *PROCEED,* TAGGE...KNOWING I HAVE THE COMPLETE *LOYALTY* OF ONE OF THE EMPIRE'S MOST *PROMISING* NOBLES AND MILITARY MEN.

PERHAPS IT IS A TRICK OF THE CHAMBER'S SUBDUED LIGHT, BUT AS THE SITH LORD AND GENERAL TAGGE DEPART...THE TRANCE-BOUND FACE OF ORMAN TAGGE SEEMS TO TWIST WITH HATRED AND RAGE!

SHORTLY, A **SHUTTLE CRAFT** ROARS OUT OF THE DOCKING BAY OF DARTH VADER'S CRUISER... CARRYING THE **NEW** BARON TAGGE BACK TO HIS OWN SHIP.

PEACE WITH AN **ENEMY**, SIR...? I'M **MOST** SURPRISED.

I EXPECTED YOU TO TAKE THIS OPPORTUNITY TO **CRUSH** THE TAGGE LINE FOREVER.

ANY PETTY TYRANT CAN **OBLITERATE** A FOE, WERMIS... I AM A **MASTER OF THE FORCE.**

FROM THIS MOMENT ON, AN ENTIRE **FAMILY** WHICH STRUGGLED AGAINST ME WILL NOW SERVE AS... MY **PAWNS.**

TIME PASSES. TIME IN WHICH THE FALLEN JEDI MOVES AT HIS OWN PACE ON HIS OWN DARK COURSE. TIME IN WHICH A FORMER MOISTURE FARMER FROM TATOOINE SERVES THE **REBEL ALLIANCE** ANY WAY HE CAN.

BLUE LEADER TO BLUE FLIGHT... I FIGURE WE'RE GOOD FOR FIVE MINUTES MORE **PATROL** WITHOUT TAXING OUR FUEL. DO YOU **COPY?** OVER.

ROGER, BLUE LEADER, BUT ARE YOU CONCERNED ABOUT **FUEL**....OR THE FACT THAT **HAN SOLO** IS BACK AT THE BASE WITH THE **PRINCESS?**

IT IS A QUESTION LUKE SKYWALKER IS *SPARED* ANSWERING... AS SCANNING SCOPES SUDDENLY COME TO *LIFE* WITH THE PRESENCE OF OTHER SHIPS!

TIE FIGHTERS AND THEIR *PREY*... ON THE EDGE OF THE YAVIN SYSTEM!

BUT NOT FOR *LONG*... AS LUKE'S PATROL MOVES IN *FAST*, LASER CANNONS *BLAZING!*

WE CAUGHT 'EM *NAPPING*, BLUE FLIGHT! ESCORT THAT *CIVILIAN* THEY WERE TRYING TO ZAP--

--I'M FOLLOWING THE LAST *STRAGGLER* TO SEE WHERE HE *CAME* FROM!

THE *ANSWER* IS NOT LONG COMING.

IMPERIAL BATTLE CRUISER...! BUT THEY'RE ALREADY BUILDING UP SPEED TO JUMP INTO *WARP*... THEY'LL BE *GONE* BEFORE I CAN GET *HELP* HERE.

GENERAL DODONNA ORDERED US TO *AVOID* ONE-SIDED ENGAGEMENTS... MIGHT AS WELL HEAD *BACK* AND SEE JUST *WHO* WE SAVED!

THERE SEEMS TO BE A *COMMOTION* OUTSIDE ON THE LANDING STRIP, HAN. I'D LIKE TO SEE WHAT'S HAPPENING.

IN THE *MIDDLE* OF MY STORY OF HOW CHEWIE AN' ME TRICKED *JABBA THE HUT* INTO TRADING A KILO OF SPICE FOR A THREE-LEGGED *BAN-THA*?

THIS IS THE LAST TIME I TRY TO ENTERTAIN INVALID *ROYALTY!*

MY LEG'S ALMOST *HEALED* SINCE IT WAS INJURED ON THAT LAST MISSION...* I DON'T THINK I NEED ANY *HELP* WALKING.

YOU'RE TOO *VALUABLE* TO THE ALLIANCE TO RISK A *RELAPSE*, PRINCESS. RELAX AND *ENJOY* IT...LIKE *ME*.

*ONE WE'VE YET TO CHRONICLE -- ARCHIE.

SHORTLY, ON THE LANDING FIELD IN FRONT OF THE GREAT STONE RUINS WHICH HOUSE REBEL HEADQUARTERS, ON THE FOURTH MOON OF YAVIN...

WHERE DID THAT *SHIP* COME FROM, THREEPIO?

MASTER LUKE AND HIS PATROL SEEM TO HAVE *RESCUED* IT, YOUR HIGHNESS --

--ARTOO WAS SO ANXIOUS TO SEE THE *PASSENGERS*, HE BARELY TOOK TIME TO BLEEP OUT THE DETAILS TO ME.

I AM *SISTER DOMINA*... PRIESTESS IN THE *ORDER OF THE SACRED CIRCLE.*

WE HAVE RISKED VIOLATING THE IMPERIAL BLOCKADE TO SEEK YOUR *COUNCIL*... AND, PERHAPS, YOUR *AID.*

AND JUDGING BY *YOUR* SWIFT ACTIONS AGAINST OUR IMPERIAL PURSUERS, AS WELL AS THE PERSONAL *AURA* I SENSE ABOUT YOU --

--COMING HERE WAS *NOT* A MISTAKE.

WELL...UH... I WAS ONLY DOING MY *JOB*....! BUT... IF YOU'RE ON A DIPLOMATIC MISSION ....YOU'LL WANT TO SEE...UH... GENERAL DODONNA OR...ER... SENATOR ORGANA...!

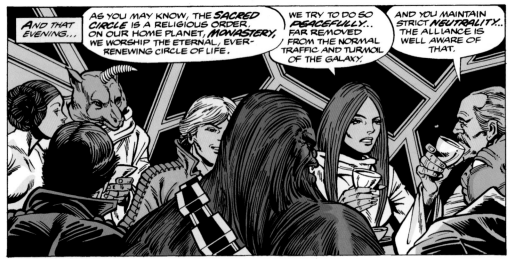

AND THAT EVENING...

AS YOU MAY KNOW, THE *SACRED CIRCLE* IS A RELIGIOUS ORDER. ON OUR HOME PLANET, *MONASTERY,* WE WORSHIP THE ETERNAL, EVER-RENEWING CIRCLE OF LIFE.

WE TRY TO DO SO *PEACEFULLY*... FAR REMOVED FROM THE NORMAL TRAFFIC AND TURMOIL OF THE GALAXY.

AND YOU MAINTAIN STRICT *NEUTRALITY*... THE ALLIANCE IS WELL AWARE OF THAT.

UNTIL *RECENTLY,* GENERAL. THE EMPIRE HAS SENT AN *ENVOY* TO MONASTERY... OVERTURES ARE BEING MADE TO PERSUADE US TO *SIDE* WITH THEM.

A GALACTIC WAR, SUCH AS YOU HAVE BEGUN, COULD WELL *SUNDER* THE CIRCLE OF LIFE ...WITH OUR MANY FOLLOWERS IN MANY SYSTEMS, OUR INFLUENCE MIGHT TIP THE BALANCE TO *END* SUCH A WAR SWIFTLY.

SISTER DOMINA, IMPERIAL *TYRANNY* CAN BE EVEN *MORE* CORRUPTING AND DANGEROUS TO THE NATURAL CYCLE THAN OUR *REBEL-LION!*

YOU CAN *SEE* THE RESULTS ON WORLDS WHERE THEY HOLD *FULL SWAY!* IF YOUR ORDER NEEDS *PROOF,* I'M CERTAINLY *WELL* ENOUGH TO TRAVEL TO--!

THAT'S THE *RESPONSE* WE HOPED FOR, SENATOR.

THE ORDER WISHED TO HEAR FROM *BOTH* SIDES BEFORE MAKING A DECISION. BUT THE EMPIRE HAS A STRONG AND *PERSUASIVE* REPRESENTATIVE.... A LARGE FACTION HAS BEEN *IMPRESSED.*

AND HE IS NOT THE SORT TO LET HIS WORK BE *UNDONE!*

DARTH VADER!

174

GENERAL DODONNA, YOU'VE GOT TO SEND *ME* ON THIS MISSION...!

THIS IS *DIPLOMACY*, LUKE... *POLITICS*. PRINCESS LEIA'S TIME IN THE IMPERIAL SENATE MAKES *HER* THE BEST QUALIFIED.

I SUPPOSE SHE COULD USE A *BODYGUARD*...

THERE IS A *PROBLEM*, I FEAR. MONASTERY IS A *CLOISTERED* WORLD... USUALLY NOT *OPEN* TO VISITORS. WE ALLOWED THE EMPIRE ONLY A *SINGLE* REPRESENTATIVE --

-- THE SAME MUST BE TRUE FOR THE *ALLIANCE*. HOWEVER --

-- I SENSE IN LUKE SKYWALKER AN *OPENESS* AND *SINCERITY* THE MOST SKILLFUL DIPLOMATS RARELY POSSESS.

THIS WOULD MAKE A MARKED *CONTRAST* TO LORD VADER... A CONTRAST THE ELDERS OF THE SACRED CIRCLE -- WITH THEIR APPRECIATION OF THE NATURAL, UNCOMPLICATED FLOW OF LIFE -- WOULD FIND *IMPRESSIVE*.

CERTAINLY, I *PERSONALLY* FIND THIS SO... BUT, OF COURSE, WHO *FINALLY* ACCOMPANIES US BACK TO MONASTERY IS YOUR *OWN* DECISION.

AND THE FOLLOWING MORNING... THAT DECISION IS MADE.

GENERAL DODONNA...! HOW COULD YOU AND THE COUNCIL *DO* THIS?!

PERHAPS WE THOUGHT YOUR ARGUMENTS WERE *TINGED* SLIGHTLY WITH JEALOUSY, YOUR HIGHNESS.

DON'T *WORRY*... ARTOO DEETOO IS *WITH* LUKE, PROGRAMMED WITH A MOST *CONVINCING* SET OF PROOFS AGAINST THE EMPIRE.

THAT-- PLUS THE FACT THAT HE SEEMS THE *CHOICE* THE ORDER'S REPRESENTATIVE FAVORS-- SHOULD ENABLE HIM TO DO THE JOB *WELL.*

BUT JUST IN CASE... WE'RE TAKING *OTHER* MEASURES. *MONASTERY* MAY BE OFF-LIMITS, BUT THAT DOESN'T MEAN WE CAN'T HAVE A *SHIP* IN THE SYSTEM...

"...ONE THAT'S NOT TOO *CONSPICUOUS...* LIKE A *SPICE FREIGHTER.*"

WE'RE COMING OUT OF *WARP,* YOUR ROYALNESS... ONE MORE *ITEM* FOR A VERY LONG BILL I'M GOING TO SUBMIT TO YOUR ALLIANCE *ACCOUNTANTS* ONE OF THESE DAYS!

AND I THOUGHT YOU WERE DOING THIS IN CASE *LUKE* NEEDED *HELP,* HAN.

FOR *SURE,* PRINCESS... BUT I'M STILL *MERCENARY* ENOUGH THAT I'D LIKE TO TURN A *PROFIT* ON IT IF I CAN.

THE RINGED PLANET IS *MONASTERY,* BY THE WAY. THE KID SHOULD BE *DOWN* THERE BY NOW... IF HE'S IN *TROUBLE,* WE OUGHT TO LEARN ABOUT IT *SOON!*

WE WON'T IF THE ULTRA-FREQUENCY LASERWAVE LINK THE TECHNOS ON YAVIN DEVISED DOESN'T *FUNCTION* PROPERLY.

THREEPIO, WE'D *BETTER TEST* IT NOW.

AS YOU *WISH*, YOUR HIGHNESS ...IT'S AN ODD SENSATION TO FIND ALL MY CIRCUITS SUDDENLY LOCKED INTO A *COMMUNICATIONS SYSTEM.*

ARTOO...? ARE YOU *RECEIVING* ME? COME IN, ARTOO... WE *MUST* KNOW IF THE *CONTACT* IS ESTABLISHED, ARTOO DEETOO, YOU MALICIOUS LITTLE MASS OF MICROCIRCUITRY... *ANSWER* ME!

VIRDOOP-A-DEET!

"OF ALL THE *ARROGANCE!* HE SAYS THE CONNECTION IS FINE...BUT HE'S TOO *BUSY* TO COMMUNICATE NOW!"

SISTER DOMINA...! *DOWN!*

BLEEET!

177

THANK THE *FORCE* YOUR PLANET'S BAN ON *WEAPONS* DIDN'T EXTEND TO MY *LIGHTSABER*, SISTER!

URAAMP!

I KNOW THAT'S BECAUSE IN AN AGE OF *BLASTERS*, IT'S CONSIDERED JUST A *CEREMONIAL* WEAPON--

SHRAAAANK!

I JUST HOPE THE ORDER OF THE SACRED CIRCLE UNDERSTANDS THAT PRESERVING OUR *LIVES* SEEMS LIKE A WORTHWHILE *CEREMONY* TO ME!

WHAT *WAS* THIS THING, SISTER DOMINA...?

A *NIGHTSHRIKE*... THEY USUALLY PREY ON OTHER CREATURES IN THE GREAT *RAIN FORESTS*.

I CAN'T IMAGINE WHY IT WAS OUT DURING THE *DAY*... THE SUNLIGHT MUST HAVE DRIVEN IT *MAD*, MADE IT *ATTACK*.

PERHAPS IT IS AN *OMEN*... A HINT OF HOW *DISRUPTIVE* TO THE NATURAL ORDER EVEN *ONE* REBEL CAN BE.

CERTAINLY IT DEMONSTRATES THEIR LACK OF *RESPECT* FOR THE ORDER OF THE SACRED CIRCLE...BY SENDING AN UNRULY *CHILD* INSTEAD OF A SEASONED *DIPLOMAT!*

DARTH VADER!

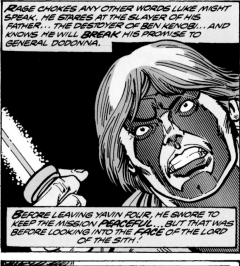

RAGE CHOKES ANY OTHER WORDS LUKE MIGHT SPEAK. HE STARES AT THE SLAYER OF HIS FATHER... THE DESTROYER OF BEN KENOBI.... AND KNOWS HE WILL *BREAK* HIS PROMISE TO GENERAL DODONNA.

BEFORE LEAVING YAVIN FOUR, HE SWORE TO KEEP THE MISSION PEACEFUL...BUT THAT WAS BEFORE LOOKING INTO THE FACE OF THE LORD OF THE SITH!

BUT IF THE URGE TO REVENGE MAKES LUKE FORSAKE EVERYTHING...SOMEONE ELSE IS READY TO REMIND HIM!

FREEP! BRRRT!

THE NUDGE IS ENOUGH. LUKE'S ANGER REMAINS... BUT IT COMES UNDER CONTROL.

ONCE THIS BUSINESS IS *SETTLED,* JUST AS SOON AS YOU'RE OFF*MONASTERY...* WE'LL *MEET,* LORD VADER, THAT'S A *PROMISE!*

YOUR PROMISES ARE OF NO *IN-TEREST* TO ME, STRIPLING,... I CHOOSE MY *OWN* TIME PLACES, AND I DIDN'T COME HERE TO IDLY *BANTER* WITH A YOUNG HOTHEAD--

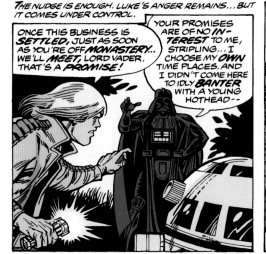

--BUT TO WELCOME *SISTER DOMINA* BACK. WE'VE BEEN AT *ODDS* IN THE PAST... BUT SHE'S DONE ME A GREAT *SERVICE* TODAY.

THIS,...*REPRESENTATIVE* YOU'VE BROUGHT BACK FROM THE ALLIANCE SHOULD MAKE MY PRESENTATION TO THE HIGH CIRCLE OF ELDERS APPEAR ALL THE *BETTER.*

BLAST IT ALL! HE'S *RIGHT...* PRINCESS LEIA SHOULD BE DOING THIS, NOT *ME.* I'M *WAY* OUT OF MY DEPTH!

NO, LUKE SKYWALKER--

IN ALL THE REBEL ALLIANCE, ONLY *YOU* CAN FULFILL WHAT MUST BE *DONE* HERE.

I *KNOW* THIS... AS A *PRIESTESS*... AS A *WOMAN!*

AND MOVING TO A *SLIDEWAY...* SISTER DOMINA, JOINING THE GREETING PARTY, LEADS THE BOY FROM TATOOINE TOWARD THEIR *DESTINATION.*

THE *TEMPLE* OF THE SACRED CIRCLE...! IT IS WHERE WE WORSHIP AND ABIDE.

QUARTERS HAVE BEEN ARRANGED FOR YOU, LUKE... REST *WELL.* TOMORROW YOU WILL FACE THE *HIGH ELDERS.*

SOON...

QUITE A *PLACE,* ARTOO... AND THAT SISTER DOMINA'S QUITE A LADY. KIND OF MAKES ME BELIEVE I CAN PULL THIS *OFF...!*

SHE'S *BEAUTIFUL,* TOO!

--ALMOST AS BEAUTIFUL AS THE *PRINCESS.* NOT THAT I'D *FORGET* LEIA... IT'S JUST THAT SOMETIMES I CAN'T FIGURE WHERE I *STAND* WITH HER, ESPECIALLY WHEN *HAN'S* AROUND...

TURN IT *OFF,* THREEPIO! OBVIOUSLY GENERAL DODONNA DIDN'T *TELL* LUKE ABOUT THE LASERWAVE LINK WITH ARTOO...! PROBABLY SO WE COULD *AID* HIM--

--WITHOUT ANY... ER... *EMBARRASSMENT.*

NIGHT FALLS ON THE PLANET OF MONASTERY; A SHOWER OF MOONS, PART OF THE PLANET'S GREAT RING, GLOW LUSHLY. ONE BY ONE THE TEMPLE LIGHTS DIM... EXCEPT IN A TOWER ROOM.

YOU USED THE *FORCE* TO MAKE THAT NIGHTSHRIKE ATTACK, LORD VADER,... IT WILL *IMPRESS* THE MORE *SUPERSTITIOUS* OF OUR FOLLOWERS.

BUT WEREN'T YOU AFRAID YOUNG SKYWALKER WOULD *EXPOSE* IT...? MY INSTINCTS AS A PRIESTESS TELL ME HE, *TOO*, IS FAMILIAR WITH THE FORCE.

TRUE. BUT HE IS STILL A *NOVICE*, WORSE YET,... HE IS A *ROMANTIC*. YOUR OVERTURES TO HIM *PLAY* ON THAT,... IT CONFUSES HIS *THOUGHTS* AND ULTIMATELY, HIS *ABILITIES*.

STRANGE. MY FAMILY PLACED ME IN THE ORDER SO I COULD MAINTAIN MY *INNOCENCE*... BE FREE OF THE GALACTIC EMPIRE'S MANY *INTRIGUES*.

YET HERE I AM, *DEEP* IN AN INTRIGUE OF MY OWN... READY TO *BETRAY* THE ORDER.

TO *AVENGE* THE DEATH OF TWO BROTHERS... INCLUDING THE ONE YOU LOVED *MOST*. SUCH DESIRES *OFTEN* OVERWHELM EVERYTHING ELSE--

--PARTICULARLY IN A LONG, PROUD LINE LIKE *YOURS*.

YES. WHY *ELSE* WOULD I HAVE ALLIED MYSELF WITH THE MAN MY BROTHER, *BARON TAGGE*, HATED?

BUT FOR *ALL* YOU DID AGAINST ORMAN, YOU WEREN'T RESPONSIBLE FOR HIS *DEATH*... *LUKE SKYWALKER* WAS!

THE LORD OF THE SITH *LEAVES* THE YOUNGEST MEMBER OF THE HOUSE OF TAGGE, STRIDING SWIFTLY TO A BALCONY WHERE HE CAN BE *ALONE*.

MY OPENING MOVES ARE *COMPLETE*, WERMIS... THE PLAYERS ARE *ALL* IN POSITION.

LET THE GAME *TRULY* BEGIN!

NEXT ISSUE: RED QUEEN RISING!

40¢ 36 JUNE 02817

APPROVED BY THE COMICS CODE AUTHORITY

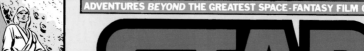

ADVENTURES *BEYOND* THE GREATEST SPACE-FANTASY FILM OF ALL!

STAR WARS

INFANTINO/WIACEK

THIS TIME THE FORCE IS *AGAINST* LUKE!
RED QUEEN RISING!

Long ago in a galaxy far, far away. . .there exists a state of cosmic *civil war*. A brave alliance of *underground freedom fighters* has challenged the tyranny and oppression of the awesome *Galactic Empire*. This is their story!

LucasFilm PRESENTS: STAR WARS THE GREATEST SPACE FANTASY OF ALL!

CONTINUING THE SAGA BEGUN IN THE FILM BY *GEORGE LUCAS* RELEASED BY *TWENTIETH CENTURY-FOX*

ARCHIE GOODWIN
writer/editor

CARMINE INFANTINO *and* GENE DAY
artists

JOHN COSTANZA
letterer

PETRA GOLDBERG
colorist

JIM SHOOTER
consulting ed.

THE *MILLENNIUM FALCON* FLOATS IN WIDE ORBIT AROUND A RINGED WORLD CALLED *MONASTERY*. AND TO HAN SOLO'S *DISMAY*... IT NO LONGER DOES THIS *ALONE!*

ATTENTION, FREIGHTER! STAND BY FOR IMPERIAL INSPECTION!

WELL, KIDS, IT'S NICE TO KNOW OUR *SCANNERS* ARE WORKING PERFECTLY--

--THIS MAKES IT PRETTY *DEFINITE* THAT ONE OF THE EMPIRE'S *BATTLE CRUISERS* IS MOVING IN ON US!

Red Queen Rising!

YOU KNOW WE COULDN'T TAKE *FLIGHT*... NOT WHEN OUR MISSION IS TO BE LONG RANGE *BACK-UP* FOR LUKE WHILE HE'S DOWN ON THAT PLANET.

YEAH, I *KNOW.* THAT DOESN'T MEAN I HAVE TO BE *HAPPY* ABOUT IT.

OUR ONLY HOPE NOW IS THAT THEY BUY OUR *COVER STORY*--

--BUT IT MAY BE HARD FOR THEM TO *BELIEVE* WE'RE A SIMPLE FREIGHTER MAKING *REPAIRS* IF THEY FIND AN ACKNOWLEDGED *LEADER* OF THE REBEL ALLIANCE ABOARD.

TIME TO GO INTO *HIDING,* PRINCESS!

VDWROWRK!

YOU *HEARD,* CHEWIE... THEY'RE PULLING US IN WITH THEIR *TRACTOR BEAM.*

DOWN INTO THE *BIN,* YOUR *ROYALNESS*... PRETEND YOU'RE A CONTAINER OF *SPICE.*

I *BEG* YOUR PARDON, CAPTAIN SOLO... BUT WHAT SHOULD *I* DO WHEN THE IMPERIALS COME ABOARD?

YOU SHOULD BE ABLE TO KEEP THAT ULTRA-FREQUENCY *LASER-WAVE LINK* TO ARTOO DETOO *OPEN,* BRONZE BRITCHES--

TELL THE STORM-TROOPERS YOU'RE RECHARGING YOUR *FRAMISTATS* OR SOMETHIN'!

BE *BOLD...* BE *CREATIVE!* YOU KNOW... *LIE!*

THIS IS *IMPERIAL* CAPTAIN *WERMIS,* FREIGHTER. LOWER YOUR *RAMP* AND STAND READY TO BE *BOARDED*--

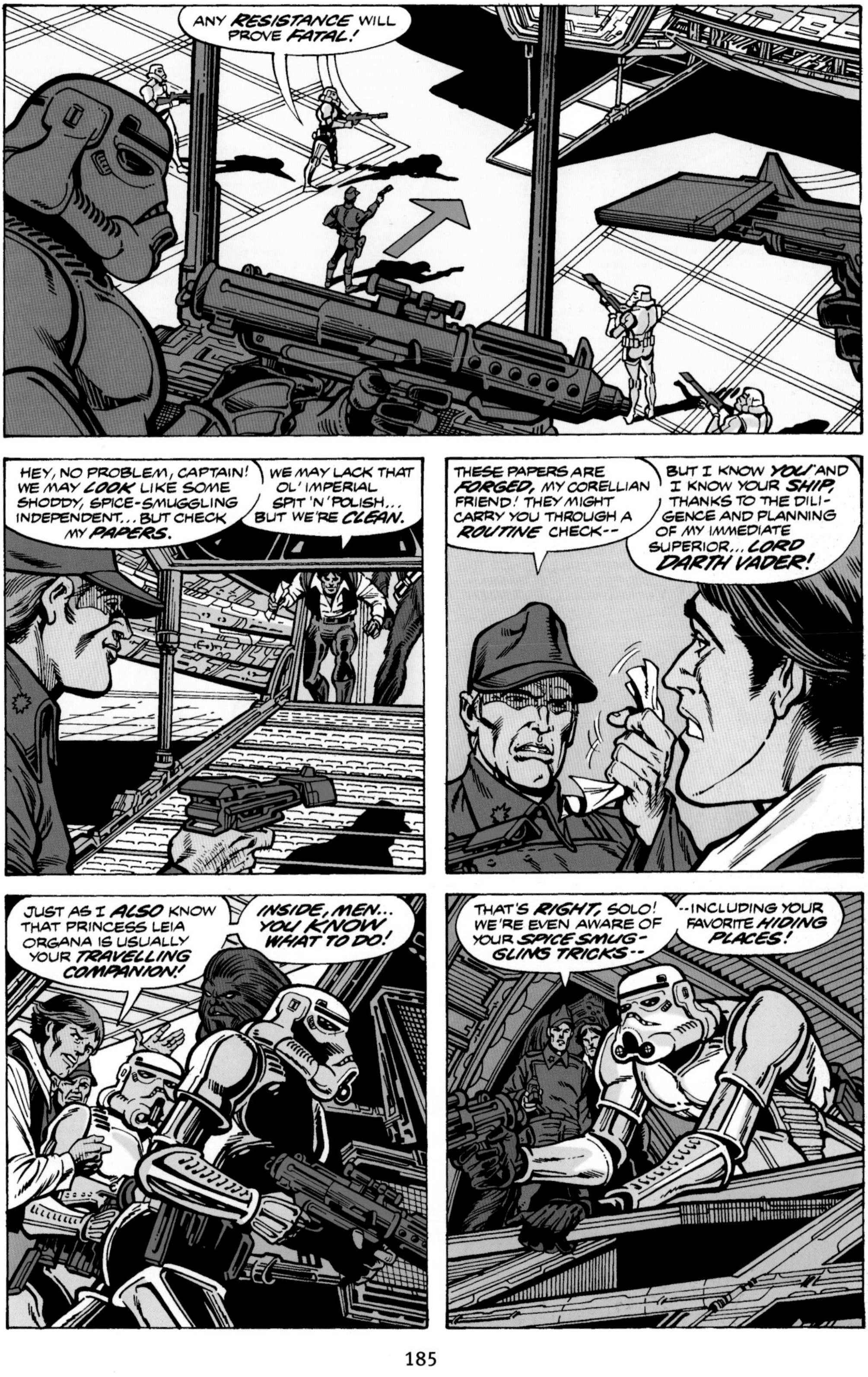
ANY RESISTANCE WILL PROVE FATAL!
HEY, NO PROBLEM, CAPTAIN! WE MAY LOOK LIKE SOME SHODDY, SPICE-SMUGGLING INDEPENDENT... BUT CHECK MY PAPERS.
WE MAY LACK THAT OL' IMPERIAL SPIT 'N' POLISH... BUT WE'RE CLEAN.
THESE PAPERS ARE FORGED, MY CORELLIAN FRIEND! THEY MIGHT CARRY YOU THROUGH A ROUTINE CHECK--
BUT I KNOW YOU AND I KNOW YOUR SHIP, THANKS TO THE DILI-GENCE AND PLANNING OF MY IMMEDIATE SUPERIOR... LORD DARTH VADER!
JUST AS I ALSO KNOW THAT PRINCESS LEIA ORGANA IS USUALLY YOUR TRAVELLING COMPANION!
INSIDE, MEN... YOU KNOW WHAT TO DO!
THAT'S RIGHT, SOLO! WE'RE EVEN AWARE OF YOUR SPICE SMUG-GLING TRICKS--
--INCLUDING YOUR FAVORITE HIDING PLACES!

ON THE WORLD OF MONASTERY, IT IS *DAWN*. BEYOND THE TEMPLE OF THE ORDER OF THE SACRED CIRCLE LIES A GREAT RAIN FOREST... AND HERE, A RESTLESS *LUKE SKYWALKER* HAS CHOSEN TO WANDER.

I CAN'T *SLEEP*, ARTOO... NOT WHEN WE'VE GOT TO PRESENT OUR CASE AGAINST THE *EMPIRE* TO THE TEMPLE ELDERS THIS MORNING.

THIS RELIGIOUS ORDER HAS A LOT OF *INFLUENCE* AROUND THE GALAXY... IF WE MESS UP, THEY MAY SEE THE REBELLION AS A *THREAT* TO THE NATURAL CIRCLE OF LIFE THAT THEY WORSHIP.

BLIT-OA VOOP!

ARE YOU TRYING TO REMIND ME THAT YOU'VE BEEN PROGRAMMED WITH ENOUGH *PROOF* TO SHOW THE EMPIRE IS AN EVEN *BIGGER* THREAT...? THAT'S *FINE*, ARTOO--

--BUT IT'S *ME*, I'M *WORRIED* ABOUT... BEING IN WAY OVER MY HEAD PLAYING *DIPLOMAT!* ESPECIALLY SINCE THE *IMPERIAL* REPRESENTATIVE HERE...IS *DARTH VADER!*

STILL... *SISTER DOMINA* OF THE ORDER THOUGHT MY LACK OF EXPERIENCE MIGHT BE A *VIRTUE*, FIGURED *SINCERITY* WOULD COUNT FOR MORE WITH THE ELDERS THAN--

WHAT'S THAT *AHEAD* OF US?

IT IS A *GLADE* AMID THE TALL TREES THAT STAND LIKE CATHEDRAL COLUMNS... AND BEFORE THE CALM POOL IN ITS CENTER, THE PRIESTESS KNOWN AS SISTER DOMINA SEEMS TO *MEDITATE*.

CERTAINLY THE WORLD AND THE FOREST APPEAR *CLOSED* FROM HER THOUGHTS...

...OR SHE WOULD BE AWARE THAT *DEATH* SLOWLY, STEALTHILY CREEPS TOWARD HER!

THEN, WITH A COUGHING SNARL...THE BEAST LEAPS!

SO, TOO, DOES *LUKE SKYWALKER!* HE HAS RUN HARD AND FAST TO *PROPEL* HIMSELF INTO THE CREATURE WITH AS MUCH *FORCE* AS POSSIBLE. HARDLY ENOUGH TO *STOP* IT...

...BUT *JUST* ENOUGH TO THROW IT OFF TARGET!

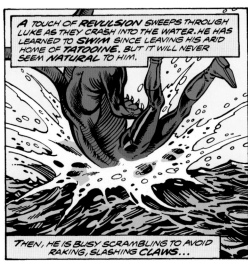

A TOUCH OF *REVULSION* SWEEPS THROUGH LUKE AS THEY CRASH INTO THE WATER. HE HAS LEARNED TO *SWIM* SINCE LEAVING HIS ARID HOME OF *TATOOINE.* BUT IT WILL NEVER SEEM *NATURAL* TO HIM.

THEN, HE IS BUSY SCRAMBLING TO AVOID RAKING, SLASHING *CLAWS*...

...BOLTING TO HIS FEET IN MERCIFULLY *SHALLOW* WATER, KNOWING HE MUST STRIKE *FIRST*...

...OR DIE!

RRAAMP!

WET, WEARY, LUKE TURNS... TO FIND HIS VICTORY HAS BEEN WITNESSED, AND OBVIOUSLY *CONDEMNED.*

BROTHERS, SISTERS... BACK TO THE *TEMPLE.* THE FOREST POOL WILL OBVIOUSLY NOT BE *FIT* FOR OUR DAWN MEDITATION.

LUKE... YOU COULDN'T *KNOW,* BUT THAT SABER CAT WAS A *PET!* HARMLESS... ALLOWED TO ROAM HERE AT WILL!

HARMLESS...?! IT WAS LEAPING TO *KILL* YOU! LET ME GO *AFTER* THEM... *EXPLAIN...!*

DON'T... YOU'RE TOO *ANGRY.* YOU MIGHT MAKE THINGS *WORSE,* LUKE.

RELAX. CALM DOWN, I'M *CERTAIN* THAT WHEN WE MEET WITH THE ELDERS ...ALL WILL GO AS IT *SHOULD.*

IT'S *GOT* TO, SISTER DOMINA...! THIS IS TOO *IMPORTANT* FOR ME TO FOUL UP!

I'LL SEE YOU BACK AT THE *TEMPLE...* AFTER I'VE CLEANED UP.

I COULD ALMOST FEEL *SORRY* FOR HIM. HE'S SO *NAIVE... TRUSTING.*

BUT I TRUST YOU THEN REMEMBER, *HE--* AND HIS REBEL FRIENDS-- ARE RESPONSIBLE FOR THE DEATH OF YOUR *BROTHER...* BARON ORMAN TAGGE!

THE HOUSE OF TAGGE *AVENGES* ITS OWN, LORD VADER... EVEN WITH MY UPBRINGING AS A PRIESTESS OF THE SACRED CIRCLE, I COULD *NEVER* FORGET THAT.

IT IS THE *REASON* I AM ALLIED WITH YOU... I WON'T *WEAKEN.*

WITHIN THE DARK PRISON OF HIS BREATHMASK... THE LORD OF THE SITH SMILES. THE GAME STILL GOES AS PLANNED.

IT IS AN *INTRICATE* GAME. ONE IN WHICH HE MOVES FORMER *RIVALS* FOR THE EMPEROR'S FAVOR LIKE *PAWNS*. RIVALS SUCH AS *BARON TAGGE*...

...WHO HAS BEEN *RESCUED* FROM NEAR-DEATH ABOARD A REBEL-DESTROYED SHIP.* NOW, ELABORATE *LIFE SUPPORT CAPSULES* SUSTAIN HIM AND HIS SCIENTIST BROTHER...

*AS ESTABLISHED *LAST ISSUE*--ARCHIE.

LIFE SUPPORT CAPSULES... AND THE *WHIM* OF DARTH VADER.

A CHANGE IN THE BARON'S *CONDITION*...? CAPTAIN *WERMIS* SHOULD BE NOTIFIED, SINCE LORD VADER IS ABSENT--

--BUT HE'S BUSY EXAMINING THAT *FREIGHTER* WE CAPTURED.

AND THAT EXAMINATION IS NOT GOING AS *PLANNED*...

I-IT *CAN'T BE*...! LORD VADER WAS *CERTAIN* THE ALLIANCE WOULD WANT PRINCESS LEIA *NEARBY* TO THE SITUATION ON MONASTERY...!

SHE MAY *BE*, SIR... BUT NOT ON THIS *SHIP*-- AND NOT IN THESE HIDDEN *STORAGE BINS*!

WE COULD BRING IN A *SCANNING TEAM* BUT--

A WASTE OF *TIME*! ALL LIKELY PLACES HAVE BEEN *THOROUGHLY* EXAMINED!

ANYONE CAN MAKE A *MISTAKE*, CAPTAIN... MY MATE AND I UNDERSTAND THE *PRESSURES* UPON AN IMPERIAL OFFICER.

RATHER THAN REPORT THIS FALSE SEARCH AND SEIZURE TO YOUR *SUPERIORS*... WE'LL JUST GO QUIETLY ON OUR WAY AS IF *NOTHING* HAD HAPPENED.

THE ONLY PLACE YOU AND THAT MOUNTAIN OF *FUR* ARE GOING, CORELLIAN...IS TO A *DETENTION CELL!*

TAKE THEM *AWAY!* TELL THE OTHER GUARDS IN THE BAY TO GET BACK TO THEIR REGULAR DUTIES... *LORD VADER* WILL DEAL WITH THIS PAIR WHEN HE *RETURNS!*

CAPTAIN WERMIS STALKS ANGRILY OFF THE MILLENNIUM FALCON. A LONG *SILENCE* FALLS OVER ITS DESERTED INTERIOR.

I'D NEVER *ADMIT* IT TO HAN SOLO...BUT THERE *ARE* ADVANTAGES TO TRAVELLING WITH A *SMUGGLER!*

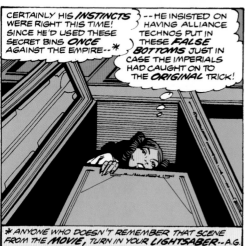

CERTAINLY HIS *INSTINCTS* WERE RIGHT THIS TIME! SINCE HE'D USED THESE SECRET BINS *ONCE* AGAINST THE EMPIRE--*

--HE INSISTED ON HAVING ALLIANCE TECHNOS PUT IN THESE *FALSE BOTTOMS* JUST IN CASE THE IMPERIALS HAD CAUGHT ON TO THE *ORIGINAL* TRICK!

* ANYONE WHO DOESN'T REMEMBER THAT SCENE FROM THE *MOVIE,* TURN IN YOUR *LIGHTSABER*--A.G.

THREEPIO! WAKE UP! WE'VE GOT TO USE THE *LASERWAVE* LINK TO *WARN* LUKE THAT DARTH VADER IS UP TO *MORE* IN THIS SYSTEM THAN PLAYING *DIPLOMAT!*

OH...*EXCUSE* ME, YOUR HIGHNESS. THE STORMTROOPERS ORDERED ME TO *SHUT DOWN.* I THOUGHT IT BEST TO *COMPLY* SO THEY WOULDN'T *REMOVE* ME FROM THE SHIP.

AND, MOMENTS LATER, ON *MONASTERY...*

LUKE...! LISTEN *CAREFULLY!* THREEPIO HAS PATCHED MY *VOICE* THROUGH ARTOO'S AUDIO-AMPLIFICATION SYSTEM--

--BUT I CAN'T TALK *LONG* WITHOUT BEING *TRACED!*

LEIA...?!

190

WHAT'S GOING *ON*...? I THOUGHT I WAS WORKING *ALONE*...

GENERAL DODONNA WANTED ME ABLE TO GIVE YOU *ADVICE* IF THE DIPLOMATIC SITUATION TURNED STICKY... BUT WE THOUGHT IF WE TOLD YOU ABOUT THIS, IT MIGHT *INHIBIT* YOU FROM ACTING ON YOUR OWN.

I DON'T KNOW... MAYBE I COULD *USE* A LITTLE INHIBITING. THINGS HAVE BEEN HAPPENING HERE THAT--

BE *ALERT*, LUKE! I'VE GOT TO SEE WHAT I CAN DO FOR HAN AND CHEWBACCA... WE'RE ON LORD VADER'S CRUISER!

HE OBVIOUSLY HAS SOME SCHEME TO TRAP US *ALL*... BUT HE'S CLOSEST TO *YOU*! MAYBE THE ORDER OF THE SACRED CIRCLE CAN HELP...!

WITH A CLICK, PRINCESS LEIA SIGNS OFF, BUT BEFORE LUKE CAN TAKE ACTION...

IT'S TIME TO MEET WITH THE TEMPLE *ELDERS*.

SISTER DOMINA, I'VE GOT TO *TALK* WITH YOU! DARTH VADER IS--

-- ALREADY ON HIS WAY TO THE GATHERING CHAMBER. ANYTHING YOU WISH TO BRING UP CAN BE SETTLED *THERE*, LUKE.

*S*WIFTLY, THE PRIESTESS MOVES INTO THE CORRIDOR BEFORE LUKE CAN SAY MORE...

...AND, AS SHE LEADS THE WAY TO THE MEETING, DOMINA TAGGE *SMILES*. IT IS HER FIRST GENUINE SMILE SINCE THE DAY HER *BROTHER* VISITED...

... HER YOUNGEST BROTHER, ULRIC, THE IMPERIAL GENERAL. HE CAME IN PLACE OF THE ONE BROTHER DOMINA TRULY LOVED,' THE HEAD OF THE FAMILY...
BARON ORMAN TAGGE.

..., AND TO SUGGEST THAT IF **RETRIBUTION** INTERESTED HER, THE **BEST** HOPE WAS TO MAKE **PEACE** WITH THE LORD OF THE SITH.

SKYWALKER IS **MINE**, DOMINA TAGGE. BUT YOU'LL HAVE THE PLEASURE OF KNOWING YOU DELIVERED HIM TO ME... AND OF DEALING A GREAT **BLOW** TO HIS CAUSE!

HE CAME, BARELY CONCEALING HIS PRIDE IN BEING THE **NEW** BARON, TO EXPLAIN HOW ORMAN HAD DIED BECAUSE OF THE REBELS AND ONE LUKE SKYWALKER IN PARTICULAR...

IT WASN'T AS MUCH AS SHE WOULD HAVE LIKED... BUT IT WAS ENOUGH. NOW DARTH VADER BECAME THE ONE REGULAR VISITOR SHE WAS ALLOWED IN THE MONASTERY'S CLOISTERED SECLUSION. UNTIL...

YOU ARE **READY.** I HAVE IMPARTED ENOUGH KNOWLEDGE AND SKILL TO YOU TO DO WHAT MUST BE DONE **WITHIN**...

THEN LET'S SEE THIS THING **FINISHED**, MY LORD!

AND ONLY IN WEAKER MOMENTS WOULD SHE RECALL AN INCIDENT FROM LONG, LONG AGO, BEFORE SHE **ENTERED** THE ORDER OF THE SACRED CIRCLE AND THE PROTECTED EXISTENCE IT OFFERED...

MARRY INTO THE IMPERIAL FAMILY WHEN SHE'S OLD ENOUGH...?! SILAS, I'LL **KILL** YOU IF YOU EVER SUGGEST ANYTHING LIKE THAT AGAIN!

DOMINA'S THE ONE PURE AND INNOCENT THING IN THE TAGGE FAMILY... I WON'T SEE HER CORRUPTED IN **ANY** WAY! EVER!

SISTER DOMINA SIGHS. THAT INNOCENCE IS LONG GONE NOW, SACRIFICED TO THE NEED FOR VENGEANCE. PERHAPS IF ORMAN HAD BEEN LESS PROTECTIVE, SHE WOULDN'T HAVE FELT HIS LOSS SO STRONGLY. BUT FEEL IT SHE *DOES*...

...AND *NOTHING* WILL STAND IN THE WAY OF MAKING THOSE RESPONSIBLE *PAY!*

WAIT HERE, LUKE... UNTIL WE SUMMON YOU.

THE PRIESTESS OF THE SACRED CIRCLE DISAPPEARS INTO THE GREAT CHAMBER BEYOND. LONG, ANXIOUS MOMENTS PASS FOR AN ALREADY NERVOUS FIGHTER PILOT TURNED UNLIKELY DIPLOMAT...

ALL CIRCUITS *FUNCTIONING*, ARTOO...? NO PROBLEM WITH THE HOLOGRAPHIC *EVIDENCE* YOU'LL BE PROJECTING...?

THEN WE OUGHTTA BE ALL RIGHT. WHATEVER DARTH VADER'S UP TO, HE CAN'T PULL ANYTHING IN THIS MEETING WITHOUT LOOKING BAD HIMSEL--

THEY ARE *READY* FOR YOU, REBEL.

BUT WHAT WAITS BEHIND THE CHAMBER DOORS IS NOT *QUITE* WHAT THE STAR WARRIOR FROM TATOOINE *EXPECTED!*

YOU ARE ENTITLED TO *SURPRISE*, LUKE SKYWALKER. THE MEMBERS OF THE ORDER HAVE JUST VOTED TO *REVOKE* THE CIRCLE OF ELDER'S AUTHORITY...

...AND NAMED *ME* AS ALL-HIGH PRIESTESS!

AND MY FIRST DUTY IS TO SEE THAT *YOU* AND THE REBEL ALLIANCE ARE *ELIMINATED* AS THREATS TO THE NATURAL CYCLE OF GALACTIC LIFE!

BLEET-DA-DEEP!

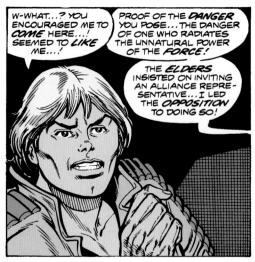

W-WHAT...? YOU ENCOURAGED ME TO *COME* HERE...! SEEMED TO *LIKE* ME....!

PROOF OF THE *DANGER* YOU POSE...THE DANGER OF ONE WHO RADIATES THE UNNATURAL POWER OF THE *FORCE!*

THE *ELDERS* INSISTED ON INVITING AN ALLIANCE REPRE-SENTATIVE...I LED THE *OPPOSITION* TO DOING SO!

AND SINCE YOUR ARRIVAL... I'VE BEEN PROVEN *RIGHT!* FROM THE MOMENT YOU SET FOOT ON MONASTERY... THERE HAVE BEEN *DIS-RUPTIONS* IN THE SACRED CIRCLE OF LIFE!

I TRIED TO BE FAIR AND OPENMINDED BY BEING ONE OF THOSE WHO *BROUGHT* YOU HERE...

...BUT WITH THE INCIDENT IN THE MEDITATION GROVE THIS MORNING, I AND THE ORDER'S MEMBERS HAVE SEEN *ENOUGH!*

YOU'RE A *MENACE,* LUKE SKYWALKER...AND BY PROCLAIMING YOU A *HERO,* THE REBELS CON-DEMN THEIR WHOLE CAUSE!

WAIT A MINUTE! THE *FORCE* IS AT WORK HERE ALL RIGHT...WITHOUT YOU CHARMING AND DIS-TRACTING ME, I CAN *SENSE* IT NOW!

IT'S BEEN USED TO SLOWLY CORRUPT AND WEAKEN THE JUDGMENT OF EVERY-ONE HERE! AND THE ONLY ONE WHO WOULD USE IT IN *THAT* WAY--

--IS *DARTH VADER!* HE USED THIS WHOLE BUSINESS TO *TRAP* ME AND MY FRIENDS AND TURN YOUR ORDER TO SERVING THE *EMPIRE!*

YOU'VE LEARNED THE WAY OF *DIPLOMAT* SWIFTLY, NOVICE...MEET ACCUSATION WITH *ACCUSATION!*

BUT IF YOU'RE *CHALLENGING* ME, I AM WILLING TO SETTLE THE MATTER IN A WAY *COMPATIBLE* WITH THE NATURAL CYCLE WORSHIPPED HERE--

...FOR WHAT IS MORE NATURAL IN THE GREAT CIRCLE OF LIFE... THAN *DEATH?*

YOURS OR MINE, PUPPY....! LET NATURE AND THE CLASH OF OUR *LIGHTSABERS* DECIDE!

194

I'M READY!

FOR ALL YOUR TWISTING AND SCHEMING... YOU'VE JUST HANDED ME THE ONE THING I WANT *MOST!*

HOLD! YOU WERE ALLOWED TO KEEP THOSE SABERS BECAUSE IN AN AGE OF *BLASTERS* THEY SEEM MERELY CEREMONIAL WEAPONS--

--BUT THEY WILL NOT BE USED IN THIS TEMPLE OF *PEACE!*

AS ALL-HIGH PRIESTESS I GIVE MY *SANCTION* FOR THIS DUEL TO BE FOUGHT...WHERE THE GREAT CIRCLE OF LIFE WILL NOT BE DISTURBED OR PROFANED.

THE TWO OF YOU WILL MEET IN THE *CRYSTAL VALLEY*... AT *SUNDOWN.*

*T*HIS NOT PRECISELY AS VADER PLANNED...

...STILL, A GOOD PLAN *ALLOWS* FOR VARIATION. THERE IS ONLY SO MUCH HE CAN ABSOLUTELY CONTROL...

BARON TAGGE SEEMS TO HAVE COMPLETELY *RECOVERED?* MEDICAL SECTION, LORD VADER LEFT ME NO *INSTRUCTIONS* ON THE MATTER!

JUST KEEP HIM IN THE LIFE SUPPORT CAPSULE. I'M ON MY WAY THER--

VOWM! BLOM!

THAT'S FROM THE DECKS *BELOW...!* W-WHAT IN THE EMPEROR'S NAME--?!

CAPTAIN WERMIS! WE'VE HAD *EXPLOSIONS* IN SUPPLY HOLDS E AND F! THEY HELD HIGHLY *INCENDIARY* STOCK... FIRE'S *SPREADING!*

GET ALL AVAILABLE PERSONNEL DOWN THERE TO *FIGHT* IT!

ALARMS SOUND THROUGHOUT THE GIANT STAR DESTROYER. ITS STERILE CORRIDORS ECHO WITH THE CLATTER OF MANY FEET. CONFUSION AND FRENZY REIGN...

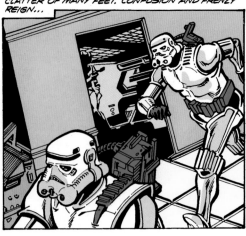

...EXCEPT IN ONE SHADOWED ALCOVE.

THOSE TIMED CHARGES ON THE *PROTON GRENADES* I TOOK FROM THE BAY GUARDS I SURPRISED DID THE *TRICK...!*

NOW, WHILE EVERYONE'S DIVERTED TO *ONE* PART OF THE SHIP--

-- I CAN STRIKE AT *ANOTHER!*

AND THIS STRIKE FREES THE CONTROL PANEL, CRUCIAL TO THE ESCAPE LEIA ORGANA PLANS FOR HER FRIENDS...

...BUT HER ACTIONS HAVE ALREADY HAD EFFECT *BEYOND* HER PLANS.

CONCUSSION FROM THOSE BLASTS *SHATTERED* THE LIFE SUPPORT CAPSULES! *SILAS* TAGGE IS STILL UNCONSCIOUS, B-BUT...

...WHERE'S THE *BARON?!*

SIR, COULD IT BE THE HOUSE OF TAGGE HAD *AGENTS* ABOARD... DELIBERATELY SABOTAGED US TO *FREE* HIM?

WE *KNOW* IT CAN'T BE REBELS... THE ONLY ONES ON THAT SHIP WE CAPTURED ARE *LOCKED AWAY!*

TROOPER, YOU JUST VOICED MY VERY *OWN* SUSPICIONS!

ACTUALLY, CAPTAIN WERMIS HAD NO SUCH SUSPICION... BUT IT SOUNDS REASONABLE ENOUGH TO BE TRUE. HE PRAYS IT WILL SOUND REASONABLE TO LORD VADER. HE IS STILL TRYING TO DECIDE HOW BEST TO FRAME HIS REPORT SO AS TO ESCAPE *BLAME*...

...WHEN *NEW* DISASTER FALLS!

SOMETHING'S HAPPENED TO THE *ARTIFICIAL GRAVITY!*

ONE PERSON ABOARD THE MASSIVE EMPIRE VESSEL IS *PREPARED* FOR THIS TURN OF EVENTS ...THE ONE WHO *CAUSED* IT.

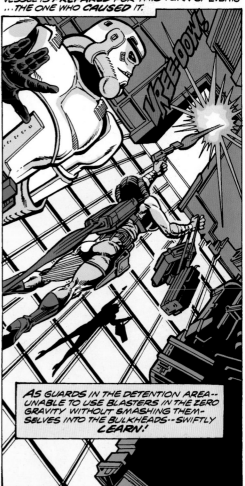

AS GUARDS IN THE DETENTION AREA-- UNABLE TO USE BLASTERS IN THE ZERO GRAVITY WITHOUT SMASHING THEM- SELVES INTO THE BULKHEADS--SWIFTLY *LEARN!*

HAN! CHEWBACCA! UNLESS YOU'VE GOTTEN FOND OF THE EMPIRE'S BRAND OF *FOOD PASTE*... STRAP THESE PROPULSION PACKS ON! *QUICKLY!*

GEE, YOUR MAJESTICNESS ...YOU THOUGHT OF EVERY- THING!

CERTAINLY! I HAD THAT ESCAPE YOU AND LUKE IMPROVISED FROM THE *DEATH STAR* TO REMIND ME WHAT IT WOULD BE LIKE IF *I DIDN'T!*

I HAVE FOND MEMORIES OF THAT ESCAPE, OF COURSE... I GOT *PAID* FOR IT.

DO YOU *REALLY* THINK WE'RE GONNA GET OUT OF HERE WITH- OUT ANY *TROUBLE?* WHAT ABOUT THE *TRACTOR BEAM?*

THERE IS TROUBLE... BUT NONE OF IT INSURMOUNTABLE. AND BY THE TIME WERMIS'S CREW BECOMES AWARE OF WHAT'S HAPPENING AND ACTIVATES THE TRACTOR BEAM...IT IS TOO LATE.

YOU PULLED IT *OFF,* PRINCESS! BUT I STILL CAN'T BELIEVE THERE'S NOT A *KICKER* SOMEWHERE.

WE HAD A LOT IN OUR *FAVOR,* HAN... PARTICULARLY *SUR- PRISE.* THE CRUISER'S *CAPTAIN* DIDN'T REACT TO IT VERY WELL--

I'D BET FROM THE CONFUSED WAY HE HAD HIS TROOPS RUSHING AROUND... HE HASN'T HAD MUCH *BATTLE* EXPERIENCE.

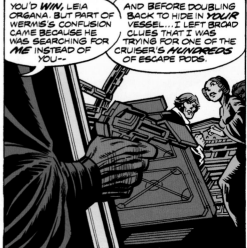

YOU'D *WIN,* LEIA ORGANA. BUT PART OF WERMIS'S CONFUSION CAME BECAUSE HE WAS SEARCHING FOR *ME* INSTEAD OF YOU--

AND BEFORE DOUBLING BACK TO HIDE IN *YOUR* VESSEL...I LEFT BROAD CLUES THAT I WAS TRYING FOR ONE OF THE CRUISER'S *HUNDREDS* OF ESCAPE PODS.

DON'T **STARE**, PRINCESS... SURELY YOU REMEMBER **BARON TAGGE**? IT HASN'T BEEN SO LONG SINCE WE **CLASHED** ON METALORN.✱

NOW, HOWEVER, WE'RE TRAVELING COMPANIONS... STRAIGHT DOWN TO **MONASTERY!** I OVERHEARD ENOUGH OF THIS DROID SPEAKING WITH HIS **CONTACT** THERE...TO KNOW I'M **NEEDED!**

N-NO....! THAT WILL VIOLATE THEIR **CLOISTER**...WHATEVER TROUBLE **LUKE** IS IN, THAT MIGHT BE ENOUGH TO **FINISH** HIM!

✱ **STAR WARS #30** --ARCHIE.

SKYWALKER...?! HIS FATE IS NO MORE MY CONCERN THAN **BLASTING** YOU WILL BE, IF YOU SHOULD **DELAY** ME!

EASY, YOUR HIGHNESS... THIS COCKPIT IS NO PLACE FOR A **FIREFIGHT.** TRUST AN OLD SMUGGLING HAND TO GET US DOWN **UNNOTICED...**

SUNDOWN! A PROCESSION SETS OUT FROM THE TEMPLE OF THE SACRED CIRCLE...MOVING TOWARD WHAT WILL BE A **KILLING GROUND.**

DARTH VADER HAS TAUGHT HER **WELL,** DOMINA TAGGE THINKS. **TOO** WELL, PERHAPS, FOR IN LETTING HER DECIDE THE **SITE** FOR THE DUEL...

...HE HAS GIVEN HER THE OPPORTUNITY TO SEE THAT NOT ONE BUT **TWO** OF HER FAMILY'S ENEMIES WILL PERISH! WHY SETTLE FOR THE **REBEL** WHEN SHE CAN BRING DOWN THE **SITH** LORD AS WELL?!

NEXT ISSUE: **IN MORTAL COMBAT!**

40¢ 37 JULY 02817

APPROVED BY THE COMICS CODE AUTHORITY

ADVENTURES *BEYOND* THE GREATEST SPACE-FANTASY FILM OF ALL!

STAR WARS

IN MORTAL COMBAT!

INFANTINO / WIACEK

Long ago in a galaxy far, far away. . .there exists a state of cosmic *civil war*. A brave alliance of *underground freedom fighters* has challenged the tyranny and oppression of the awesome *Galactic Empire*. This is their story!

LucasFilm PRESENTS: **STAR WARS** ™ THE GREATEST SPACE FANTASY OF ALL!

CONTINUING THE SAGA BEGUN IN THE FILM *BY GEORGE LUCAS* RELEASED BY *TWENTIETH CENTURY-FOX*

SUNSET ON THE RINGED PLANET OF *MONASTERY*, CLOISTERED HOMEWORLD OF THE ORDER OF THE SACRED CIRCLE. A DIPLOMATIC MISSION FOR THE REBEL ALLIANCE HAS BROUGHT LUKE SKYWALKER HERE. THE BAROQUE SCHEMING OF DARTH VADER MAY NOW SEE THAT MISSION END...

IN MORTAL COMBAT!

THERE! BELOW THE EVENING MISTS LIES THE *CRYSTAL VALLEY.*

TWO SEPARATE PATHS LEAD DOWN TO IT FROM THIS POINT. YOU EACH WILL TAKE ONE, WHEN YOU *MEET* IN THE VALLEY--

--YOUR *DUEL* MAY BEGIN!

ARCHIE GOODWIN writer/editor • **CARMINE INFANTINO** and **GENE DAY** artists • **JOHN COSTANZA** letterer • **NEL YOMTOV** colorist • **JIM SHOOTER** consulting editor

LF 607

WITH NO SOUND BUT THE HISS OF HIS BREATHMASK, THE HUM OF HIS LIGHTSABER, THE SITH LORD STRIDES INSTANTLY FORWARD...

...HIS DARK THOUGHTS SOLELY HIS OWN.

YOUR TURN, REBEL.

YEAH...

...AFTER ALL THE FANCY *MANIPULATING* YOU AND VADER PUT ME THROUGH TO BRING THIS ABOUT--

--A LITTLE HONEST *FIGHTING* WILL BE A PLEASURE!

VLITTA DOOP

I...I'M SORRY, ARTOO, YOU CAN'T GO WITH ME, NOT *THIS* TIME.

DOMINA TAGGE SMILES. EVERYTHING HAS GONE PERFECTLY. BY COOPERATING WITH LORD VADER SHE HAS GAINED THE *POWER* SHE NEEDED...

HIS INFLUENCE HAS MADE ME *LEADER* OF THE ORDER--

--AND, AS AGREED, I'VE SANCTIONED THIS COMBAT.

BUT HE CARELESSLY LET *ME* CHOOSE THE SITE. AND DOWN *THERE*... NO ONE CAN SURVIVE.

INSTEAD OF SETTLING FOR VENGEANCE ON *ONE* ENEMY OF MY BROTHER--

--I'LL SEE THEM *BOTH* DESTROYED!

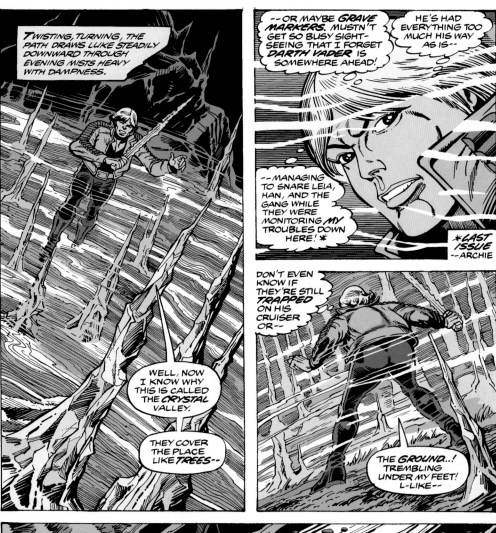

TWISTING, TURNING, THE PATH DRAWS LUKE STEADILY DOWNWARD THROUGH EVENING MISTS HEAVY WITH DAMPNESS.

--OR MAYBE *GRAVE MARKERS.* MUSTN'T GET SO BUSY SIGHT-SEEING THAT I FORGET *DARTH VADER* IS SOMEWHERE AHEAD!

HE'S HAD EVERYTHING TOO MUCH HIS WAY AS IS--

--MANAGING TO SNARE LEIA, HAN, AND THE GANG WHILE THEY WERE MONITORING *MY* TROUBLES DOWN HERE! *

*LAST ISSUE --ARCHIE

WELL, NOW I KNOW WHY THIS IS CALLED THE *CRYSTAL* VALLEY.

THEY COVER THE PLACE LIKE *TREES*--

DON'T EVEN KNOW IF THEY'RE STILL *TRAPPED* ON HIS CRUISER OR--

THE *GROUND..!* TREMBLING UNDER MY FEET! L-LIKE--

SHRAKRAAACK!

203

T-THAT *CRYSTAL*...! SEEMED TO *BURST* FROM THE GROUND!

MOISTURE FROM THIS HEAVY DEW AND MIST MUST CAUSE SOME SORT OF *CHEMICAL REACTION*--

--MAKES THEM GROW *FAST*... ALMOST *EXPLOSIVELY*!

AND THE FORCE OF THE NEW ONES THRUSTING UP... MAKES THE OLD ONES NEARBY *SHATTER* AND *FALL*!

KR-KOW!

EITHER COULD GET YOU FATALLY *SKEWERED*--

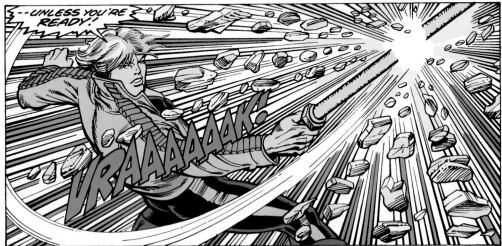

--UNLESS YOU'RE *READY*!

VRAAAAAAK!

BUT HOW READY CAN YOU *STAY* WHEN ONE OF THESE CRYSTALS CAN THRUST UP OR CRASH DOWN--

WROOOM!

--FROM ANY *PLACE* AT ANY *MOMENT*?!

UNLESS THE FORCE IS WITH *BOTH* OF US... DARTH VADER AND I MAY NOT *LIVE* TO BATTLE EACH OTHER!

BUT THE DARK LORD HAS *HALTED* HIS DESCENT INTO THE VALLEY. HE STANDS WAITING...

...PATIENTLY, EXPECTANTLY. WAITING. UNTIL IN MONASTERY'S TWILIGHT SKY...

...A *LIGHT* FLICKERS AND GROWS IN SIZE. THE LIGHT OF AN APPROACHING *SPACECRAFT.*

FROM UNYIELDING BLACK METAL... A HISS OF SATISFACTION. WITH SO MUCH THAT *MIGHT* HAVE GONE WRONG IN HIS COMPLEX SCHEMING...

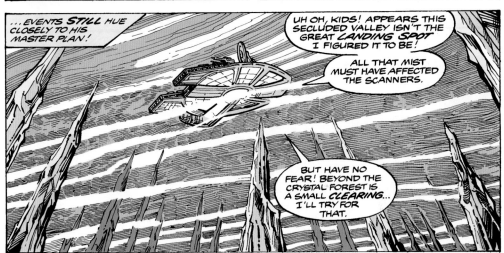

...EVENTS *STILL* HUE CLOSELY TO HIS *MASTER PLAN!*

UH OH, KIDS! APPEARS THIS SECLUDED VALLEY ISN'T THE GREAT *LANDING SPOT* I FIGURED IT TO BE!

ALL THAT MIST MUST HAVE AFFECTED THE SCANNERS.

BUT HAVE NO FEAR! BEYOND THE CRYSTAL FOREST IS A SMALL *CLEARING...* I'LL TRY FOR THAT.

IF YOU'RE *UP* TO SOMETHING, CORELLIAN... IT'LL BE YOUR *LAST* TRICK!

NOTHING STANDS IN MY WAY... NOT WITH MY *SISTER* IN JEOPARDY!

DESPITE MY FAMILY'S *RIVALRY* WITH DARTH VADER FOR THE EMPEROR'S FAVOR... DOMINA HAS REMAINED INNOCENT, PROTECTED. I'LL *KILL* TO SEE THAT DOESN'T CHANGE!

UNLESS YOU'RE A LOT *NICER* TO ME, BARON OL' BUDDY... YOU WON'T GET THE CHANCE.

THE MIDDLE OF A TOUGH *LANDING* IS NO PLACE TO THREATEN THE *PILOT!*

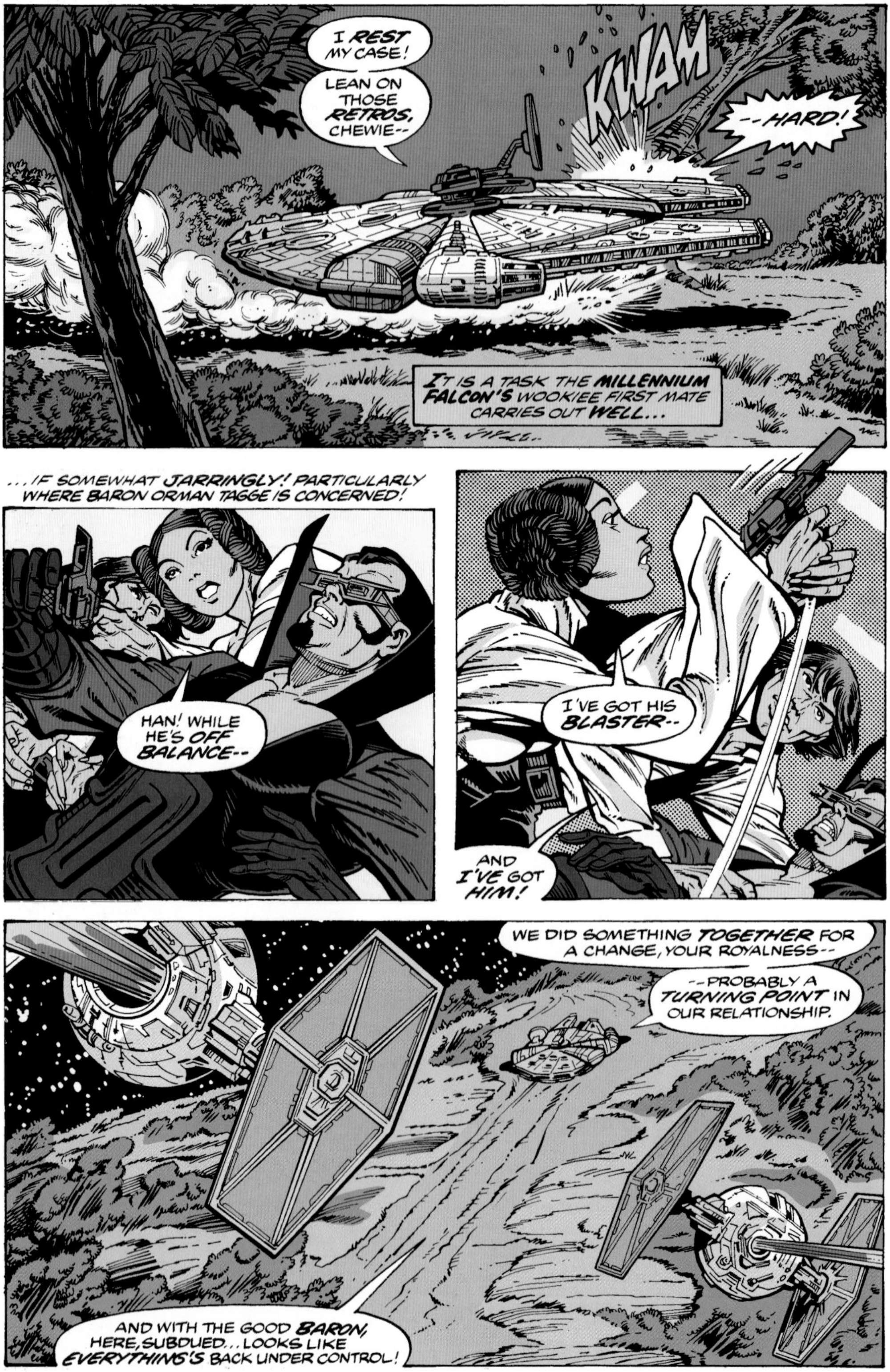

I REST MY CASE!
LEAN ON THOSE RETROS, CHEWIE--
KWAM
--HARD!
IT IS A TASK THE MILLENNIUM FALCON'S WOOKIEE FIRST MATE CARRIES OUT WELL...
...IF SOMEWHAT JARRINGLY! PARTICULARLY WHERE BARON ORMAN TAGGE IS CONCERNED!
HAN! WHILE HE'S OFF BALANCE--
I'VE GOT HIS BLASTER--
AND I'VE GOT HIM!
WE DID SOMETHING TOGETHER FOR A CHANGE, YOUR ROYALNESS--
--PROBABLY A TURNING POINT IN OUR RELATIONSHIP.
AND WITH THE GOOD BARON, HERE, SUBDUED... LOOKS LIKE EVERYTHINS'S BACK UNDER CONTROL!

BOWRK!

WATTA YOU *MEAN* I'D BETTER LOOK AGAIN? WE JUST--

OH, THOSE *TIE* FIGHTERS, WELL...NOBODY'S PERFECT.

CAPTAIN SOLO? I STILL HAVE THE LASERWAVE LINK *OPEN* TO ARTOO-DETOO.

THE LITTLE FELLOW REPORTS--

NOT *NOW*, THREEPIO...OR WE MAY NOT BE *AROUND* FOR ANY REPORTS!

THEN HAN IS AT THE *FALCON'S* QUAD LASER CANNON...

...JUST AS THE TWO IMPERIAL SHIPS ARE AT THE *FALCON!*

PA-KWOM

I GUESS THE CAPTAIN OF DARTH VADER'S *CRUISER* TOOK OUR *ESCAPE* PRETTY HARD--

VRA-DOW!

--VIOLATING A RELIGIOUS ORDER'S *CLOISTER* LIKE THIS! IT'S SURE TO BE A *DIPLOMATIC* SCANDAL.

OF COURSE, WE MAY BE TOO LONG *VAPORIZED* TO ENJOY THE EMPIRE'S EMBARRASSMENT!

I DON'T SUPPOSE THIS IS THE TIME TO POINT OUT TO THE CAPTAIN THAT WE, *TOO*, ARE IN VIOLATION.

THE IRONY *MIGHT* ELUDE HIM--

"-- JUST AS THAT REMAINING *TIE FIGHTER* SEEMS TO BE DOING!"

I *HEARD* THAT, YOUR WORSHIP--

VRADOM VRDOM

AND IF I DIDN'T KNOW THESE LITTLE DIGS WERE JUST YOUR WAY OF DIS-GUISING YOUR *TRUE* FEELINGS--

-- I MIGHT BE *INSULTED!*

KA-WOOM

I KNOW THAT KIND OF SHARPSHOOTING LEAVES YOU *STUNNED*, KIDS, BUT RELAX--

--IT'S OKAY TO *CHEER*.

EXCEPT THAT WHILE EVERYTHING *ELSE* WAS BREAKING LOOSE--

"...SO WAS *BARON TAGGE!* HE'S RACING TOWARD THAT FOREST OF CRYSTAL RIGHT NOW!"

"THEN MAYBE THE JOKE'S ON *HIM*, PRINCESS. 'CAUSE ACCORDING TO THE SCOPES..."

"... THE PLACE IS IN A CONSTANT STATE OF *ERUPTION!* ANYONE WHO GETS HIMSELF IN THERE BETTER BE UNNATURALLY *LUCKY* ...OR POSITIVELY *INVINCIBLE.*

"*PREFERABLY BOTH!*"

KRAKOW

AND JUST AS LUKE IS REACHING THE *SAME* CONCLUSION...

ARTOO! YOU FOLLOWED ME AFTER ALL...?! THAT'S--

LESS *RISKY* THAN YOU MIGHT IMAGINE, SIR... GIVEN HIS COMPUTERIZED SENSORY SYSTEM.

STILL...IT'S FAR FROM *FLAWLESS.* THAT'S WHY *I'M* SPEAKING UP VIA THE LASERWAVE LINK--

WE'RE *NEARBY,* SIR! AND BY HOMING IN ON ME, ARTOO CAN *LEAD* YOU TO US, GIVEN YOUR PREDICAMENT... IT'S THE ONLY HOPE!

NO, THREEPIO!

DARTH VADER'S PLAYED US ALL FOR *PAWNS,* BUT I'VE GOT THE CHANCE TO *FIGHT* HIM HERE--

AND WHATEVER THE CONSEQUENCES... I'M GOING TO *DO* IT!

LUKE! THAT MAY BE *EXACTLY* WHAT HE--

I'M SORRY, YOUR HIGHNESS, HE'S BROKEN TRANSMISSION!

MEANWHILE...

WRRAK

T-THE CRYSTAL!

CAN'T MOVE *FAST* ENOUGH ...IT'S GOING TO--

CRUSH YOU, ORMAN TAGGE...? NO, ITS GREAT BULK IS GOING TO STOP INCHES SHORT OF THAT--

IT WILL PRESS YOU DOWN... DRIVING YOU FINALLY ONTO YOUR BACK!

IT'S NOT P-POSSIBLE...!

TO A MASTER OF THE FORCE... ALL THINGS ARE POSSIBLE.

INCLUDING LURING YOU HERE... TO THIS SPOT, AT THIS TIME.

IN THE EMPEROR'S NAME... WHY? YOU COULD HAVE SLAIN ME LONG AGO!

AN UNIMAGINATIVE VENGEANCE, BARON... YOU'VE TROUBLED ME ENOUGH TO DESERVE BETTER.

FOR INSTANCE: THIS FATE THAT'S BEFALLEN YOU--

--IS ACTUALLY WHAT YOUR DEAR LITTLE SISTER PLANNED TO HAVE HAPPEN TO ME.

DOMINA...? B-BUT... SHE'S NOT LIKE THAT! SHE'S INNOCENT ...BEYOND SUCH SCHEMING!

NO MORE, TAGGE.

WITH A BIT OF -GUIDANCE FROM ME, ANXIOUS TO AVENGE WHAT SHE THINKS IS YOUR DEATH... SHE'S CHANGED! AS THIS VISI-CUBE SHOWS--

N-NO,...! THE ONE UNSULLIED, UNCORRUPTED THING IN OUR ENTIRE LINE...!

FINISH ME, VADER! YOU'VE RUINED THE ONLY PERSON IN THIS GALAXY I LOVED! FINISH ME NOW!

SOON. BUT FIRST... YOU'LL FULFILL A FINAL TASK.

THE SUN IS GONE. NIGHT ON MONASTERY IS MADE BEAUTIFUL BY ITS SOFTLY GLOWING RING OF MOONS. BUT THAT BEAUTY IS LOST ON TWO FIGURES URGENTLY, DESPERATELY SKIRTING THE CRYSTAL VALLEY...

FASTER, HAN! FROM WHAT THREEPIO LEARNED FROM ARTOO... WE CAN STILL *STOP* THIS DUEL!

BUT WE'VE GOT TO LET DOMINA TAGGE KNOW HER BROTHER IS *ALIVE*... THAT LUKE DIDN'T CAUSE HIS DEATH, AS DARTH VADER MADE HER BELIEVE!

HAN DOESN'T VOICE A RESPONSE THAT OCCURS TO HIM. IT'S NO DOUBT IN LEIA'S MIND AS WELL...

THEIR EFFORT COULD ALREADY BE *TOO LATE* TO SAVE LUKE FROM THE VALLEY...

...OR WORSE!

THAT *SHARD*...! IT DIDN'T FALL OR ERUPT--

I-IT... *HURTLED* THROUGH THE AIR...! ALMOST AS IF IT WERE THROWN--

WAAMP

-- BY THE FORCE!

211

NO OTHER WORDS ARE SPOKEN, FOR PERHAPS A HEARTBEAT... BOTH FIGURES ARE STILL.

THEN...THEY MOVE!

SHDAAAAAKKKK!

SWIFTLY, INEVITABLY... LIKE *LIGHTNING* STRIKING!

AND IN THE STRAINING PRESS OF COMBAT... A *TRUTH* COMES TO LUKE SKYWALKER.

I CAN *FEEL* THE FORCE AROUND VADER... IT'S SO *STRONG!* SURROUNDS HIM LIKE A *WALL!* B-BUT... *BEYOND* THAT... I SENSE SOMETHING ELSE... *FEAR!*

H-HE'S ACTUALLY *AFRAID* OF ME! IF THAT'S SO... *I CAN WIN!* IT WON'T BE EASY... BUT I CAN *DO* IT!

BUT IN HIS PROBING OF THE ONE HE FIGHTS...

...THE YOUNG WARRIOR FORGETS *ANOTHER* FACTOR! HE FALLS...

...HIS FOE DOES *NOT!*

FWAM!

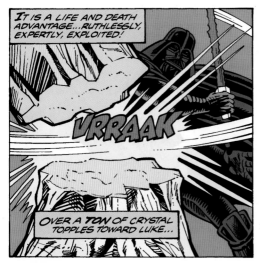

IT IS A LIFE AND DEATH ADVANTAGE...RUTHLESSLY, EXPERTLY, EXPLOITED!

VRRAAK

OVER A *TON* OF CRYSTAL TOPPLES TOWARD LUKE...

WOM

BUT THE LESSONS OF BEN KENOBI ARE *WITH* HIM...

HIS ACTIONS GROW FROM INSTINCT, FROM FEELING, FROM HIS INNER SELF...

ZAMP!

...FROM THE *FORCE!*

HIS ARMORED ENEMY MOVES WITH SKILL, WITH DARING...

...BUT NOW IT IS THE YOUNGER MAN WHO PRESSES THE BATTLE!

HE'S OUT TO *FLATTEN* ME...!

BUT IF I FALL BACK *WITH* HIS KICK AND COME UP *FAST*--

SHRRAAAKK

THE BLADE HITS GLANCINGLY... NOT A KILLING STROKE. MERELY A *DEVASTATING* ONE!

213

Then, from out of the surrounding crystals...

VADJOT DABIP WRRT

ARTOO?! You're supposed to be making your way back to the FALCON!

No one ever had a more LOYAL friend--

But I can't afford ANY distraction now--

--not when I need all my concentration to FINISH DARTH VADER!

Threepio on the LINKUP, sir! Artoo is frantic because his sensory receptors DETECT something--

--your human vision apparently CAN'T! He fears--

My mind's being CLOUDED by the Force! Now that I'm not FIGHTING, I can SENSE it! And I can tell--

An alarmed SCREECH erupts from the little droid!

NO! This doesn't have to be! Don't make me--

The looming figure's lightsaber SWINGS... and Luke has no choice!

WAAAMP

His only defense is... a FATAL THRUST!

The Sith Lord's towering form SAGS... begins to fall...

...BUT IT IS *BARON ORMAN TAGGE* WHO CRASHES TO THE GROUND!

I KNEW IT...! BUT I REALIZED IT TOO LATE! IT'S THE REASON I SENSED *FEAR* EARLIER! TAGGE DUELED ME BEFORE... * HE LOST THEN. HE FEARED IT MIGHT HAPPEN AGAIN!

B-BUT...THAT *STILL* DOESN'T EXPLAIN--

THE *PURPOSE* OF THE ILLUSION...? THE *REASON* HE WAS MADE TO FIGHT IN *MY* PLACE?

* STAR WARS #33 --ARCHIE.

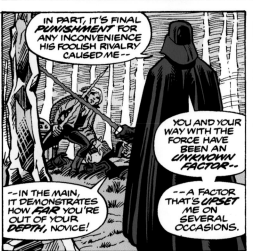

IN PART, IT'S FINAL *PUNISHMENT* FOR ANY INCONVENIENCE HIS FOOLISH RIVALRY CAUSED ME--

YOU AND YOUR WAY WITH THE FORCE HAVE BEEN AN *UNKNOWN FACTOR*--

--A FACTOR THAT'S *UPSET* ME ON SEVERAL OCCASIONS.

--IN THE MAIN, IT DEMONSTRATES HOW *FAR* YOU'RE OUT OF YOUR *DEPTH*, NOVICE!

NO *MORE*, LUKE SKYWALKER!... I'VE THOROUGHLY *TESTED* YOU... MADE YOU PERFORM IN A HOSTILE ENVIRONMENT... PROBED YOUR EMOTIONS BY PLACING YOUR FRIENDS IN JEOPARDY. I NOW KNOW YOUR LIMITS...AND YOUR LIMITATIONS!

THEN YOU KNOW SOMETHING *ELSE*. I'M LEARNING...! I CAN *CHANGE*... I CAN *GROW*!

WHEN YOUR ONLY *INSTRUCTOR* IS DEAD... BY MY HANDS?

AN AMUSING NOTION, PUPPY. HAVE YOU THE *COURAGE* TO PURSUE IT?

COME! ONLY A FEW *STEPS* SEPARATE US.

I'LL *GIVE* YOU THE FIRST BLOW!

RAGE FLARES WITHIN LUKE. HE TENSES TO CHARGE, THEN INSTEAD... LEAPS *BACK*!

LOOK *OUT*, ARTOO! HE MEANT TO TRICK ME *INTO* THAT!

WHTOOM!

NOW I'LL SHOW WHAT I'VE LEARNED--

THE ONLY WAY TO **WIN** THIS BATTLE... IS TO STOP PLAYING DARTH VADER'S OWN GAME!

MOVE IT, LITTLE FRIEND... WE'RE GETTING **OUT** OF HERE!

WHILE ABOVE THE VALLEY... INFORMATION HAS BEEN DELIVERED, INTENSE ARGUMENTS MADE!

YOU WASTE **WORDS**, LEIA ORGANA! THE SITH LORD MAY HAVE PLAYED ME FOR A **FOOL** AS YOU SAY--

BUT ALONG WITH MY BROTHER AND YOUR YOUNG REBEL--

--HE'S **DOOMED** HIMSELF! THERE'S NO WAY TO BRING AID INTO THE CRYSTAL FOREST...OR FOR HIM TO GET **OUT!**

SOMEONE FORGOT TO **TELL** VADER...!

THE UNIQUE TIE FIGHTER DISAPPEARS INTO THE HEAVENS, LEAVING **SILENCE** IN ITS WAKE... SOME SHOCKED, SOME ANGRY.

THEN...

KID...! LUKE....! YOU **MADE** IT!

THE **FORCE** WAS WITH ME, HAN. UNFORTUNATELY... IT WAS WITH **DARTH VADER** TOO!

B-BUT...MY **BROTHER!** IF YOU COULD SAVE YOURSELF--

--WHY COULDN'T YOU SAVE **HIM?!**

LUKE TRIES TO EXPLAIN. BUT **UNDERSTANDING** NEVER LIGHTS THE EYES OF DOMINA TAGGE... ONLY COLD FURY.

LORD VADER'S CORRUPTIVE TOUCH RUNS DEEP, EVEN THE **TRUTH** CAN'T SHAKE IT.

GO! I'M FINISHED AS ALL-HIGH PRIESTESS...BUT I CAN NEVER FORGET OR FORGIVE THE DEATH OF MY BROTHER, NO MATTER **WHAT** THE CIRCUMSTANCES

THE ORDER OF THE SACRED CIRCLE WON'T TURN ITS INFLUENCE AGAINST THE REBEL ALLIANCE NOW--

--BUT MY WRATH WILL **ALWAYS** BE AGAINST **YOU**, LUKE SKYWALKER!

AND SHORTLY, LIKE THE IMPERIAL CRAFT BEFORE IT... THE *MILLENNIUM FALCON* SOARS TOWARD SPACE.

FRANKLY, KID... I DON'T *GET* IT! SEEMS TO ME VADER WENT TO A LOT OF TROUBLE FOR *NOTHING.*

NOT IF YOU REGARD THE *FORCE* AS THE GREATEST POWER IN THE GALAXY, AS *HE* DOES, HAN... IT'S WORTH *ANYTHING* TO LEARN HOW MUCH OF IT HE *SHARES* WITH ME.

UNTIL *CERTAIN*, HE HAD TO BE CAUTIOUS... OUR PAST ENCOUNTERS PROVED THAT. SO THIS TIME, THROUGH HIS CONTROL OF DOMINA TAGGE, HE ARRANGED THE PHYSICAL DISTRACTIONS LIKE MY DUEL--

--ALONG WITH THE *MENTAL* ONES OF MY MISSION GOING WRONG AND ALL OF YOU BEING IN DANGER.

THANKS TO ARTOO... I CAUGHT ON BEFORE HE LURED ME INTO A *FINAL FIGHT* I'M NOT *READY* FOR!

BUT, WITH ALL HE LEARNED... HE WON'T HAVE TO BE *CAUTIOUS* AGAIN.

I'M AFRAID THAT MEANS ROUGH TIMES AHEAD... FOR ME *AND* THE REBEL ALLIANCE!

YOU MEAN UP TILL NOW IT'S BEEN *EASY*? I'M NO BEN KENOBI, LUKE... BUT I'VE GOT SOME *PHILOSOPHY* FOR YOU.

WORRYIN' ABOUT THE FUTURE CAN BE A LOT WORSE--

--THAN *LIVIN'* IT AS IT COMES!

AND IF YOU'VE GOT AN OLD CYNIC LIKE *ME* SPOUTING WISDOM... YOU MUST HAVE A *LOT* MORE GOIN' FOR YOU THAN YOU THINK!

EPILOGUE: IN THE DISTANT, ISOLATED DREXEL SYSTEM... A DERELICT HAS BEEN DISCOVERED.

NO MISTAKE! IT'S CRIMSON JACK'S *PIRATE SHIP!* I'D KNOW THAT CONVERTED IMPERIAL CRUISER ANYWHERE.

MAYBE THE BOARDING CREW WILL SALVAGE *SOMETHING*... BUT FROM HERE IT LOOKS LIKE WE'LL BE RETURNING HOME WITH VERY *BAD* NEWS.

* WE SAW IT *PUT* IN THIS SHAPE BACK IN *STAR WARS* #15 --ARCH.

AND ONE RECIPIENT OF THAT BAD NEWS IS... *JABBA THE HUT!*

I WAS A BACKER WHO HELPED JACK *REFIT* THAT CRUISER!

A MAJOR INVESTMENT *DESTROYED...!* INCLUDING ITS TREASURE HOLDS!

BLAM

AT LEAST THE SHIP'S *LOG* SURVIVED...AND MAKES CLEAR *WHO* DID THIS!

HARD TO BELIEVE *ONE MAN* COULD CONTINUALLY BRING ME SO MUCH *GRIEF!* HARSH ACTION IS REQUIRED!

ONCE REQUIRED... IT IS NOT *LONG* BEGINNING!

CRAZY BOUNTY HUNTER!

JABBA TOOK THE *PRICE* OFF OUR HEADS *WEEKS* AGO...!*

*FOR REASONS RECOUNTED IN *STAR WARS* #28--ARCH AGAIN.

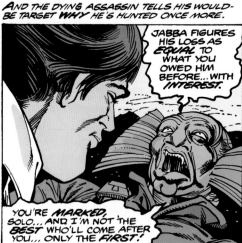

AND THE DYING ASSASSIN TELLS HIS WOULD-BE TARGET *WHY* HE'S HUNTED ONCE MORE.

JABBA FIGURES HIS LOSS AS *EQUAL* TO WHAT YOU OWED HIM BEFORE...WITH *INTEREST.*

YOU'RE *MARKED,* SOLO...AND I'M NOT THE *BEST* WHO'LL COME AFTER YOU... ONLY THE *FIRST!*

WELL, CHEWIE... LOOKS LIKE THE ONLY PLACE WE'RE WELCOME IS WITH THE *REBELS.*

NOT THE *SAFEST* OF SPOTS, WITH DARTH VADER AND THE EMPIRE AROUND.

BUT YA GOTTA ADMIT... IT WON'T BE *DULL!*

NEXT: THE MOST EAGERLY AWAITED SAGA OF THEM ALL BEGINS! MARVEL'S ADAPTATION OF...

THE EMPIRE STRIKES BACK!

AUG # 38 40¢

STAR WARS

LUKE AND LEIA TRAPPED IN A LIVING STARSHIP!
RIDERS IN THE VOID!

Long ago in a galaxy far, far away. . .there exists a state of cosmic *civil war*. A brave alliance of *underground freedom fighters* has challenged the tyranny and oppression of the awesome *Galactic Empire*. This is their story!

LucasFilm PRESENTS: **STAR WARS**™ THE GREATEST SPACE FANTASY OF ALL!

CONTINUING THE SAGA BEGUN IN THE FILM BY GEORGE LUCAS RELEASED BY TWENTIETH CENTURY-FOX

ARCHIE GOODWIN — WRITER/EDITOR
MICHAEL GOLDEN — PLOTTER/PENCILLER
TERRY AUSTIN — INKER
JOE ROSEN — LETTERER
MICHAEL GOLDEN — COLORIST
DANNY FINGEROTH — ASST. EDITOR
JIM SHOOTER — EDITOR-IN-CHIEF

ORDINARILY, A LONE SPICE TANKER PLYING THE OUTWORLD TRADE ROUTES IS OF SMALL CONCERN TO THE EMPIRE...

BUT ORDINARILY, SUCH A TANKER DOESN'T HAVE ITS HOLDS LINED WITH MEDICAL SUPPLIES BOUND FOR THE REBEL ALLIANCE...

...OR TWO PROMINENT MEMBERS OF THE REBELLION AT ITS HELM.

LUKE....! WE'VE BEEN BETRAYED!

RIDERS IN THE VOID!

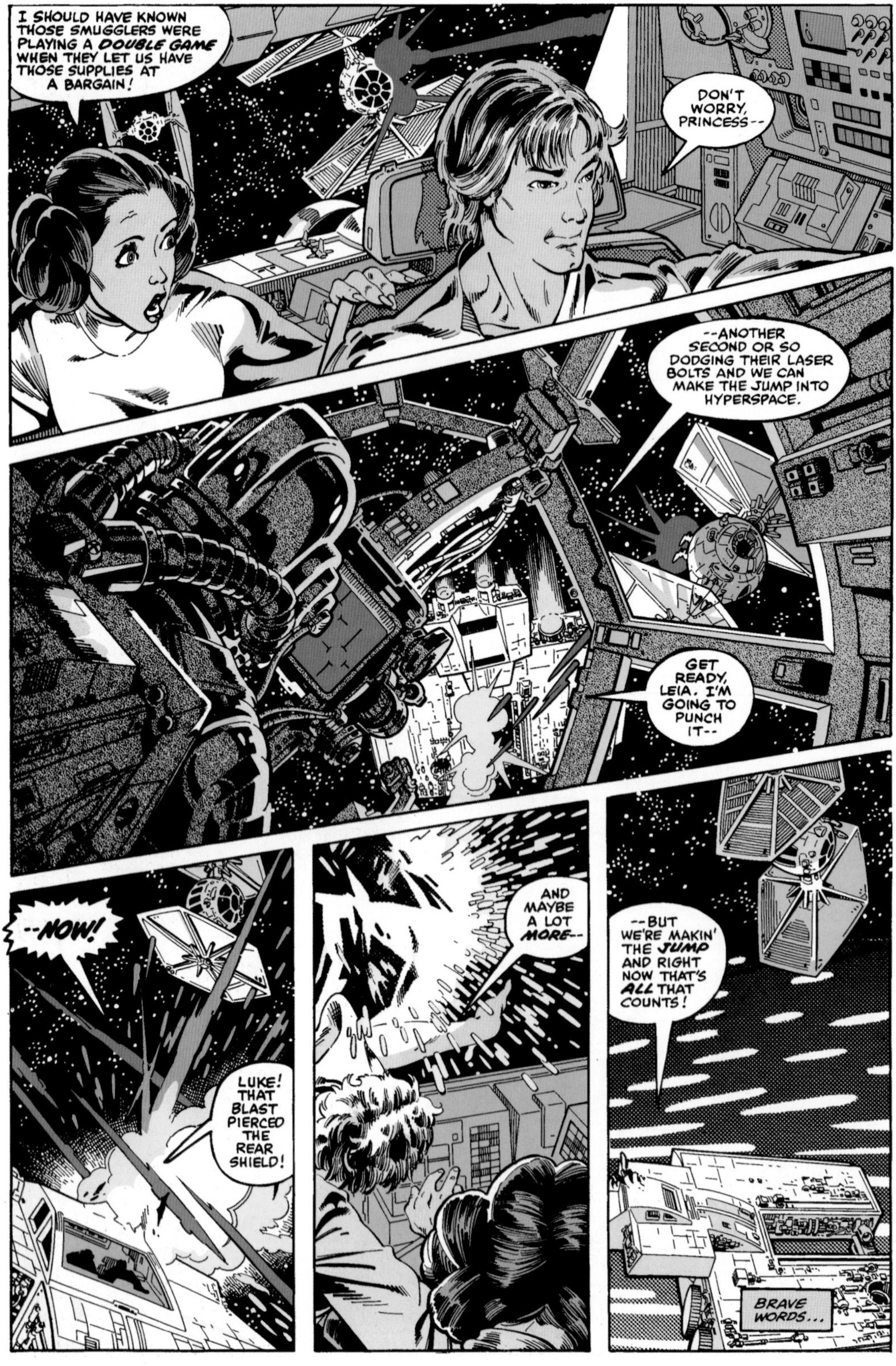

I SHOULD HAVE KNOWN THOSE SMUGGLERS WERE PLAYING A DOUBLE GAME WHEN THEY LET US HAVE THOSE SUPPLIES AT A BARGAIN!
DON'T WORRY, PRINCESS--
--ANOTHER SECOND OR SO DODGING THEIR LASER BOLTS AND WE CAN MAKE THE JUMP INTO HYPERSPACE.
GET READY, LEIA. I'M GOING TO PUNCH IT--
--NOW!
LUKE! THAT BLAST PIERCED THE REAR SHIELD!
AND MAYBE A LOT MORE--
--BUT WE'RE MAKIN' THE JUMP AND RIGHT NOW THAT'S ALL THAT COUNTS!
BRAVE WORDS...

I'M *TRYING...!* BUT... INSTRUMENTS ARE GOING CRAZY...NOTHING'S RE-SPONDING...LIKE IT SHOULD!

I-IT FEELS LIKE WE'RE SHAKING *APART...!* EVERY *CIRCUIT* IS BLOWING....!

LET'S GET *OUT* OF THIS!

STILL, THE YOUNG STAR WARRIOR FIGHTS TO MANUALLY OVERRIDE THE SHIPBOARD COMPUTER SYSTEM! UNTIL...

...*GOT* IT! WE'RE DROPPING BACK TO SUB-LIGHT!

THANK THE *FORCE...!*

UH...I'M NOT SO CERTAIN THE FORCE WAS *WITH* US, PRINCESS.

THAT HIT WE TOOK DEFINITELY AFFECTED THE *HYPERDRIVE.* WE'VE JUMPED WAY TOO FAST--

--AND MUCH TOO *FAR!*

THE *STARS...!* THEY'RE GONE! W-WE'RE *BEYOND* THE GALAXY... LOST SOMEWHERE IN THE *VOID!*

AND I HAD TO KILL ALL *POWER* TO STOP US. IT'LL TAKE MAJOR REPAIRS TO GET US GOING AGAIN.

I'LL TRY THE *EMERGENCY BEACON,* BUT WE'RE BOUND TO BE *LIGHT YEARS* FROM ANY KIND OF--

LUKE...! THERE'S *SOMETHING...* ONE STAR I DIDN'T *SEE* BEFORE!

223

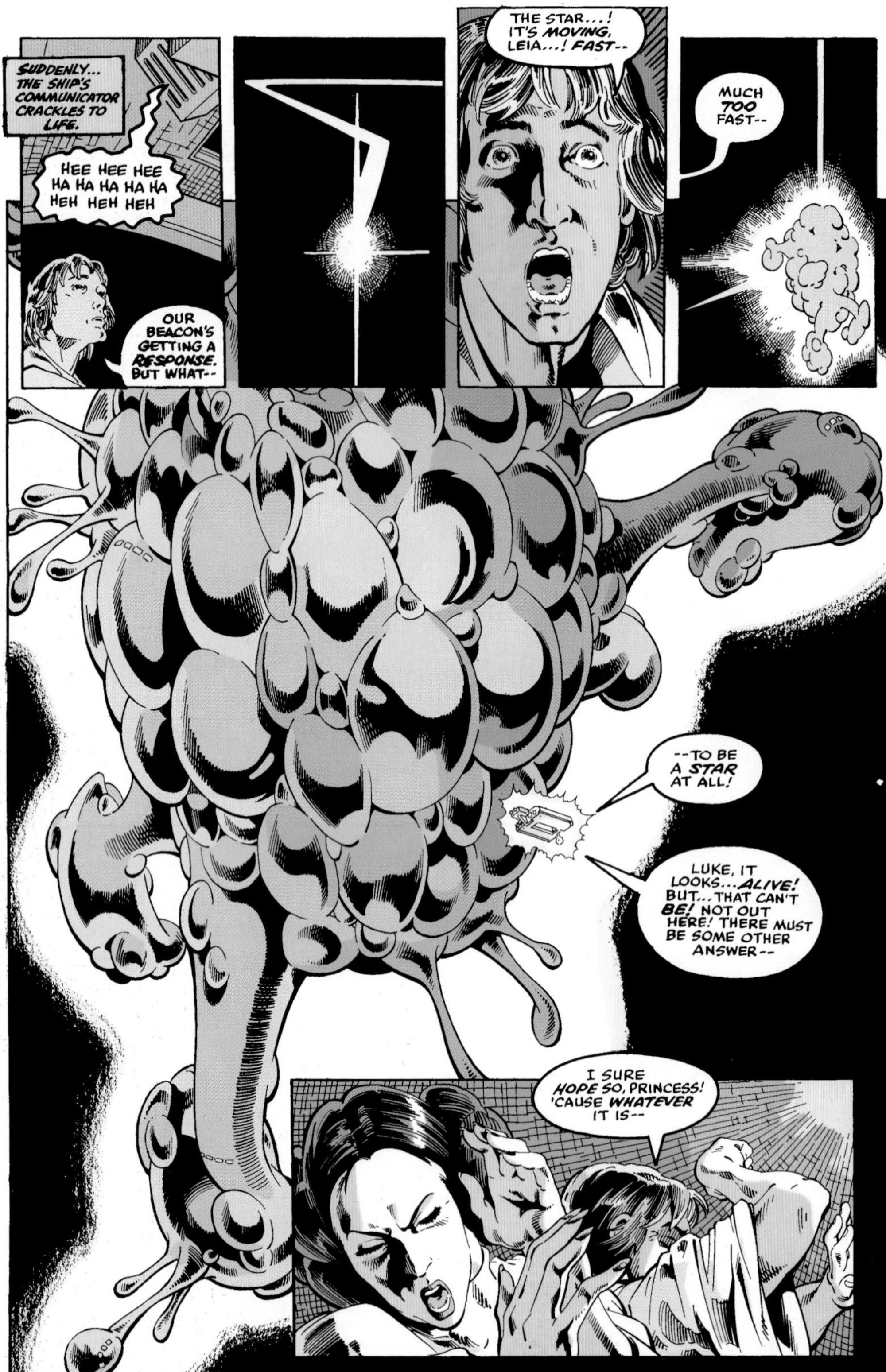
SUDDENLY... THE SHIP'S COMMUNICATOR CRACKLES TO LIFE.
HEE HEE HEE HA HA HA HA HA HEH HEH HEH
OUR BEACON'S GETTING A RESPONSE. BUT WHAT--
THE STAR...! IT'S MOVING, LEIA...! FAST--
MUCH TOO FAST--
--TO BE A STAR AT ALL!
LUKE, IT LOOKS...ALIVE! BUT... THAT CAN'T BE! NOT OUT HERE! THERE MUST BE SOME OTHER ANSWER--
I SURE HOPE SO, PRINCESS! 'CAUSE WHATEVER IT IS--

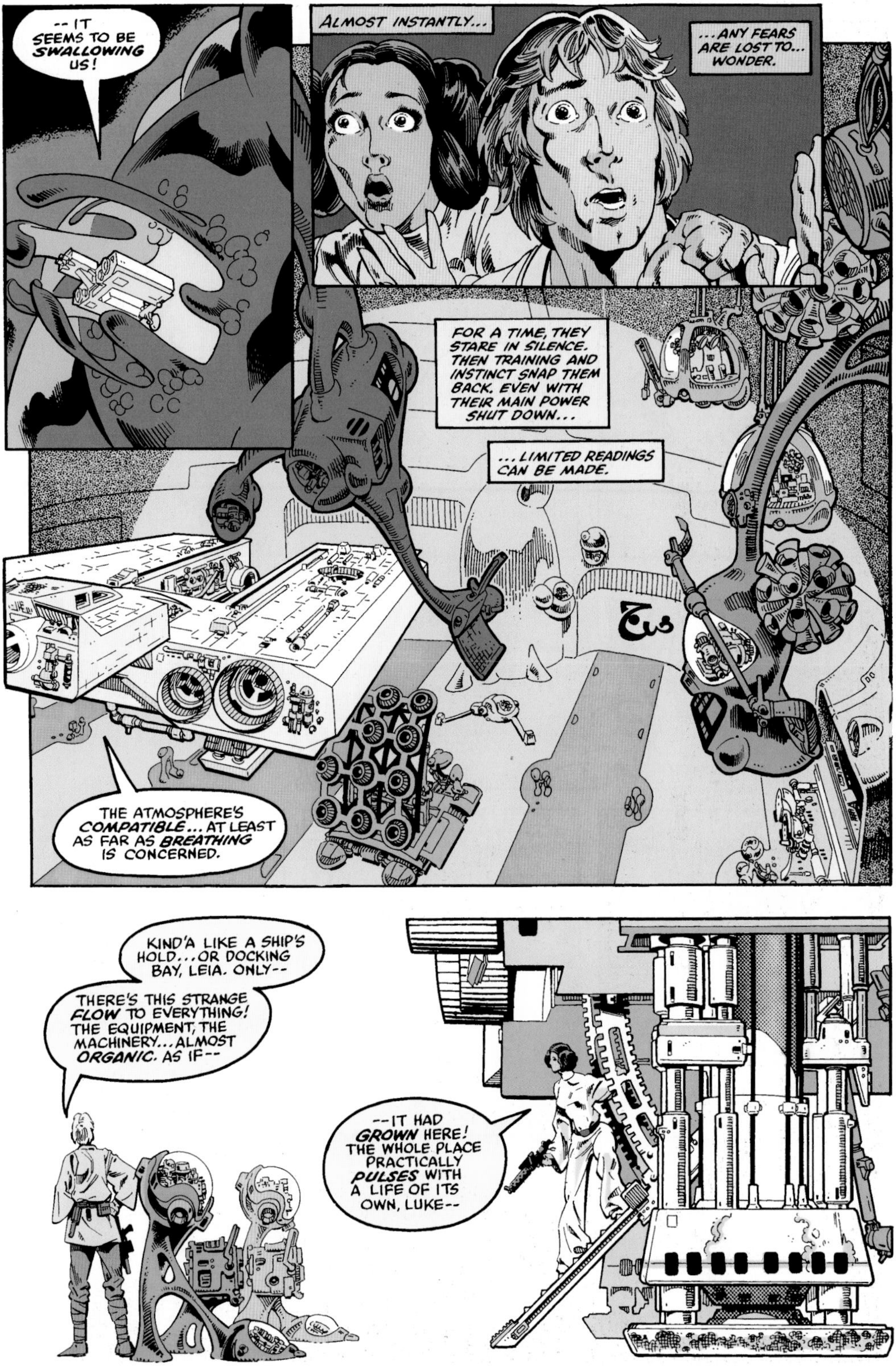

--IT SEEMS TO BE SWALLOWING US!
ALMOST INSTANTLY...
...ANY FEARS ARE LOST TO... WONDER.
FOR A TIME, THEY STARE IN SILENCE. THEN TRAINING AND INSTINCT SNAP THEM BACK. EVEN WITH THEIR MAIN POWER SHUT DOWN...
...LIMITED READINGS CAN BE MADE.
THE ATMOSPHERE'S COMPATIBLE... AT LEAST AS FAR AS BREATHING IS CONCERNED.
KIND'A LIKE A SHIP'S HOLD...OR DOCKING BAY, LEIA. ONLY--
THERE'S THIS STRANGE FLOW TO EVERYTHING! THE EQUIPMENT, THE MACHINERY... ALMOST ORGANIC. AS IF--
--IT HAD GROWN HERE! THE WHOLE PLACE PRACTICALLY PULSES WITH A LIFE OF ITS OWN, LUKE--

--AND THOUGH IT MAY SOUND JUST A TOUCH PROVINCIAL FOR A FORMER SENATOR AND A SEASONED INTERGALACTIC TRAVELER--

--I DON'T *LIKE* IT.

IN FACT, I GET A VERY UNCOMFORTABLE FEELING OF BEING WATCHED... OR STUDIED.

WELL, *SOMETHING* DEFINITELY BROUGHT US HERE. BUT IF ITS PURPOSE WAS TO *HARM* US--

--IT SURELY WOULD'VE DONE IT BEFORE NOW.

HAHAHAHAHAHAHAHAHA

THE LAUGHTER SEEMS TO FLOW ALL AROUND THEM...

AND THEN...

...THE MADNESS BEGINS.

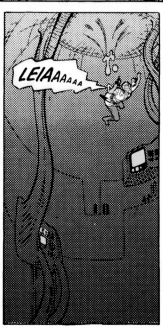

*LEIA*AAAAAA

LUKE! WHERE *ARE* YOU? *LUKE?!*

ALL RIGHT, LEIA ORGANA... *CALMLY* DOES IT.

IF OUR LAUGHING HOST THINKS YOU'RE MORE *VULNERABLE* SEPARATED FROM LUKE, HE, SHE, OR IT BETTER--

HEEHEEHEEHEEHEEHEEHEE

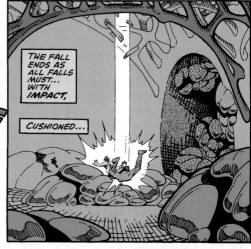

THE FALL ENDS AS ALL FALLS MUST... WITH IMPACT,

CUSHIONED...

...BUT ALL THE SAME, STUNNING.

STILL, HE IS YOUNG, HIS BODY IS STRONG...

...AND HIS SENSES ARE HONED BY THE WAYS OF THE FORCE.

W- WHO...?

SHRAAAKK!

227

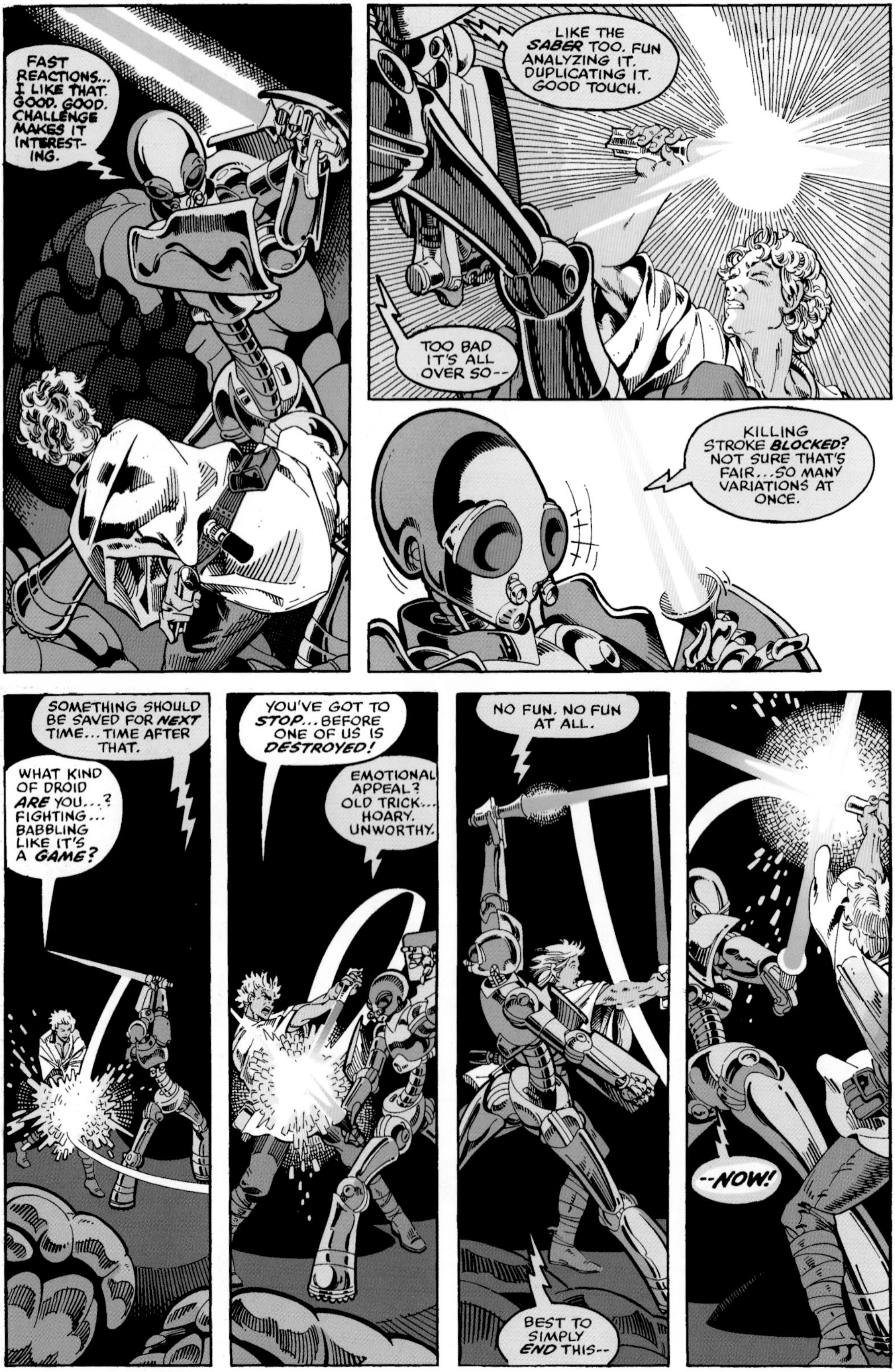
FAST REACTIONS... I LIKE THAT. GOOD. GOOD. CHALLENGE MAKES IT INTEREST-ING.
LIKE THE SABER TOO. FUN ANALYZING IT. DUPLICATING IT. GOOD TOUCH.
TOO BAD IT'S ALL OVER SO--
KILLING STROKE BLOCKED? NOT SURE THAT'S FAIR...SO MANY VARIATIONS AT ONCE.
SOMETHING SHOULD BE SAVED FOR NEXT TIME...TIME AFTER THAT.
WHAT KIND OF DROID ARE YOU...? FIGHTING... BABBLING LIKE IT'S A GAME?
YOU'VE GOT TO STOP... BEFORE ONE OF US IS DESTROYED!
EMOTIONAL APPEAL? OLD TRICK... HOARY. UNWORTHY.
NO FUN. NO FUN AT ALL.
BEST TO SIMPLY END THIS--
--NOW!

I—IT *NEARLY* DID! SEEMS TO ANALYZE AND ADJUST CONSTANTLY TO MY MOVES—— ——AND THE LONGER WE BATTLE, THE *BETTER* IT GETS!

I WON'T BE *ALIVE* TO HELP LEIA... IF I DON'T DO SOMETHING *FAST!*

A *MISSED* STROKE! YOU WOULDN'T LEAVE YOURSELF *OPEN* LIKE THAT UNLESS——

HESITATION, SUSPICION OF DECEIT. NO LONGER THAN A HEARTBEAT...

...BUT LONG ENOUGH FOR LUKE TO WHIRL... AND *WIN!*

THE DROID DIES...

...BUT THE VOICE WHICH SPOKE *THROUGH* IT STILL SCREAMS ON.

IMPOSSIBLE! *IMPOSSIBLE!* IT'S NOT IN THE *PROGRAMMING* FOR YOU TO WIN. ONLY IF——

YOU'RE *REAL!* YOU *EXIST!* *ENEMIES! ENEMIES!* ENEMIES IN THE *SHIP!*

THE SHRIEKING SOUNDS THROUGHOUT THE MECHO-ORGANIC VESSEL, RISING IN VOLUME, IN SHEER HYSTERIA.

THE SHIP IS MINE... THE SHIP IS ME!

NO ONE *ELSE* BELONGS! NO ONE! *NO* ONE!

A *BREACH* OPENS TO THE VACUUM OF SPACE...

...SUCKING OUT *ATMOSPHERE* WITH HURRICANE FURY. AND CAUGHT WITHIN THE HOWLING GALE...

...*LUKE* IS PULLED TOWARD THE AIRLESS VOID SOMEWHERE BEYOND!

HE IS NOT *ALONE*.

OUT... *OUT!* I AM THE SHIP... THE SHIP MUST *SURVIVE!*

W-WIND IS... *IMPOSSIBLE* TO FIGHT...!

OH, LUKE... *LUKE!* WHERE *ARE* YOU.

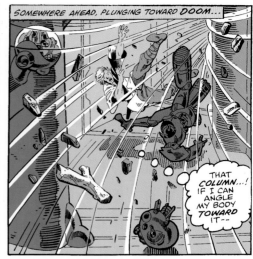

SOMEWHERE AHEAD, PLUNGING TOWARD *DOOM*...

THAT *COLUMN*...! IF I CAN ANGLE MY BODY *TOWARD* IT --

~AAAAGH!~

IT'S PAINFUL, BUT... IT *SUCCEEDS*.

AIR CURRENTS WILL *HOLD* ME HERE AS LONG AS I DON'T MOVE TOO --

NO!

BEHIND ME --

-- IT'S *LEIA!*

THIS WAY, PRINCESS... TWIST THIS WAY!

THEN I CAN GRAB --

-- YOUR *HAND!*

LUKE! LET *GO!* YOU'LL BE PULLED ALONG *WITH* ME!

I WON'T LET YOU *DIE*... I *WON'T!*

PLEASE, LUKE...! SAVE YOURSELF! PLEASE!

NO!

I LOVE YOU, LEIA--

I CAN'T LOSE YOU! I--

YOU'RE SLIPPING!

LUKE...! I-IT'S... NO... USE...!

TRUE.

EXCEPT...

...OTHER FORCES ARE INVOLVED.

FORCES STRANGE...AND SEEMINGLY WHIMSICAL.

I DON'T BELIEVE IT...! ONE MOMENT WE'RE ON THE VERGE OF DEATH--

--THE NEXT, EVERYTHING STOPS! AS IF IT NEVER HAPPENED!

INSANITY...!

'LEAST IT'S WORKING IN OUR FAVOR NOW. BUT I CAN'T FIGURE WHY--

YOU...CARE FOR EACH OTHER. I HAD FORGOTTEN ABOUT SUCH... CARING. I'VE FORGOTTEN MANY THINGS--

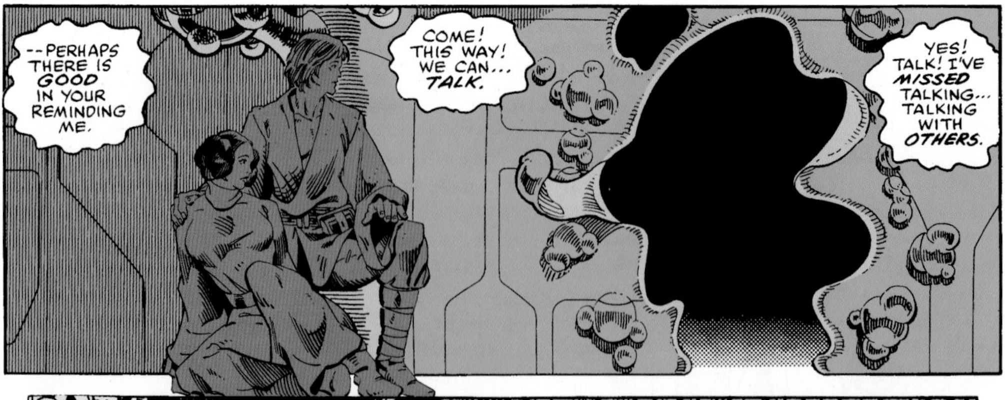
--PERHAPS THERE IS GOOD IN YOUR REMINDING ME.
COME! THIS WAY! WE CAN... TALK.
YES! TALK! I'VE MISSED TALKING... TALKING WITH OTHERS.

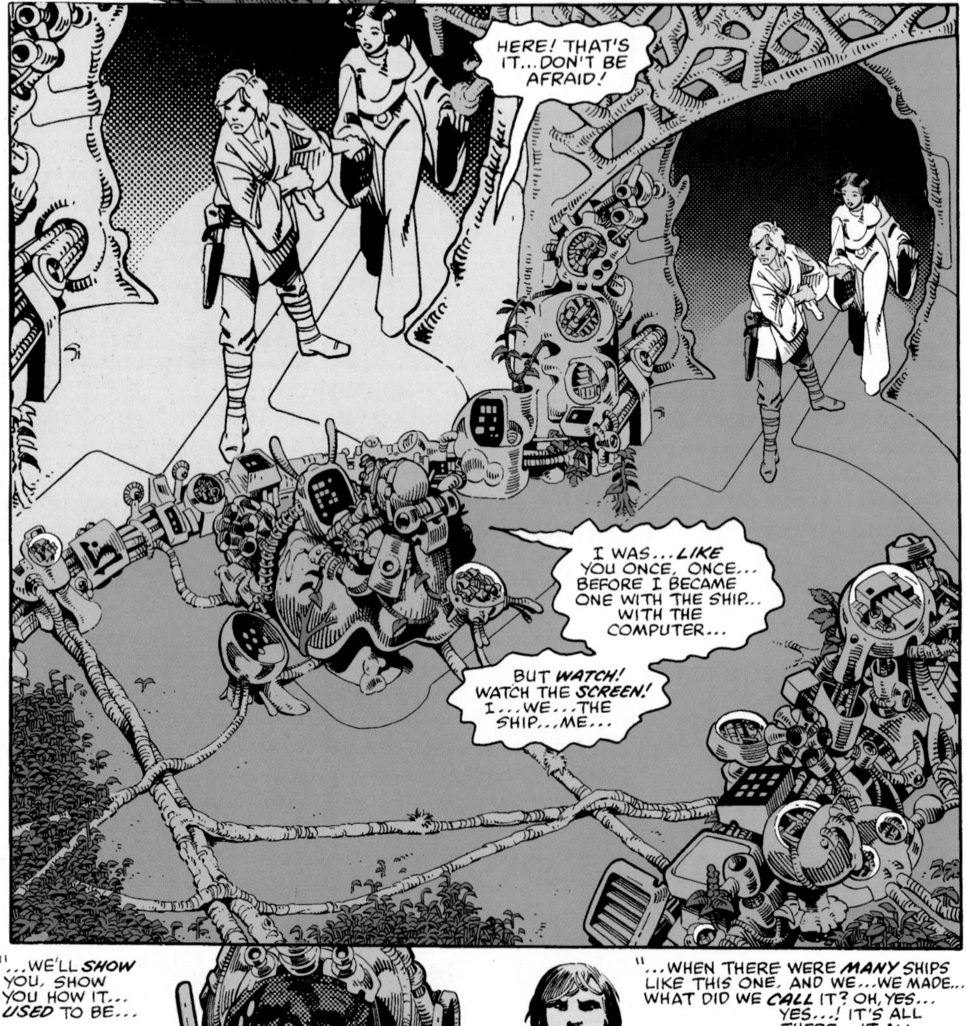
HERE! THAT'S IT... DON'T BE AFRAID!
I WAS... LIKE YOU ONCE, ONCE... BEFORE I BECAME ONE WITH THE SHIP... WITH THE COMPUTER...
BUT WATCH! WATCH THE SCREEN! I... WE... THE SHIP... ME...

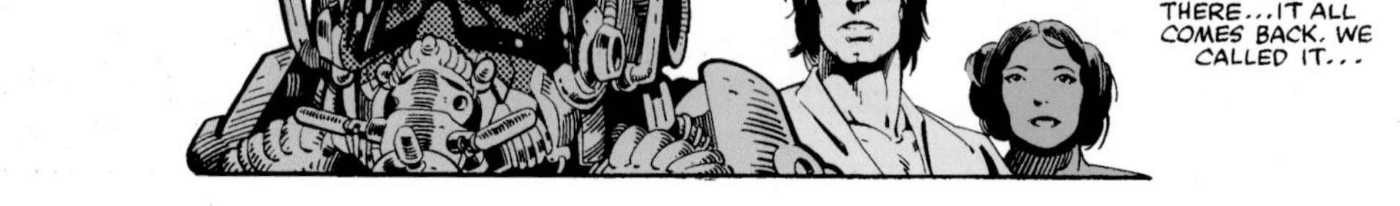
"...WE'LL SHOW YOU, SHOW YOU HOW IT... USED TO BE...
"...WHEN THERE WERE MANY SHIPS LIKE THIS ONE, AND WE... WE MADE... WHAT DID WE CALL IT? OH, YES... YES...! IT'S ALL THERE... IT ALL COMES BACK. WE CALLED IT...

"...WAR.

"BUT ONE BY ONE, THE SHIPS *DESTROYED* EACH OTHER...

"UNTIL, AFTER ONE LAST BATTLE... ONLY *MY* SHIP SURVIVED. THE WAR WAS *OVER.*

"MY CREW AND I CAME HOME *VICTORS,* ONLY TO FIND...

"...AS A FINAL GESTURE, OUR ENEMY HAD RELEASED A *PLAGUE BOMB.*

"THERE WAS NO ONE LEFT. FAMILIES, FRIENDS, EVERY LAST SOUL...DEAD, AND THE PLAGUE WAS STILL *ACTIVE.* IT CONTAINED CORROSIVE AGENTS WHICH COULD PENETRATE SPACE ARMOR. I MADE IT BACK TO THE SHIP IN TIME. NO ONE *ELSE* DID.

"I FLED, *SOMEONE* HAD TO SURVIVE, OTHERWISE...IT ALL MEANT NOTHING. THE PLAGUE COULD SPREAD FROM PLANET TO PLANET THROUGH-OUT MY GALAXY. I HAD TO GO *BEYOND,...* OUTSIDE, THE SHIP AND I...RIDING... RIDING THROUGH THE VOID...."

WE *FUSED* IN TIME... THE COMPUTER, THE SHIP, AND I. MY CONSCIOUSNESS SYMBIOTICALLY LINKED TO ITS ORGANIC, SELF-PERPETUATING CONTROL SYSTEMS.

ALL OF US RIDING... ENDLESSLY RIDING... AWAY FROM PLAGUES. TIME *IS* NOTHING AND WE HAVE OUR *GAMES,* OUR--

LUKE... ON THE SCREEN! THAT'S--

-- OUR *GALAXY!* WHILE HE'S BEEN TALKING, WE'VE BEEN TRAVELING *BACK!*

PERHAPS. PERHAPS. OR PERHAPS IT'S AN *AMUSEMENT* THE COMPUTER IS CREATING.

WHAT...?!

OUR *GAMES!* THAT'S WHAT I THOUGHT YOU TWO WERE. THAT'S WHAT *THIS* MAY BE.

NO! IT'S STILL *THERE* AS WE DROP OUT OF HYPERDRIVE. IT'S REAL... IT'S OUR *HOME!*

233

AND HOME, UNFORTUNATELY, IS WHERE THE GALACTIC EMPIRE AND ITS AGENTS WAIT.

THAT'S *IT*, CAPTAIN! THE HUGE MASS THAT'S HAD OUR SCANNERS GOING WILD.

APPEARING IN NEARLY THE SAME SPOT WHERE WE LOST THOSE *REBELS* EARLIER...!

IT CAN'T BE *COINCIDENCE!* THIS IS SOME MONSTROUS *TRICK* OF THE REBEL ALLIANCE!

W-WE'RE GETTING CONFUSED *LIFE READINGS*, SIR, AND ON THE *COMMUNICATOR--*

--THERE'S *LAUGHTER.* INSANE LAUGHTER!

LEIA! THAT'S THE IMPERIAL CRUISER THAT WAS *PURSUING* US BEFORE!

SHIP...! YOU'RE IN *DANGER!* GET *OUT* OF HERE OR ELSE--

TOO LATE.

THE STAR DESTROYER CAPTAIN DEALS WITH THE *UNKNOWN* IN THE SAME WAY IN WHICH THE EMPIRE HANDLES *MOST PROBLEMS* ...

...*VIOLENTLY!*

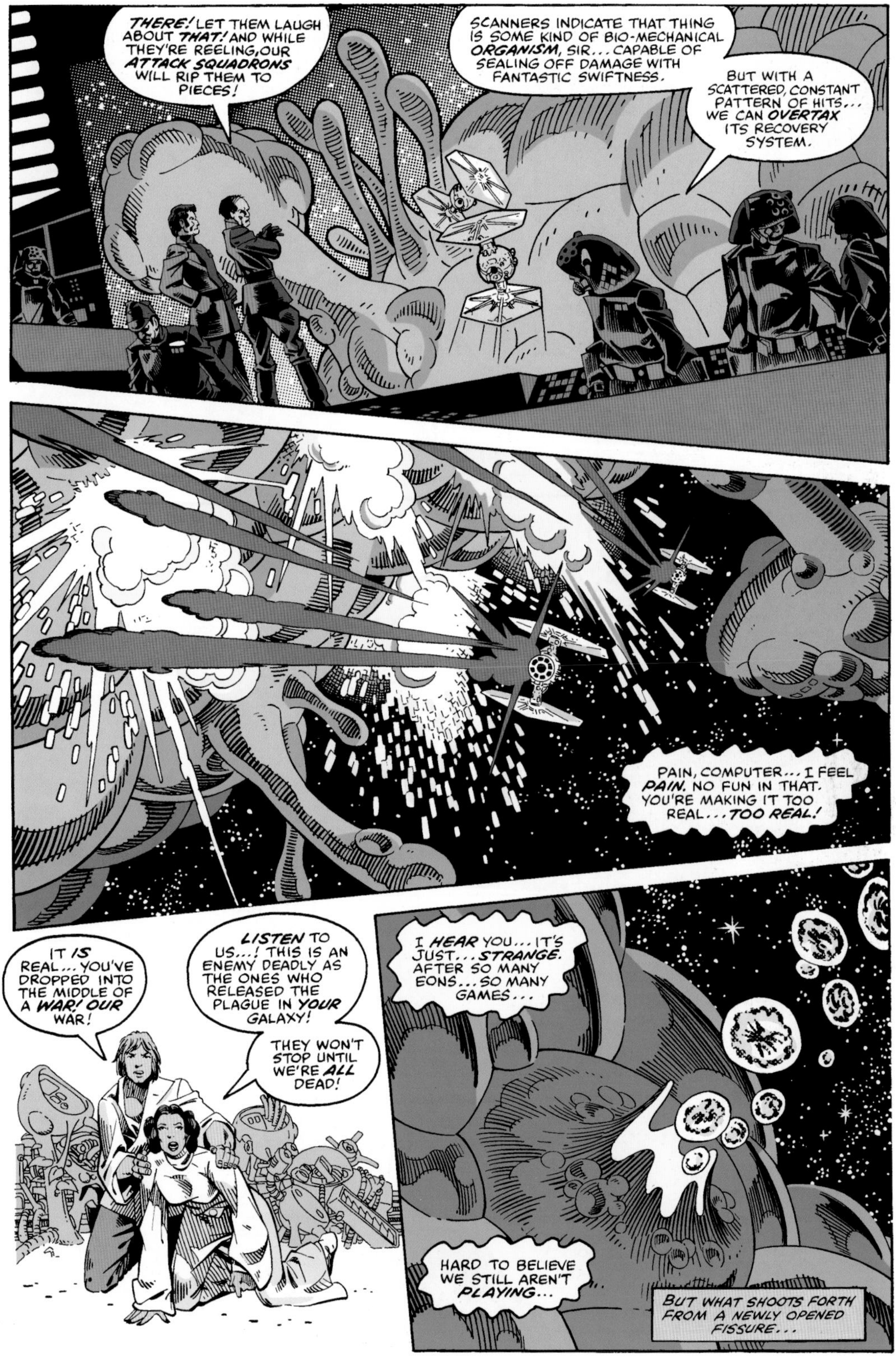
THERE! LET THEM LAUGH ABOUT THAT! AND WHILE THEY'RE REELING, OUR ATTACK SQUADRONS WILL RIP THEM TO PIECES!
SCANNERS INDICATE THAT THING IS SOME KIND OF BIO-MECHANICAL ORGANISM, SIR... CAPABLE OF SEALING OFF DAMAGE WITH FANTASTIC SWIFTNESS.
BUT WITH A SCATTERED, CONSTANT PATTERN OF HITS... WE CAN OVERTAX ITS RECOVERY SYSTEM.
PAIN, COMPUTER... I FEEL PAIN. NO FUN IN THAT. YOU'RE MAKING IT TOO REAL... TOO REAL!
IT IS REAL... YOU'VE DROPPED INTO THE MIDDLE OF A WAR! OUR WAR!
LISTEN TO US...! THIS IS AN ENEMY DEADLY AS THE ONES WHO RELEASED THE PLAGUE IN YOUR GALAXY!
THEY WON'T STOP UNTIL WE'RE ALL DEAD!
I HEAR YOU... IT'S JUST... STRANGE. AFTER SO MANY EONS... SO MANY GAMES...
HARD TO BELIEVE WE STILL AREN'T PLAYING...
BUT WHAT SHOOTS FORTH FROM A NEWLY OPENED FISSURE...

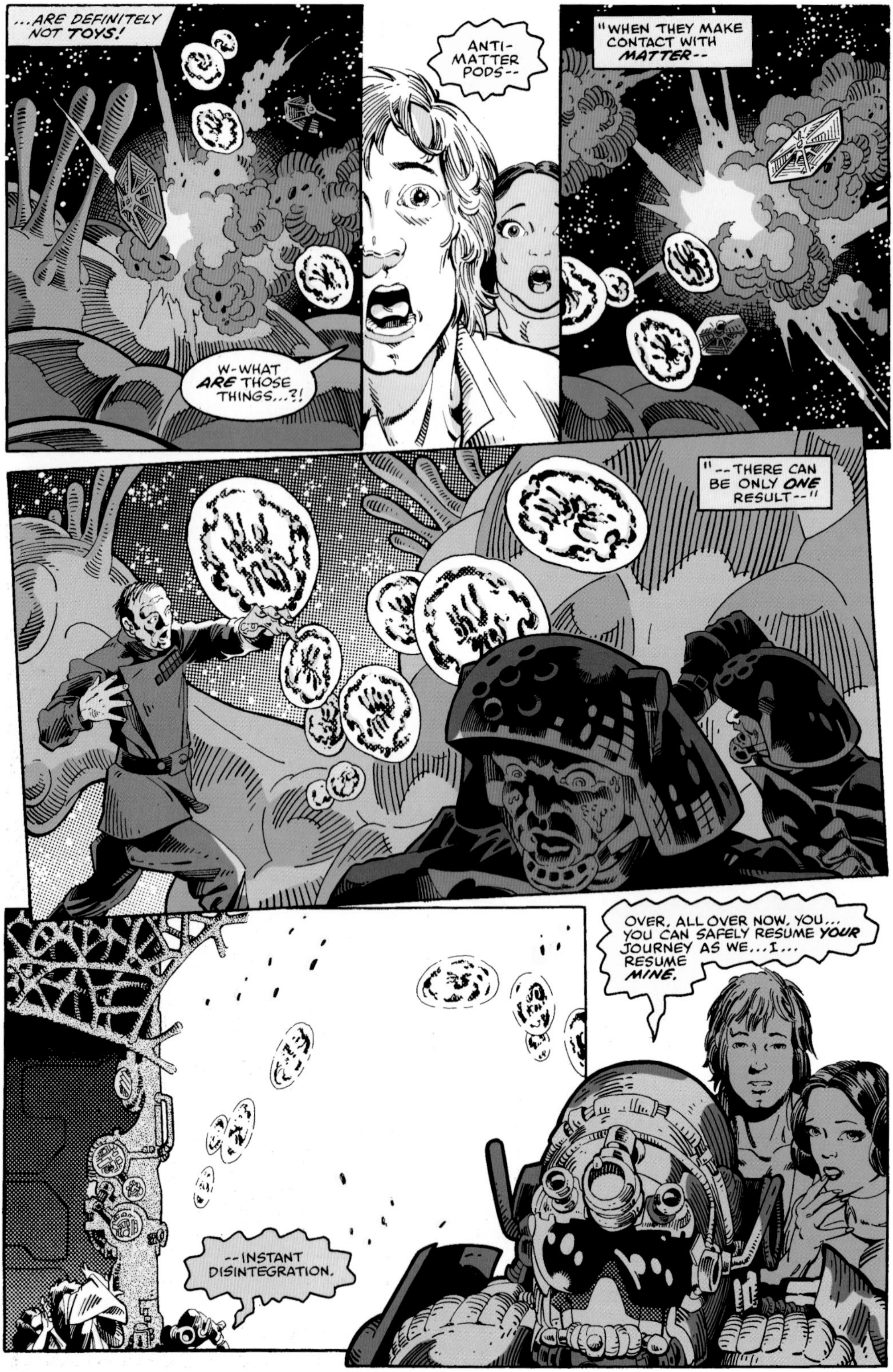
...ARE DEFINITELY NOT TOYS!
W-WHAT ARE THOSE THINGS...?!
ANTI-MATTER PODS--
"WHEN THEY MAKE CONTACT WITH MATTER--
"--THERE CAN BE ONLY ONE RESULT--"
--INSTANT DISINTEGRATION.
OVER. ALL OVER NOW. YOU... YOU CAN SAFELY RESUME YOUR JOURNEY AS WE... I... RESUME MINE.

YOUR SHIP HAS BEEN *REPAIRED*... YOU SHOULD HAVE NO FURTHER TROUBLE.

BUT WHAT ABOUT *YOU*...?

THIS IS A BIG GALAXY, WHY NOT STAY *HERE*?

YOUR GALAXY IS TOO *REAL*, MY FRIENDS, IT REMINDS ME OF *ANOTHER*--

--WHICH I TRAVELED LIGHT YEARS TO *ESCAPE*. I WISH YOU WELL,... BUT I SEE NOW I *BELONG* TO THE VOID.

RIDING,... ME, THE SHIP, THE COMPUTER, OUR GAMES.

MAY YOU IN TIME WIN *HAPPINESS* HERE! MINE,... OURS... IS *OUT THERE*.

AND LAUGHTER RISES FROM THE COMMUNICATOR. PERHAPS MAD. PERHAPS NOT.

IT IS DIFFICULT TO TELL...

...FOR VERY SHORTLY, IT IS GONE.

NEXT: THE EMPIRE STRIKES BACK!

50¢
39
SEPT
02817
APPROVED BY THE COMICS CODE AUTHORITY
STAR WARS
BEGINNING! THE OFFICIAL COMICS ADAPTATION OF THE MOST EAGERLY-AWAITED SPACE FANTASY OF ALL!
THE EMPIRE STRIKES BACK

Long ago in a galaxy far, far away. . .there exists a state of cosmic *civil war*. A brave alliance of *underground freedom fighters* has challenged the tyranny and oppression of the awesome *Galactic Empire*. This is their story!

LucasFilm PRESENTS: STAR WARS ™ **THE GREATEST SPACE FANTASY OF ALL!**

ARCHIE GOODWIN ★ AL WILLIAMSON & CARLOS GARZON ★ JIM NOVAK ★ GLYNIS WEIN ★ JO DUFFY ★ JAMES SHOOTER

WRITER/EDITOR — ARTISTS — LETTERER — COLORIST — ASST. EDITOR — EDITOR-IN-CHIEF

STAR WARS THE EMPIRE STRIKES BACK ™

BEGINNING! THE OFFICIAL COMICS ADAPTATION BASED ON THE SCRIPT BY *LEIGH BRACKETT* AND *LAWRENCE KASDAN* FROM THE STORY BY *GEORGE LUCAS!*

A TWENTIETH CENTURY-FOX RELEASE.

TM: ©LUCASFILM LTD. 1980 (LFL)

After the destruction of its most feared battle station the Empire has declared martial law throughout the galaxy.

A thousand worlds have felt the oppressive hand of the Emperor as he attempts to crush the growing Rebellion.

As the Imperial grip of tyranny tightens, Princess Leia and the small band of freedom fighters search for a more secure base of operations...

HOTH! A WORLD OF FROZEN LANDSCAPES AND SUB-ZERO TEMPERATURES. ON PATROL, LUKE SKYWALKER PAUSES, SCANNING THE SKY WITH HIS MACROBINOCULARS...

EASY, GIRL! IT'S JUST ANOTHER *METEORITE!*

THEY FALL ON THIS PLACE ABOUT AS REGULARLY AS THE SNOW.

CALMING HIS NERVOUS TAUNTAUN, THE YOUNG REBEL ACTIVATES HIS COMLINK TRANSMITTER...

YOU READ ME, HAN...? I'M ABOUT TO PACK IT IN... AFTER I CHECK OUT A METEORITE THAT JUST HIT. HAVEN'T PICKED UP ANY LIFE READINGS.

KID, THERE ISN'T ENOUGH LIFE ON THIS ICE CUBE TO FILL THE *MILLENNIUM FALCON'S* HOLD! MY SENTRY MARKERS ARE PLACED... I'LL SEE YOU AT THE BASE!

NO SOONER DOES LUKE SIGN OFF... THAN HIS MOUNT SKITTERS WORSE THAN EVER.

WHAT'S GOTTEN INTO YOU? THERE'S *NOTHING* OUT HERE EXCEPT YOU AND M--

SON OF A JUMPIN'--

AND BEFORE HE CAN DRAW HIS BLASTER, SOMETHING HUGE AND HEAVY SLAMS INTO HIS FACE...

...AND A MONSTROUS *HOWLING* FILLS THE AIR!

SOMEWHERE ACROSS THE HORIZON, A *CRATER* SMOULDERS AND STEAMS...

IT IS A CRATER THAT LUKE SKYWALKER WILL NOW NEVER INVESTIGATE...

...AND IT WAS *NOT* MADE BY ONE OF THE METEORITES WHICH FREQUENTLY BOMBARD THE PLANET'S SURFACE.

ELSEWHERE, WITHIN CAVERNS OF LASER-BLASTED ICE... *ACTIVITY* REIGNS. A STRONGHOLD IS UNDER CONSTRUCTION. ONLY A FEW PAUSE IN THEIR WORK AS A LONE RIDER RETURNS...

WE THOUGHT CORELLIANS WERE TOUGH, SOLO... YOU ACTUALLY LOOK *COLD.*

COLD ISN'T THE *WORD* FOR IT! I'LL TAKE A GOOD FIGHT ANY DAY OVER ALL THIS HIDIN' AND FREEZIN'!

HAN STRIDES PAST SNOWSPEEDERS AND X-WING FIGHTERS TO THE REAR OF THE GREAT HANGAR... WHERE A BATTERED *FREIGHTER* STANDS.

HEY, *CHEWIE!* HOW'S IT COMING WITH THE *FALCON'S* LIFTERS? SOONER THEY'RE FIXED... THE SOONER WE'RE *OUT* OF HERE.

RAARRGHHH!

ALL RIGHT, ALL RIGHT! I'LL GO REPORT... THEN GIVE YOU A HAND!

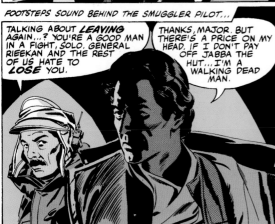

FOOTSTEPS SOUND BEHIND THE SMUGGLER PILOT...

TALKING ABOUT *LEAVING* AGAIN...? YOU'RE A GOOD MAN IN A FIGHT, SOLO. GENERAL RIEEKAN AND THE REST OF US HATE TO *LOSE* YOU.

THANKS, MAJOR. BUT THERE'S A PRICE ON MY HEAD. IF I DON'T PAY OFF JABBA THE HUT... I'M A WALKING DEAD MAN.

YES, WE HEARD ABOUT THAT *BOUNTY HUNTER* ON ORD MANTELL. A DEATH MARK IS NOT AN EASY THING TO LIVE WITH...

GOOD LUCK, SOLO.

I GUESS THIS IS *IT*, YOUR HIGHNESS.

I SUPPOSE IT IS.

WELL, DON'T GO ALL *MUSHY* ON ME.

SO LONG, PRINCESS.

HAN... *WAIT!* DOES... DOES *LUKE* KNOW?

HE WILL WHEN HE GETS BACK. AND DON'T GIVE ME ANY LOOKS. EVERY DAY, JABBA SENDS OUT MORE REMOTES, GANK KILLERS, AND WHO KNOWS WHAT ELSE.

I'VE GOT TO GET THIS PRICE OFF MY HEAD WHILE I STILL *HAVE* ONE.

BUT... YOU'RE A NATURAL LEADER. WE STILL NEED YOU.

NO, YOUR WORSHIP, THAT'S NOT WHY YOU CAME AFTER ME. I THINK YOU WERE AFRAID I WAS LEAVING YOU WITHOUT EVEN A KISS.

WHAT? I'D JUST AS SOON KISS A *WOOKIEE!*

THERE'S NO ACCOUNTING FOR TASTE. BELIEVE ME, YOU COULD *USE* A GOOD KISS. YOU'VE BEEN SO BUSY GIVING ORDERS, YOU'VE FORGOTTEN HOW TO BE A *WOMAN.*

BUT NOW IT'S TOO LATE, SWEETHEART, YOUR BIG *OPPORTUNITY* IS FLYING OUT OF HERE.

SOMEHOW, I'LL SURVIVE. PARTICULARLY SINCE IT'S NOW OBVIOUS THAT YOU DON'T EVEN *CARE* ABOUT THE--

SPARE ME ANOTHER LECTURE ABOUT THE *REBELLION.* IT'S ALL YOU EVER THINK ABOUT. YOU'RE AS COLD AS THIS PLANET.

AND YOU THINK *YOU'RE* THE ONE TO APPLY SOME HEAT?

SURE, IF I WERE INTERESTED, BUT I DON'T THINK IT'D BE MUCH *FUN.*

WE'LL MEET AGAIN. MAYBE BY THEN YOU'LL HAVE WARMED UP A LITTLE.

YOU HAVE ALL THE BREEDING OF A *BANTHA*... BUT NOT AS MUCH CLASS! ENJOY YOUR *TRIP,* HOTSHOT!

LEIA ORGANA STORMS AWAY IN THE OPPOSITE DIRECTION, NEVER HEARING THE CRUMBLING OF AN ICY WALL BEHIND HER...

...OR GLIMPSING WHAT *CAUSES* IT.

CONSCIOUSNESS RETURNS TO LUKE SKYWALKER. BLOOD POUNDS THICKLY IN HIS HEAD. SOLID ICE BINDS HIS ANKLES. SOMETHING SHIMMERS IN HIS PAIN-WRACKED VISION, AGONIZINGLY OUT OF REACH...

L-LIGHTSABER.... IF I COULD JUST *REACH* IT.... I COULD... COULD...

CAN'T....! ONLY ABOUT A METER... MIGHT AS WELL BE... A LIGHT YEAR!

A GROWLING MOAN ECHOES OFF THE FROZEN WALLS THAT SURROUND HIM. *SOMETHING* IS MOVING CLOSER. HE MOMENTARILY PANICS... STRUGGLING FUTILELY. UNTIL... HE HEARS A QUIET, CALM VOICE.

LUKE, YOU MUST RELAX... *THINK* THE SABER INTO YOUR HAND.

LET THE *FORCE* FLOW, LUKE.

GOTTA RELAX... RELAX...

THE GROWL ECHOES AGAIN... NEARER. *TOO NEAR.* BUT THAT IS NOT IN LUKE'S MIND NOW... ONLY THE *SABER.* THE SABER *MOVING.* AND SUDDENLY...

...IT *IS.*

AND AS A MENACING SHADOW LOOMS... THE WARRIOR FROM *TATOOINE* BRINGS HIS FATHER'S LIGHTBLADE SIZZLING INTO THE ICE THAT GRIPS HIM!

LUKE **FALLS**, CRASHING HEAVILY INTO THE SNOW... AS SOMETHING **HUGE** RUSHES TOWARD HIM!

HE **ROLLS**, SLASHING OUT WITH HIS LIGHTBLADE...

...AND A **SCREAM** OF **PAIN** FILLS THE ICY GORGE.

IT STILL ECHOES IN HIS MIND AS HE SOMEHOW STAGGERS TO SAFETY...

...LIMPING INTO THE GATHERING GRAYNESS THAT HERALDS THE APPROACH OF SUB-ZERO **NIGHT** ON HOTH.

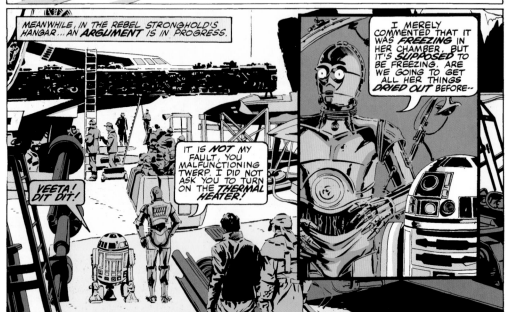

MEANWHILE, IN THE REBEL STRONGHOLD'S HANGAR... AN **ARGUMENT** IS IN PROGRESS.

IT IS **NOT** MY FAULT, YOU MALFUNCTIONING TWERP. I DID NOT ASK YOU TO TURN ON THE **THERMAL HEATER!**

VEETA! DIT DIT!

I MERELY COMMENTED THAT IT WAS **FREEZING** IN HER CHAMBER, BUT IT'S **SUPPOSED** TO BE FREEZING. ARE WE GOING TO GET ALL HER THINGS **DRIED OUT** BEFORE--

AH, HERE WE ARE.

CAPTAIN SOLO, SIR? THE PRINCESS HAS BEEN TRYING TO REACH YOU ON THE COMMUNICATOR. IT MUST BE MALFUNCTIONING.

I SHUT IT OFF. WHAT'S TROUBLING HER ROYAL HOLINESS NOW?

SHE HOPED MASTER LUKE MIGHT BE WITH YOU. IT'S ALMOST NIGHT OUTSIDE AND IF HE'S NOT *BACK* YET...

HAN KNOWS *EXACTLY* WHAT THAT MEANS. AND AN URGENT CHECK WITH THE WATCH OFFICER...

...CONFIRMS THE *WORST.*

UNLESS WE FIND HIM FAST... LUKE IS *DEAD.* ARE THE SPEEDERS READY?

MAYBE BY MORNING... ADAPTING THEM TO THE COLD IS PROVING DIFFICULT, AND WE'VE HAD *OTHER* PROBLEMS... SOMETHING *ATTACKED* ONE OF THE TAUNTAUNS.

RIGHT NOW I'M ONLY CONCERNED ABOUT THE KID. WE'LL HAVE TO SEND *RIDERS* OUT. I'LL TAKE SECTOR FOUR.

SOLO, THE TEMPERATURE IS FALLING TOO RAPIDLY. THE *NIGHT STORMS* WILL START BEFORE ANY OF YOU REACH THE FIRST MARKER.

THEN I'LL SEE YOU IN HELL.

247

IN THE FADING TWILIGHT ON HOTH'S FROZEN PLAINS... A FIGURE STAGGERS, TRYING TO STAY UPRIGHT AGAINST BLASTS OF CUTTING WIND AND SNOW, TRYING TO KEEP MOVING ON LEGS LONG NUMBED...

TRYING... AND *FAILING.*

C-CAN'T... KEEP GOING... *CAN'T*...

YOU *MUST*, YOUNG LUKE! THIS WAY... LOOK AT ME. YOU MUST SURVIVE...

B-BEN...? I'M SO COLD, BEN... SO COLD...

YOU MUST GO TO THE *DAGOBAH SYSTEM.* YOU WILL LEARN FROM *YODA*, THE JEDI MASTER... THE ONE WHO TAUGHT ME.

YOU MUST, LUKE... YOU'RE OUR ONLY HOPE.

B-BENNNNNNNN...!

THE VISION IS GONE, AND WITH IT, THE LAST OF LUKE SKYWALKER'S RESISTANCE...

... EVEN AS A RIDER ON A WEARY, EXHAUSTION-SPENT TAUNTAUN APPEARS ON THE HORIZON.

KID...?!

LEAPING FROM HIS MOUNT, HAN RUSHES TO THE UNMOVING FIGURE IN THE SNOW.

COME **ON**, BUDDY. GIVE ME A SIGN YOU'RE ALIVE. YOU WOULDN'T LEAVE ME OUT HERE ALL **ALONE**, WOULD YOU?

THE FAINTEST OF GROANS BRINGS A SMILE TO THE CORELLIAN'S FACE...

A SMILE THAT SWIFTLY **FADES** AS HE TURNS TO FIND...

COLD'S **FINISHED** MY TAUNTAUN! LET'S GO, KID... WE HAVEN'T GOT MUCH TIME.

BLASTED COMLINK IS **USELESS** IN THIS STORM!

IF I DON'T GET SOME **SHELTER** UP FAST... JABBA THE HUT WON'T NEED THOSE BOUNTY HUNTERS!

AND AS HAN STRUGGLES TO PULL EQUIPMENT FROM THE DEAD ANIMAL'S PACK, **NIGHT** IN ALL ITS FIERCENESS COMES TO HOTH...

... A FACT CHILLING AS THE STORM WINDS TO THOSE KEEPING VIGIL AT THE REBEL STRONGHOLD.

ARTOO, YOU MUST COME INSIDE... YOUR RANGE IS PROBABLY TOO **LIMITED** TO PICK UP ANY SIGNALS. THERE'S NOTHING MORE YOU CAN DO.

ARTOO, THEY **MUST** CLOSE THE SHIELD DOORS, WILL YOU HURRY...? MY **JOINTS** ARE FREEZING UP!

ALL PATROLS ARE NOW IN, YOUR HIGHNESS... EXCEPT SOLO AND SKYWALKER. I'M SORRY. THE SPEEDERS SHOULD BE READY AT DAWN. THEY'LL MAKE THE SEARCH EASIER.

IS THERE ANY CHANCE OF THEIR *SURVIVING* UNTIL MORNING, MAJOR DERLIN?

ARTOO HAS ALREADY COMPUTED IT, YOUR MAJESTY. HE SAYS THE CHANCES OF SURVIVAL ARE 725 TO 1.

ACTUALLY, ARTOO, I DON'T THINK WE NEEDED TO *KNOW* THAT.

MORNING! AN ALLIANCE SNOWSPEEDER STREAKS ACROSS THE BLEAK LANDSCAPE...

ECHO BASE... THIS IS ROGUE TWO. DO YOU *COPY?* OVER.

READ YOU CLEAR, ROGUE TWO. HAVE YOU *GOT* SOMETHING? OVER.

NOT MUCH, ECHO BASE. READINGS ARE FAINT... BUT IT COULD BE *LIFE FORMS.* I'M SWITCHING TO A MORE LOCALIZED BAND TO SEE IF I CAN PICK UP ANY--

NICE OF YOU GUYS TO DROP BY. HOPE WE DIDN'T GET YOU UP TOO EARLY.

ECHO BASE... THIS IS ROGUE TWO. I FOUND THEM. REPEAT. I *FOUND* THEM.

WITHIN THE HOUR, LUKE SKYWALKER IS IN THE BASE MEDICAL CENTER, DRIFTING IN DELIRIUM AS *TREATMENT* BEGINS...

WATCH OUT...! SNOW CREATURES... DANGEROUS....! YODA... GO TO YODA... ONLY HOPE...

MASTER LUKE SOUNDS SOMEWHAT GARBLED, I DO HOPE HE'S ALL THERE... IF YOU TAKE MY MEANING, IT WOULD BE MOST UNFORTUNATE IF HE HAD DEVELOPED A SHORT CIRCUIT.

THE KID RAN INTO SOMETHING *MEAN*... AND IT WASN'T THE COLD.

IS HE GOING TO BE *ALL RIGHT*, TOO-ONEBEE?

THE SURGEON DROID TURNS HIS PHOTORECEPTORS ON THE CONCERNED TRIO BEYOND THE VIEW-WALL.... COMMANDER SKYWALKER HAS BEEN IN DORMO-SHOCK... BUT IS RESPONDING WELL TO THE BACTA. HE IS PRESENTLY OUT OF DANGER.

HAN, IF YOU HADN'T *FOUND* HIM....! I DON'T KNOW HOW TO--

FORGET IT. WE'D BETTER LEARN WHAT *ATTACKED* HIM.... IF THIS SNOWBALL'S GOT NASTY NATIVES, THEY COULD BE *ANYWHERE.*

AN OBSERVATION ABOUT TO BE PROVEN ABSOLUTELY *VALID.* FOR AS A CERTAIN R2-D2 UNIT MOVES ALONG ONE OF THE STRONGHOLD'S CORRIDORS...

FREETA-DOOOOOP!

ARTOO'S ELECTRONIC SHRIEK BRINGS REBEL GUARDS RUNNING. SWIFTLY, SUDDENLY... WHAT WAS ONCE A CORRIDOR BECOMES A *BATTLEGROUND!*

SECURITY CONTROL... THIS IS SECTION J! ALERT ALL INTERIOR PATROLS. *ALERT ALL PATROLS!*

SHORTLY, AT THE BASE COMMAND CENTER...

...STUN BLASTS FINALLY *STOPPED* IT, YOUR HIGHNESS. EVOLVING IN HOTH'S EXTREME COLD HAS GIVEN IT SUB-NORMAL LIFE FUNCTIONS... WE'VE HAD TO ADJUST OUR *SENSORS* TO DETECT THEM.

ALL UNEXPLORED CAVE AREAS SHOULD BE IMMEDIATELY *SCANNED,* GENERAL RIEEKAN... THOUGH I'M NOT SURE I'M GOING TO BE HAPPY KNOWING HOW *MANY* THERE ARE!

OF COURSE, *ARTOO* WOULD BE IN THE *MIDDLE* OF THIS!

PRINCESS! GENERAL! LOOK AT THIS *SCOPE...* WE'VE GOT A *VISITOR!*

IT'S IN ZONE TWELVE, MOVING EAST... TOWARD ADVANCE STATION THREE-EIGHT.

AND IT'S *METAL...* DEFINITELY *NOT* ONE OF THOSE CREATURES. STATION THREE-EIGHT... THIS IS ECHO COMMAND COME *IN* STATION THREE-EIGHT!

THIS IS THREE-EIGHT, ECHO COMMAND! WE HAVE *VISUAL CONTACT!* IT LOOKS LIKE--

N-NO....!

AND THERE IS ONLY *SILENCE* FROM ADVANCE STATION THREE-EIGHT.

IMMEDIATELY... A SNOWSPEEDER PATROL MOVES OUT TO INVESTIGATE.

BUT AS THE LEAD CRAFT PEELS OFF TOWARD ITS ASSIGNED SECTOR...

...IT IS CAREFULLY *TRACKED!*

AND AS THE ISOLATED SPEEDER COMES TO A STOP BEHIND A DISTANT RIDGE, THE OMINOUS TRACKER STALKS FORWARD...

...CIRCUITRY BUZZING WITH AN AWARENESS THAT OUT OF THE HALTED VEHICLE.... *LIFE* WILL EMERGE.

WAAARK!

AND THAT LIFE WILL BE AN EASY, CERTAIN, *TARGET!*

THEN, JUST A FRACTION OF AN INSTANT TOO LATE, ITS SENSORS REGISTERS THAT THE TARGET...

BA-WOM!

...IS ALSO A *DECOY!*

...I DIDN'T HIT IT THAT HARD. MUST'VE HAD SOME KIND'A *SELF-DESTRUCT.* DOESN'T LEAVE MUCH TO *IDENTIFY.*

AN IMPERIAL *PROBE DROID!*

HEY, C'MON. LET'S NOT PANIC. WE DON'T *KNOW* THAT.

BUT WE DON'T KNOW THAT IT *WASN'T.*

SOMEWHERE IN DEEP SPACE, THE FLEET HOVERS, WAITING. WAITING FOR A HINT, A CLUE. UNTIL, ABOARD THE HULKING, OMINOUS CRUISER THAT LOOMS LARGER THAN EVEN THE SURROUNDING STAR DESTROYERS...

I THINK WE'VE *FOUND* SOMETHING, ADMIRAL OZZEL...

THE REPORT WE HAVE IS ONLY A *FRAGMENT*...FROM A PROBE DROID IN THE HOTH SYSTEM, SIR, BUT IT'S THE BEST LEAD WE'VE HAD IN--

WE'VE *THOUSANDS* OF PROBE DROIDS SEARCHING THE GALAXY, CAPTAIN PIETT...I WANT *PROOF*, NOT LEADS! I DON'T INTEND TO CONTINUE CHASING ENDLESSLY AROUND THE COSMOS.

THE *HOTH* SYSTEM. THAT'S IT.

B-BUT, MY LORD...! THERE ARE SO MANY UNCHARTED SETTLE-MENTS, IT COULD MERELY BE *SMUGGLERS* OR--

THAT IS THE ONE, AND *SKYWALKER* IS THERE! BRING IN THE PATROL SHIPS, ADMIRAL, AND TELL GENERAL VEERS TO ALERT HIS TROOPS...

...WE'RE PROCEEDING TO THE HOTH SYSTEM, *FULL SPEED!*

NEXT ISSUE: BATTLEGROUND HOTH!

50¢ | 40
OCT
02817

STAR
WARS

CONTINUING THE
OFFICIAL COMICS ADAPTATION OF
THE EMPIRE
STRIKES BACK!

BATTLEGROUND
HOTH!

Long ago in a galaxy far, far away. . .there exists a state of cosmic *civil war*. A brave alliance of *underground freedom fighters* has challenged the tyranny and oppression of the awesome *Galactic Empire*. This is their story!

LucasFilm PRESENTS: STAR WARS — *THE GREATEST* **SPACE FANTASY** OF ALL!

ARCHIE GOODWIN ° **AL WILLIAMSON** AND **CARLOS GARZON** ° **GLYNIS WEIN** ° **RICK VEITCH** ° **DAN FINGEROTH** ° **JAMES SHOOTER**
WRITER/EDITOR | ARTISTS | COLORIST | LETTERER | ASST. EDITOR | EDITOR-IN-CHIEF

STAR **THE EMPIRE STRIKES BACK** WARS™

WITH THE *DESTRUCTION* OF THEIR DEATH STAR, THE EMPEROR'S FORCES TIGHTEN THE REINS OF TYRANNY THROUGHOUT THE GALAXY. MEANWHILE, ON THE FROZEN PLANET OF *HOTH*, PRINCESS LEIA AND HER FREEDOM FIGHTERS STRUGGLE TO KEEP THE REBELLION GROWING, AS LUKE FALLS VICTIM TO ONE OF THE WORLD'S *ICE MONSTERS* AND THEIR NEWLY ESTABLISHED BASE IS MENACED BY AN IMPERIAL *PROBE DROID*...

TM: © LUCASFILM LTD. 1980 (LFL)

CHAPTER TWO:
BATTLEGROUND HOTH!

ALARMS SOUND AT REGULAR INTERVALS THROUGHOUT THE LASER-BLASTED WALLS OF THE *REBEL* STRONGHOLD. EVERYWHERE THERE IS THE ECHO OF TROOPS, DROIDS, AND TRANSPORT SPEEDERS ON THE MOVE.

A FULL-SCALE **ALERT** IS IN EFFECT.

IN JUST A FEW DAYS TIME, **TWO** THREATS TO THE ALLIANCE PRESENCE ON HOTH HAVE ARISEN, AND AT THIS MOMENT, AFTER CONSIDERABLE STRUGGLE...

...ONLY **ONE** CAN BE CONSIDERED UNDER CONTROL.

JUST *LISTEN* TO THOSE ICE CREATURES **HOWL,** ARTOO! SEE HOW YOUR CHIRPS AND WHISTLES **UPSET** THEM?

THEY'RE ALL BEING ENTICED INTO THE *TRAP* BY HIGH-PITCHED SOUNDS, AND IF *THAT* SATISFIES YOUR MORBID CURIOSITY... WE **WERE** ON THE WAY TO THE MEDICAL CENTER...

WHERE...

HOLD STILL FOR ONE MOMENT, COMMANDER SKYWALKER...

THERE, YES...

THE BACTA ARE GROWING WELL. THOSE SCARS SHOULD BE GONE IN A DAY OR SO.

THE SURGEON DROID TOO-ONEBEE, SLIDES BACK, AND LEIA ORGANA MOVES FORWARD WITH COMPASSION AND CONCERN. AND PERHAPS, SOMETHING MORE.

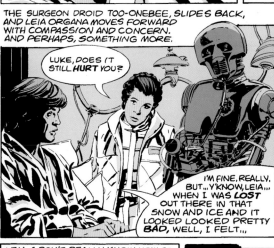

LUKE, DOES IT STILL HURT YOU?

I'M FINE, REALLY, BUT... Y'KNOW, LEIA... WHEN I WAS LOST OUT THERE IN THAT SNOW AND ICE AND IT LOOKED LOOKED PRETTY BAD, WELL, I FELT...

I FELT AFRAID FOR YOU...

LEIA, I DON'T REALLY KNOW HOW TO SAY THIS. BUT YOU MUST KNOW THAT YOU... WELL... YOU'RE THE ONLY ONE I... I...

UNCERTAIN, BUT DRAWN BY THE MOMENT, THE PRINCESS LEANS CLOSE TO THE YOUNG REBEL HERO...

MASTER LUKE! IT'S SO GOOD TO SEE YOU FUNCTIONAL AGAIN!

VA-DOOT BIP!

AND THE MOMENT PASSES. THE ONE-TIME SENATOR FROM ALDERAAN TURNS TO LEAVE...

LEIA... WAIT!... W-WHAT WOULD YOU THINK IF... I WENT AWAY FOR A WHILE? TO ANOTHER SYSTEM... A PLACE CALLED DAGOBAH... I'VE GOT TO--

WHAT? THAT'S JUST FINE! FIRST HAN... NOW YOU! I COULD GET MORE LOYALTY IF I RECRUITED SOME OF THOSE ICE CREATURES WE'VE TRAPPED!

AH! SHE'S BEING **CHARMING** AGAIN, HI, KID! YOU LOOK STRONG ENOUGH TO WRESTLE A GUNDARK!

VAAARRK!

THANKS TO **YOU**, HAN, BETWEEN THE DEATH STAR TRENCH AND RESCUING ME AFTER I WANDERED AWAY **DELIRIOUS** FROM THAT MONSTER'S LAIR... THAT'S **TWO** I OWE YOU.

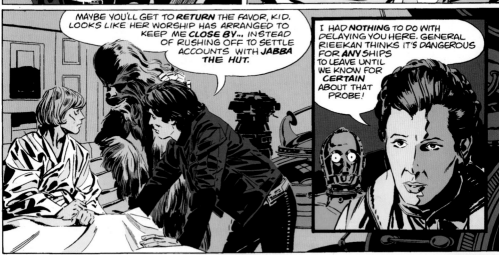

MAYBE YOU'LL GET TO **RETURN** THE FAVOR, KID. LOOKS LIKE HER WORSHIP HAS ARRANGED TO KEEP ME **CLOSE BY**... INSTEAD OF RUSHING OFF TO SETTLE ACCOUNTS WITH **JABBA THE HUT**.

I HAD **NOTHING** TO DO WITH DELAYING YOU HERE. GENERAL RIEEKAN THINKS IT'S DANGEROUS FOR **ANY** SHIPS TO LEAVE UNTIL WE KNOW FOR **CERTAIN** ABOUT THAT PROBE!

MAKES A GOOD **STORY**, LADY... BUT I THINK YOU JUST CAN'T **BEAR** TO LET ME OUT OF YOUR SIGHT. ESPECIALLY AFTER EXPRESSING YOUR **TRUE** FEELINGS WHEN WE WERE **ALONE** THE OTHER DAY.

I **MUST** BE RIGHT OR YOU WOULDN'T BE SO **STEAMED**. LOOK THAT WAY TO **YOU**, LUKE...?

WELL... YEAH... IT DOES, KIND OF...

FOR AN INSTANT, THERE IS HURT IN LEIA ORGANA'S EYES. THEN SHE BECOMES THE PRINCESS AND ALLIANCE LEADER AGAIN. COOL...

...DEFIANT.

I GUESS *NEITHER* OF YOU UNDERSTANDS EVERYTHING ABOUT WOMEN...

DO YOU?!

ON THE EDGE OF THE HOTH SYSTEM, A HEARTBEAT BEFORE... THIS WAS BARREN SPACE. NOW... SIX *SHIPS* APPEAR.

FIVE ARE HUGE IMPERIAL *STAR DESTROYERS.* THE SIXTH DWARFS EVEN *THESE!*

WHAT *IS* IT, VEERS?

LORD VADER, THE FLEET HAS MOVED OUT OF *LIGHT-SPEED...*

COM-SCAN HAS DETECTED AN *ENERGY FIELD* PROTECTING AN AREA OF THE SIXTH PLANET. THE FIELD IS STRONG ENOUGH TO *DEFLECT* ANY BOMBARDMENT.

THE REBEL SCUM ARE *ALERTED* TO OUR PRESENCE. OZZEL CAME OUT OF LIGHT-SPEED TOO *CLOSE* TO THE SYSTEM!

HE FELT *SURPRISE* WAS A WISER--

HE IS AS *CLUMSY* AS HE IS STUPID! A CLEAN BOMBARDMENT IS NOW *IMPOSSIBLE!* PREPARE YOUR TROOPS FOR A *SURFACE ATTACK!*

AND WITH A *SWIRL* OF HIS FLOWING CAPE, THE SITH LORD STALKS FROM THE CUBICLE...

...TO FACE THE ADMIRAL OF HIS FLEET.

MY LORD, THE SHIPS ARE ALL OUT OF LIGHT AND... AND... *AGHHHHH!*

CAPTAIN PIETT! MAKE READY TO LAND *ASSAULT TROOPS* BEYOND THE ENERGY FIELD... THEN DEPLOY OUR VESSELS SO THAT *NOTHING* CAN GET OFF THAT PLANET!

CHOKING... GASPING... THE IMPERIAL OFFICER FALLS!

SWIFTLY! YOU'RE IN *COMMAND* NOW!

--*ADMIRAL* PIETT!

WHILE *ON* THE SIXTH PLANET... THE ALERT IS NOW IN ITS *FINAL STAGE.* ACTIVITY IS AT ITS ZENITH. AND PRINCESS LEIA IS ADDRESSING PART OF HER COMMAND...

THE LARGE TRANSPORT SHIPS WILL LEAVE AS SOON AS THEY'RE LOADED. THE ENERGY SHIELD CAN ONLY BE OPENED FOR A *SPLIT SECOND* SO YOU ESCORTS HAVE TO STICK *CLOSE!*

FIGHTER ESCORTS AGAINST IMPERIAL *STAR DESTROYERS?*

YOU'LL HAVE SOME HELP FROM THE *ION CANNON.* ONCE YOU CLEAR THE ENERGY FIELD ... PROCEED TO THE RENDEZVOUS POINT. GOOD LUCK!

AND IF THAT GOOD LUCK IS EXTENDED TO A CERTAIN SMUGGLER CAPTAIN AND HIS WOOKIEE FIRST MATE ...

...LEIA DOESN'T *SAY* SO AS SHE FINISHES THE BRIEFING AND MOVES PAST WHERE THE *MILLENNIUM FALCON* IS BEING REPAIRED.

THAT SHOULD *DO* IT, CHEWIE. LET'S GIVE THE LIFTERS A TRY.

GROWWK!

AWRIGHT! *AWRIGHT!* SO THAT *DOESN'T* DO IT!

MEANWHILE, ON PATROL ABOVE HOTH'S GLISTENING WHITE SURFACE ...

SIR! REBEL SHIPS COMING INTO OUR SECTOR ... A TRANSPORT AND ESCORTS!

GOOD. OUR FIRST *CATCH* OF THE DAY.

263

ECHO C-130 IS APPROACHING THE SHIELD, GENERAL RIEEKAN.

STAND BY TO **OPEN** IT, AND SIGNAL **ION CONTROL--**

"...TO START FIRING THE **INSTANT** IT DOES!"

AND FROM THE GIANT WEAPON, CRIMSON ENERGY BOLTS BLAST SPACEWARD...

...STREAKING AHEAD OF TRANSPORT AND FIGHTERS TO STRIKE **ON TARGET!**

CHEERS FILL THE ALLIANCE CENTER BELOW. STILL, ALL REALIZE THIS IS ONLY THE OPENING ROUND IN A DESPERATELY ONE-SIDED BATTLE...

...WHERE VICTORY CAN ONLY BE MEASURED BY **HOW LONG** THEY HOLD OFF THE ENEMY.

CHEWIE, TAKE CARE OF YOURSELF...AND WATCH OUT FOR THIS GUY, WILL YOU?

WAAARRK!

HAN, I HOPE YOU MAKE YOUR **PEACE** WITH JABBA...EVEN IF IT DOES THROW HALF THE GALAXY'S **BOUNTY HUNTERS** OUT OF WORK.

'GIVE 'EM HELL, KID!

LUKE STARES AT HIS FRIEND AND RIVAL. THERE SEEMS TO BE **MORE** THAT EACH WANTS TO SAY. SO MUCH HAS HAPPENED SINCE FATE THREW THEM TOGETHER IN THE CANTINA AT MOS EISLEY SO LONG AGO. THEN...

ATTENTION! ALL SPEEDER PILOTS TO YOUR CRAFTS! ON WITHDRAW SIGNAL... ASSEMBLE AT SOUTH SLOPE. YOUR FIGHTERS WILL BE WAITING WHEN **EVACUATION** IS COMPLETE.

AND THERE IS ONLY TIME FOR LUKE TO RUSH ACROSS THE HANGER...

YEAH... I KNOW WHAT YOU MEAN.

...TO JOIN HIS GUNNER, DACK.

EVERYTHING **OKAY**...?

GLAD TO SEE YOU BACK AND WELL, SIR... NOW I FEEL LIKE WE CAN TAKE ON THE WHOLE EMPIRE!

WHY IS IT WHEN THINGS SEEM TO GET SETTLED... EVERYTHING FALLS APART? TAKE GOOD CARE OF MASTER LUKE WHEN HE JOINS YOU AT HIS FIGHTER... AND TAKE GOOD CARE OF YOURSELF, TOO!

VOOOO **DOOP**!

OUTSIDE, THE ALLIANCE GROUND DEFENSES PRE- PARE FOR THE INEVITABLE...

OUR **POWER GENERATOR** WILL BE THEIR PRIME OBJECTIVE, SO--

WAIT! OUT ON THE HORIZON... IT LOOKS LIKE...

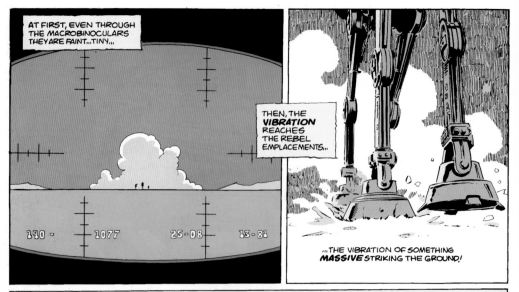

AT FIRST, EVEN THROUGH THE MACROBINOCULARS THEY ARE FAINT... TINY...

THEN, THE **VIBRATION** REACHES THE REBEL EMPLACEMENTS...

...THE VIBRATION OF SOMETHING **MASSIVE** STRIKING THE GROUND!

POINT RIDER FIVE TO ECHO DEFENSE! **ENEMY CONTACT! ENEMY CONTACT!**

IMPERIAL **WALKERS** ADVANCING ON YOUR POSITION!

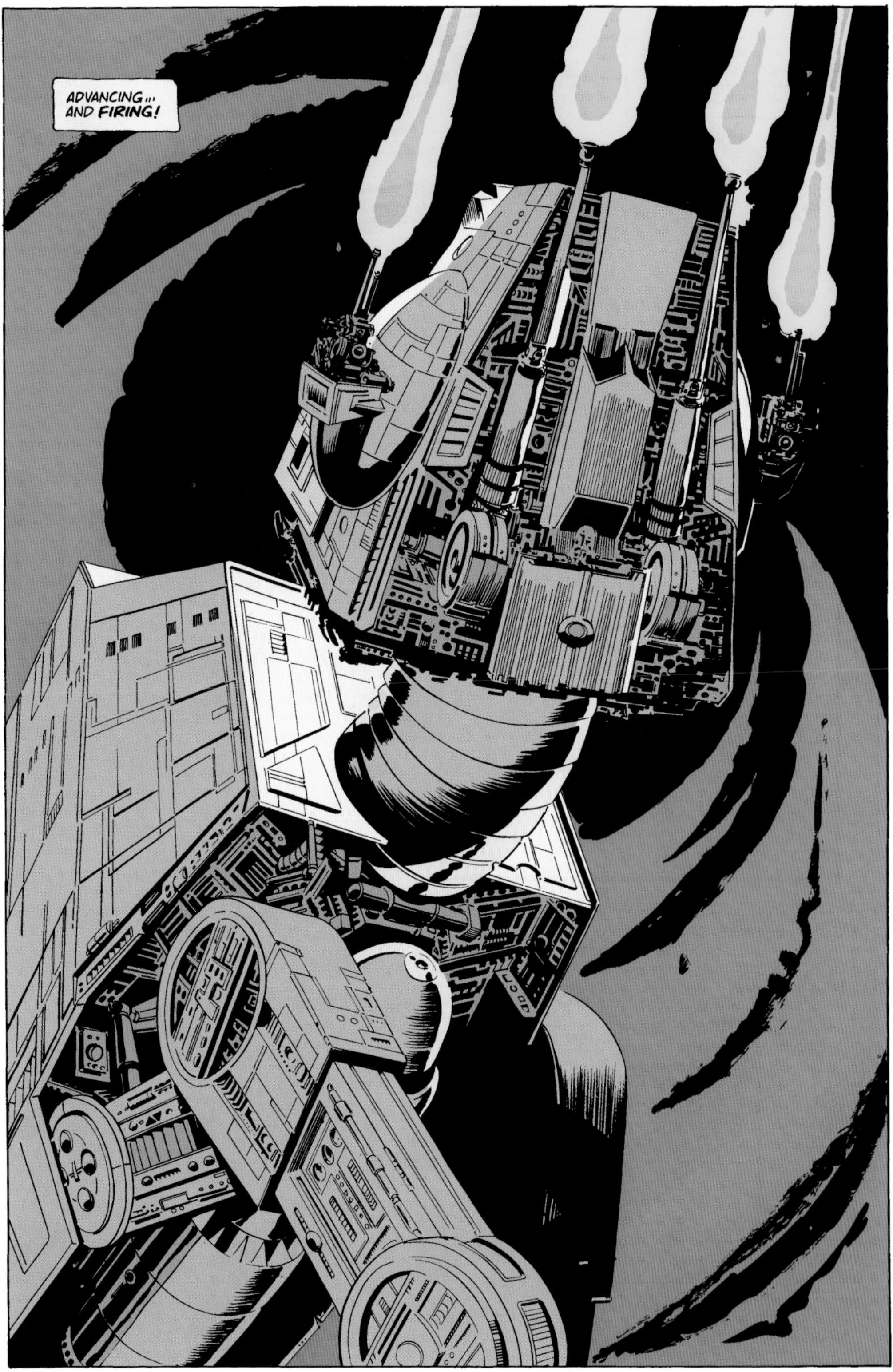
ADVANCING... AND FIRING!

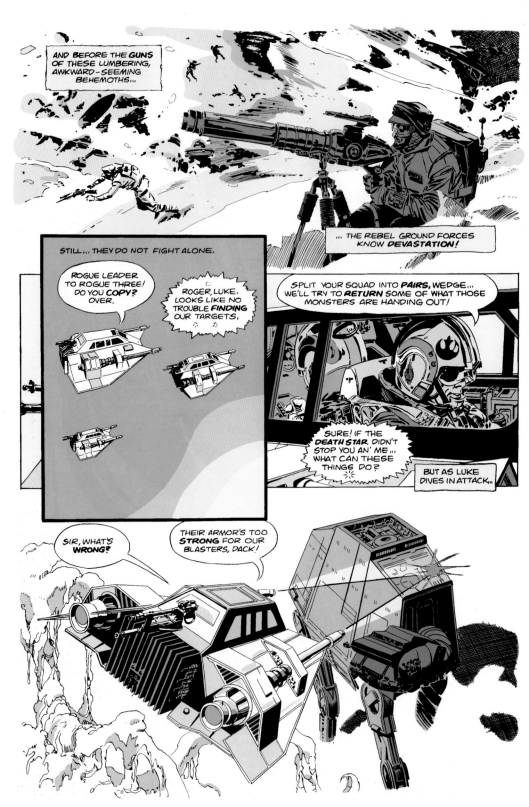

AND BEFORE THE **GUNS** OF THESE LUMBERING, AWKWARD-SEEMING BEHEMOTHS...

... THE REBEL GROUND FORCES KNOW **DEVASTATION!**

STILL... THEY DO NOT FIGHT ALONE.

ROGUE LEADER TO ROGUE THREE! DO YOU **COPY?** OVER.

ROGER, LUKE. LOOKS LIKE NO TROUBLE **FINDING** OUR TARGETS.

SPLIT YOUR SQUAD INTO **PAIRS,** WEDGE... WE'LL TRY TO **RETURN** SOME OF WHAT THOSE MONSTERS ARE HANDING OUT!

SURE! IF THE **DEATH STAR** DIDN'T STOP YOU AN' ME... WHAT CAN THESE THINGS DO?

BUT AS LUKE DIVES IN ATTACK...

SIR, WHAT'S **WRONG?**

THEIR ARMOR'S TOO **STRONG** FOR OUR BLASTERS, DACK!

268

A SITUATION RAPIDLY EXPERIENCED BY EVERY SNOWSPEEDER...

FOR MANY,,,THE EXPERIENCE IS **FATAL.**

NO BETTER LUCK WITH **MY** GUNS, SIR!

WE'VE GOT TO CHANGE **TACTICS,** DACK, ONCE WE'RE IN THE CLEAR I'VE GOT AN IDEA WHAT TO--

BUT AS THE SNOWSPEEDER SOARS FROM THE STRIDING MECHANICAL GIANT,,,,

WE'VE TAKEN A **HIT!** DACK, WHAT'S THE **DAMAGE** BACK THERE?

DACK,,,?!

THE RELENTLESS ENEMY BARRAGE IS FELT EVERY-WHERE,,, INCLUDING THE ALLIANCE STRONGHOLD'S ALMOST DESERTED **HANGAR.**

FIRST CHANCE WE GET,,, WE'RE GIVING THIS CRATE A **COMPLETE** OVERHAUL, BUT UNDER THE CIRCUMSTANCES, PAL,,, THAT WELD'S TIGHT ENOUGH,

IN FACT, I'D BET IT'S GONNA HOLD A LOT **LONGER** THAN THIS JOINT'S CEILING!

IN THE COMMAND CENTER... THINGS LOOK NO BETTER.

I'M NOT SURE WE CAN PROTECT TWO TRANSPORTS AT A TIME, PRINCESS.

IT'S *RISKY*, GENERAL RIEEKAN... BUT OUR HOLDING ACTION IS FALTERING.

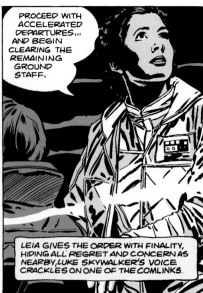

PROCEED WITH ACCELERATED DEPARTURES... AND BEGIN CLEARING THE REMAINING GROUND STAFF.

LEIA GIVES THE ORDER WITH FINALITY, HIDING ALL REGRET AND CONCERN AS NEARBY, LUKE SKYWALKER'S VOICE CRACKLES ON ONE OF THE COMLINKS.

I'M STILL FLYING, ROGUE GROUP... BUT THEY GOT *DACK!*

USE YOUR HARPOONS AND TOW CABLES... GO FOR THEIR *LEGS!*

IT'S OUR ONLY HOPE OF *STOPPING* THEM!

READ YOU *CLEAR*, ROGUE LEADER, THIS IS ROGUE THREE... *GOING IN!*

AND WEDGE--LAST SURVIVOR, ALONG WITH LUKE, OF THE BATTLE OF THE DEATH STAR-- SENDS HIS SPEEDER ZOOMING IN FRONT OF THE LEAD WALKER!

ACTIVATE HARPOON! FIRE CABLE!

CABLE AWAY!

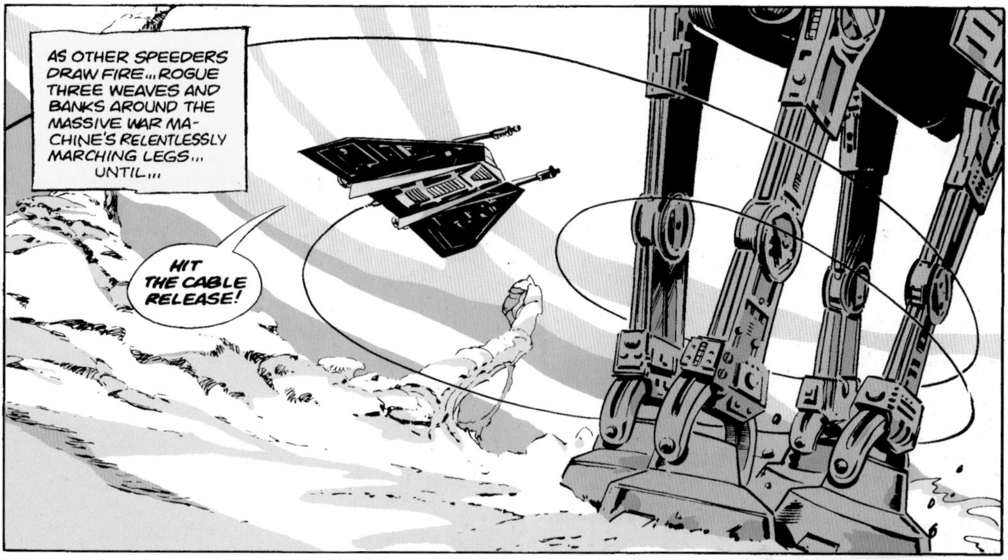
AS OTHER SPEEDERS DRAW FIRE... ROGUE THREE WEAVES AND BANKS AROUND THE MASSIVE WAR MACHINE'S RELENTLESSLY MARCHING LEGS... UNTIL...
HIT THE CABLE RELEASE!

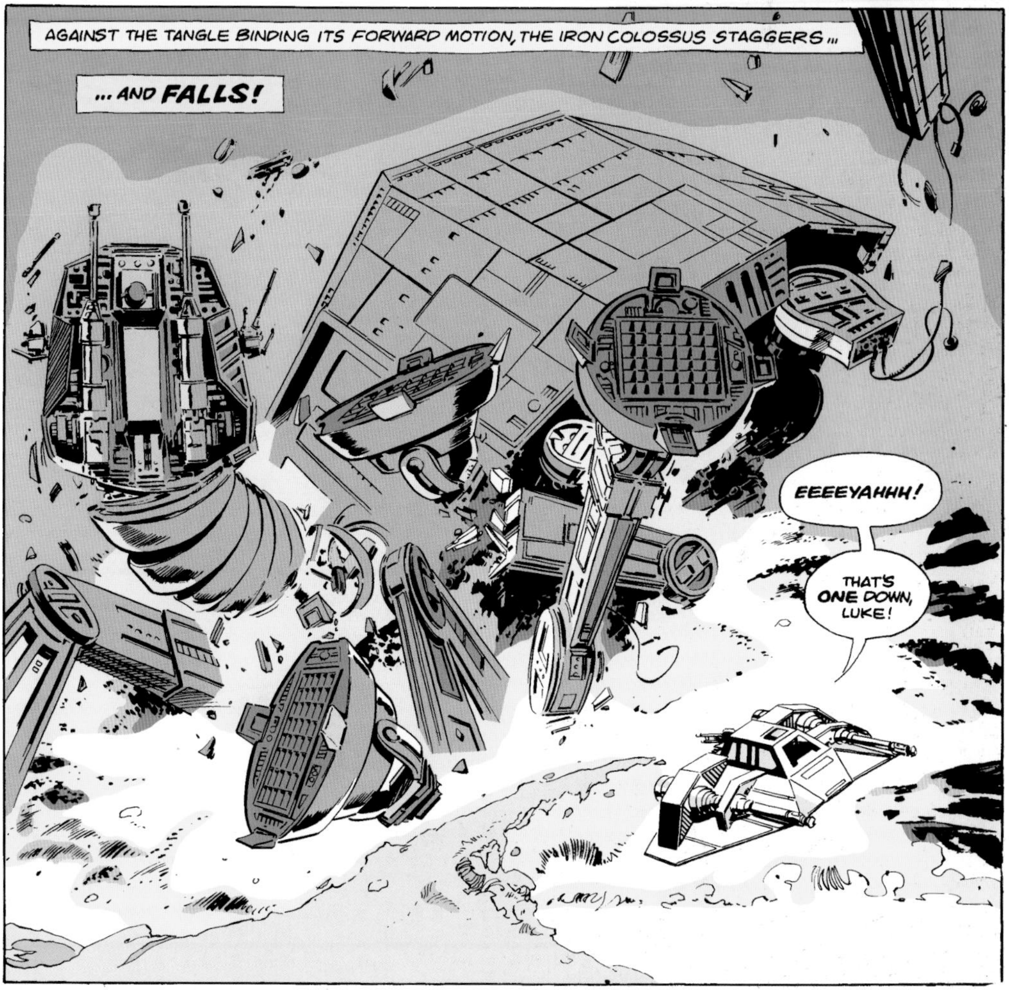
AGAINST THE TANGLE BINDING ITS FORWARD MOTION, THE IRON COLOSSUS STAGGERS...
... AND FALLS!
EEEEYAHHH!
THAT'S ONE DOWN, LUKE!

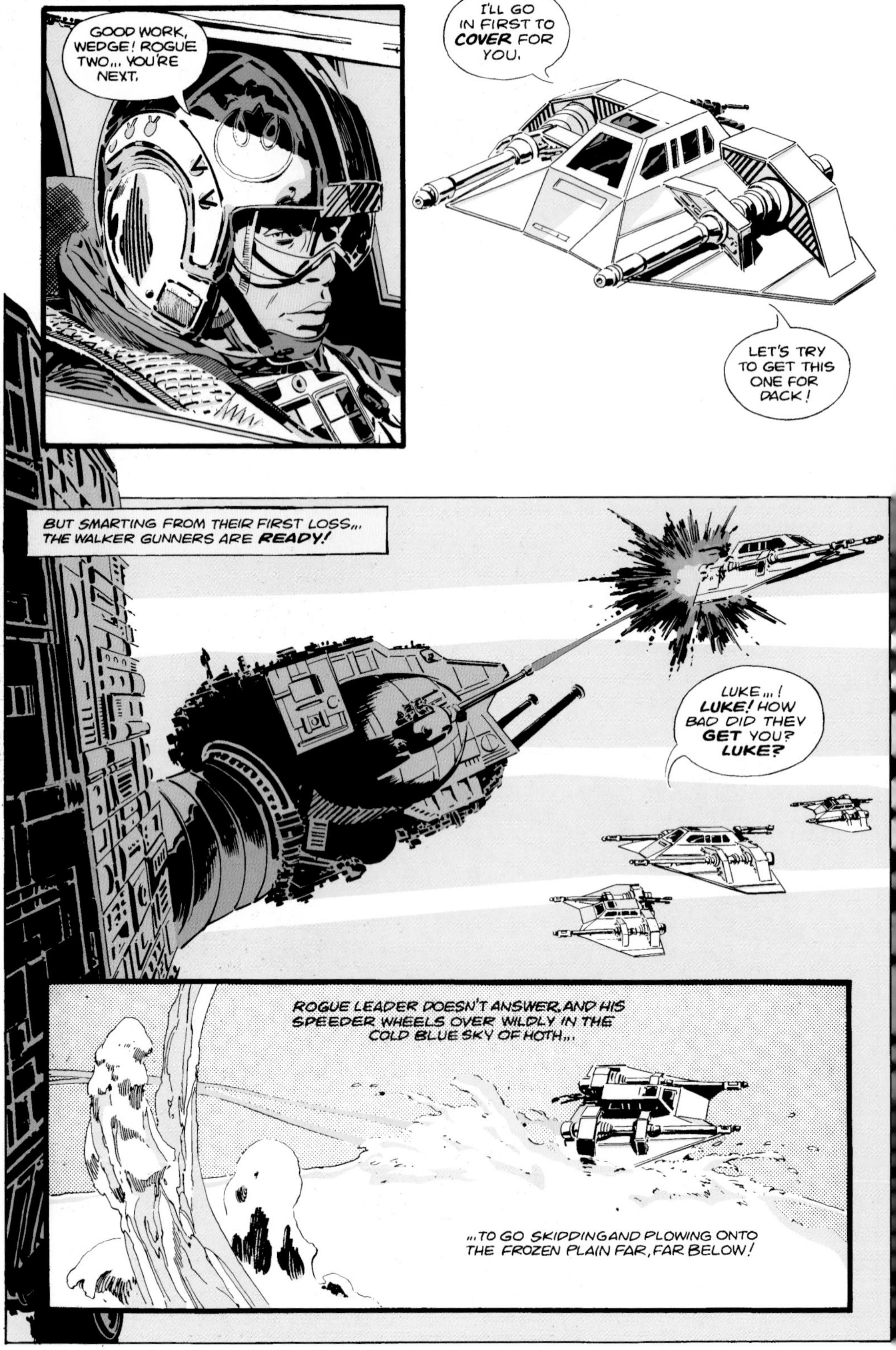
GOOD WORK, WEDGE! ROGUE TWO... YOU'RE NEXT.
I'LL GO IN FIRST TO COVER FOR YOU.
LET'S TRY TO GET THIS ONE FOR DACK!
BUT SMARTING FROM THEIR FIRST LOSS... THE WALKER GUNNERS ARE READY!
LUKE...! LUKE! HOW BAD DID THEY GET YOU? LUKE?
ROGUE LEADER DOESN'T ANSWER, AND HIS SPEEDER WHEELS OVER WILDLY IN THE COLD BLUE SKY OF HOTH...
...TO GO SKIDDING AND PLOWING ONTO THE FROZEN PLAIN FAR, FAR BELOW!

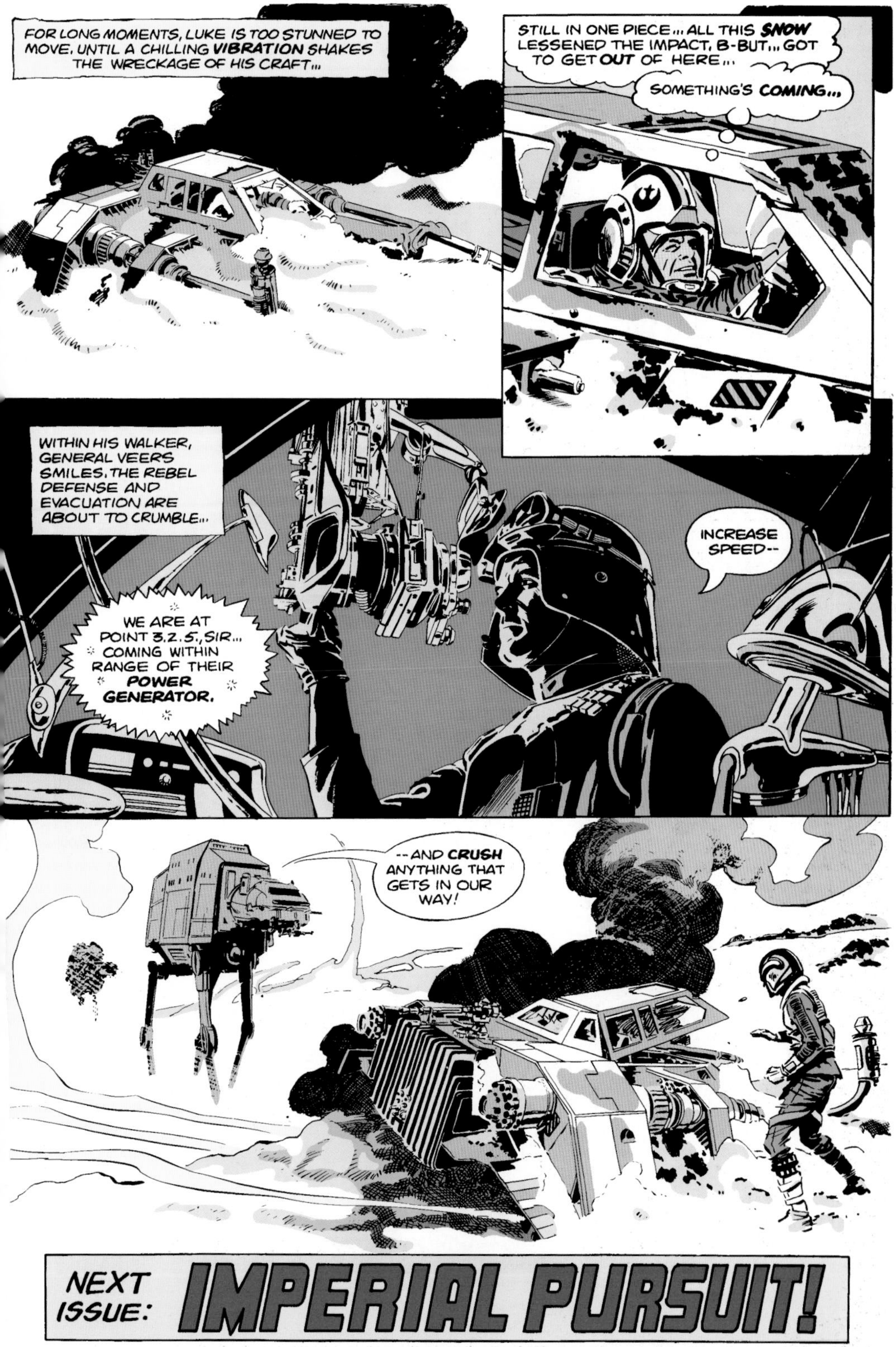
FOR LONG MOMENTS, LUKE IS TOO STUNNED TO MOVE, UNTIL A CHILLING **VIBRATION** SHAKES THE WRECKAGE OF HIS CRAFT...
STILL IN ONE PIECE... ALL THIS **SNOW** LESSENED THE IMPACT. B-BUT... GOT TO GET **OUT** OF HERE...
SOMETHING'S **COMING...**
WITHIN HIS WALKER, GENERAL VEERS SMILES. THE REBEL DEFENSE AND EVACUATION ARE ABOUT TO CRUMBLE...
WE ARE AT POINT 3.2.5., SIR... COMING WITHIN RANGE OF THEIR **POWER GENERATOR.**
INCREASE SPEED--
--AND **CRUSH** ANYTHING THAT GETS IN OUR WAY!
NEXT ISSUE: IMPERIAL PURSUIT!

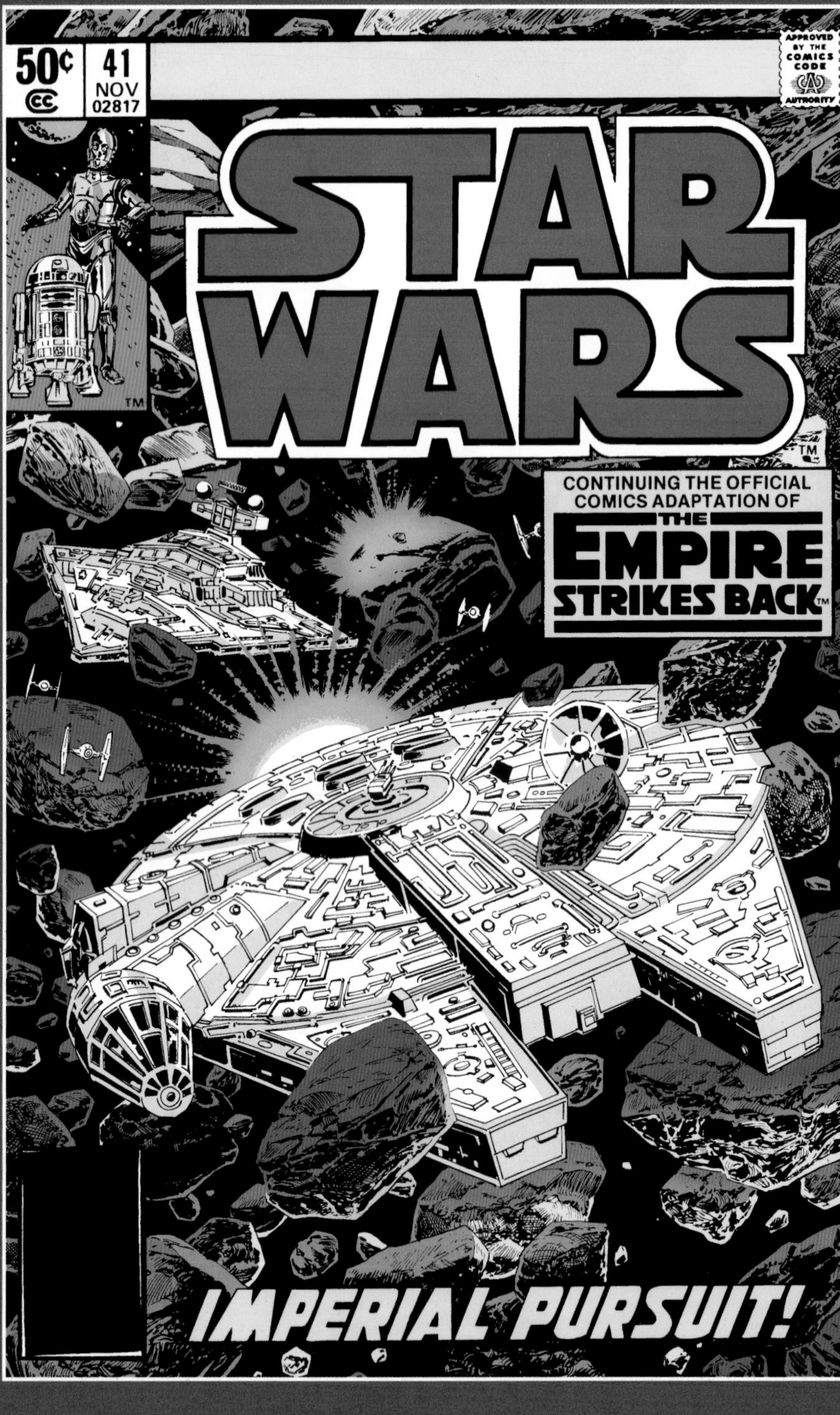
50¢
41
NOV
02817
APPROVED BY THE COMICS CODE AUTHORITY
STAR WARS
CONTINUING THE OFFICIAL COMICS ADAPTATION OF
THE EMPIRE STRIKES BACK
IMPERIAL PURSUIT!

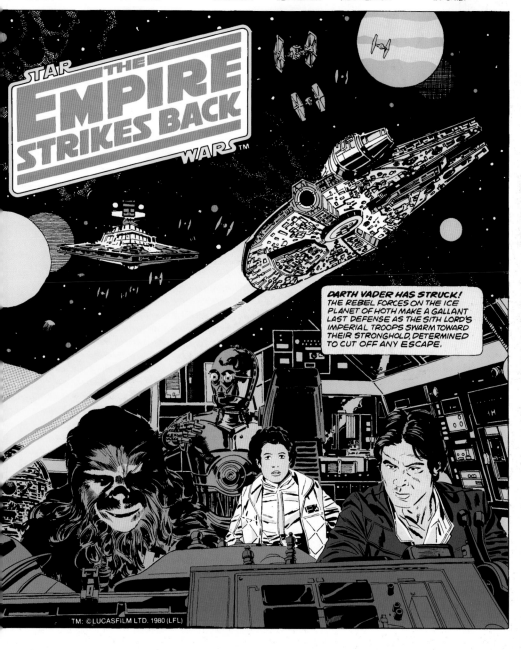

Long ago in a galaxy far, far away. . .there exists a state of cosmic *civil war*. A brave alliance of *underground freedom fighters* has challenged the tyranny and oppression of the awesome *Galactic Empire*. This is their story!

LucasFilm PRESENTS: STAR WARS — *THE GREATEST SPACE FANTASY OF ALL!*

ARCHIE GOODWIN WRITER/EDITOR • AL WILLIAMSON AND CARLOS GARZON ARTISTS • GLYNIS WEIN COLORIST • RICK VEITCH LETTERER • DAN FINGEROTH ASST. EDITOR • JAMES SHOOTER EDITOR-IN-CHIEF

THE EMPIRE STRIKES BACK

DARTH VADER HAS STRUCK! THE REBEL FORCES ON THE ICE PLANET OF HOTH MAKE A GALLANT LAST DEFENSE AS THE SITH LORD'S IMPERIAL TROOPS SWARM TOWARD THEIR STRONGHOLD, DETERMINED TO CUT OFF ANY ESCAPE.

TM: ©LUCASFILM LTD. 1980 (LFL)

CHAPTER THREE IMPERIAL PURSUIT!

THUNDER ECHOES ON THE FROZEN PLAIN BEFORE THE ALLIANCE BASE... AS THE EMPIRE'S MONSTROUS MECHANIZED WAR MACHINES MOVE RELENTLESSLY FORWARD, THEIR *GOAL* IS THE REBEL POWER GENERATOR...

...LUKE SKYWALKER AND HIS DOWNED SNOW-SPEEDER ARE SCARCELY WORTH THEIR NOTICE, SMALL CONSOLATION... SINCE ANYTHING IN THEIR COURSE WILL BE GROUND UNDERFOOT REGARDLESS!

A THOUGHT VERY MUCH IN THE YOUNG FLIGHT COMMANDER'S MIND AS HE SUDDENLY RUSHES *BACK* TO HIS WRECKED CRAFT.

GOT TO TAKE THE *CHANCE...!* IF OUR GENERATOR GOES... SO DOES THE POWER SHIELD! AND INSTEAD OF AN ORDERLY WITHDRAWAL ...WE'LL HAVE A *SLAUGHTER!*

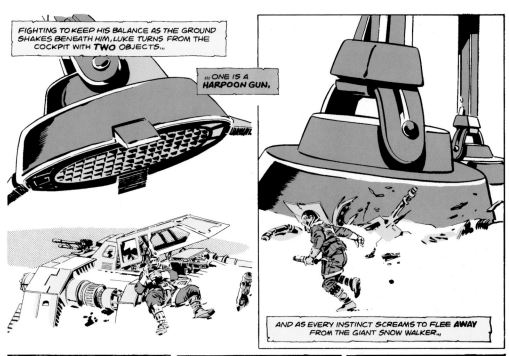

FIGHTING TO KEEP HIS BALANCE AS THE GROUND SHAKES BENEATH HIM, LUKE TURNS FROM THE COCKPIT WITH **TWO** OBJECTS...

...ONE IS A **HARPOON GUN,**

AND AS EVERY INSTINCT SCREAMS TO FLEE **AWAY** FROM THE GIANT SNOW WALKER...

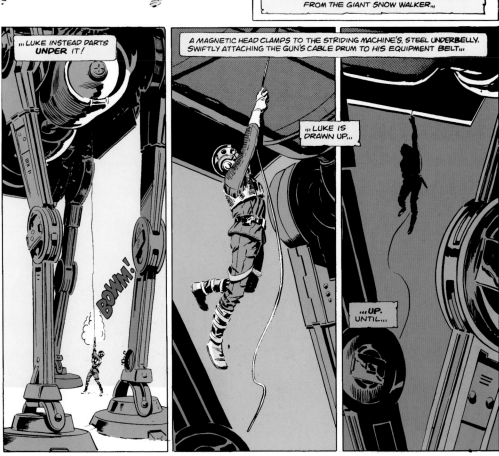

...LUKE INSTEAD DARTS **UNDER** IT!

BOWM!

A MAGNETIC HEAD CLAMPS TO THE STRIDING MACHINE'S STEEL UNDERBELLY, SWIFTLY ATTACHING THE GUN'S CABLE DRUM TO HIS EQUIPMENT BELT...

...LUKE IS DRAWN UP,...

...UP, UNTIL,...

...HE CAN USE HIS LASER BLADE TO SLICE OPEN A SMALL HATCH AND INSERT THE **SECOND** OBJECT TAKEN FROM HIS SPEEDER...

...A **CONCUSSION CHARGE!**

NOT A MOMENT TO SPARE FOR NICETIES LIKE SLIDING BACK DOWN...!

DROPPING THOSE CHARGES FROM OUR SPEEDERS, THEY COULDN'T CRACK THE WALKER'S PROTECTIVE ARMOR, BUT NOW THAT I'VE GOT ONE INSIDE...

LUKE LANDS HARD, ROLLING, AS TWO MONSTROUS LEGS PASS OVER HIM...

THEN...

THAT BUYS LEIA AND THE OTHERS A LITTLE MORE **TIME**--

--BUT IS IT **ENOUGH?!**

278

REBEL COMMAND! AND THE INCREASING THUNDER OF LASER BLASTS, HAN SOLO PUSHES FORWARD THROUGH ICE AND DEBRIS...

I HEARD THE CENTER TOOK A HIT, ARE YOU **ALL RIGHT?**

SO FAR. I... I DIDN'T EXPECT YOU'D BE CONCERNED. WITH REPAIRS TO THE **FALCON** TO WORRY ABOUT AND--

COME ON! A LITTLE MORE POUNDING AND THE WHOLE PLACE WILL GO TO **PIECES.** YOU'VE GOT TO GET TO YOUR SHIP.

W-WAIT!

GIVE THE EVACUATION CODE SIGNAL... AND GET TO THE TRANSPORT!

YES, YOUR HIGHNESS! ALL UNITS... ALL UNITS! DISENGAGE... **DISENGAGE!** BEGIN **RETREAT ACTION!**

THAT MEANS YOU TOO, BRONZE BRITCHES! LET'S HIT THE CORRIDORS!

PERHAPS YOU'RE **RIGHT,** SIR... THINGS ARE DEFINITELY FALLING APART **HERE!**

BUT ONCE **IN** THE CORRIDORS...

BETTER FORGET THE **TRANSPORT**, YOUR **ROYALNESS**... WE'RE CUT OFF FROM REACHING IT BUT **GOOD!**

RETURNING TO THE COMMAND CENTER IS OUT OF THE QUESTION NOW. ANY **IDEAS**, FLYBOY?

IF WE'RE **LUCKY**... WE CAN STILL MAKE IT TO THE **FALCON!**

FEELS LIKE THEY NAILED THE **MAIN GENERATOR**... NO MORE **SHIELD!** IMPERIALS CAN LAND AT WILL... THEY'RE GONNA SWARM IN HERE LIKE FLIES AROUND A **BANTHA!**

AND AT THE STRONGHOLD'S MAIN HANGAR, AN ANXIOUSLY PACING **WOOKIEE** IS THINKING THE SAME THING... AS THE CAVERN CRUMBLES **MORE** UNDER THE EMPIRE'S MOUNTING ASSAULT!

THEN...

AWWRK?

IT'S **US** ALL RIGHT, YOU BIG FURBALL! START CRANKIN' HER UP... I WANNA SET SOME KINDA' **RECORD** FOR FAST TAKE-OFFS!

THERE IS GOOD REASON FOR HASTE. SOMEWHERE BEHIND THEM, THE LAST DEFENSES **FALL** BEFORE ADVANCING STORMTROOPERS...

NOW JOINED **PERSONALLY** BY THEIR SUPREME COMMANDER.

280

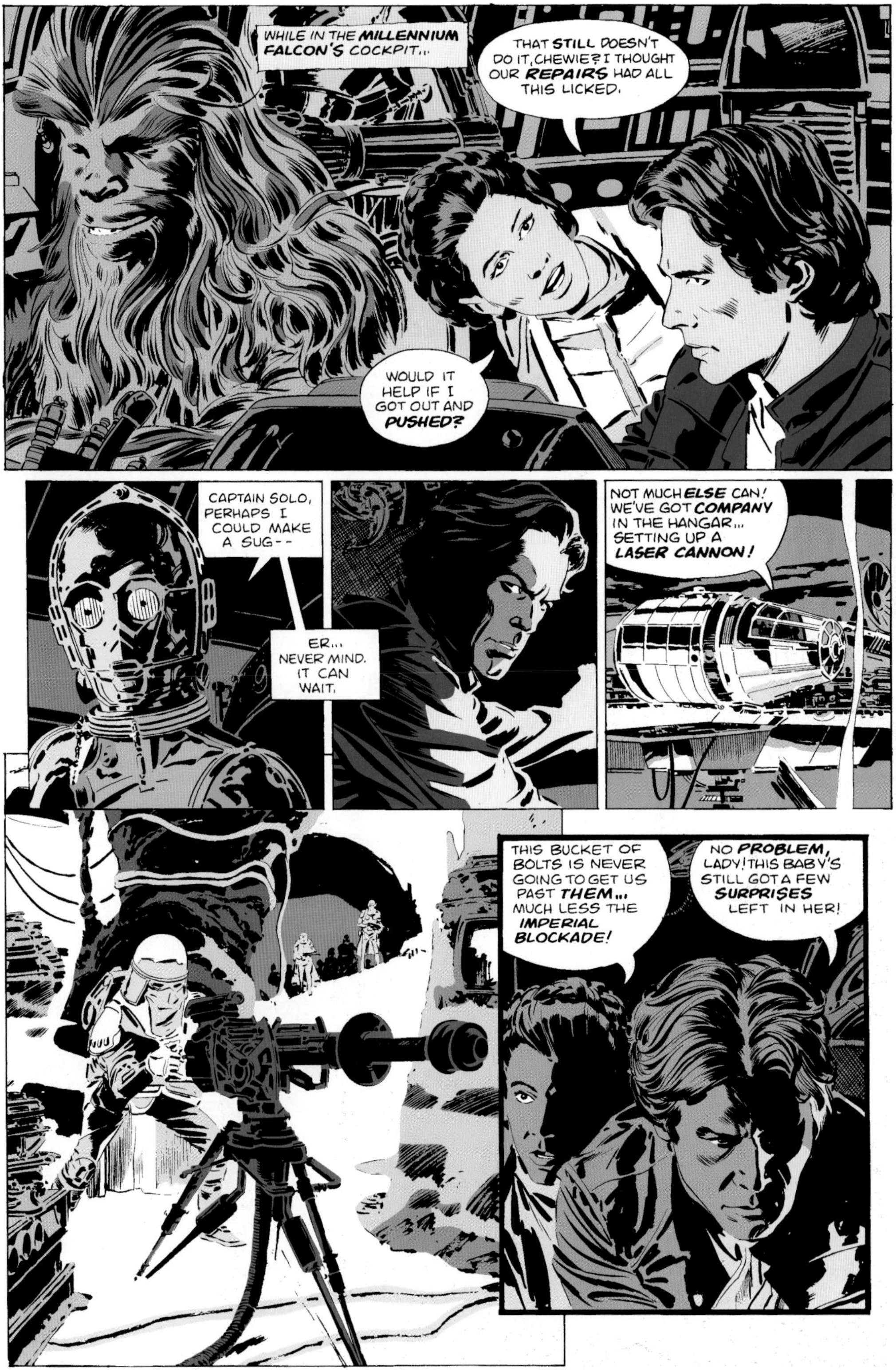
WHILE IN THE MILLENNIUM FALCON'S COCKPIT...
THAT STILL DOESN'T DO IT, CHEWIE? I THOUGHT OUR REPAIRS HAD ALL THIS LICKED.
WOULD IT HELP IF I GOT OUT AND PUSHED?
CAPTAIN SOLO, PERHAPS I COULD MAKE A SUG--
ER... NEVER MIND. IT CAN WAIT.
NOT MUCH ELSE CAN! WE'VE GOT COMPANY IN THE HANGAR... SETTING UP A LASER CANNON!
THIS BUCKET OF BOLTS IS NEVER GOING TO GET US PAST THEM... MUCH LESS THE IMPERIAL BLOCKADE!
NO PROBLEM, LADY! THIS BABY'S STILL GOT A FEW SURPRISES LEFT IN HER!

I'LL BE SURPRISED IF WE START **MOVING!**

CHEWIE, WE'LL JUST HAVE TO SWITCH OVER TO AUXILIARY AND HOPE FOR THE BEST!

SOMEDAY YOU'RE GOING TO BE WRONG AND I HOPE I'M THERE TO **SEE** IT.

PUNCH IT, CHEWIE!

THE ICE CAVERN EXPLODES WITH THE SOUND OF THE **MILLENNIUM FALCON'S** MAIN ENGINES, AND AS IMPERIAL TROOPS REEL FROM THE CONCUSSION...

...THE SMUGGLING CRAFT SOARS **CLEAR!** CLIMBING TOWARD THE SKIES...

...CLIMBING PAST A GROUP OF REBEL PILOTS WHO HAVE REACHED THEIR HIDDEN FIGHTER CRAFT.

AT LEAST HAN GOT AWAY, WEDGE, YOU AND THE OTHERS TAKE TO YOUR SHIPS!

GOOD LUCK, LUKE! SEE YOU AT THE RENDEZVOUS!

FROM THE DIRECTION OF HIS OWN X-WING COMES A NAGGING ELECTRONIC BLEEP...

ACTIVATE THE POWER AND STOP **WORRYING,** ARTOO, WE'LL SOON BE AIRBORNE.

BUT AS THE **FALCON** BECOMES A TWINKLE IN HOTH'S COLD BLUE SKY, LUKE WONDERS WHEN HE'LL SEE HIS FRIENDS AGAIN, FOR HIS RENDEZVOUS WILL **NOT** BE THE ONE DETERMINED BY THE REBEL ALLIANCE.

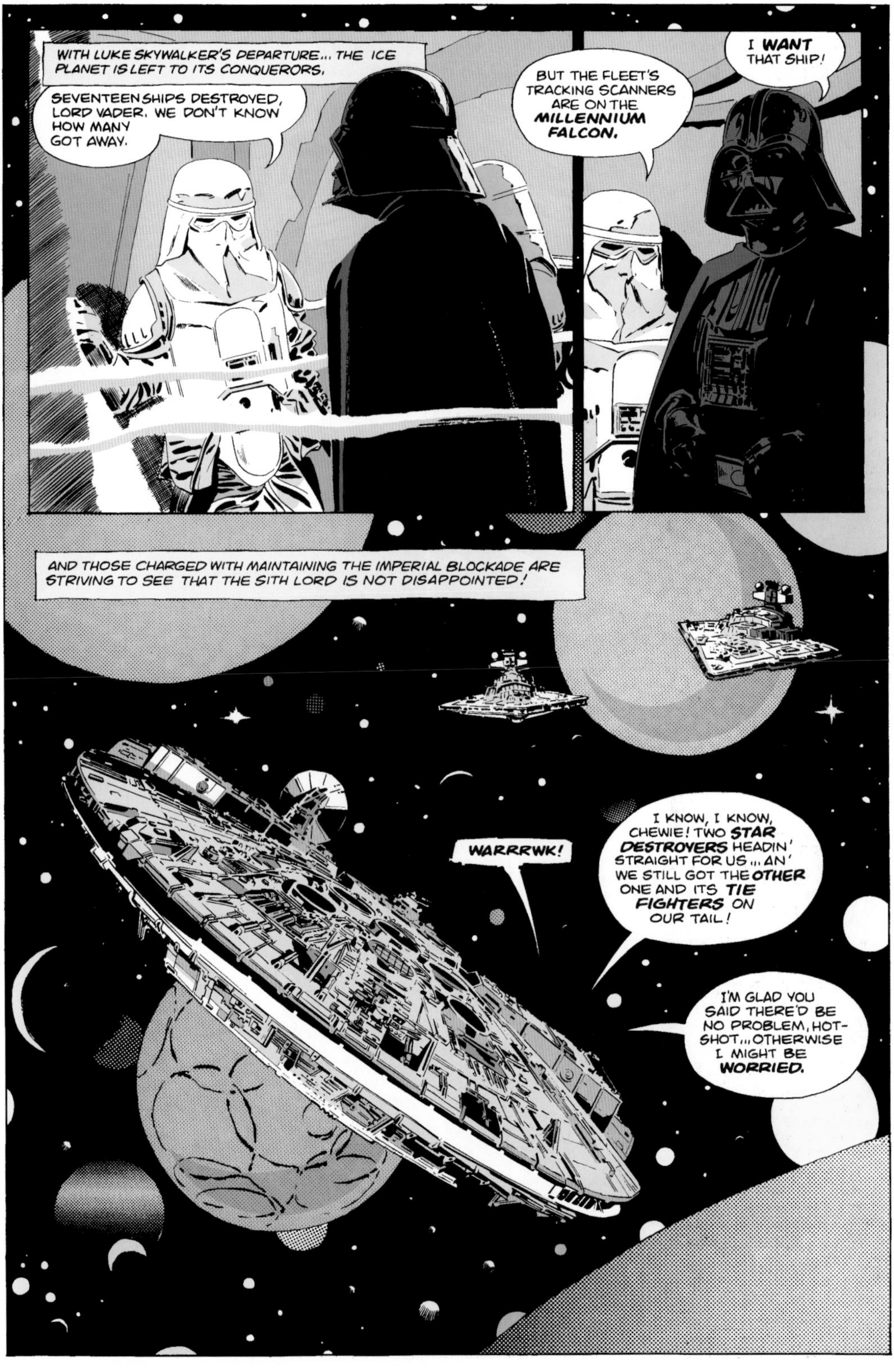
WITH LUKE SKYWALKER'S DEPARTURE... THE ICE PLANET IS LEFT TO ITS CONQUERORS.
SEVENTEEN SHIPS DESTROYED, LORD VADER. WE DON'T KNOW HOW MANY GOT AWAY.
BUT THE FLEET'S TRACKING SCANNERS ARE ON THE MILLENNIUM FALCON.
I WANT THAT SHIP!
AND THOSE CHARGED WITH MAINTAINING THE IMPERIAL BLOCKADE ARE STRIVING TO SEE THAT THE SITH LORD IS NOT DISAPPOINTED!
WARRRWK!
I KNOW, I KNOW, CHEWIE! TWO STAR DESTROYERS HEADIN' STRAIGHT FOR US... AN' WE STILL GOT THE OTHER ONE AND ITS TIE FIGHTERS ON OUR TAIL!
I'M GLAD YOU SAID THERE'D BE NO PROBLEM, HOT-SHOT... OTHERWISE I MIGHT BE WORRIED.

BUT AS THE TWO MONSTROUS VESSELS CONVERGE ON THE TINY FREIGHTER... IT SUDDENLY, SHARPLY *DIVES!*

THEY MAY BE FASTER AT SUB-LIGHT... BUT WE CAN OUTMANEUVER 'EM EVERY TIME!

CAPTAIN SOLO, I WAS WONDERING IF *NOW* WAS A GOOD TIME TO--

EITHER SHUT UP OR *SHUT DOWN!*

WE'VE STILL GOT THOSE FIGHTERS AND THEIR MOTHER SHIP NAGGIN' US!

CHEWIE... STAND BY TO MAKE THE JUMP INTO LIGHT-SPEED!

THEY'RE VERY *CLOSE...*

OH, YEAH... WATCH *THIS!*

WATCH *WHAT?*

NAAARGH?

I THINK WE'RE IN TROUBLE.

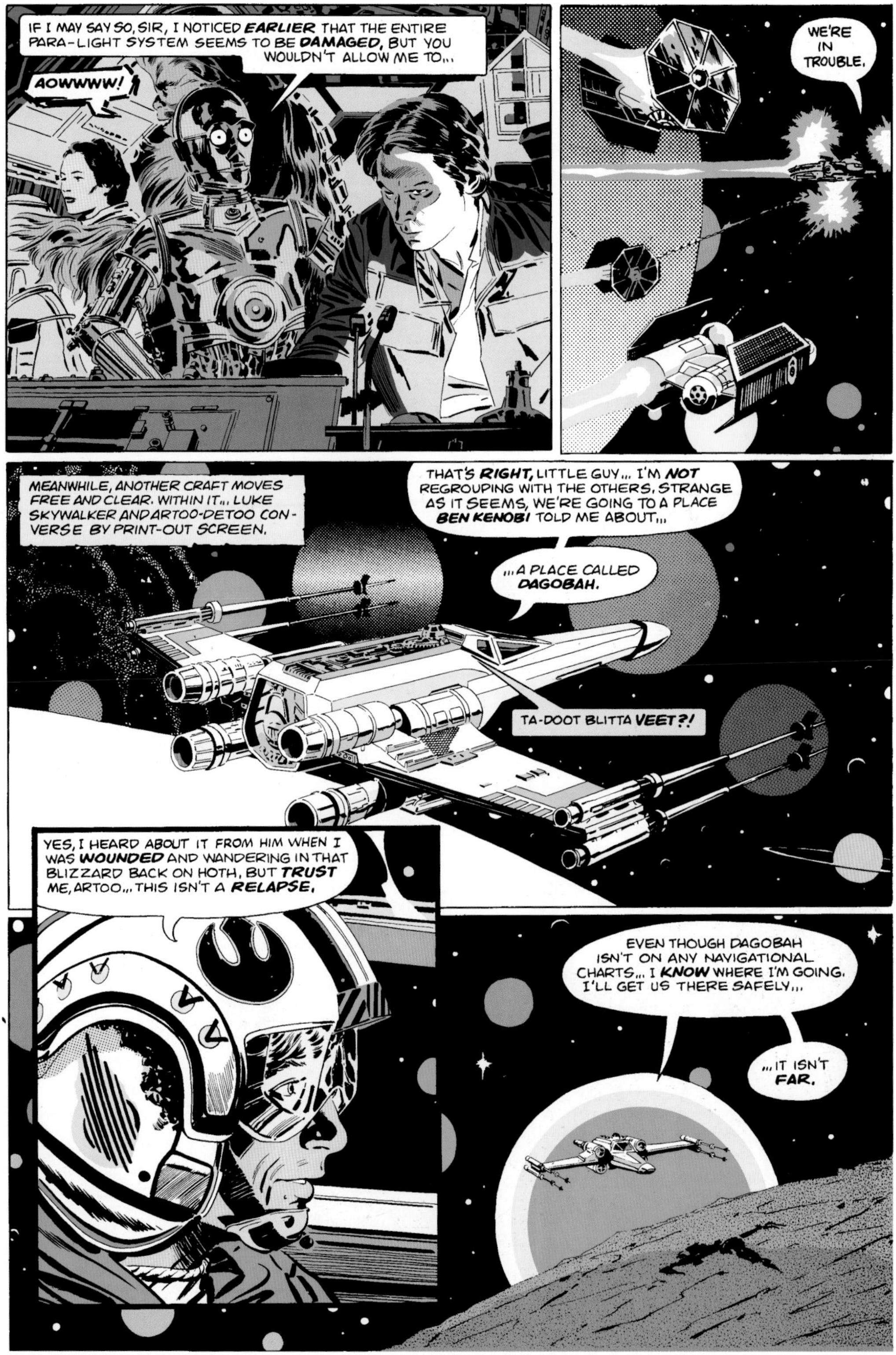

IF I MAY SAY SO, SIR, I NOTICED EARLIER THAT THE ENTIRE PARA-LIGHT SYSTEM SEEMS TO BE DAMAGED, BUT YOU WOULDN'T ALLOW ME TO...
AOWWWW!
WE'RE IN TROUBLE.
MEANWHILE, ANOTHER CRAFT MOVES FREE AND CLEAR. WITHIN IT... LUKE SKYWALKER AND ARTOO-DETOO CONVERSE BY PRINT-OUT SCREEN.
THAT'S RIGHT, LITTLE GUY... I'M NOT REGROUPING WITH THE OTHERS. STRANGE AS IT SEEMS, WE'RE GOING TO A PLACE BEN KENOBI TOLD ME ABOUT...
...A PLACE CALLED DAGOBAH.
TA-DOOT BLITTA VEET?!
YES, I HEARD ABOUT IT FROM HIM WHEN I WAS WOUNDED AND WANDERING IN THAT BLIZZARD BACK ON HOTH, BUT TRUST ME, ARTOO... THIS ISN'T A RELAPSE.
EVEN THOUGH DAGOBAH ISN'T ON ANY NAVIGATIONAL CHARTS... I KNOW WHERE I'M GOING. I'LL GET US THERE SAFELY...
...IT ISN'T FAR.

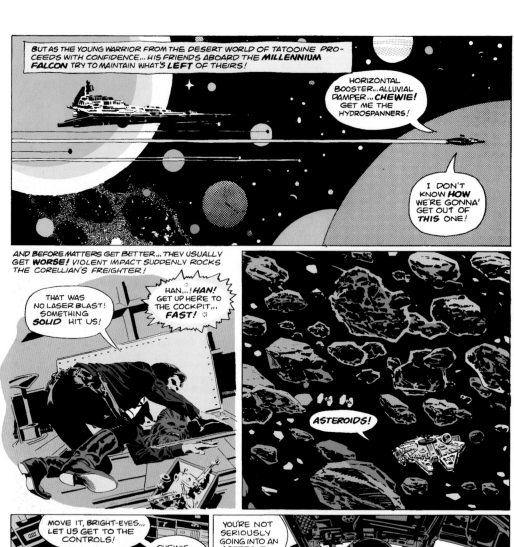

BUT AS THE YOUNG WARRIOR FROM THE DESERT WORLD OF TATOOINE *PROCEEDS* WITH CONFIDENCE... HIS FRIENDS ABOARD THE *MILLENNIUM FALCON* TRY TO MAINTAIN WHAT'S *LEFT* OF THEIRS!

HORIZONTAL BOOSTER... ALLUVIAL DAMPER... *CHEWIE!* GET ME THE HYDROSPANNERS!

I DON'T KNOW *HOW* WE'RE GONNA' GET OUT OF *THIS* ONE!

AND BEFORE MATTERS GET BETTER... THEY USUALLY GET *WORSE!* VIOLENT IMPACT SUDDENLY ROCKS THE CORELLIAN'S FREIGHTER!

THAT WAS NO LASER BLAST! SOMETHING *SOLID* HIT US!

HAN...! *HAN!* GET UP HERE TO THE COCKPIT... *FAST!*

ASTEROIDS!

MOVE IT, BRIGHT-EYES... LET US GET TO THE CONTROLS!

CHEWIE -- SET COURSE 2-7-1!

YOU'RE NOT SERIOUSLY GOING INTO AN ASTEROID FIELD?

IF I MIGHT REMIND YOU, CAPTAIN, THE PROBABILITY OF SUCCESSFULLY NAVIGATING SUCH AN OBSTACLE IS APPROXIMATELY 2,467 TO 1!

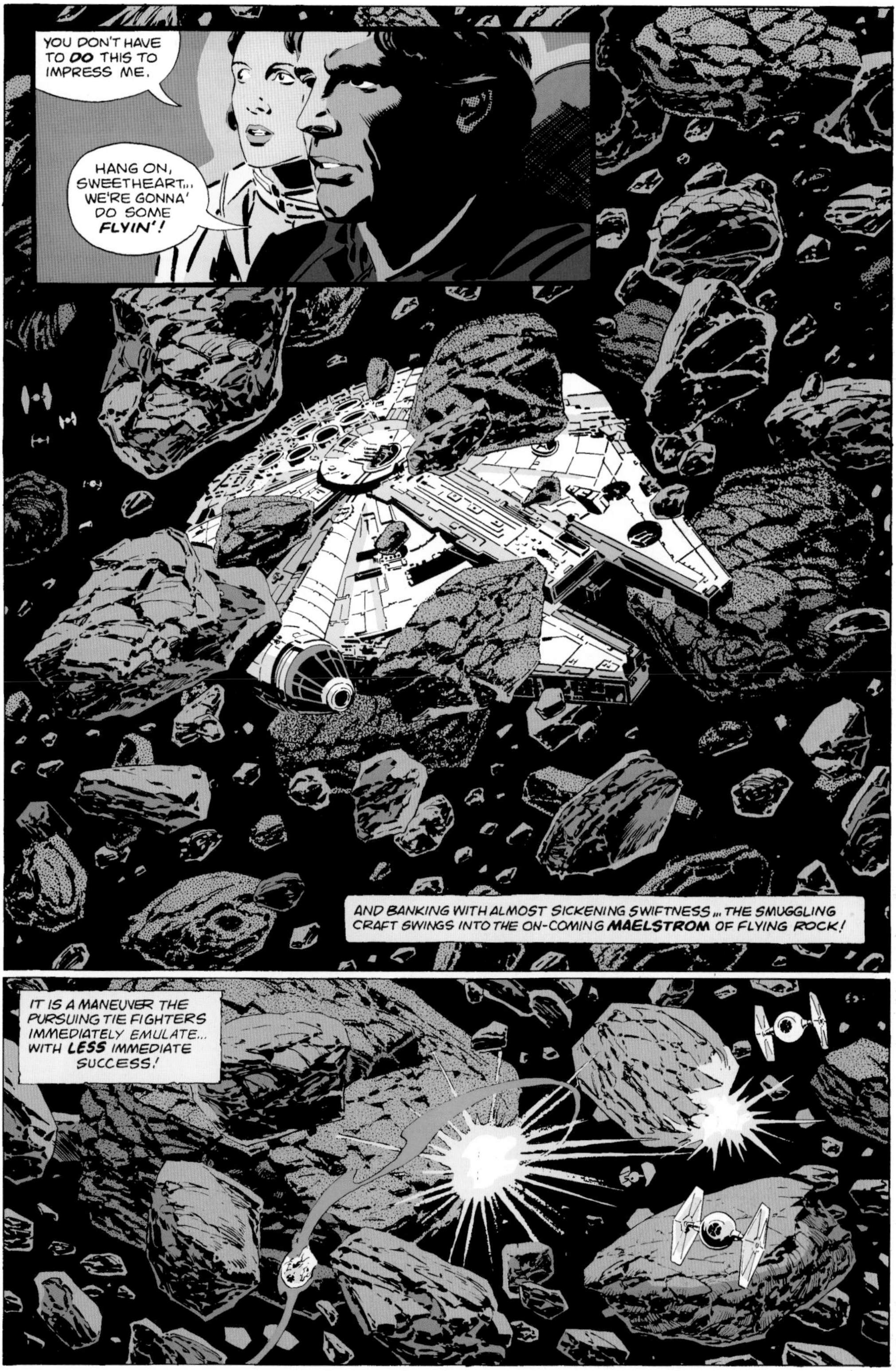
YOU DON'T HAVE TO **DO** THIS TO IMPRESS ME.
HANG ON, SWEETHEART... WE'RE GONNA' DO SOME **FLYIN'**!
AND BANKING WITH ALMOST SICKENING SWIFTNESS... THE SMUGGLING CRAFT SWINGS INTO THE ON-COMING **MAELSTROM** OF FLYING **ROCK**!
IT IS A MANEUVER THE PURSUING TIE FIGHTERS IMMEDIATELY EMULATE... WITH **LESS** IMMEDIATE SUCCESS!

MEANWHILE, NOT FAR AWAY, AT LEAST IN A GALAXY WHERE LIGHT-YEARS ARE SPANNED SIMPLY AS KILOMETERS...

COME *IN*, ADMIRAL ...

HESITANT, UNEASY, PIETT ENTERS THE PRIVATE CHAMBER. LIGHT DAZZLES HIS EYES; THE WHINE OF SERVO-LIFTS ECHOES IN HIS EARS. AND IN THE MEDITATION POD BEFORE HIM...

...HE HALF-GLIMPSES A *HELMET* BEING LOWERED ONTO THE HEAD OF THE SEATED FIGURE HE UNCERTAINLY APPROACHES.

AS THE GLEAMING BLACK MASK LOCKS IN PLACE, SWIVEL MOTORS SOUND, TURNING THE DARK FORM, BRINGING PIETT FACE-TO-FACE WITH *DARTH VADER*, LORD OF THE SITH.

OUR PURSUIT SHIPS HAVE SIGHTED THE *MILLENNIUM FALCON*, SIR... IT'S ENTERING AN *ASTEROID FIELD*.

ASTEROIDS DON'T CONCERN ME, ADMIRAL. I WANT THAT *SHIP*... NOT EXCUSES. HOW *LONG* BEFORE YOU HAVE SKYWALKER AND HIS FRIENDS BEFORE ME?

WHILE PIETT TRIES TO SUMMON HIS VOICE FROM A TIGHT, DRY THROAT, A *CAPE* IS MECHANICALLY LOWERED AND THE DARK LORD STANDS... EXPECTANTLY, IMPATIENTLY.

S-SOON, MY LORD...

YES, ADMIRAL... *SOON*.

BUT AT **THIS** MOMENT,... IT SEEMS A MORE PRESSING DOOM MAY OVERTAKE THE **MILLENNIUM FALCON** AND ITS PASSENGERS!

WELL, YOUR WORSHIP... YOU **SAID** YOU WANTED TO BE THERE WHEN I WAS WRONG.

I TAKE IT **BACK.**

THAT **STAR DESTROYER** IS SLOWING DOWN... BUT WE'RE GONNA GET **PULVERIZED** IF WE STAY HERE MUCH LONGER.

I'M AGAINST THAT.

WE'VE GOT TO GET **OUT** OF THIS SHOWER. I'M GOING CLOSER TO ONE OF THOSE **BIG ONES**...

CLOSER?

CLOSER!

NAROWRRR?!

IF HE HEARS THE OTHERS, HAN SOLO GIVES NO SIGN. HE MERELY SENDS THE **FALCON** PLUNGING THROUGH LESSER ASTEROIDS TOWARD A HUGELY LOOMING GIANT!

HIS ACTION DOESN'T **LOSE** THE CLOSELY PURSUING TIE FIGHTERS...

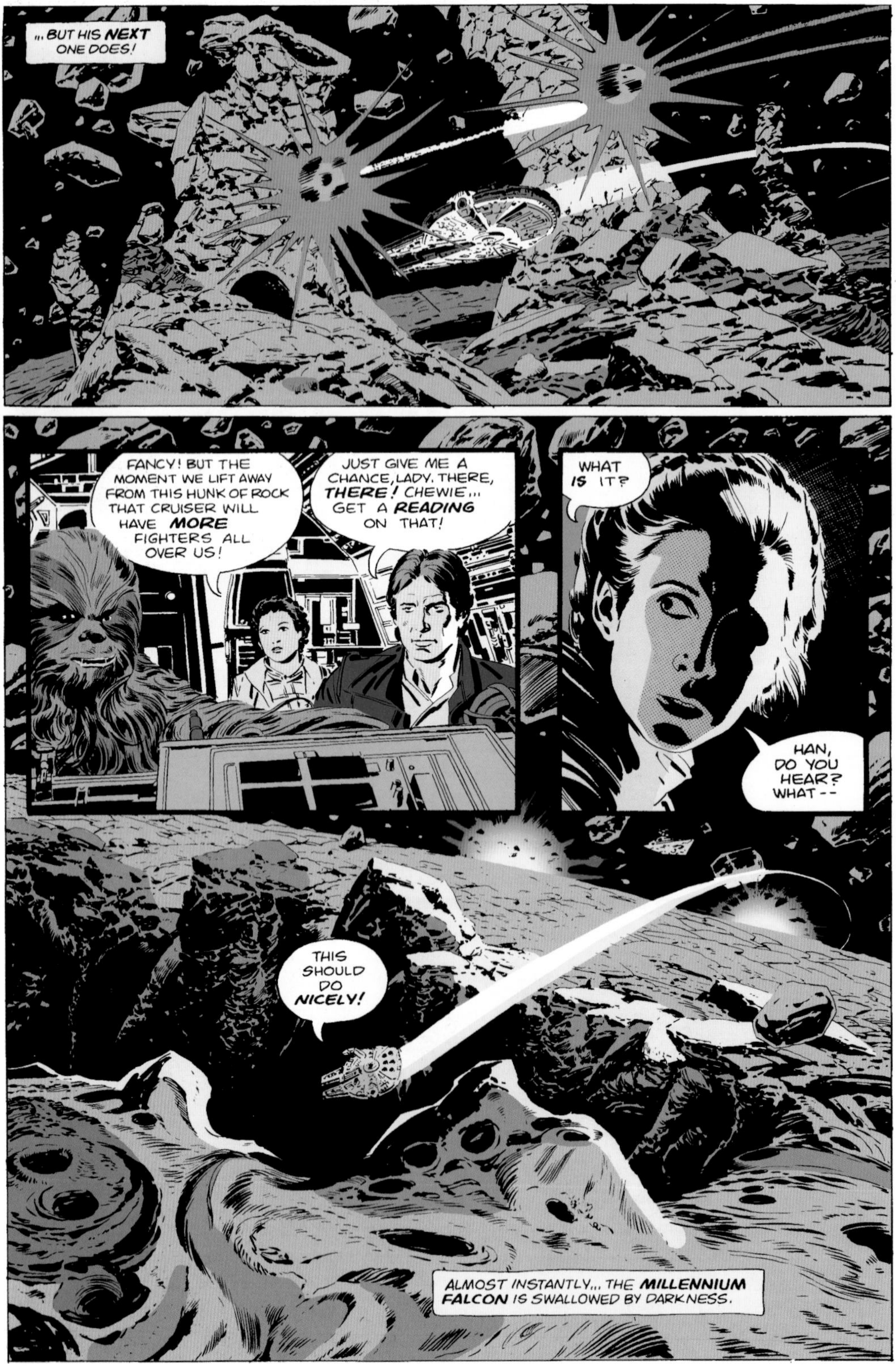
... BUT HIS NEXT ONE DOES!
FANCY! BUT THE MOMENT WE LIFT AWAY FROM THIS HUNK OF ROCK THAT CRUISER WILL HAVE MORE FIGHTERS ALL OVER US!
JUST GIVE ME A CHANCE, LADY. THERE, THERE! CHEWIE... GET A READING ON THAT!
WHAT IS IT?
HAN, DO YOU HEAR? WHAT--
THIS SHOULD DO NICELY!
ALMOST INSTANTLY... THE MILLENNIUM FALCON IS SWALLOWED BY DARKNESS.

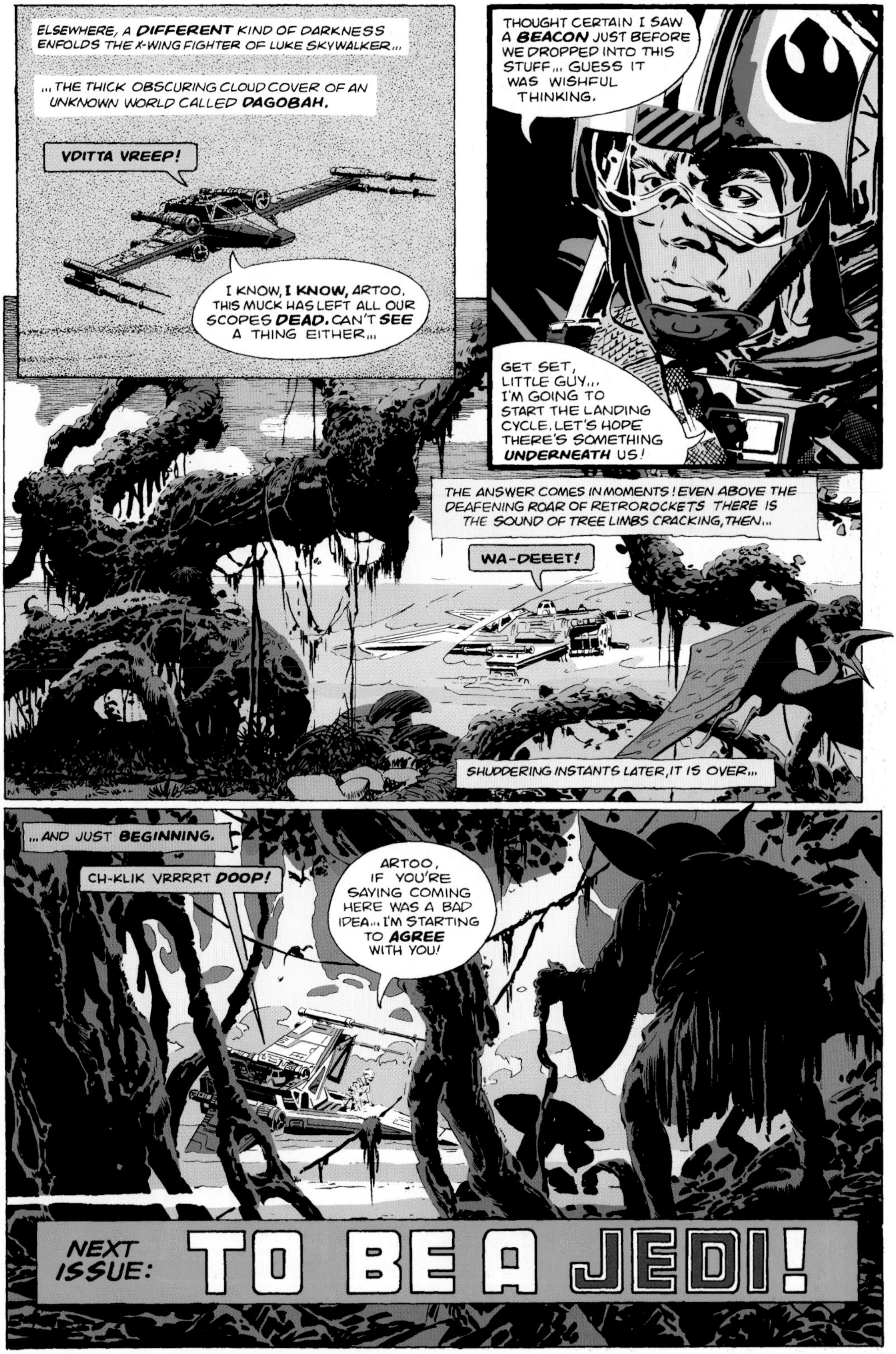

ELSEWHERE, A DIFFERENT KIND OF DARKNESS ENFOLDS THE X-WING FIGHTER OF LUKE SKYWALKER...
...THE THICK OBSCURING CLOUD COVER OF AN UNKNOWN WORLD CALLED DAGOBAH.
VDITTA VREEP!
I KNOW, I KNOW, ARTOO. THIS MUCK HAS LEFT ALL OUR SCOPES DEAD. CAN'T SEE A THING EITHER...
THOUGHT CERTAIN I SAW A BEACON JUST BEFORE WE DROPPED INTO THIS STUFF... GUESS IT WAS WISHFUL THINKING.
GET SET, LITTLE GUY... I'M GOING TO START THE LANDING CYCLE. LET'S HOPE THERE'S SOMETHING UNDERNEATH US!
THE ANSWER COMES IN MOMENTS! EVEN ABOVE THE DEAFENING ROAR OF RETROROCKETS THERE IS THE SOUND OF TREE LIMBS CRACKING, THEN...
WA-DEEET!
SHUDDERING INSTANTS LATER, IT IS OVER...
...AND JUST BEGINNING.
CH-KLIK VRRRRT DOOP!
ARTOO, IF YOU'RE SAYING COMING HERE WAS A BAD IDEA... I'M STARTING TO AGREE WITH YOU!
NEXT ISSUE: TO BE A JEDI!

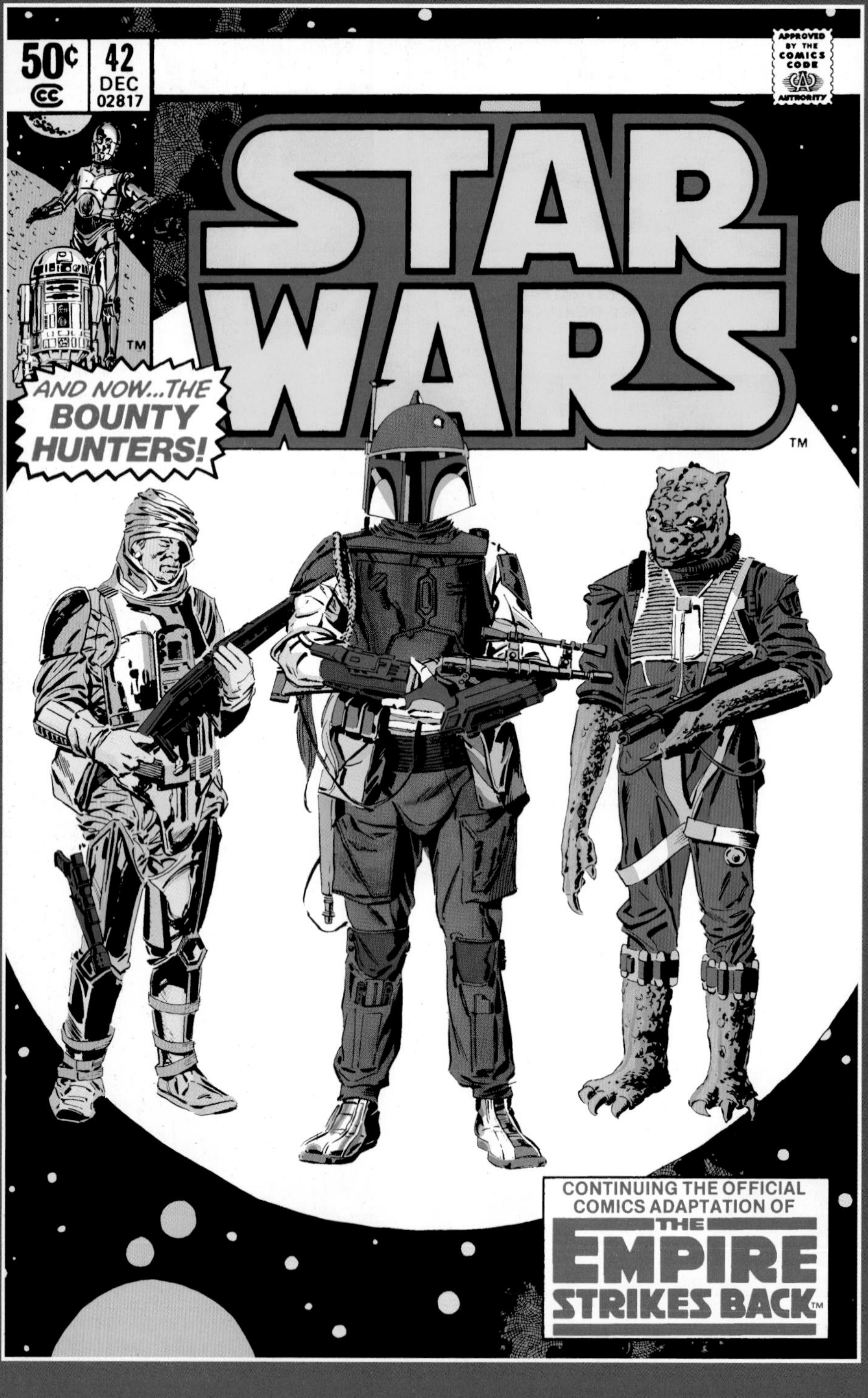
50¢
42
DEC
02817
APPROVED BY THE COMICS CODE AUTHORITY
STAR WARS
AND NOW...THE BOUNTY HUNTERS!
CONTINUING THE OFFICIAL COMICS ADAPTATION OF
THE EMPIRE STRIKES BACK

Long ago in a galaxy far, far away. . .there exists a state of cosmic *civil war*. A brave alliance of *underground freedom fighters* has challenged the tyranny and oppression of the awesome *Galactic Empire*. This is their story!

LucasFilm PRESENTS: STAR WARS

THE GREATEST SPACE FANTASY OF ALL!

ARCHIE GOODWIN WRITER/EDITOR ° **AL WILLIAMSON** AND **CARLOS GARZON** ARTISTS ° **GLYNIS WEIN** COLORIST ° **RICK VEITCH** LETTERER ° **JAMES SHOOTER** EDITOR-IN-CHIEF

STAR THE EMPIRE STRIKES BACK WARS™

FAILING TO CRUSH THE REBELS BY ATTACKING THEIR BASE ON THE ICE PLANET, HOTH, DARTH VADER'S FLEET HOTLY PURSUES THE *MILLENNIUM FALCON.* BUT AS THE SHADOW OF THE DARK LORD THREATENS TO ENGULF PRINCESS LEIA AND THE OTHERS ABOARD, *LUKE* IS UNAWARE... GUIDED BY THE FORCE ON A MISSION OF HIS OWN. NOW, STRANGE *NEW DANGERS* LOOM... BOTH FOR HIM AND HIS FRIENDS.

CHAPTER FOUR: TO BE A JEDI!

"YOU MUST GO TO THE *DAGOBAH SYSTEM*, LUKE. YOU WILL LEARN FROM *YODA*... THE ONE WHO TAUGHT ME." LUKE CAN ALMOST HEAR OBI-WAN KENOBI'S WORDS AGAIN... AS HE HEARD THEM THE FIRST TIME WANDERING WOUNDED AND DELIRIOUS ON BLIZZARD-SWEPT HOTH.

SOMEHOW, HAVING REACHED HIS GOAL... IT SEEMS *HARDER* TO BELIEVE.

GETTING OUT OF HERE WILL TAKE SOME *DOING*, ARTOO! THIS SEEMS LIKE A STRANGE PLACE TO FIND A *JEDI MASTER*.

ALTHOUGH... THERE'S SOMETHING *FAMILIAR* ABOUT IT. I FEEL LIKE--

YOU FEEL LIKE WHAT...?

LIKE... WE'RE BEING WATCHED!

WA-REEEET!

AWAY PUT YOUR WEAPON... I MEAN YOU NO HARM. BUT I AM WONDERING... WHY ARE YOU HERE? PERHAPS HELP YOU I CAN.

I... I DON'T THINK SO. YOU SEE, I'M LOOKING FOR A GREAT WARRIOR.

A GREAT WARRIOR...? NOT MANY OF THOSE. WARS DON'T MAKE ONE GREAT.

HEY! THAT FOOD CONCENTRATE STICK WAS GOING TO BE MY DINNER!

THE WIZENED LITTLE INTRUDER SEEMS UNIMPRESSED, PARTICULARLY WHEN HE STARTS TO CHEW AND PROMPTLY SPITS OUT THE BITE TAKEN.

≩PEEWH!≩ HOW YOU GET SO BIG EATING FOOD OF THIS KIND? COME, COME! I TAKE YOU TO GOOD FOOD... HELP YOU FIND YOUR FRIEND.

I'M NOT LOOKING FOR A FRIEND. I'M LOOKING FOR A JEDI MASTER.

OH, A JEDI MASTER, DIFFERENT ALTOGETHER. YODA, YOU SEEK YODA, I TAKE YOU TO HIM... COME.

YOU... KNOW HIM?

...UNTIL HE COMES UP WITH A POWER LAMP, AND OVER ARTOO'S ELECTRONIC PROTESTS, WALKS OFF WITH IT. LUKE HESITATES A MOMENT...THEN FOLLOWS.

SETTLE DOWN, ARTOO...WATCH OVER THE SHIP, I CAN TAKE CARE OF MYSELF... I'LL BE SAFE.

HEH... SAFE, QUITE SAFE... HEH, HEH, YES... OF COURSE.

FA-DITTA VOOP?!

THE GNOME-LIKE CREATURE MERELY RUMMAGES ON THROUGH THE SUPPLY PACK...

FAR AWAY FROM THE MISTS OF DAGOBAH WHICH ENVELOP LUKE, TWO IMPERIAL CRUISERS MOVE THROUGH THE ASTEROID FIELD TO WHICH THEY HAVE TRACKED THE *MILLENNIUM FALCON*...

...BOMBING AS THEY GO!

ONE TARGET: A PARTICULARLY LARGE *CRATER* ON A PARTICULARLY LARGE ASTEROID.

BUT THEIR CHARGES FALL *STRAIGHT* INTO THE CRATER'S NEARLY BOTTOMLESS DEPTHS... *MISSING* A CAVE IN ITS WALL.

OH, MY! THEY'VE *FOUND* US! ISN'T IT ENOUGH THAT THIS ASTEROID IS ALREADY *UNSTABLE*?!

RELAX, BRIGHT EYES! THOSE *TREMORS* WHEN WE LANDED WERE NOTHING, AND THE CRUISERS ARE MOVING *AWAY*...

THEY'RE JUST TRYING TO STIR SOMETHING UP. WE'RE *SAFE*.

WHERE HAVE I HEARD *THAT* BEFORE, MR. SOLO?

THANKS FOR THE VOTE OF CONFIDENCE, YOUR WORSHIP.

THREEPIO, HAS THIS FLYING SHORT CIRCUIT *TOLD* YOU ANYTHING?

WHERE'S ARTOO WHEN I NEED HIM? I DON'T KNOW *WHERE* YOUR SHIP LEARNED TO COMMUNICATE, CAPTAIN... BUT ITS *DIALECT* LEAVES SOMETHING TO BE DESIRED.

I BELIEVE, SIR, IT'S SAYING THAT THE *POWER COUPLING* ON THE NEGATIVE AXIS HAS BEEN *POLARIZED*.

I'M AFRAID YOU'LL HAVE TO *REPLACE* IT.

OF COURSE I'LL HAVE TO REPLACE IT.

CHEWIE...

REPLACE IT!

BUT EVENTUALLY, EVERYONE IS ENLISTED INTO THE REPAIR WORK... *ROYALTY* INCLUDED. AND THE WORK SEEMS TO ABSORB HER... ESPECIALLY WHENEVER *HAN* TRIES TO APPROACH,

EASY, YOUR WORSHIP, I WAS JUST GOING TO OFFER SOME HELP,

WOULD YOU PLEASE STOP *CALLING* ME THAT--?

--YOU MAKE IT SO DIFFICULT SOMETIMES, HAN.

I DO... I REALLY DO, YOU COULD BE A LITTLE *NICER,* THOUGH... COME ON! ADMIT IT... SOMETIMES YOU THINK I'M *ALL RIGHT.*

SOMETIMES, MAYBE... WHEN YOU AREN'T ACTING LIKE A SCOUNDREL,

SCOUNDREL. I LIKE THE SOUND OF THAT, AND I THINK YOU LIKE ME *BECAUSE* I'M A SCOUNDREL, I BET YOU HAVEN'T HAD *ENOUGH* SCOUNDRELS IN YOUR LIFE...

AND AS THIS PARTICULAR SCOUNDREL MOVES *CLOSER*... PRINCESS LEIA ORGANA FINDS IT DIFFICULT TO *ARGUE* THE POINT.

AND SWIFTLY... THE *TIME* FOR ARGUING IS LONG PAST,

THEN, SHE BREAKS NERVOUSLY AWAY, PERHAPS *FRIGHTENED* BY WHAT SHE FEELS...

OR PERHAPS BY HOW MUCH SHE WISHES THE FEELING WOULD *CONTINUE.*

MEANWHILE, BEYOND THE *MILLENNIUM FALCON'S* REFUGE, DARTH VADER RESOLUTELY REFUSES TO ABANDON THE HUNT ...DESPITE THE *TOLL* TAKEN ON HIS FLEET BY THE ASTEROID FIELD!

MY LORD...! I-IT'S ... THE *EMPEROR!* HE COMMANDS YOU TO MAKE CONTACT WITH HIM.

MOVE OUT TO A POSITION WHERE WE CAN SEND A CLEAR TRANSMISSION--

--AND CODE THE SIGNAL TO MY PRIVATE CHAMBER.

AND SHORTLY, *WITHIN* THAT CHAMBER...

WHAT IS THY *BIDDING*, MY MASTER?

THERE IS A GRAVE DISTURBANCE IN THE *FORCE!* WE HAVE A NEW ENEMY WHO COULD BRING ABOUT OUR *DESTRUCTION*--

--THE *SON OF SKY-WALKER!* YOU MUST DESTROY *HIM*, MY SERVANT... OR HE WILL BE OUR UNDOING.

HE'S NOT A JEDI... JUST A BOY. OBI-WAN COULD NOT HAVE TAUGHT HIM VERY MUCH.

YET WITH THE FORCE SO STRONG WITHIN HIM... HE COULD BE A POWERFUL *ALLY*. IF HE COULD BE *TURNED*...

FOR A LONG MOMENT THE HUGE HOLOGRAPH IMAGE FLICKERS SILENTLY, THEN...

YES... *YES*. HE WOULD BE A GREAT ASSET. CAN IT BE DONE?

HE WILL *JOIN* US, MY MASTER--

--OR *DIE!*

298

ON MIST-SHROUDED DAGOBAH, THE *OBJECT* OF THE EMPEROR'S CONCERN AND INTEREST CONTINUES HIS OWN *SEARCH*. A SEARCH THAT NOW BRINGS HIM TO A *CLEARING* IN THE GNARLED SWAMP TREES... AND A SMALL HOUSE OF MUD.

...LOOK, I'M SURE YOUR FOOD'S DELICIOUS, BUT CAN'T WE GO ON TO *YODA* FIRST? HOW FAR AWAY *IS* HE?

NOT FAR, NOT FAR, PATIENCE. IT IS THE *JEDI'S* TIME TO EAT, TOO, SOON YOU WILL SEE HIM.

BUT WHY WISH YOU TO *BECOME* A JEDI?

BECAUSE OF MY FATHER, I GUESS.

OH, YOUR *FATHER*... A POWERFUL JEDI WAS HE, *POWERFUL* JEDI.

HOW COULD *YOU* KNOW MY FATHER? YOU DON'T EVEN KNOW WHO *I* AM. AND I... I DON'T EVEN KNOW WHAT I'M *DOING* HERE!

NO *GOOD* THIS! THIS WILL NOT DO, I CANNOT *TEACH* HIM. THE BOY HAS NO *PATIENCE!*

A *CHILL* GOES THROUGH LUKE SKYWALKER AS HIS WIZENED LITTLE GUIDE SPEAKS SEEMINGLY TO HIMSELF... AND IS *ANSWERED* BY THE VOICE OF *BEN KENOBI!*

HE WILL *LEARN* PATIENCE. WE'VE DISCUSSED THIS BEFORE.

SO MUCH *ANGER* IN HIM ...JUST LIKE HIS FATHER.

Y-YOU'RE... *YODA!* WHY DIDN'T YOU *TELL* ME? I'M READY... I CAN *BE* A JEDI! RIGHT, BEN...? *BEN...?*

READY ARE YOU? WHAT KNOW YOU OF *READY?* I HAVE TRAINED JEDI FOR *800 YEARS*... MY OWN COUNSEL I'LL KEEP ON *WHO* IS TO BE TRAINED.

TO BECOME A JEDI TAKES THE **DEEPEST COMMITMENT.** ALL HIS LIFE, THIS ONE HAS LOOKED AWAY... TO THE HORIZON, TO THE SKY, TO THE FUTURE. NEVER HIS MIND ON WHERE HE WAS... WHAT HE WAS DOING.

ADVENTURE... EXCITEMENT... A **JEDI** CRAVES NOT THESE THINGS!

HE WILL LEARN, YODA. WE HAVE COME THIS FAR... HE IS OUR ONLY HOPE.

I KNOW I'M RECKLESS... BUT I'VE LEARNED A LOT ALREADY. I WON'T FAIL YOU... I'M NOT AFRAID.

YOU WILL BE, MY YOUNG ONE. HEH... YOU **WILL** BE.

FOG ENCLOSES THE MUD HOUSE ON DAGOBAH...

...MUCH AS NEW **MENACE** SURROUNDS HAN SOLO'S SHIP HIDDEN DEEP WITHIN THE ASTEROID CAVERN.

SOMETHING WAS **DEFINITELY** CRAWLING AROUND ON THE HULL... BUT MAYBE WE'RE CRAZY TO COME **OUT** HERE TO SEE ABOUT IT!

WE'VE JUST GOT THIS BUCKET READY TO **ROLL** AGAIN... I'M NOT LETTING SOME **VARMINT** TEAR IT APART!

THERE!

LOOKS LIKE SOME KIND OF **MYNOCK.**

GREAT. THERE'LL BE **MORE** OF THEM... THEY ALWAYS TRAVEL IN GROUPS. AND THERE'S NOTHING THEY LIKE BETTER THAN TO ATTACH THEMSELVES TO **SHIPS.** JUST WHAT WE **NEED!**

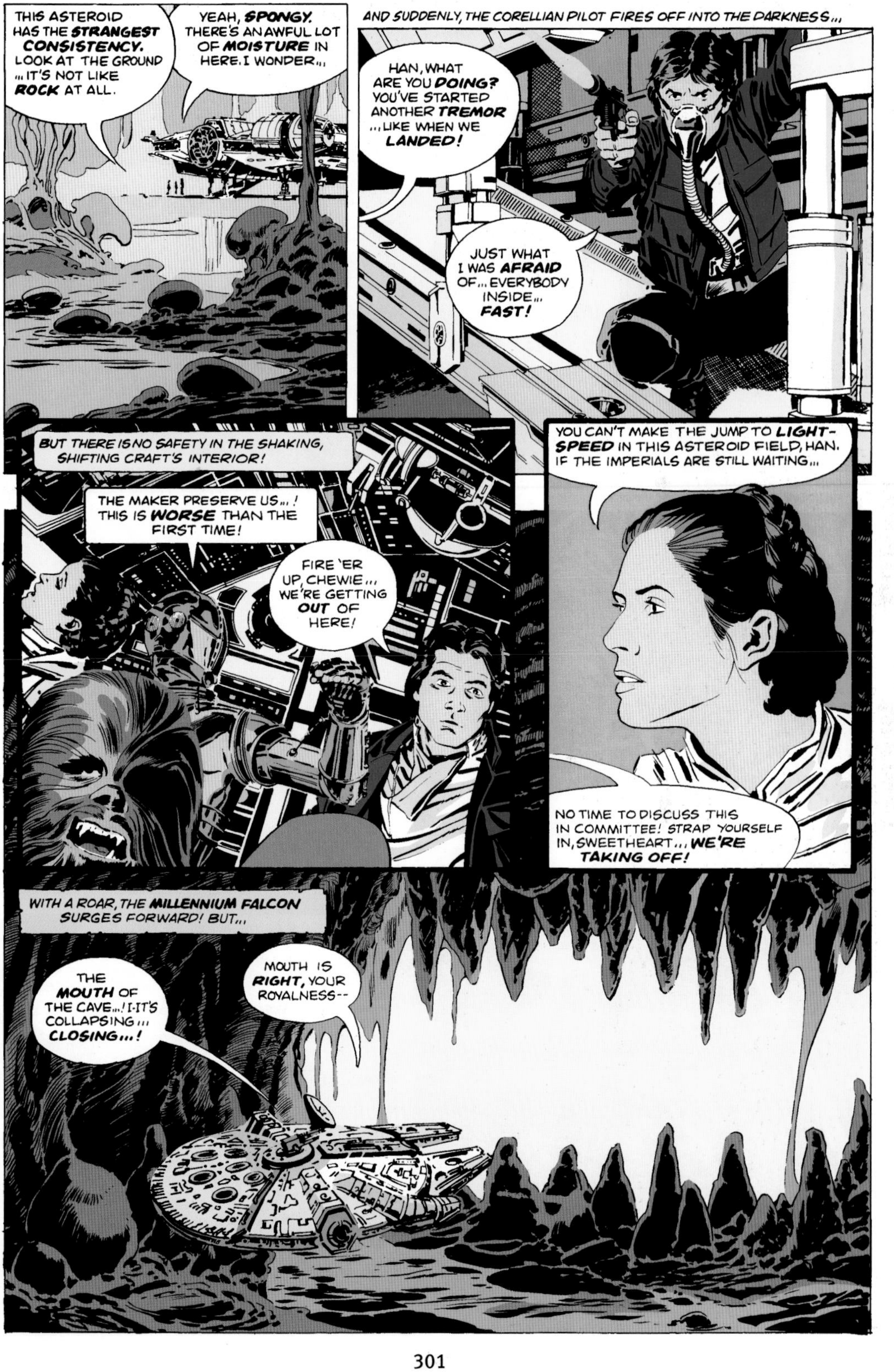
THIS ASTEROID HAS THE STRANGEST CONSISTENCY. LOOK AT THE GROUND ...IT'S NOT LIKE ROCK AT ALL.
YEAH, SPONGY. THERE'S AN AWFUL LOT OF MOISTURE IN HERE. I WONDER...
AND SUDDENLY, THE CORELLIAN PILOT FIRES OFF INTO THE DARKNESS...
HAN, WHAT ARE YOU DOING? YOU'VE STARTED ANOTHER TREMOR ...LIKE WHEN WE LANDED!
JUST WHAT I WAS AFRAID OF... EVERYBODY INSIDE... FAST!
BUT THERE IS NO SAFETY IN THE SHAKING, SHIFTING CRAFT'S INTERIOR!
THE MAKER PRESERVE US...! THIS IS WORSE THAN THE FIRST TIME!
FIRE 'ER UP, CHEWIE... WE'RE GETTING OUT OF HERE!
YOU CAN'T MAKE THE JUMP TO LIGHT-SPEED IN THIS ASTEROID FIELD, HAN. IF THE IMPERIALS ARE STILL WAITING...
NO TIME TO DISCUSS THIS IN COMMITTEE! STRAP YOURSELF IN, SWEETHEART... WE'RE TAKING OFF!
WITH A ROAR, THE MILLENNIUM FALCON SURGES FORWARD! BUT...
THE MOUTH OF THE CAVE...! I-IT'S COLLAPSING... CLOSING...!
MOUTH IS RIGHT, YOUR ROYALNESS--

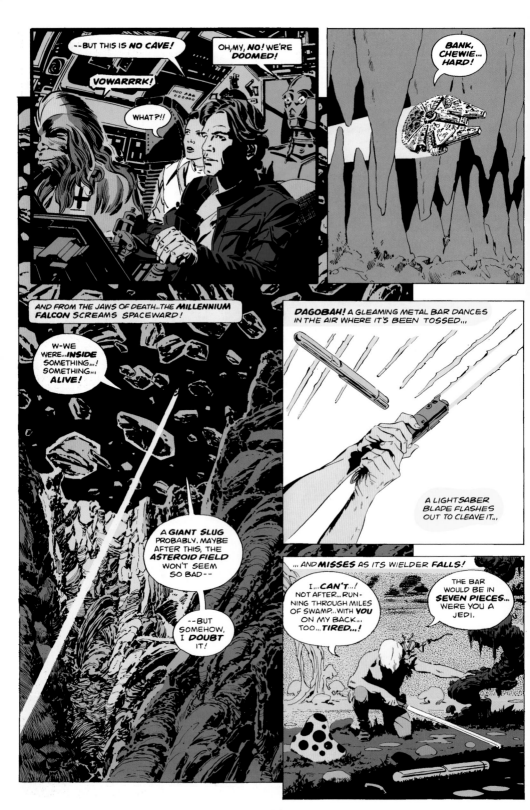

--BUT THIS IS *NO CAVE!*

OH, MY, *NO!* WE'RE *DOOMED!*

VOWARRRK!

WHAT?!!

BANK, CHEWIE... *HARD!*

AND FROM THE JAWS OF DEATH...THE *MILLENNIUM FALCON* SCREAMS SPACEWARD!

W-WE WERE...*INSIDE* SOMETHING...! SOMETHING... *ALIVE!*

A *GIANT SLUG* PROBABLY. MAYBE AFTER THIS, THE *ASTEROID FIELD* WON'T SEEM SO BAD--

--BUT SOMEHOW, I *DOUBT* IT!

DAGOBAH! A GLEAMING METAL BAR DANCES IN THE AIR WHERE IT'S BEEN TOSSED...

A LIGHTSABER BLADE FLASHES OUT TO CLEAVE IT...

... AND *MISSES* AS ITS WIELDER *FALLS!*

I...*CAN'T*...! NOT AFTER... RUNNING THROUGH MILES OF SWAMP...WITH *YOU* ON MY BACK... TOO...*TIRED*...!

THE BAR WOULD BE IN *SEVEN PIECES*... WERE YOU A *JEDI.*

302

I... I THOUGHT... I WAS IN... GOOD SHAPE...!

YES, BUT BY WHAT *STANDARD* ASK I? FORGET YOUR OLD MEASURES--

--UNLEARN. HEH. *UNLEARN!*

AND AS TIME PASSES, LUKE DOES THAT AND MORE. *MUCH MORE.* PUSHED BY THE UNYIELDING LITTLE JEDI MASTER TO CONCENTRATE, TO OPEN HIMSELF TO THE *FORCE...* THE YOUNG MAN FROM TATOOINE BEGINS TO *GROW* IN WAYS HE NEVER DREAMED POSSIBLE,

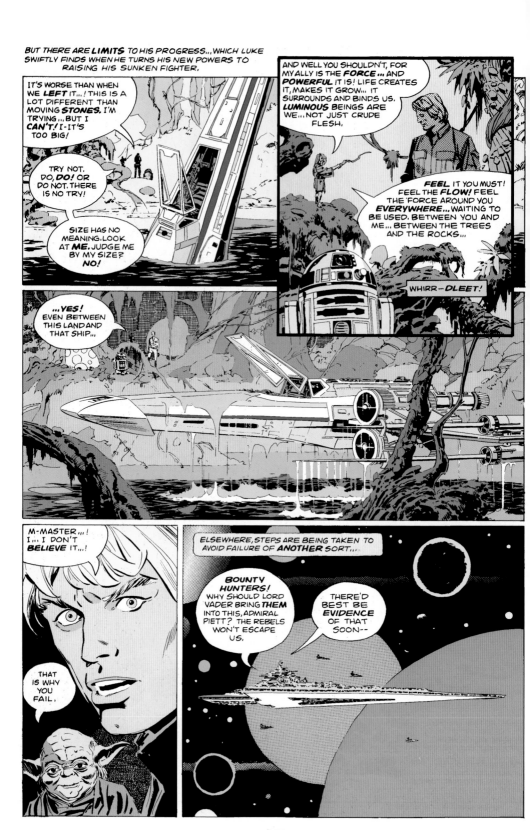

BUT THERE ARE **LIMITS** TO HIS PROGRESS...,WHICH LUKE SWIFTLY FINDS WHEN HE TURNS HIS NEW POWERS TO RAISING HIS SUNKEN FIGHTER.

IT'S WORSE THAN WHEN WE **LEFT** IT...! THIS IS A LOT DIFFERENT THAN MOVING **STONES.** I'M TRYING..., BUT I **CAN'T!** I-IT'S TOO BIG!

TRY NOT, DO, **DO!** OR DO NOT. THERE IS NO TRY!

SIZE HAS NO MEANING. LOOK AT **ME.** JUDGE ME BY MY SIZE? **NO!**

AND WELL YOU SHOULDN'T, FOR MY ALLY IS THE **FORCE**... AND **POWERFUL** IT IS! LIFE CREATES IT, MAKES IT GROW... IT SURROUNDS AND BINDS US. **LUMINOUS** BEINGS ARE WE..., NOT JUST CRUDE FLESH.

FEEL IT YOU MUST! FEEL THE **FLOW!** FEEL THE 'FORCE AROUND YOU **EVERYWHERE**... WAITING TO BE USED. BETWEEN YOU AND ME..., BETWEEN THE TREES AND THE ROCKS...

WHIRR—**DLEET!**

...**YES!** EVEN BETWEEN THIS LAND AND THAT SHIP...

M-MASTER...! I... I DON'T **BELIEVE** IT...!

THAT IS WHY YOU **FAIL.**

ELSEWHERE, STEPS ARE BEING TAKEN TO AVOID FAILURE OF **ANOTHER** SORT...

BOUNTY HUNTERS! WHY SHOULD LORD VADER BRING **THEM** INTO THIS, ADMIRAL PIETT? THE REBELS WON'T ESCAPE US.

THERE'D BEST BE **EVIDENCE** OF THAT SOON--

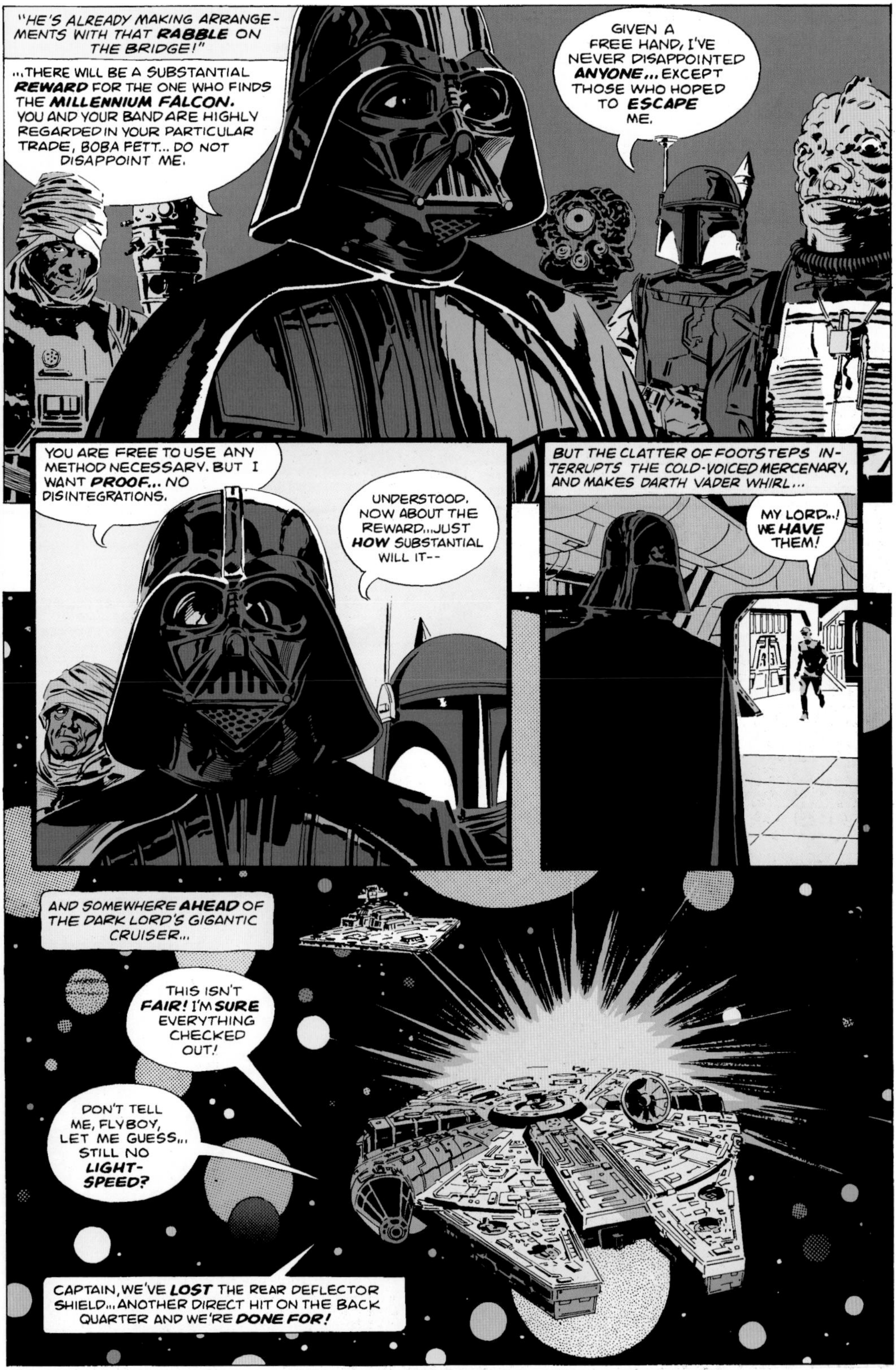
"HE'S ALREADY MAKING ARRANGEMENTS WITH THAT RABBLE ON THE BRIDGE!"
...THERE WILL BE A SUBSTANTIAL REWARD FOR THE ONE WHO FINDS THE MILLENNIUM FALCON. YOU AND YOUR BAND ARE HIGHLY REGARDED IN YOUR PARTICULAR TRADE, BOBA FETT... DO NOT DISAPPOINT ME.
GIVEN A FREE HAND, I'VE NEVER DISAPPOINTED ANYONE... EXCEPT THOSE WHO HOPED TO ESCAPE ME.
YOU ARE FREE TO USE ANY METHOD NECESSARY. BUT I WANT PROOF... NO DISINTEGRATIONS.
UNDERSTOOD. NOW ABOUT THE REWARD...JUST HOW SUBSTANTIAL WILL IT--
BUT THE CLATTER OF FOOTSTEPS INTERRUPTS THE COLD-VOICED MERCENARY, AND MAKES DARTH VADER WHIRL...
MY LORD..! WE HAVE THEM!
AND SOMEWHERE AHEAD OF THE DARK LORD'S GIGANTIC CRUISER...
THIS ISN'T FAIR! I'M SURE EVERYTHING CHECKED OUT!
DON'T TELL ME, FLYBOY, LET ME GUESS... STILL NO LIGHT-SPEED?
CAPTAIN, WE'VE LOST THE REAR DEFLECTOR SHIELD... ANOTHER DIRECT HIT ON THE BACK QUARTER AND WE'RE DONE FOR!

FOR AN INSTANT THE CORELLIAN PILOT IS SILENT, THOUGHTFUL. THEN...

ALL RIGHT, CHEWIE! SWING THIS BUCKET **AROUND** ... FULL POWER ON THE **FRONT SHIELD!**

YOU'RE NOT GOING TO **ATTACK** THEM?!

SIR, IF I MIGHT POINT OUT, THE ODDS OF **SURVIVING** A DIRECT ASSAULT ON AN IMPERIAL STAR DESTROYER ARE--

A CURT **GROWL** FROM THE SHIP'S WOOKIEE FIRST MATE INDUCES SEE-THREEPIO TO KEEP HIS **ODDS** TO HIMSELF...

...AS THE TINY FREIGHTER SCREAMS LOW ACROSS THE IMPERIAL WARSHIP'S HULL WITH SEEMINGLY **SUICIDAL** INTENT!

WE'RE GOING TO **COLLIDE!**

SHIELDS UP... HE'S **INSANE!**

LOOK OUT!

THEN SUDDENLY...

CAPTAIN...! I-IT'S **GONE!** DOESN'T APPEAR ON ANY OF OUR TRACKING SCOPES. PERHAPS THEY WENT INTO **LIGHT-SPEED** AT THE LAST INSTANT...

THEN WHY DID THEY **ATTACK?** THEY COULD HAVE GONE INTO HYPERSPACE AS SOON AS THEY CLEARED THE **ASTEROID FIELD!** THERE'S GOT TO BE A MORE **LOGICAL** EXPLANATION, BUT--

SIR, LORD VADER DEMANDS AN **UPDATE** ON OUR PURSUIT, SIR...? SIR...?

WITH THE RESIGNED AIR OF A MAN TOTALLY WITHOUT HOPE... THE CRUISER COMMANDER MOVES TO REPORT HIS FAILURE.

306

WHILE ON THE PLANET DAGOBAH... THERE IS SOME SUCCESS.

FOUR! WHERE ONCE YOU MISSED ENTIRELY! MUCH PROGRESS DO YOU MAKE, YOUNG ONE... STRONGER DO YOU GROW!

BUT IT'S TAKING SO **LONG!** A **JEDI** COULD DO SEVEN! LET ME TRY AGAIN! THIS TIME I'M **ANGRY** ENOUGH TO--

NO! **NO!** ANGER, FEAR, AGGRESSION... THE **DARK SIDE** OF THE FORCE ARE THEY! EASILY DO **THEY** FLOW... QUICK TO JOIN YOU IN A FIGHT. **BEWARE**...A HEAVY PRICE IS PAID FOR THE POWER THEY BRING.

EASIER, QUICKER, MORE SEDUCTIVE IS THE DARK SIDE... BUT ONCE YOU START DOWN THAT PATH, **FOREVER** WILL IT DOMINATE! **CONSUME** YOU IT WILL! AS IT DID OBI-WAN'S APPRENTICE...

LUKE LISTENS TO YODA AND TRIES TO GROW CALM. YET IT'S SO HARD NOT TO BE IMPATIENT, SO HARD...

AND THERE WOULD BE SMALL COMFORT IN KNOWING THAT HIS **ENEMY** EXPERIENCES SIMILAR FRUSTRATIONS AS HIS FLEET RENDEZVOUS.

LORD VADER, OUR COMPLETE SCAN HAS FOUND **NOTHING.** THE **MILLENNIUM FALCON** MUST HAVE GONE INTO LIGHT-SPEED.

IT'S NO DOUBT ON THE OTHER SIDE OF THE GALAXY BY NOW.

ALERT ALL COMMANDS...CALCULATE EVERY POSSIBLE DESTINATION ALONG THEIR LAST-KNOWN TRAJECTORY! DISBURSE THE FLEET TO **SEARCH** FOR THEM! DON'T FAIL ME AGAIN... I'VE HAD **QUITE** ENOUGH.

ADMIRAL PIETT AND HIS OTHER OFFICERS HASTEN TO OBEY...

... SO THAT WITHIN RECORD TIME EACH OF THE GATHERED VESSELS IS GOING ITS SEPARATE WAY, INCLUDING ONE STAR DESTROYER THAT UNKNOWINGLY CARRIES **ADDED CARGO.**

YOU KNOW, HOTSHOT, ASIDE FROM IMPRESSING ME WITH HOW **FAST** YOU MANAGED TO BRAKE AND SHUT DOWN THIS FLYING DISASTER... I'M NOT SURE WHAT YOU'VE **ACCOMPLISHED.**

WATCH AND **LEARN,** SWEET-HEART. IT'S STANDARD IMPERIAL PROCEDURE TO DUMP THEIR **GARBAGE** BEFORE GOING INTO LIGHT-SPEED...

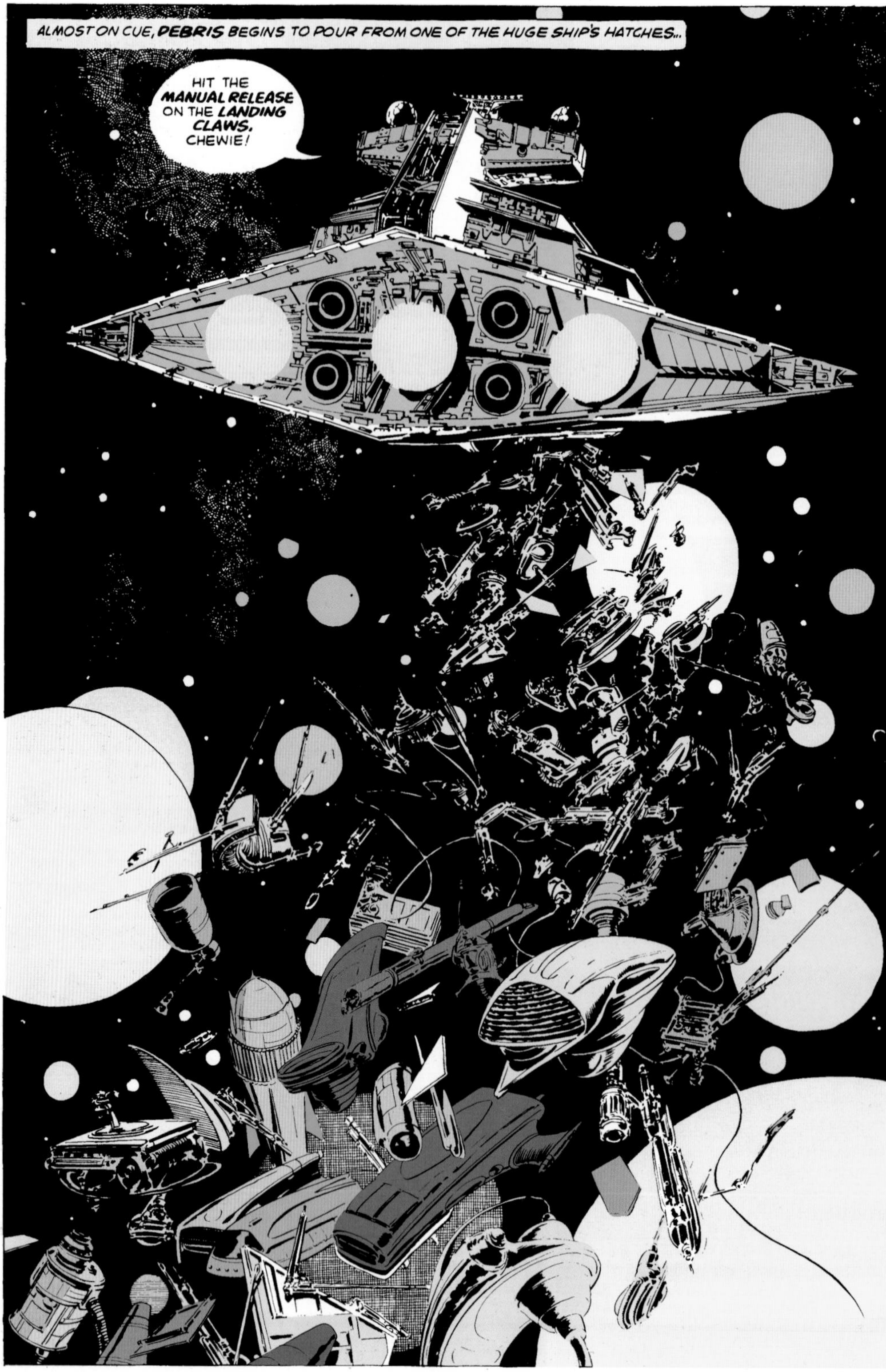
ALMOST ON CUE, DEBRIS BEGINS TO POUR FROM ONE OF THE HUGE SHIP'S HATCHES...
HIT THE MANUAL RELEASE ON THE LANDING CLAWS, CHEWIE!

AND WHEN THE STREAM OF SPENT GENERATORS, UNSALVAGEABLE PARTS, AND OTHER ACCUMULATED JUNK IS JETTISONED,...THE **MILLENNIUM FALCON** ARTFULLY DRIFTS AWAY WITH IT!

NOT **BAD**, FLYBOY! YOU **DO** HAVE YOUR MOMENTS,.. NOT **MANY**, BUT YOU **DO** HAVE THEM.

NOW WHAT?

LEMME CHECK THE COMPUTER LOG... **AHA!** THE BESPIN SYSTEM. IT'S A FAIR DISTANCE,,. BUT MANAGEABLE. I **KNOW** A FELLA THERE,,,

CAN YOU **TRUST** HIM, HAN?

LANDO CALRISSIAN. GAMBLER, CON ARTIST, ALL-AROUND SCOUNDREL ,,, **YOUR** KIND OF GUY, PRINCESS.

OF **COURSE** NOT. BUT LANDO AND I GO WAY BACK,,. BELIEVE ME, HE HAS NO LOVE FOR THE **EMPIRE.**

YET AS THE **MILLENNIUM FALCON** MOVES TOWARD SAFETY, THE SAME FLOATING DEBRIS WHICH MASKS IT FROM THE DEPARTING IMPERIALS HIDES A **SECOND SHIP** FROM VIEW, A SHIP WHICH FOLLOWS THE **FALCON.**

IT IS CALLED THE **SLAVE 1.** IT IS OWNED BY THE BOUNTY HUNTER NAMED **BOBA FETT.**

NEXT ISSUE **BETRAYAL AT BESPIN!**

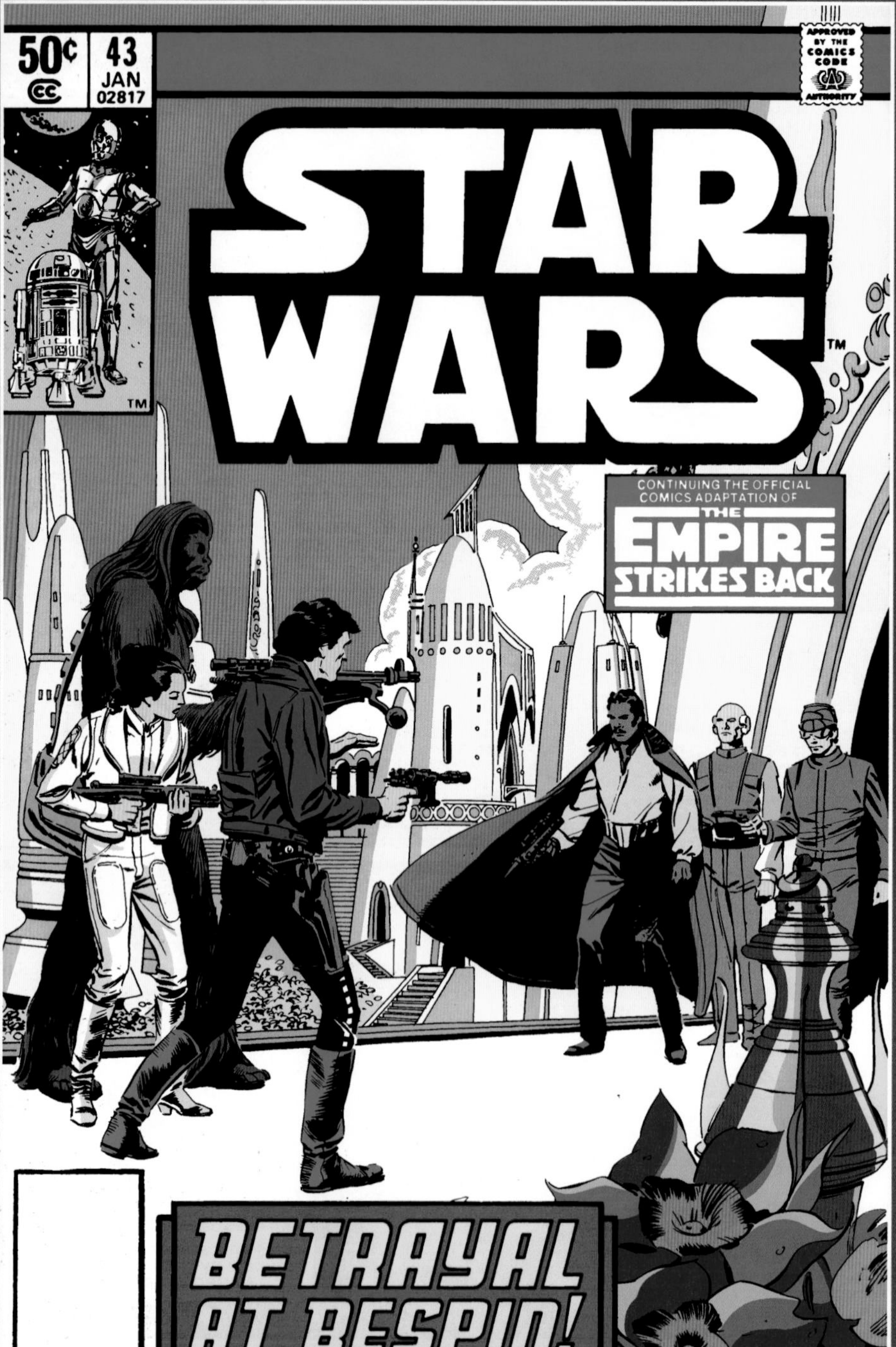

50¢
43
JAN
02817
APPROVED BY THE COMICS CODE AUTHORITY
STAR WARS™
CONTINUING THE OFFICIAL COMICS ADAPTATION OF
THE EMPIRE STRIKES BACK
BETRAYAL AT BESPIN!

LucasFilm PRESENTS: **STAR WARS**™ *THE GREATEST* **SPACE FANTASY** *OF ALL!*

ARCHIE GOODWIN WRITER/EDITOR	**AL WILLIAMSON** AND **CARLOS GARZON** ARTISTS	**GLYNIS WEIN** COLORIST	**RICK VEITCH** LETTERER	**JAMES SHOOTER** EDITOR-IN-CHIEF

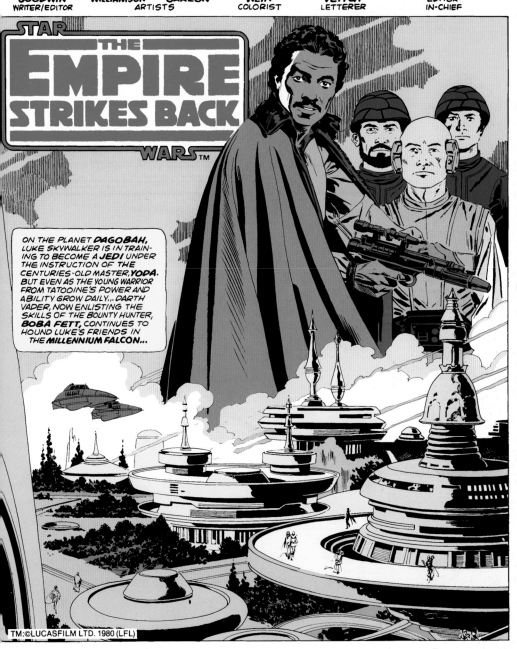

STAR THE **EMPIRE STRIKES BACK** WARS™

ON THE PLANET *DAGOBAH,* LUKE SKYWALKER IS IN TRAINING TO BECOME A *JEDI* UNDER THE INSTRUCTION OF THE CENTURIES-OLD MASTER, *YODA.* BUT EVEN AS THE YOUNG WARRIOR FROM TATOOINE'S POWER AND ABILITY GROW DAILY... *DARTH VADER,* NOW ENLISTING THE SKILLS OF THE BOUNTY HUNTER, *BOBA FETT,* CONTINUES TO HOUND LUKE'S FRIENDS IN THE *MILLENNIUM FALCON*...

CHAPTER FIVE: BETRAYAL AT BESPIN

CLOUDS, SHOT WITH PINK REFLECTED FROM THE GASEOUS SURFACE OF THE PLANET BESPIN MILES BELOW, *PART*... AND FOR THE FIRST TIME THE FUGITIVES ABOARD THE CORELLIAN SMUGGLING SHIP BEHOLD THE SANCTUARY THEY'VE BEEN DESPERATELY SEEKING.

CLOUD CITY, YOUR ROYALNESS...! IT'S A TIBANNA GAS MINE. LANDO WON IT IN A SABACC MATCH... OR SO HE CLAIMS. LANDO AND I GO--

-- *WAY BACK,* SO YOU KEEP SAYING, HAN, NO DOUBT THAT'S A *WELCOMING COMMITTEE* FROM HIM I SEE FLYING OUR WAY.

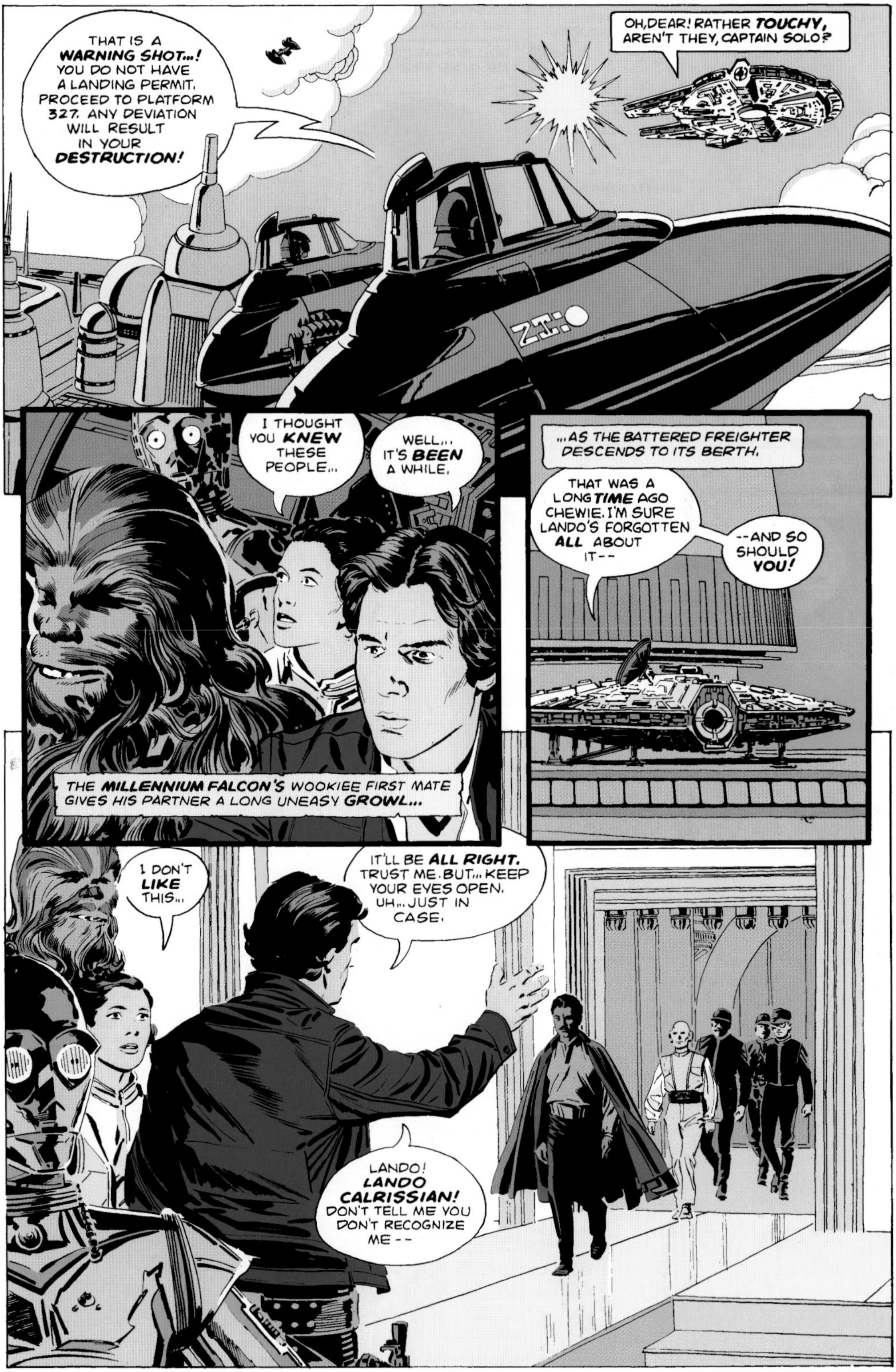
THAT IS A WARNING SHOT...! YOU DO NOT HAVE A LANDING PERMIT. PROCEED TO PLATFORM 327. ANY DEVIATION WILL RESULT IN YOUR DESTRUCTION!
OH, DEAR! RATHER TOUCHY, AREN'T THEY, CAPTAIN SOLO?
I THOUGHT YOU KNEW THESE PEOPLE...
WELL... IT'S BEEN A WHILE.
THE MILLENNIUM FALCON'S WOOKIEE FIRST MATE GIVES HIS PARTNER A LONG UNEASY GROWL...
...AS THE BATTERED FREIGHTER DESCENDS TO ITS BERTH.
THAT WAS A LONG TIME AGO CHEWIE. I'M SURE LANDO'S FORGOTTEN ALL ABOUT IT--
--AND SO SHOULD YOU!
I DON'T LIKE THIS...
IT'LL BE ALL RIGHT. TRUST ME. BUT... KEEP YOUR EYES OPEN. UH... JUST IN CASE.
LANDO! LANDO CALRISSIAN! DON'T TELL ME YOU DON'T RECOGNIZE ME --

HAN SOLO! YOU SLIMY, DOUBLE-CROSSING, NO-GOOD SWINDLER--

I CAN EXPLAIN **EVERYTHING**, BUDDY. NO NEED FOR HARD FEELINGS ABOUT THE PAST, I ALWAYS SAID YOU WERE A **GENTLEMAN--**

I'LL **BET!**

SUDDENLY, LANDO CAN HOLD HIS SCOWL NO LONGER, **LAUGHTER** FILLS THE MORNING AIR...AND BLASTERS ARE SWIFTLY LOWERED.

YOU SONUVAGUN! YOU REALLY HAD ME **GOIN'** FOR A SECOND!

THAT **STILL** LEAVES YOU A COUPLE OF BLUFFS AHEAD, ACE! COME ON... INTRODUCE ME TO YOUR FRIENDS.

CHEWBACCA, HE ALREADY KNOWS. AND OF THE OTHER TWO TRAVELERS, THE MINING FACILITY'S ADMINISTRATOR IS MOST OBVIOUSLY CHARMED BY PRINCESS **LEIA ORGANA**.

THE LADY'S WITH **ME**, LANDO...AND I DON'T INTEND TO GAMBLE HER AWAY, SO YOU MIGHT JUST AS WELL **FORGET** SHE EXISTS...

WE'RE ONLY GONNA BE HERE LONG ENOUGH TO MAKE **REPAIRS.**

REPAIRS? WHAT **HAVE** YOU DONE TO **MY** SHIP?

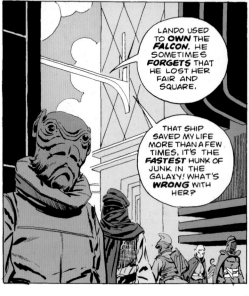

LANDO USED TO **OWN** THE **FALCON**. HE SOMETIMES **FORGETS** THAT HE LOST HER FAIR AND SQUARE.

THAT SHIP SAVED MY LIFE MORE THAN A FEW TIMES. IT'S THE **FASTEST** HUNK OF JUNK IN THE GALAXY! WHAT'S **WRONG** WITH HER?

HYPERDRIVE.

I'LL HAVE MY PEOPLE GET TO WORK RIGHT AWAY. HATE THE THOUGHT OF THE **MILLENNIUM FALCON** WITHOUT HER HEART!

THINGS *LOOK* PROSPEROUS, LANDO. HOW'S YOUR MINING OPERATION DOING?

NOT AS WELL AS I'D LIKE. WE'RE A *SMALL* OUTPOST AND NOT VERY SELF-SUFFICIENT. I'VE HAD *SUPPLY PROBLEMS* THAT...

HEY! WHAT ARE YOU *GRINNING* AT, SOLO?

NOTHING. EXCEPT I NEVER WOULD'VE GUESSED THAT UNDER THAT *WILD SCHEMER* I USED TO KNOW WAS A RESPONSIBLE *LEADER* AND *BUSINESSMAN...!* YOU WEAR IT WELL.

SEEING YOU AGAIN SURE BRINGS *BACK* THINGS... YEAH, I *AM* RESPONSIBLE THESE DAYS. AND YOU KNOW WHAT...?

YOU WERE RIGHT ALL ALONG, HAN... IT'S *OVER-RATED!*

BUT AS THE LAUGHING GROUP MOVES ALONG--NO ONE NOTICES THAT *SEE-THREEPIO* HAS NOT KEPT UP WITH THEM.

THAT *BLEEPING*... IT'S AN *R2 UNIT!* I'D ALMOST *FORGOTTEN* WHAT THEY SOUND LIKE.

SEEMS TO BE FROM THAT *DOOR* AHEAD...

THE BRONZE TRANSLATOR DROID IS *WRONG* --WHAT WAITS BEYOND THE DOOR IS DEFINITELY *NOT* AN R2 UNIT!

OH, MY! THOSE LOOK LIKE--

THE SENTENCE IS CUT SHORT BY THE UGLY WHINE OF *LASER BOLTS!*

DAGOBAH! A TREE LOOMS BEFORE LUKE SKYWALKER. DARK, GNARLED, OMINOUS, MORE SO THAN ANY OTHER HE HAS SEEN ON THIS STRANGE, SWAMP-LIKE PLANET WHERE HE IS BEING TUTORED IN THE WAYS OF THE FORCE.

SOMETHING'S NOT *RIGHT*, YODA. I FEEL DANGER ... *DEATH* ... COLD...

THIS TREE IS *STRONG* WITH THE DARK SIDE OF THE FORCE... A SERVANT OF *EVIL* IT IS. INTO IT YOU *MUST* GO.

WHAT'S *IN* THERE, MASTER?

ONLY WHAT *YOU* TAKE WITH YOU. YOUR WEAPON... YOU WON'T *NEED* IT.

BUT PEERING AT THE GAPING CAVERN BENEATH THE TREE'S GIGANTIC ROOTS, LUKE CANNOT BRING HIMSELF TO STEP IN *UNARMED*...

THEN, THE DARKNESS *SWALLOWS* HIM, DEEP, VAST, *UNNATURAL* IN ITS TOTALITY, AND WITH THE SUDDEN HISS OF A *LIGHTSABER* IGNITING...

DARTH VADER!

...LUKE FINDS IT CONCEALS FAR *MORE* THAN HE EVER DARED IMAGINE!

THE LOOMING FIGURE *CHARGES*... BUT IT *IS* LUKE WHOSE STROKE IS TRUE!

THE BLACK HELMET-MASK SEPARATES FROM THE BODY, FALLING WITH A DREAM-LIKE MOTION TO *SHATTER* UPON THE CAVERN FLOOR...

...AND REVEAL THE GREATEST *NIGHT-MARE* OF ALL!

N-NO... THAT'S *MY* FACE...!

CLOUD CARS PASS LAZILY OUTSIDE THE WINDOW OF THE SUITE LANDO CALRISSIAN HAS PROVIDED THE FUGITIVE REBELS. FOR SOME TIME HAN SOLO HAS BEEN CONTENT TO IDLY *WATCH* THEM, UNTIL NOW, WHEN THE DOOR TO *LEIA'S* ROOM OPENS BEHIND HIM...

HAN, HAS *THREEPIO* TURNED UP YET...?

HUH...? OH YEAH... HE'S BEEN GONE *TOO LONG* TO BE JUST *LOST.*

BUT BEFORE WE ORGANIZE THE *SEARCH PARTIES*... LET ME GET A *LOOK* AT YOU! YOU LOOK *GREAT!*

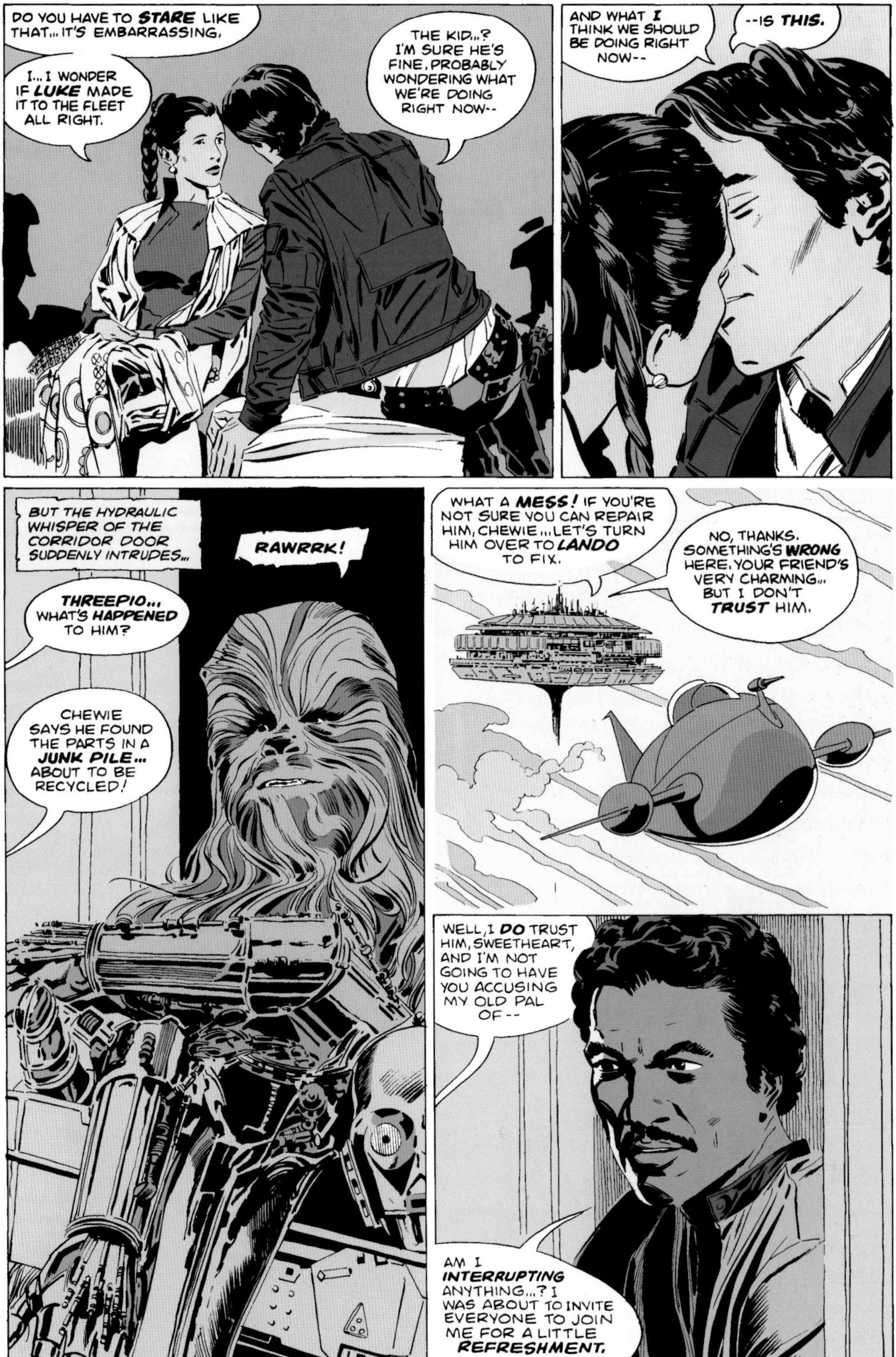

DO YOU HAVE TO STARE LIKE THAT... IT'S EMBARRASSING.
I... I WONDER IF LUKE MADE IT TO THE FLEET ALL RIGHT.
THE KID...? I'M SURE HE'S FINE, PROBABLY WONDERING WHAT WE'RE DOING RIGHT NOW--
AND WHAT I THINK WE SHOULD BE DOING RIGHT NOW--
--IS THIS.
BUT THE HYDRAULIC WHISPER OF THE CORRIDOR DOOR SUDDENLY INTRUDES...
RAWRRK!
THREEPIO... WHAT'S HAPPENED TO HIM?
CHEWIE SAYS HE FOUND THE PARTS IN A JUNK PILE... ABOUT TO BE RECYCLED!
WHAT A MESS! IF YOU'RE NOT SURE YOU CAN REPAIR HIM, CHEWIE... LET'S TURN HIM OVER TO LANDO TO FIX.
NO, THANKS. SOMETHING'S WRONG HERE. YOUR FRIEND'S VERY CHARMING... BUT I DON'T TRUST HIM.
WELL, I DO TRUST HIM, SWEETHEART, AND I'M NOT GOING TO HAVE YOU ACCUSING MY OLD PAL OF--
AM I INTERRUPTING ANYTHING...? I WAS ABOUT TO INVITE EVERYONE TO JOIN ME FOR A LITTLE REFRESHMENT.

AWAY ON DAGOBAH, LUKE SKYWALKER **MEDITATES.** SHAKEN BY HIS STRANGE VISION IN THE DARK TREE CAVERN, HE HAS APPLIED HIMSELF TO HIS TRAINING WITH MORE INTENSITY THAN EVER...

YODA... FOR A MOMENT I THOUGHT I SAW **BEN...!** BUT THEN IT FADED.

FREE YOUR MIND AND **RETURN** HE WILL. BUT CONTROL, **CONTROL!** MANY IMAGES WILL FILL YOUR MIND, YOU MUST LEARN OF WHAT YOU SEE.

I... I SEE... A **CITY** IN THE CLOUDS... **BESPIN!** MY **FRIENDS** ARE THERE... B-BUT... THEY'RE IN **PAIN...** SUFFERING...!

IT IS THE **FUTURE** YOU SEE.

WILL THEY **DIE?** I CAN'T LET THAT **HAPPEN...** I'VE GOT TO **GO** TO THEM... THEY'RE MY **FRIENDS!**

AND THEREFORE DECIDE YOU MUST HOW **BEST** TO SERVE THEM! IF YOU LEAVE NOW, HELP THEM YOU COULD--

--BUT YOU WOULD DESTROY **ALL** FOR WHICH THEY HAVE FOUGHT AND SUFFERED!

BUT AS A **CHILL** PASSES THROUGH THE APPRENTICE JEDI, THE OBJECTS OF HIS CONCERN STROLL IN PLEASANT SUNLIGHT ON A CLOUD CITY WALKWAY...

IT'S A LOVELY OUTPOST, LANDO.

WE'RE PROUD OF IT. THE AIR IS QUITE SPECIAL HERE... STIMULATING, YOU COULD GROW TO LIKE IT.

ONLY UNTIL THE **FALCON'S** REPAIRED, OLD BUDDY. THIS IS A **FREE STATION,** NOT EVEN PART OF THE **MINING** GUILD--

--AREN'T YOU AFRAID THE *EMPIRE* WILL SOMEDAY LEARN OF YOUR UNOFFICIAL LITTLE OPERATION AND SHUT YOU DOWN?

THAT'S ALWAYS BEEN A *DANGER...* LOOMING OVER EVERYTHING WE'VE BUILT HERE LIKE A SHADOW.

BUT CIRCUMSTANCES HAVE DEVELOPED WHICH WILL INSURE *SECURITY.* YOU SEE, I'VE JUST MADE A *DEAL--*

--IT'LL KEEP THE EMPIRE OUT OF HERE *FOREVER.*

CHEWBACCA TRIES TO SNARL A *WARNING* AS SOMETHING STRIKES HIS SENSES, BUT THE DOORS TO THE DINING HALL ARE ALREADY SWINGING OPEN, AND *BEHIND* THEM...

SORRY, FRIEND... I HAD NO *CHOICE.* THEY ARRIVED RIGHT BEFORE YOU DID.

YEAH, LANDO--

...*I'M* SORRY, TOO!

THE DRAW...THE SHOT... ARE FANTASTICALLY SWIFT PERHAPS THE *BEST* HAN HAS EVER MADE IN A LONG CAREER OF BEING GOOD WITH A BLASTER...

AGAINST ANY *OTHER* OPPONENT, THEY WOULD HAVE BEEN DEVAS-TATING. ANY BUT *DARTH VADER,* LORD OF THE SITH!

THE BOLTS ARE DEFLECTED AWAY TO EXPLODE HARMLESSLY AGAINST THE WALLS...

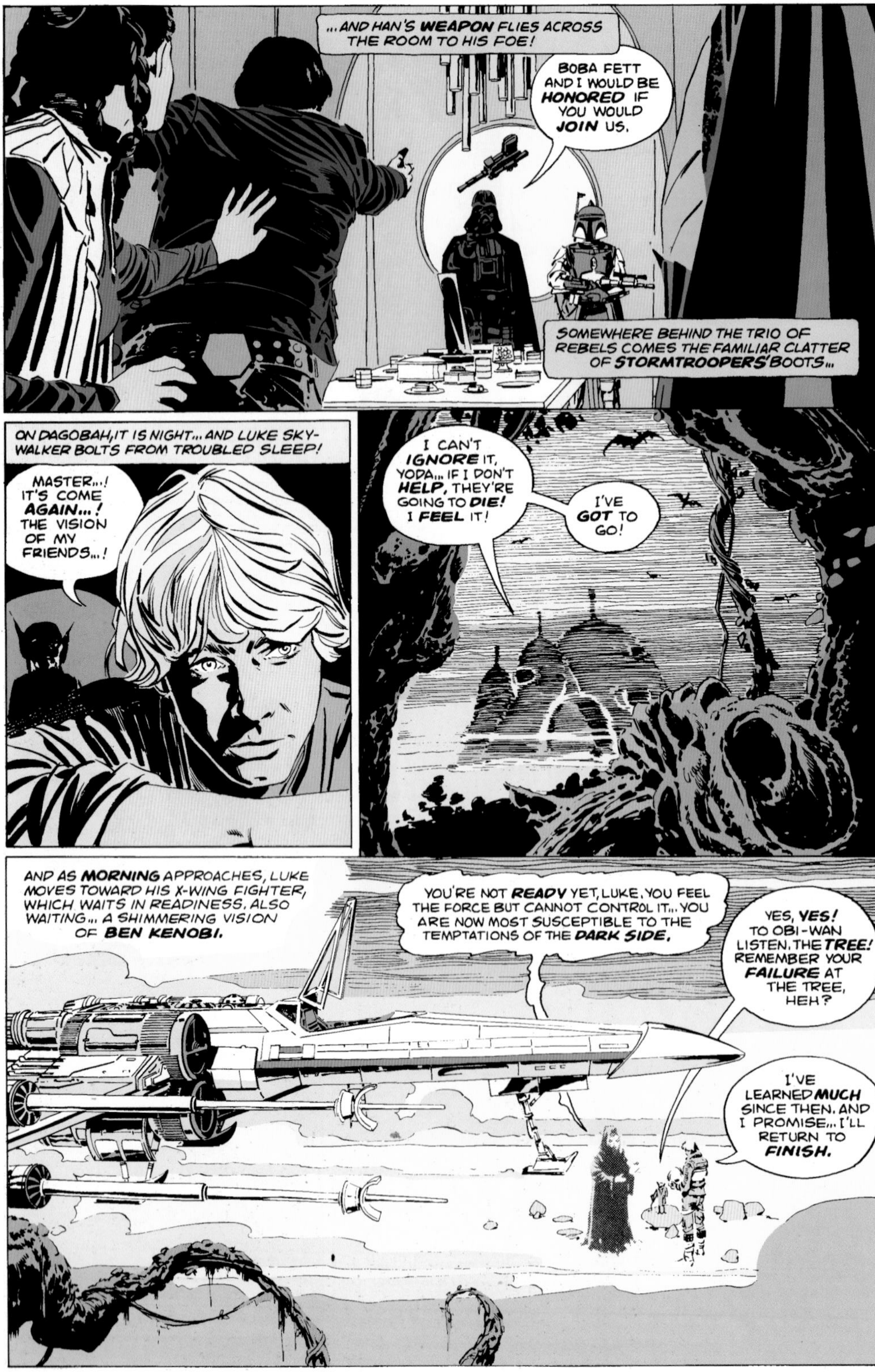
...AND HAN'S WEAPON FLIES ACROSS THE ROOM TO HIS FOE!
BOBA FETT AND I WOULD BE HONORED IF YOU WOULD JOIN US.
SOMEWHERE BEHIND THE TRIO OF REBELS COMES THE FAMILIAR CLATTER OF STORMTROOPERS' BOOTS...
ON DAGOBAH, IT IS NIGHT... AND LUKE SKY-WALKER BOLTS FROM TROUBLED SLEEP!
MASTER...! IT'S COME AGAIN...! THE VISION OF MY FRIENDS...!
I CAN'T IGNORE IT, YODA... IF I DON'T HELP, THEY'RE GOING TO DIE! I FEEL IT!
I'VE GOT TO GO!
AND AS MORNING APPROACHES, LUKE MOVES TOWARD HIS X-WING FIGHTER, WHICH WAITS IN READINESS. ALSO WAITING... A SHIMMERING VISION OF BEN KENOBI.
YOU'RE NOT READY YET, LUKE. YOU FEEL THE FORCE BUT CANNOT CONTROL IT... YOU ARE NOW MOST SUSCEPTIBLE TO THE TEMPTATIONS OF THE DARK SIDE.
YES, YES! TO OBI-WAN LISTEN. THE TREE! REMEMBER YOUR FAILURE AT THE TREE, HEH?
I'VE LEARNED MUCH SINCE THEN. AND I PROMISE... I'LL RETURN TO FINISH.

ONLY A FULLY-TRAINED **JEDI KNIGHT** WILL CONQUER VADER AND HIS EMPEROR! CHOOSE THE QUICK AND EASY PATH AND YOU'LL BECOME AN AGENT OF **EVIL**, PLUNGING THE GALAXY INTO THE ABYSS OF HATE AND DESPAIR.

YOU ARE THE **LAST JEDI**, LUKE. BE **PATIENT.**

AND **SACRIFICE** HAN AND LEIA...? I CAN'T, BEN... I **CAN'T!**

TURMOIL RAGING WITHIN HIM, THE YOUNG HERO OF THE DEATH STAR BATTLE CLIMBS INTO THE X-WING COCKPIT... AND READIES FOR TAKE-OFF.

LUKE, I CANNOT **PROTECT** YOU. IF YOU CHOOSE TO FACE VADER..., YOU DO IT **ALONE.** USE THE FORCE FOR **DEFENSE...** DON'T GIVE IN TO HATE, ANGER, FEAR. THEY LEAD THE WAY TO THE DARK SIDE.

I-I'LL **REMEMBER**, BEN. AND... I GIVE YOU MY **WORD** I'LL BE BACK!

THEN, WITH A ROAR OF ROCKET ENGINES... THE FIGHTER CRAFT SOARS UP INTO THE MISTS.

HE'S STILL RECKLESS, YODA... THINGS ARE GOING TO GET **WORSE** I FEAR. BUT THE BOY IS OUR **LAST** HOPE.

NO, OBI-WAN... THERE IS **ANOTHER.**

IN THE CLOUD CITY ABOVE BESPIN..., **SCREAMS** ARE HEARD. THEY COME FROM HAN SOLO.

DARTH VADER LISTENS FOR A WHILE WITHOUT GREAT INTEREST, THEN **TURNS...**

...TO JOIN **BOBA FETT** AND **LANDO CALRISSIAN.**

HIS PAIN IS GREAT, BOUNTY HUNTER... WITHOUT BEING PERMANENT. BUT YOU DON'T GET **HIM**... UNTIL I HAVE **SKYWALKER.**

I'M CONCERNED THAT THE CAPTAIN NOT BE **DAMAGED**, LORD VADER. JABBA THE HUT PAYS **DOUBLE** IF HE'S ALIVE.

WHAT ABOUT **LEIA** AND THE **WOOKIEE**...?

YOUR MEN SAID SOMETHING ABOUT THEM NEVER *LEAVING* THIS CITY. KEEPING THEM *PRISONER* HERE WASN'T A CONDITION OF OUR AGREEMENT... NOR WAS GIVING *HAN* TO THIS BOUNTY HUNTER!

LANDO IS TOO MUCH OF A *SURVIVOR* TO DO ANYTHING BUT KEEP *SILENT*, UNTIL THE DARK LORD AND BOBA FETT DEPART.

YOU KNOW, LOBOT, THIS DEAL'S GETTING *WORSE* ALL THE TIME.

I'VE GOT A *BAD FEELING* ABOUT THIS!

I HOPE YOU DON'T THINK YOU'RE BEING TREATED *UNFAIRLY*, CALRISSIAN--

--IT WOULD BE MOST UNFORTUNATE IF I HAD TO LEAVE A *PERMANENT GARRISON* AT YOUR OUTPOST.

THE CLOUD CITY DETENTION CELLS. CHEWBACCA COVERS MOUNTING CONCERN BY CONCENTRATING ON THE INTRICATE TASK OF REPAIRING AN UNAPPRECIATIVE ROBOTS...

WHAT HAVE YOU *DONE*, YOU FLEA-BITTEN FURBALL... MY HEAD'S ON *BACKWARD!*

IS THERE NO *END* TO A DROID'S SUFFERING? BLASTED TO PIECES FOR ACCIDENTALLY BUMPING INTO SOME *STORMTROOPERS*... AND NOW *DEFORMED* BY AN OVERGROWN MOPHEAD!

THEN... THE *DOOR* HISSES OPEN! AND CHEWIE AND HIS FELLOW PRISONER, *LEIA ORGANA*, SEE...

WAAAARRK!

HAN!

AND AS THE *STORMTROOPERS* LEAVE...

I'M... *ALL RIGHT...* HAD ME HOWLING ON THE *SCAN GRID*... BUT THEY NEVER ASKED ME ANY *QUESTIONS*, OR--

LANDO! GET *OUT* OF HERE!

SHUT UP AND LISTEN,...! I'M DOING WHAT I *CAN* TO MAKE THINGS EASIER. I DIDN'T KNOW ABOUT THE *PRICE* ON YOUR HEAD, BUT VADER HAS AGREED TO--

322

YOU DON'T **KNOW** MUCH IF YOU THINK DARTH VADER WANTS ALL OF US ANYTHING BUT **DEAD** BEFORE THIS THING IS OVER!

HE DOESN'T WANT YOU AT **ALL**, HAN! HE'S SETTING A **TRAP** FOR SOME YOUNG REBEL NAMED **SKYWALKER**... YOU PEOPLE ARE THE **BAIT**.

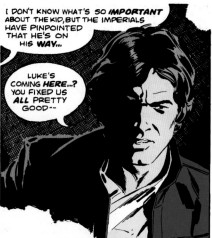

I DON'T KNOW WHAT'S **SO IMPORTANT** ABOUT THE KID, BUT THE IMPERIALS HAVE PINPOINTED THAT HE'S ON HIS **WAY**...

LUKE'S COMING **HERE**...? YOU FIXED US **ALL** PRETTY GOOD--

-- FRIEND!

FOR A MOMENT IT'S A **FIGHT**... UNTIL LANDO'S GUARDS MOVE IN, CLUBBING WITH **THEIR** BLASTERS!

OKAY,... **ENOUGH!** I'VE DONE AS MUCH AS I CAN. I WISH IT WERE MORE ... BUT I'VE GOT MY **OWN** PROBLEMS.

I'VE ALREADY STUCK MY **NECK** OUT FARTHER THAN I SHOULD.

YEAH, YEAH, LANDO ... YOU'RE A **REAL HERO!**

WHIRLING, THE CLOUD CITY ADMINISTRATOR STALKS OUT...

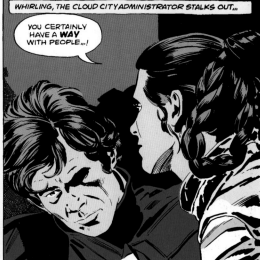

YOU CERTAINLY HAVE A **WAY** WITH PEOPLE...!

LEAVING THE DETENTION AREA, LANDO FINDS HE'S **WANTED**, WANTED BY THE LAST PERSON HE CARES TO SEE,...AND THE ONLY ONE HE DARES NOT REFUSE.

LORD VADER, THE X-WING CLASS SHIP YOU'VE HAD US MONITOR IS NOW APPROACHING.

GOOD. ALLOW SKYWALKER TO LAND, WE'LL BE **READY** FOR HIM SHORTLY.

THIS FACILITY IS **CRUDE**, CALRISSIAN,... BUT IT SHOULD MEET MY NEEDS.

BRING IN **SOLO**.

WE ONLY USE THIS PLACE FOR **CARBON FREEZING**, IF YOU PUT HIM THROUGH THAT,... IT MIGHT **KILL** HIM.

I DON'T WISH THE EMPEROR'S PRIZE TO BE **DAMAGED**... WE'LL **TEST** IT FIRST.

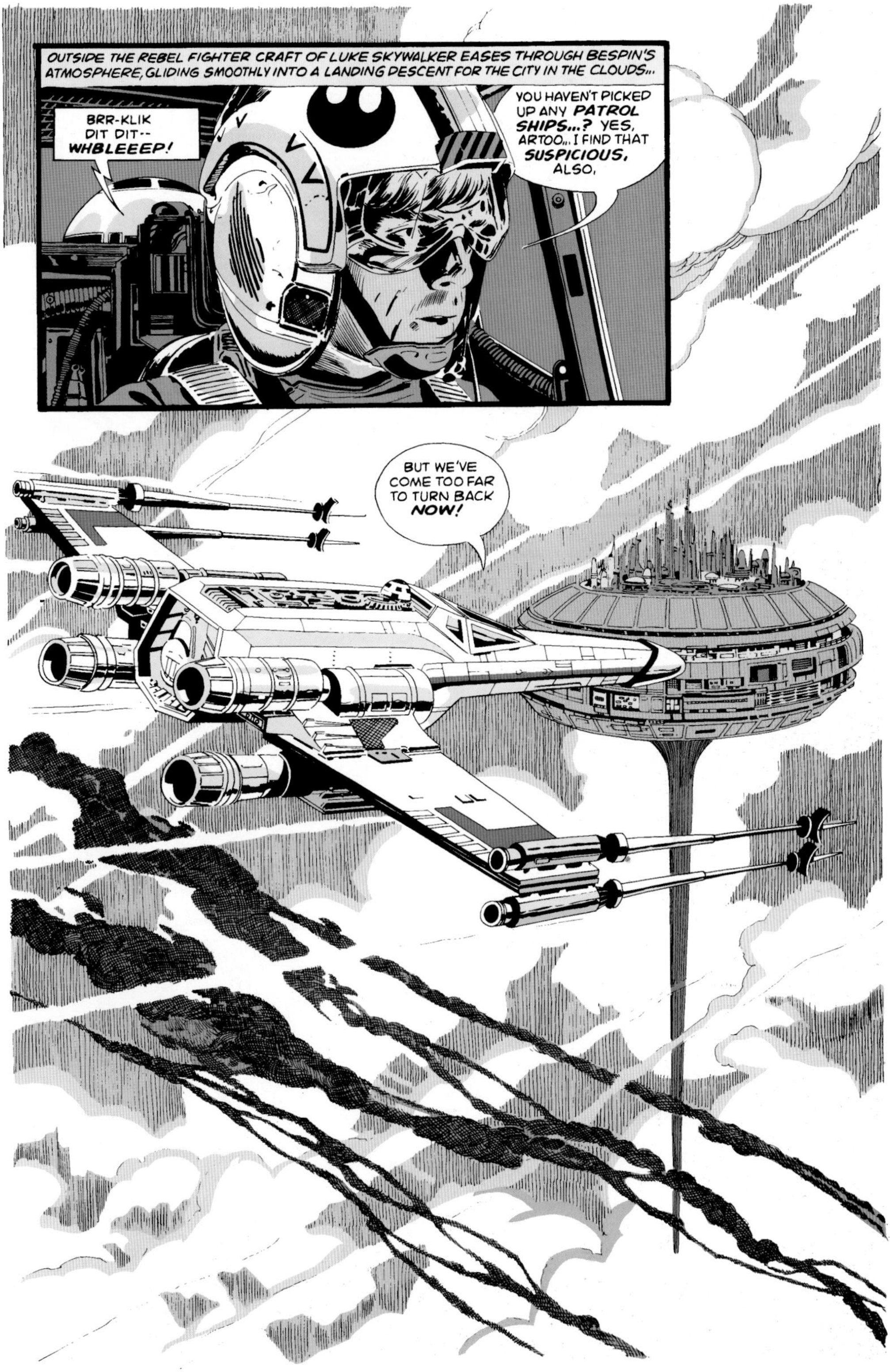
OUTSIDE THE REBEL FIGHTER CRAFT OF LUKE SKYWALKER EASES THROUGH BESPIN'S ATMOSPHERE, GLIDING SMOOTHLY INTO A LANDING DESCENT FOR THE CITY IN THE CLOUDS...
BRR-KLIK DIT DIT-- WHBLEEEP!
YOU HAVEN'T PICKED UP ANY PATROL SHIPS...? YES, ARTOO... I FIND THAT SUSPICIOUS, ALSO.
BUT WE'VE COME TOO FAR TO TURN BACK NOW!

RESPONDING INSTANTLY TO THEIR LEADER'S COMMAND... STORMTROOPERS BRING HAN. TOO SOON THE TEST OF THE CARBON-FREEZING CHAMBER IS READY TO *BEGIN*... BEFORE AN AUDIENCE OF THE WILLING AND THE *UNWILLING.*

THE EMPIRE WILL *COMPENSATE* YOU FOR THE LOSS.

PUT HIM IN THE *CHAMBER!*

NO!

WHAT IF SOLO DOESN'T *SURVIVE*, LORD VADER? BEYOND WHAT YOU'RE PAYING... HE'S WORTH A *LOT* TO ME.

LEIA'S CRY TRIGGERS THE GIANT WOOKIEE INTO ACTION. TROOPERS POUR FORWARD FOR THE KILL... UNTIL *HAN* INTERCEDES.

THANK THE *MAKER!*

NO, BIG BUDDY, COME ON, SAVE YOUR STRENGTH FOR *ANOTHER* TIME... WHEN THE *ODDS* ARE BETTER.

NOWRRRRRAGH!

YEAH... I KNOW... I FEEL THE SAME WAY.

HAN... OH, *HAN*...! I *LOVE* YOU...! I COULDN'T TELL YOU BEFORE... BUT IT'S *TRUE.*

JUST *REMEMBER* THAT, LEIA--

--'CAUSE I'LL BE *BACK.*

SWIFTLY THE CAPTAIN OF THE **MILLENNIUM FALCON** IS STRAPPED TO THE CHAMBER'S HYDRAULIC LIFT PLATFORM. HE HAS TIME FOR A BRIEF GLANCE AT HIS FRIENDS. THEN, TO THEIR HORROR, THE PLATFORM **DROPS**...

...AND **FIERY LIQUID** CASCADES DOWN INTO THE OPENING FROM THE JETS ABOVE!

THEY'RE ENCASING HIM IN **CARBONITE**... IT'S A HIGH-QUALITY ALLOY. MUCH BETTER THAN MY OWN. HE SHOULD BE QUITE WELL PROTECTED... IF HE SURVIVED THE **FREEZING PROCESS.**

AND NO ONE AT THE SCENE KNOWS BETTER WHAT A **BIG** "IF" THAT IS THAN **LANDO CALRISSIAN**...

...WHO WINCES IN **SORROW** AT HOW FAR THE PRICE OF SUCCESS HAS TAKEN HIM.

ELSEWHERE, A DOOR FROM THE LANDING AREA SLIDES BACK. FOR A MOMENT, LUKE SKYWALKER **HESITATES**, LETTING HIS FEELINGS REACH OUT TO THE SILENT, OMINOUSLY DESERTED CORRIDORS BEYOND...

...THEN, HE MOVES GRIMLY AND URGENTLY FORWARD INTO CLOUD CITY... AND **WHATEVER** LIES AHEAD.

NEXT ISSUE: **DUEL A DARK LORD!**

50¢ CC 44 FEB 02817

STAR WARS ™

AT LAST! THE INCREDIBLE CONCLUSION OF THE OFFICIAL COMICS ADAPTATION OF...

THE **EMPIRE** STRIKES BACK ™

DUEL A DARK LORD!

Long ago in a galaxy far, far away. . .there exists a state of cosmic *civil war*. A brave alliance of *underground freedom fighters* has challenged the tyranny and oppression of the awesome *Galactic Empire*. This is their story!

LucasFilm PRESENTS: STAR WARS™ **THE GREATEST SPACE FANTASY OF ALL!**

ARCHIE GOODWIN	AL WILLIAMSON & CARLOS GARZON	GLYNIS WEIN	RICK VEITCH	JAMES SHOOTER
WRITER/EDITOR	ARTISTS	COLORIST	LETTERER	EDITOR-IN-CHIEF

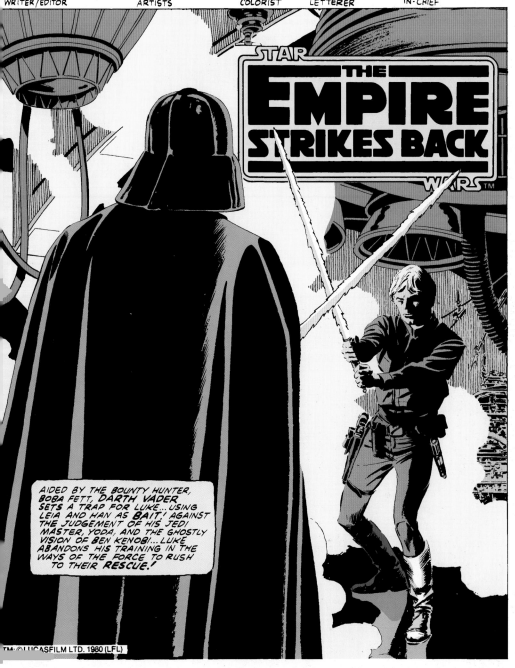

STAR **THE EMPIRE STRIKES BACK** WARS™

AIDED BY THE BOUNTY HUNTER, BOBA FETT, *DARTH VADER* SETS A TRAP FOR LUKE...USING LEIA AND HAN AS *BAIT!* AGAINST THE JUDGEMENT OF HIS JEDI MASTER, YODA, AND THE GHOSTLY VISION OF BEN KENOBI...LUKE ABANDONS HIS TRAINING IN THE WAYS OF THE FORCE TO RUSH TO THEIR *RESCUE!*

CHAPTER SIX: DUEL A DARK LORD!

OMINOUS SILENCE HANGS OVER THE **CARBON-FREEZING CHAMBER** OF BESPIN'S CLOUD CITY. THE PROCESS IS COMPLETE...THE **RESULTS** NOW STAND FOR ALL PRESENT TO VIEW, AS ADMINISTRATOR LANDO CALRISSIAN TENSELY CHECKS READ-OUT GAUGES AND TRIES TO DE-TERMINE IF THE OLD FRIEND HE BETRAYED TO SAVE HIS OUTPOST CITY IS **DEAD** OR...

HE'S **ALIVE**...! AND IN PERFECT **HIBERNATION!**

THEN SOLO IS ALL **YOURS**, BOUNTY HUNTER... TAKE HIM TO **JABBA THE HUT** IF THAT'S WHAT YOU WISH.

AND NOW THAT WE'RE CERTAIN IT **PRESERVES** WITH-OUT KILLING...RESET THE CHAMBER FOR **SKYWALKER!**

MONITORS REPORT THAT HE'S JUST *LANDED*, MY LORD.

GOOD. SEE THAT HE FINDS HIS WAY *HERE*.

AND MAKE ARRANGEMENTS FOR A *PERMANENT GARRISON* TO TAKE UP RESIDENCE--

-- SO THE PRINCESS AND SOLO'S WOOKIEE COMPANION CAN STILL BE *WATCHED OVER* WHILE IN CALRISSIAN'S CARE.

THAT WASN'T OUR *BARGAIN!* YOU SAID THE EMPIRE WOULDN'T *INTERFERE* IN--

I'M *ALTERING* THE BARGAIN, PRAY I DON'T ALTER IT ANY *FURTHER.*

AND LANDO FEELS A SUDDEN *CONSTRICTION* IN HIS THROAT, PAINFUL...BUT BRIEF. MERELY A *REMINDER...* FOR NOW.

MEANWHILE, THROUGH EERILY DESERTED CORRIDORS, LUKE SKYWALKER ADVANCES CAUTIOUSLY TOWARD THE TIBANNA GAS MINING COMMUNITY'S *CENTER.* THEN...

QUIET, ARTOO THERE'S SOME KIND OF *JUNCTION* AHEAD--

SOMEONE'S *COMING!*

HAN! T-THAT'S *HAN* THEY'RE CARRYING...!

WHAT HAVE THEY *DONE* TO HIM...?!

BOBA FETT AND THE STORMTROOPER ESCORTS OF THE CARBONITE-ENTOMBED CORELLIAN WHIRL TO FIRE...

331

...ONLY TO FIND THAT THE APPRENTICE JEDI IS TOO *SWIFT!*

HIS SHOT HITS TWO TROOPERS.

BUT LUKE'S ATTEMPT TO GIVE CHASE IS CUT SHORT BY A HEAVY BARRAGE FROM *BOBA FETT...*

...AND THE SUDDEN *DESCENT* OF A BLAST SHIELD DOOR!

HE SPINS, LOOKING FOR ANOTHER WAY TO FOLLOW, AND SEES INSTEAD...

LEIA! CHEWBACCA! THREEPIO!

LUKE!

GET OUT OF HERE!

GET OUT OF *CLOUD CITY...*

IT'S A TRAP!

AGAIN A BLAST SHIELD THUNDERS DOWN, CUTTING LUKE OFF FROM THOSE HE HOPES TO SAVE...

332

CORRIDOR BY CORRIDOR, IT *CONTINUES*... SEPARATING HIM EVEN FROM ARTOO-DETOO! UNTIL AT LAST THERE IS ONLY *ONE PATH*, LEADING TO THE CARBON-FREEZING CHAMBER...

...AND WHAT LUKE NOW REALIZES WAS *INEVITABLE*.

DARTH VADER... I *FEEL* YOUR PRESENCE.

SHOW YOURSELF... OR DO YOU *FEAR* ME?

THE *FORCE* IS WITH YOU, YOUNG SKYWALKER... BUT YOU'RE NOT A *JEDI* YET!

INSTANTLY, TWO LIGHTSABERS *IGNITE*...

AND WITH A GREAT *LEAP* FROM LUKE, BORN OF HIS INTENSE TRAINING WITH YODA...

...A BATTLE, LONG COMING, IS *JOINED*!

MEANTIME, AS THE IMPERIALS HUSTLE LEIA AND CHEWBACCA, WITH HIS BURDEN OF THE BLASTER-DAMAGED SEE-THREEPIO, THROUGH THE MINING OUTPOST'S INTERSECTING BYWAYS, *LANDO* SUDDENLY SPEAKS...

CODE FORCE... *SEVEN*.

ALMOST INSTANTLY, CLOUD CITY GUARDS *SURROUND* THEM ALL.

WHAT'S *HAPPENED*, CHEWBACCA? TURN ME AROUND SO I CAN *SEE*, YOU OVERSTUFFED HAIRBALL!

AND WHAT THE TRANSLATOR DROID'S PHOTORECEPTORS SOON BEHOLD IS THE STORMTROOPERS BEING *DISARMED...*

PUT THIS BUNCH IN THE SECURITY TOWER... *QUIETLY.* NO ONE MUST KNOW.

WHAT'S GOING ON...?

LET'S SAY I'M TRYING TO CORRECT A *BIG MISTAKE.* COME ON... WE'RE GETTING *OUT* OF HERE.

LANDO, AFTER WHAT YOU DID TO *HAN,* I WOULDN'T TRUST YOU TO--

LEIA DOESN'T FINISH, BECAUSE SUDDENLY...

...CHEWBACCA IS EXPRESSING THE SAME FEELINGS MORE *STRONGLY!*

NRAWWWK!

I-I... HAD NO *CHOICE*...! BUT... THERE'S STILL A CHANCE TO... *SAVE* HAN... BOBA FETT'S SHIP... IS AT... EAST PLATFORM...!

CHEWIE! LET HIM *GO!*

BUT KEEP YOUR *EYES* ON HIM EVERY *STEP* OF THE WAY!

I'VE A FEELING I'M MAKING *ANOTHER* BIG MISTAKE...

NONETHELESS, LANDO CALRISSIAN IS SOON ON HIS FEET...

...LEADING A DESPERATE RACE TOWARD CLOUD CITY'S LANDING AREA, AND THAT RACE LEADS THEM PAST...

ARTOO! THIS WAY... HURRY!

VREETA BLIIT WA-DOOOT!

I KNOW... I KNOW, BUT MASTER LUKE CAN TAKE CARE OF HIMSELF... AT LEAST UNTIL WE CAN RESCUE CAPTAIN SOLO FROM THE BOUNTY HUNTER!

BUT WHEN THE GROUP BURSTS FROM THE EASTERN PLATFORM ELEVATOR... IT IS TO SEE BOBA FETT'S *SLAVE I* TAKING TO THE AIR!

AND A FRANTIC BARRAGE OF BLASTER FIRE CAN'T STOP IT!

IT'S NO USE... THEY'RE OUT OF *RANGE!*

NO! NO!

AND THE EMPIRE ALLOWS NO TIME TO MOURN THE *LOSS* OF HAN SOLO...

COME *ON...!* LET'S *MOVE!*

IT IS AS IF LANDO HAD NEVER SPOKEN. LEIA AND CHEWBACCA UNHEEDINGLY VENT THEIR FRUSTRATION AND ANGER AGAINST THE ADVANCING ENEMY.

LISTEN TO ME! IF WE REACH THE *FALCON*... WE CAN GO *AFTER* BOBA FETT!

THE WORDS REGISTER. THE PAIR WITHDRAW...

WHILE IN THE CARBON-FREEZING CHAMBER... LUKE SKYWALKER RELENTLESSLY *ADVANCES!*

THE FEAR DOES NOT *REACH* YOU... YOU'VE LEARNED *MORE* THAN I ANTICIPATED.

YOU'LL FIND I'M *FULL* OF SURPRISES!

AND I, *TOO!*

A LIGHTNING FEINT AND SLASH MAKE LUKE DODGE *BACKWARD*... ONTO THE UNCERTAIN *FOOTING* OF THE PLATFORM STAIRS!

THE YOUNG WARRIOR LETS HIMSELF *TUMBLE*, ROLLING WITH THE FALL, READY TO COME UP FIGHTING...

...ONLY TO HAVE THE LORD OF THE SITH LAUNCH THROUGH THE AIR *AFTER* HIM LIKE SOME HUGE DARK BIRD!

YOUR FUTURE LIES WITH *ME*, SKYWALKER. NOW YOU WILL EMBRACE THE *DARK SIDE*... OBI-WAN KNEW THIS TO BE *TRUE*.

THERE IS *MUCH* HE DID NOT TELL YOU, COME... I WILL *COMPLETE* YOUR TRAINING.

NO! I'LL *DIE* FIRST!

WITH A LOUD DEADLY HISS... *LIQUID METAL* JETS FROM OVERHEAD! THE SAME CARBONITE THAT IMPRISONED HAN SOLO... NOW STREAMING ONTO THE SPOT WHERE *LUKE* HAS BEEN MANEUVERED!

ALL TOO *EASY*--

-- PERHAPS YOU ARE NOT AS *STRONG* AS THE EMPEROR FEARED.

TIME WILL *TELL*, LORD VADER... BUT I WAS STRONG ENOUGH TO LEAP *THIS* FAR.

OBI-WAN HAS TAUGHT YOU WELL. YOU'VE CONTROLLED YOUR FEAR... NOW RELEASE YOUR *ANGER*! I DESTROYED YOUR *FAMILY*... TAKE YOUR *REVENGE*!

LUKE DROPS AGILELY INTO THE RISING STEAM, READY TO *ANSWER* THE CHALLENGE... AND FINDS ONLY THE TAUNTING *ECHO* OF DARTH VADER'S VOICE.

YOUR *HATRED* CAN GIVE YOU THE POWER TO DESTROY *ME*, NOVICE... USE IT! *USE IT!*

YET EVEN AS HE MOVES IN PURSUIT, HE RECALLS *ANOTHER* VOICE... BEN'S...

...CAUTIONING HIM NOT TO GIVE IN TO THE *DARKER EMOTIONS*. STILL, HE PRESSES ON,... INTO ONE OF THE MINING OUTPOST'S *REACTOR CONTROL ROOMS*.

YOU'VE *FOUND* ME... NOW ATTACK, *DESTROY* ME! ONLY BY TAKING YOUR REVENGE CAN YOU *SAVE* YOURSELF!

FOR A MOMENT, LUKE IS CONFUSED, UNCERTAIN. THEN HE MOVES TO *STRIKE*...

...AND THE ROOM *EXPLODES!* MACHINERY RIPS FREE AND HURTLES AT HIM, POWERED BY THE *DARK SIDE OF THE FORCE!*

IT'S USELESS TO *RESIST*. JOIN *ME*... OR JOIN OBI-WAN IN *DEATH!*

A *SABER SLASH* DISINTEGRATES ONE DEADLY MISSILE,... THE FORCE DEFLECTS OTHERS. BUT EVENTUALLY, INEVITABLY,...

...A HUGE CHUNK OF MACHINERY *SMASHES* THROUGH LUKE'S GUARD!

THE SEEMINGLY ENDLESS ABYSS OF CLOUD CITY'S *REACTOR SHAFT* YAWNS BENEATH HIM ...

...UNTIL ONE HAND CATCHES HOLD OF THE CONTROL ROOM'S EXTERIOR WALKWAY!

BLEEDING, BATTERED,... HE *DANGLES*, THEN AGONIZINGLY HE PULLS HIMSELF *UP*...

...TO FIND *DARTH VADER* ADVANCING, DRIVING HIM BACK ALONG THE WALKWAY,... OUT ONTO THE REACTOR *GANTRY*.

WHY RESIST FURTHER,...? YOU ARE *BEATEN*, LUKE. DON'T LET YOURSELF BE *DESTROYED* AS OBI-WAN DID!

CALM... MUST BE CALM...

IN THE LANDING AREA, A **DOOR** NOW SEPARATES LEIA, LANDO, AND THE OTHERS FROM THE **MILLENNIUM FALCON**. A DOOR THAT **IS SEALED**...AS STORMTROOPERS CLOSE IN!

ARTOO! PLUG INTO THE **CONTROL PANEL**... YOU CAN **OVERRIDE** THE ALERT SYSTEM!

FRA-DWEEEEEEET!

WELL, NEXT TIME **YOU** PAY MORE ATTENTION! I'M NOT SUPPOSED TO KNOW **POWER SOCKETS** FROM COMPUTER FEEDS... I'M AN INTERPRETER!

ANYONE **ELSE** GOT ANY IDEAS?

THIS WAY! THERE MAY BE **ANOTHER** APPROACH TO THE **FALCON**. LEAST I GOT A CHANCE TO USE THE **COMLINK** BACK THERE--

--AND ALERTED EVERYONE ELSE TO **EVACUATE** BEFORE MORE IMPERIALS ARRIVE!

BACK AT THE REACTOR CORE, ABOVE THE SHAFT'S HOWLING WINDS, THE STEADY CLASH OF **SABERS** CAN BE HEARD... UNTIL THE DARK LORD'S BLADE COMES SLICING THROUGH PART OF THE GANTRY EQUIPMENT TO STRIKE LUKE'S **SWORDARM!**

PAIN SEIZES THE YOUNG WARRIOR! HIS WEAPON FALLS. THE HAND THAT GRASPED IT WILL NEVER GRASP **ANYTHING** AGAIN. AND CLINGING PRECARIOUSLY WITH HIS ONE GOOD HAND...

338

...HE FACES DARTH VADER AND *DEATH.*

THERE IS NO *ESCAPE,* LUKE, DON'T MAKE ME *SLAY* YOU... *JOIN* ME, TOGETHER WE WILL BE MORE *POWERFUL* THAN THE EMPEROR--

IT WAS *MEANT* TO BE! THERE ARE *MANY* THINGS OBI-WAN HAS KEPT FROM YOU. SUCH AS WHAT HAPPENED TO YOUR *FATHER...*

TURNING OFF HIS LASER BLADE, THE LORD OF *SITH* EXTENDS HIS HAND...

BEN TOLD ME *ENOUGH.* HE TOLD ME YOU *KILLED* MY FATHER!

NO, LUKE, I *AM* YOUR FATHER.

N-NO... THAT... *CAN'T* BE! I-IT'S... IMPOSSIBLE!

SEARCH YOUR FEELINGS, YOUNGSTER, YOU *KNOW* IT TO BE TRUE.

LUKE, YOU CAN *DESTROY* THE EMPEROR... HE HAS *FORSEEN* THIS. WE CAN RULE THE *GALAXY* TOGETHER... *FATHER* AND *SON!* COME WITH ME... IT'S THE *ONLY* WAY.

NO...! NO...!

STUNNED, LUKE PONDERS, THEN SUDDENLY REALIZES THAT HE HAS NO *CHOICE...*

...AND STEPS OFF INTO NOTHINGNESS!

NEVERRRR...

VADER STARES AS THE YOUTH VANISHES INTO THE DARKNESS. IT IS *OVER.* THE SHAFT'S CHANGING AIR CURRENTS MAY CUSHION HIM MOMENTARILY, BUT SOMEWHERE BELOW ARE *EXHAUST VENTS.* CERTAINLY THE BOY WILL BE DRAGGED INTO ONE OF THESE... AND SPEWED OUT OF CLOUD CITY *MILES* ABOVE THE GASEOUS SURFACE OF BESPIN.

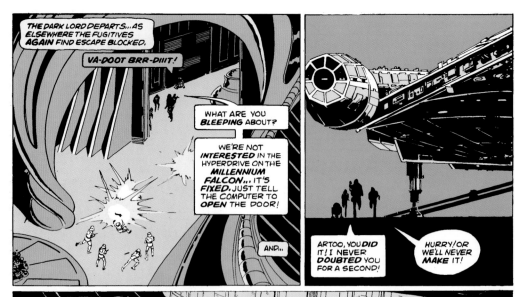

THE DARK LORD DEPARTS...AS ELSEWHERE THE FUGITIVES *AGAIN* FIND ESCAPE BLOCKED.

VA-DOOT BRR-DIIIT!

WHAT ARE YOU *BLEEPING* ABOUT?

WE'RE NOT *INTERESTED* IN THE HYPERDRIVE ON THE *MILLENNIUM FALCON*...IT'S *FIXED.* JUST TELL THE COMPUTER TO *OPEN* THE DOOR!

AND...

ARTOO, YOU *DID* IT! I NEVER *DOUBTED* YOU FOR A SECOND!

HURRY! OR WE'LL NEVER *MAKE* IT!

NO ONE HAS TO BE URGED *TWICE.* AND MOMENTS LATER, UNDER A HAIL OF LASER FIRE...THE *MILLENNIUM FALCON* SOARS FOR THE HEAVENS, LEAVING *CLOUD CITY* BEHIND!

NEAR THE END OF ONE OF THE REACTOR CORE EXHAUST VENTS IS AN *ELECTRONIC WEATHER VANE,* ONE OF MANY LINING THIS BOTTOM-MOST PART OF THE CITY...

NEAR ENOUGH FOR A SEMI-CONSCIOUS LUKE TO *GRASP* RATHER THAN PLUNGE TO HIS DOOM...

...BUT NEVER BUILT TO *HOLD* THE WEIGHT IT NOW SUPPORTS.

ALREADY IT CREAKS WITH STRAIN AND STARTS TO **GIVE**...

BEN... BEN...

BUT AS PARTS OF THE VANE FALL INTO THE **CLOUDS** BELOW...

...LUKE'S DELIRIOUS PLEA REACHES THE **WRONG** EARS.

BEN CANNOT HELP YOU **NOW**, MY YOUNG JEDI...

BRING MY **SHIP** IN.

LEIA...

...HEAR ME... LEIA...

SOMEWHERE AHEAD... THREE TIE FIGHTERS MOVE IN PURSUIT OF THE **FALCON**.

SINCE MY PEOPLE REPAIRED THIS BABY... WE CAN **OUTDISTANCE** 'EM EASILY. I KNEW THAT SET-UP WAS TOO GOOD TO LAST... I'M GONNA **MISS** IT.

L-LUKE...?

LANDO... WE'VE GOT TO GO **BACK**!

WAIT A **MINUTE**... WE CAN'T GO BACK! WHAT ABOUT THOSE **FIGHTERS**?!

WAAAAARRK!

NO ARGUMENTS... JUST **DO** IT! THAT'S A **COMMAND**!

AND TURNING BACK *INTO* ITS SHOCKED PURSUERS... THE MILLENNIUM FALCON STREAKS FOR CLOUD CITY AT FULL SUBLIGHT SPEED!

BENEATH THE AERIAL CITY... THE WEATHER VANE'S LAST SUPPORT **SNAPS!** SILENT, BARELY CONCIOUS, BEYOND HOPE...

...LUKE SKYWALKER **FALLS!**

...A FALL **BROKEN** BY A SAUCER-SHAPED SMUGGLING SHIP THAT ZOOMS IN FROM OUT OF THE DISTANCE!

WAS LANDO **READY** AT THE TOP HATCH? DID WE **CATCH** LUKE ALL RIGHT? HOW **FAR** DID HE FALL?!

THE **ANSWERS** TO LEIA'S CONCERNED QUESTIONS ARE **DELAYED**...BY A PERSISTENT TRIO OF **TIE FIGHTERS!**

GET US **OUT** OF HERE, LADY--

...AND I THINK YOUR FRIEND WILL **SURVIVE!**

THANK THE FORCE! BUT UNDER THIS POUNDING THE DEFLECTOR SHIELDS CAN'T **HOLD UP**--

WE WON'T HAVE ROOM FOR ANY **MISTAKES** JUMPING TO HYPERSPACE.

IF MY CREW SAID IT WAS FIXED,...IT'S **FIXED,** PRINCESS.

THAT SOUNDS A LITTLE TOO **FAMILIAR,** LANDO... ESPECIALLY SINCE **ANOTHER** SHIP, MUCH **BIGGER,** IS NOW TRYING TO CUT US OFF!

"IT'S *VADER*"... LUKE WHISPERS, ALMOST TO HIMSELF... BUT IT *CHILLS* EVERYONE IN THE CABIN.

GOOD, PIETT, PREPARE A *BOARDING PARTY*... AND SET ALL WEAPONS FOR *STUN*.

THEY'LL BE WITHIN RANGE OF OUR *TRACTOR BEAM*, IN A MOMENT, MY LORD... AND THEIR HYPERDRIVE WAS *DEACTIVATED* RIGHT AFTER THEIR CAPTURE WAS ORDERED.

AND ABOARD THE *FALCON*...

NOTHING'S *HAPPENING* THAT CAN'T BE!

YAWRRRK!

I-I WON'T BE ABLE TO *RESIST* HIM THIS TIME! BEN...! WHY DIDN'T YOU *TELL* ME...?

AN ANGRY WOOKIEE RUSHES BACK TO THE *REPAIR HATCH*... AS LASER BOLTS VIOLENTLY *ROCK* THE SHIP.

WHRRR-DEET *BLIT VOOP!*

WHAT DO YOU MEAN YOU *KNOW* WHAT'S WRONG...? SO DO I! MY *FOOT* ISN'T ATTACHED YET AND WE'RE *DOOMED* BECAUSE THE HYPERDRIVE ENGINES ARE *STILL* MALFUNCTIONING!

ARTOO-DETOO, COME *BACK* HERE! YOU HAVEN'T *FINISHED*! GET AWAY FROM THOSE *CONTROLS*... MASTER CALRISSIAN IS ABOUT TO TRY *AGAIN*!

WITH *CHEWBACCA* HAMMERING AWAY DOWN BELOW AND *YOU* FIDDLING ABOUT UP HERE, THERE'S NO TELLING *WHAT* MAY HAP--

THE *MILLENNIUM FALCON* GIVES A SUDDEN *WILD LURCH* AND...

BLEEEEET!

RAARGHH!

344

THAT DID IT!

AND DESPITE AN INCREDIBLE **COMMOTION** IN THE REPAIR HATCH, HAN SOLO'S FREIGHTER SPEEDS AWAY INTO INFINITY... AND **SAFETY** AT LAST!

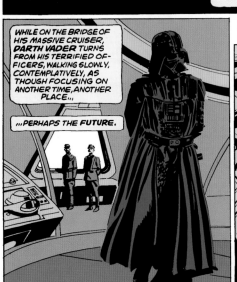

WHILE ON THE BRIDGE OF HIS MASSIVE CRUISER, **DARTH VADER** TURNS FROM HIS TERRIFIED OFFICERS, WALKING SLOWLY, CONTEMPLATIVELY, AS THOUGH FOCUSING ON ANOTHER TIME, ANOTHER PLACE...

...PERHAPS THE **FUTURE.**

SOMETIME LATER, IN A SAFE SECTOR OF SPACE... A **PATIENT** RECUPERATES FROM AN OPERATION THAT HAS GIVEN HIM A NEW HAND... ONE THAT IS MECHANIZED, CYBERNETICALLY CONTROLLED.

MASTER LUKE, IT'S **LANDO** ON THE COMLINK.

LUKE...? CHEWIE AND I ARE READY FOR **TAKE OFF.**

I'LL SEE YOU ON **TATOOINE.**

AND DON'T **WORRY,** LEIA... WE'LL **FIND** HAN!

VAROWRK!

AND AS THE **MILLENNIUM FALCON** PULLS AWAY FROM THE REBEL BATTLE CRUISER THAT HAS BEEN A TEMPORARY REFUGE... THOSE LEFT **BEHIND** HAVE MANY THOUGHTS, MANY UNCERTAINTIES, BUT FOR THIS MOMENT...

...THEY ALSO HAVE **PEACE.**

TAKE **CARE,** MY FRIENDS... MAY THE **FORCE** BE WITH YOU!

END

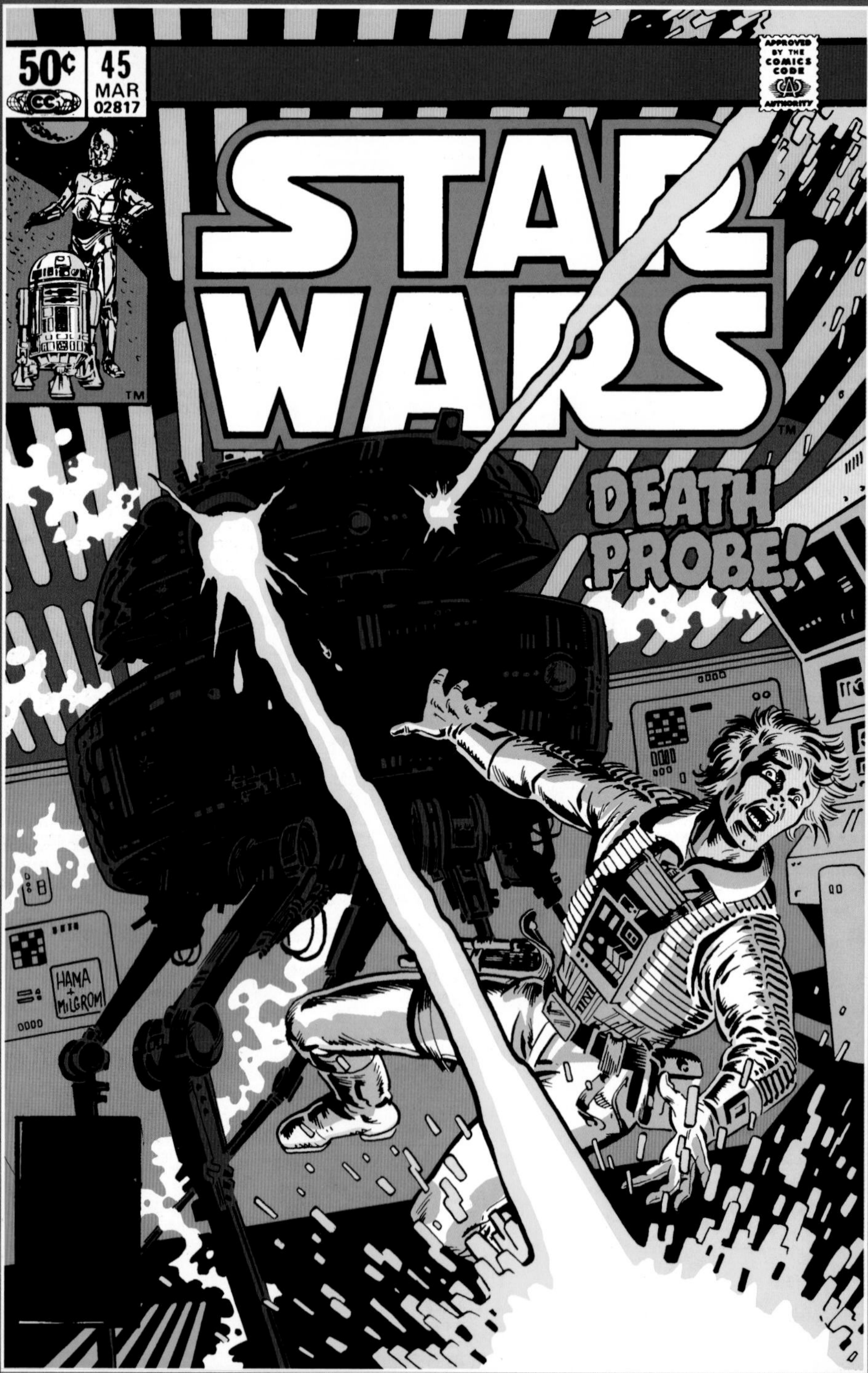
50¢
45
MAR
02817
APPROVED BY THE COMICS CODE AUTHORITY
STAR WARS
DEATH PROBE!
HAMA + MILGROM

Long ago in a galaxy far, far away. . .there exists a state of cosmic *civil war*. A brave alliance of *underground freedom fighters* has challenged the tyranny and oppression of the awesome *Galactic Empire*. This is their story!

LucasFilm PRESENTS: STAR WARS
THE GREATEST SPACE FANTASY OF ALL!

ARCHIE GOODWIN
writer
•
CARMINE INFANTINO
penciler
•
DAY & STONE
inkers
•
JOHN COSTANZA
letterer
•
GLYNIS WEIN
colorist
•
LOUISE JONES
editor
•
JIM SHOOTER
editor-in-chief

HARD TIMES IN THE GALAXY. SINCE THE FALL OF THEIR BASE ON THE ICE PLANET, HOTH, FORCES OF THE REBEL ALLIANCE FIND NEW, EVER MORE SINISTER THREATS FROM THE EMPIRE ON ALL FRONTS.

A BATTLE-DAMAGED BLOCKADE RUNNER LIMPS THROUGH DEEP SPACE, LONG RANGE SCANNERS INOPERATIVE, EACH EXHAUSTED CREW MEMBER PRAYING THEIR RETURN TO REBEL FLEET RENDEZVOUS WILL BE WITHOUT INCIDENT.

IT ALMOST IS.

DEATH PROBE

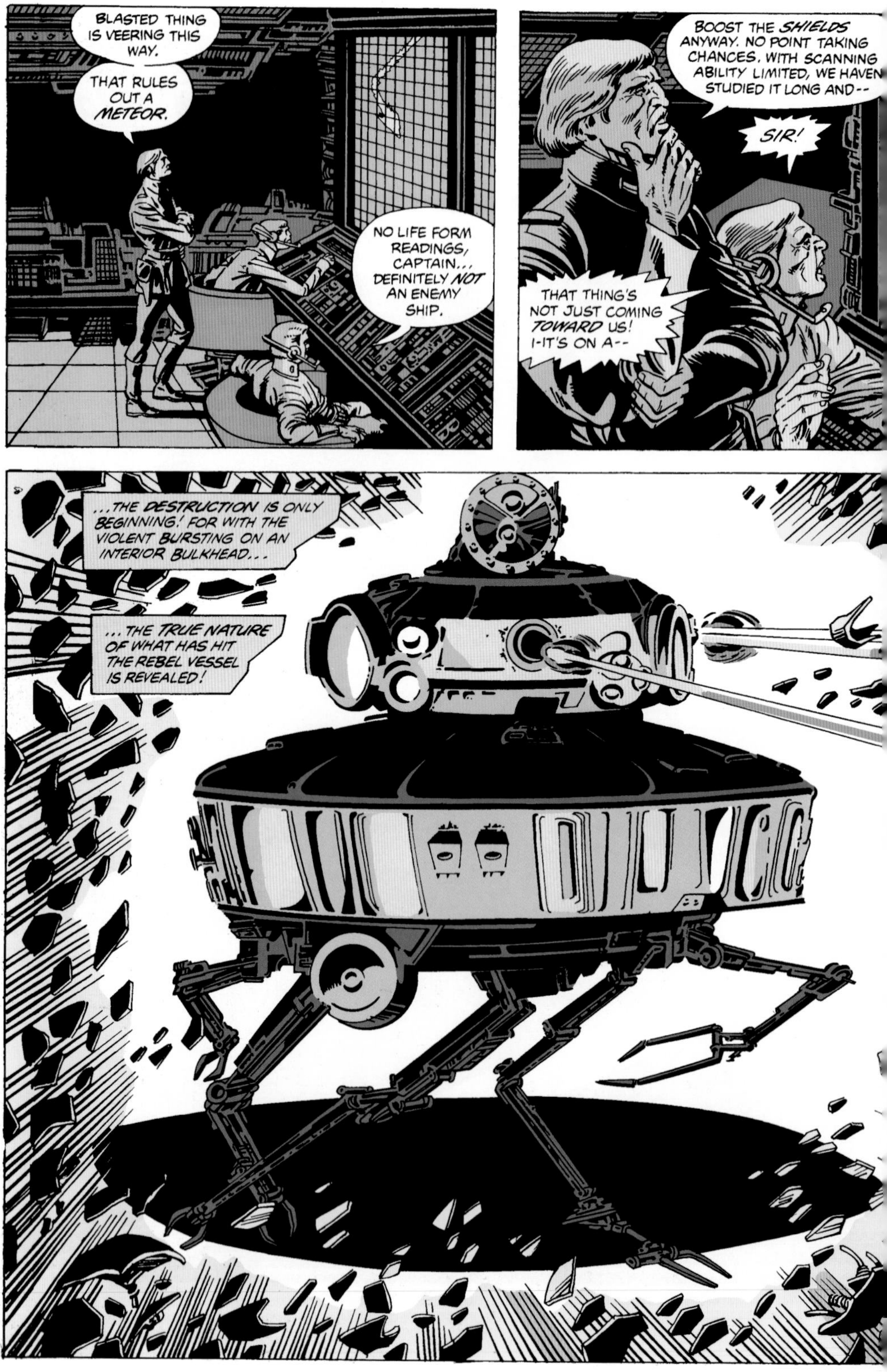
BLASTED THING IS VEERING THIS WAY.
THAT RULES OUT A METEOR.
NO LIFE FORM READINGS, CAPTAIN... DEFINITELY NOT AN ENEMY SHIP.
BOOST THE SHIELDS ANYWAY. NO POINT TAKING CHANCES. WITH SCANNING ABILITY LIMITED, WE HAVEN STUDIED IT LONG AND--
SIR!
THAT THING'S NOT JUST COMING TOWARD US! I-IT'S ON A--
...THE DESTRUCTION IS ONLY BEGINNING! FOR WITH THE VIOLENT BURSTING ON AN INTERIOR BULKHEAD...
...THE TRUE NATURE OF WHAT HAS HIT THE REBEL VESSEL IS REVEALED!

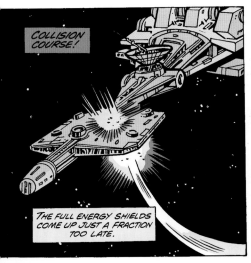

COLLISION COURSE!

THE FULL ENERGY SHIELDS COME UP JUST A FRACTION TOO LATE.

MEN DIE...

...SUCKED TO THEIR DOOM IN A SUDDEN RUSH OF ESCAPING ATMOSPHERE. AND EVEN AS THE DAMAGED COMPARTMENTS ARE SEALED OFF,...

AN IMPERIAL PROBE DROID!

B-BUT IT'S BIGGER... BETTER ARMED...! AND--

AND REAPING *DEATH* AS IT MOVES METHODICALLY, PURPOSEFULLY, THROUGH THE SHIP.

BUT WITH SO MANY TARGETS, THE PROBE ROBOT'S LOGIC CIRCUITS KEY ITS ATTACK ON *MOVEMENT...*

UNTIL IT IS SUDDENLY MADE *OBVIOUS* THAT A MAN LYING STILL IS NOT NECESSARILY *DEAD!*

IT'S ARMOR IS *HEAVIER* THAN IT LOOKS! NO TIME TO READJUST MY BLASTER... GOT TO REACH A COMMUNICATIONS TERMINAL!

DOESN'T LOOK LIKE WE CAN *CONTAIN* THAT MECHANIZED MONSTER! THE *FLEET* HAS TO KNOW!

HE IS *RAD TORLENT,* ONE OF THE SHIP'S JUNIOR OFFICERS...

HE JOINED THE REBELLION WHEN THE EMPIRE SEIZED HIS HOME PLANET OF *NEUTRA FOUR...*

ANOTHER FEW SECONDS AT THE COMMUNICATOR AND HE MIGHT HAVE BECOME A *HERO...*

...INSTEAD, HE BECOMES ONE MORE *ANONYMOUS VICTIM* IN A LONG, BITTER WAR.

A VICTIM WITH THE MISFORTUNE TO HAVE REACHED A COMMUNICA- TIONS TERMINAL IN THE COMPARTMENT THAT WAS THE PROBE DROID'S DESTINATION.

AND SEVERAL LIGHT YEARS AWAY...THAT ARRIVAL IS DULY NOTED.

IT'S PROBE *13-K,* SIR. ONE OF THE MODELS YOU HAD SPECIALLY *AUGMENTED* BY TECHNOLOGICAL SECTION.

OF *COURSE* IT IS. I WOULDN'T HAVE EXCEEDED ORDERS BY TAMPERING WITH OUR PROBE UNLESS I WAS *CERTAIN* OF WORTHWHILE RESULTS.

HERE'S THE PRINT-OUT ON ITS PROGRESS, ADMIRAL.

SATISFACTORY. *MOST* SATISFACTORY. AND THOSE FOOL TECHNOS THOUGHT WE WERE PROGRAMMING IT *BEYOND* ITS CAPABILITIES.

THE REBELS WILL SOON KNOW THE *FULLEST MEASURE* OF THOSE CAPABILITIES--

--AND THE *EMPEROR* HIMSELF WILL PRAISE THE NAME OF ADMIRAL *DAMON KRELL.*

ELSEWHERE, AN INCOMING T-65 X-WING FIGHTER KNIFES THROUGH THE VOID ON WIDE PATROL FOR THE ALLIANCE FLEET...

VA-DITTA PA-FREET BWOOOP?

NO, ARTOO, I'M NOT PUSHING MYSELF TOO HARD. AFTER ALL, I TOOK THIS FLIGHT TO *TEST* HOW WELL I'M RECOVERING...

BEING TESTED HOLDS FEW FEARS FOR THE YOUNG MAN AT THE X-WING'S CONTROLS...

FOR HE IS LUKE SKYWALKER AND HE HAS ALREADY FACED MANY TESTS, FROM HIS TRAINING IN THE WAYS OF THE FORCE BY THE DEMANDING LITTLE JEDI MASTER, YODA...

...TO THE PHYSICAL AND EMOTIONAL PAIN OF HIS SHOWDOWN DUEL AT CLOUD CITY WITH THE DARK LORD OF THE SITH, DARTH VADER...

...WHERE HE LEARNED THAT THIS MAN HE MOST HATED IN ALL THE GALAXY MIGHT WELL BE HIS FATHER!

WHATEVER THE TRUTH, LUKE CHOSE DEATH RATHER THAN JOINING THE MASTER OF THE FORCE'S DARK SIDE. THE MILLENNIUM FALCON APPEARED IN TIME TO SPARE HIM FROM THAT...

...BUT HE NOW WEARS A BIONIC HAND IN PLACE OF THE REAL ONE FOREVER LOST; A GRIM, LASTING REMINDER OF THE BATTLE AND ITS HAUNTING IMPLICATIONS.

IT FELT LIKE VADER TOLD ME THE *TRUTH*... BUT WOULDN'T THAT MEAN *BEN KENOBI* MISLED ME?

EITHER SEEMS *UNTHINKABLE*. MAKES IT SO HARD TO DECIDE WHAT I SHOULD DO *NEXT* AND--

WHRAT KA-LIIIK--

BRAAP!

THANKS FOR WAKING ME UP, ARTOO...! I SEE IT ON THE SCOPE--

--APPROACHING *SPACECRAFT*. SENSORS TAG IT AS ONE OF OUR *BLOCKADE RUNNERS*.

AND VISUAL CONFIRMATION IS AFFIRMATIVE. WE CAN *RELAX*, LITTLE GUY.

LOOKS LIKE THEY'VE TAKEN SOME *DAMAGE*. MAYBE THAT'S WHY THEY'RE NOT IN *COMMUNICATION* WITH US, OR--

SUDDENLY, THERE IS COMMUNICATION... SPIT HOSTILELY FROM ALL FORWARD LASER CANNONS!

THE MESSAGE IS LOUD, CLEAR... AND TOTALLY *DEVASTATING!*

LUKE'S SHIP DISINTEGRATES...

...HURLING PILOT AND R2-D2 DROID VIOLENTLY INTO SPACE!

MY FLYING SUIT'S LIFE SUPPORT SYSTEM IS CUTTING IN... BUT ARTOO AND I ARE GOING TO BE THRUST *MILES* APART IN SECONDS!

UNLESS...

*L*UKE'S MIND GOES CLEAR... WIPED CLEAN OF ANXIETY, OF CONFUSION. OBLIVIOUS TO THE HISS OF OXYGEN THROUGH HIS AUTOMATICALLY SEALING FACEMASK...

...THE STAR WARRIOR FROM TATOOINE FEELS THE *FORCE!*

AND MOMENTARILY, MUCH LESS MYSTICALLY... SO DOES HIS DRIFTING COMPANION.

BA-LEET!

EASY, ARTOO! I'M JUST DRAWING YOU NEAR ENOUGH--

... TO *GRAB!* OKAY? THIS SUIT CAN'T KEEP ME GOING FOR TOO *LONG*--

--BUT *TOGETHER*, WE AT LEAST HAVE A CHANCE! WITH YOU TO TRANSMIT LONG RANGE DISTRESS SIGNALS--

--SOMEONE SHOULD COME.

THE ROGUE BLOCKADE RUNNER HAS *TURNED*... MOVING BACK, SHARK-LIKE... FOR THE *KILL.*

BUT EVEN AS ITS GUNS FIRE, LUKE'S BLASTER IS OUT... DOING THE SAME!

CAN'T HURT IT WITH A HANDGUN, LITTLE PAL... BUT I CAN PROPEL US OUT OF THE WAY!

ONLY... NOT TOO *FAR!* WHEN THAT DEATH-DEALING HULK LUMBERS PAST, I WANT *YOU* ABLE TO--

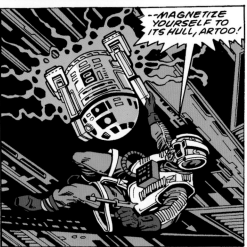

--MAGNETIZE YOURSELF TO ITS HULL, ARTOO!

GREAT!

WITH YOU TO HANG ONTO, MY *LIGHTSABER* CAN DO THE REST!

OKAY... THIS IS THE REPAIR CONDUIT BETWEEN THE INNER AND OUTER HULLS.

DON'T KNOW WHAT'S *HAPPENING* ON BOARD, BUT IT CAN'T BE WORSE THAN PLAYING FLOATING *TARGET* OUTSIDE OR--

LOOK OUT, ARTOO!

FRA-DEETA SKREEEEET!

WELDING BEAMS... FROM THE DAMAGE SEALING SYSTEMS! I ALMOST FORGOT ABOUT THEM.

YOU'D THINK THEY'D HAVE ACTIVATED IMMEDIATELY... THOSE FEW MOMENTS HESITATION PUT US RIGHT IN THEIR PATH.

YOUR SENSORS DETECTING ANY OTHER SURPRISES, ARTOO?

TA-DOOT VA-DLEEP!

AN INCOMING TRANSMISSION?

LET'S HEAR IT!

ARTOO'S AUDIO-AMPLIFICATION UNIT CUTS IN AND LUKE'S EARS ARE SUDDENLY ASSAILED BY...

IMPERIAL CODE!

CAN'T DECIPHER WHAT THEY'RE SAYING, BUT... IF IT'S BEING SENT HERE--

THIS SHIP MUST BE UNDER THE EMPIRE'S CONTROL!

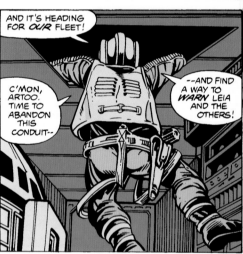

AND IT'S HEADING FOR OUR FLEET!

C'MON, ARTOO. TIME TO ABANDON THIS CONDUIT--

--AND FIND A WAY TO WARN LEIA AND THE OTHERS!

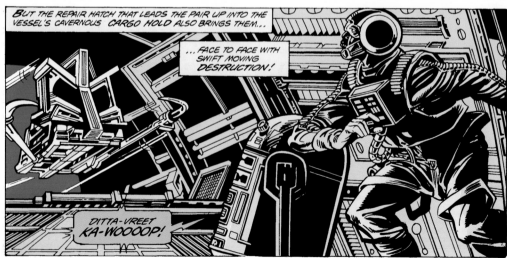

BUT THE REPAIR HATCH THAT LEADS THE PAIR UP INTO THE VESSEL'S CAVERNOUS CARGO HOLD ALSO BRINGS THEM...

...FACE TO FACE WITH SWIFT MOVING DESTRUCTION!

DITTA-VREET KA-WOOOOP!

IF YOU'RE SAYING YOU NEVER SAW A MECHANIZED HOLD-TENDER *ACT* LIKE THAT--

-- I *AGREE,* ARTOO!

MOVE! BEFORE--

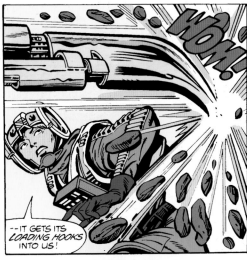

-- IT GETS ITS *LOADING HOOKS* INTO US!

ARTOO IS PUSHED CLEAR, BUT...

IT'S HURLING CARGO CASES! AND DODGING 'EM LEAVES MY *BACK* OPEN TO BE *IMPALED!*

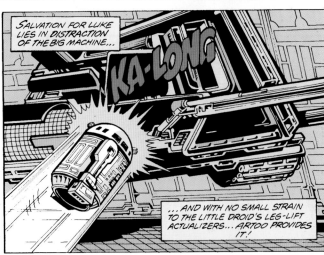

SALVATION FOR LUKE LIES IN DISTRACTION OF THE BIG MACHINE...

KA-LONG

...AND WITH NO SMALL STRAIN TO THE LITTLE DROID'S LEG-LIFT ACTUALIZERS...ARTOO PROVIDES IT!

BUT TO THE REPAIR ROBOT'S CONSTERNATION, AS THE RAMPAGING HOLD-TENDER WHIRLS *HIS* WAY...

...LUKE, WITH POWER BORN OF HIS JEDI TRAINING...

...LEAPS STRAIGHT *BACK* INTO HARM'S WAY!

FLOOOO-BRIIT?!

MUST *SEEM* LIKE I'VE BLOWN THE *CHANCE* YOU GAVE ME--

KLONG

KWONG

--BUT WE'RE CLOSE ENOUGH SO THE *WALL* INTERFERES WITH ITS *PINCER* MOVEMENT--

--LONG ENOUGH FOR ME TO DO *THIS!*

DEAD *FRONT* WAS THE ONLY ANGLE TO KNOCK OUT ITS MOTOR CONTROLS--

FOAK!

--WITH *ONE SHOT!* NO MORE MENACE, ARTOO... IT'S JUST *BURNING JUNK* NOW!

BUT...

A-A *CARGO DRUM....?!*

VWOM!

THEN LUKE HEARS THE RATTLE OF THE AUTOMATED CONVEYER OVERHEAD AND REALIZES...

THOSE THINGS CONTAIN *LIQUID PROPELLENT!* HEAD FOR THE *DOOR*, LITTLE GUY!

THIS HOLD'S GONNA BECOME AN *INFERNO!*

WHREEEET!

AND THE DROID'S SHRILL WHISTLE SIGNALS THAT THE ONLY EXIT IS SWIFTLY, SURELY CLOSING!

THE MASSIVE DOOR THUNDERS DOWN, BARELY MISSING THE LITHE, ROLLING FIGURE...

...AND FOR THE MOMENT THE YOUNG STAR WARRIOR AND HIS DROID KNOW SAFETY. FOR THE MOMENT...

STATUS REPORT ON SPECIAL PROBE 13-K...?

RESPONDING *PERFECTLY* TO ALL SECONDARY PROGRAMMING, ADMIRAL KRELL.

THEN THERE IS NO REASON NOT TO INIATE THE *FINAL CYCLE.*

THERE'S STILL SOME *TIME,* SIR.

IT MIGHT BE AMUSING TO SEE HOW 13-K RESOLVES THIS BUSINESS WITH THE *REBEL INTERLOPER* BEFORE--

WE'RE NOT DOING THIS FOR AMUSEMENT... BUT TO *DESTROY* THE REBEL FLEET.

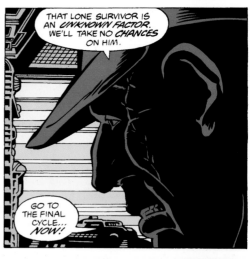

THAT LONE SURVIVOR IS AN *UNKNOWN FACTOR.* WE'LL TAKE NO *CHANCES* ON HIM.

GO TO THE FINAL CYCLE... *NOW!*

ABOARD THE BLOCKADE RUNNER, THERE IS SILENCE, GRIM AND FORBODING. LUKE STANDS STILL, NOT LISTENING, BUT... FEELING.

UNTIL...

SOMETHING *HAPPENED...* JUST NOW... B-BUT...

IMPATIENCE OVERTAKES HIM...

WHATEVER'S HAPPENING... IT'S GOT TO BE CONNECTED--

--WITH THE *MAIN COMPUTER CHAMBER!*

EVERY ATTACK ON US HAS INVOLVED THE SHIP'S *AUTOMATED* EQUIPMENT.

WHOEVER'S TAKEN OVER COULD ONLY DIRECT ALL THAT STUFF FROM--

--T-THERE!

FOR THE FIRST TIME, LUKE AND ARTOO BEHOLD THE TRUE NATURE OF THEIR ENEMY... AND REALIZE HOW TERRIBLY COMPLETE THE TAKEOVER OF THE REBEL VESSEL IS!

THAT THING'S TAPPED INTO *EVERY* SYSTEM,...MADE THE ENTIRE SHIP PRACTICALLY AN *EXTENSION* OF ITSELF!

SOMEONE'S *REALLY* AUGMENTED ITS PROGRAMMING! PROBE DROID'S WERE *NEVER* MENT TO OPERATE THIS INDEPENDENTLY!

DARTH VADER ONLY USED THEM TO *TRACK* ME AND THE OTHER REBELS!

BUT *WHATEVER* ITS CAPABILITIES... *NO* ONE'S GONNA USE THIS ONE ANYM--

¡*UNGHH!* ARTOO, YOU SPOILED MY *SHOT!* AND THAT PROBE'S WON'T GIVE US *ANOTHER!* W-WHAT--?

BRAKOW

WEE-DOOOT FRAAAT!

SHOVED BY THE LITTLE DROID, LUKE RETREATS FROM THE PROBOT'S LASER BLASTS UNTIL...

WE'VE REACHED A CORRIDOR *PRINT OUT TERMINAL*... YOU CAN USE IT TO *EXPLAIN.*

ONLY *WATCH* YOURSELF! THAT MASS OF *IMPERIAL* TECHNOLOGY CAN ALSO USE IT... TO *FRY* YOUR CIRCUITS!

BUT WHAT INSTANTLY FLASHES ONTO THE TERMINAL'S VIEWSCREEN FOR LUKE TO READ...

...MAKES CLEAR WHY FURTHER DIRECT ACTION AGAINST THEM SHOULDN'T BE NECESSARY!

THE PROBOT'S LINKED ITSELF TO THE *MAIN REACTOR* AS WELL AS THE COMPUTER... AND IT'S BUILDING IT TOWARD *CRITICAL MASS?!*

ANY ATTEMPT TO DISLODGE OR DAMAGE THE *DROID*... WILL MAKE THE REACTOR *BLOW!* AND--

OH NO!

BRR-VOOT...?

YOUR SCANNERS SAVED US, ARTOO, B-BUT--

WE'RE COMING UP ON THE *FLEET!* ONCE WE'RE *AMONG* THEM... THAT THING *MUST* INTEND TO *EXPLODE* THE SHIP!

AND IF WE DON'T *DO* SOMETHING, ARTOO... *IT WILL!*

THE ONLY WAY FOR US TO SAVE THE FLEET IS TO *FORGET* ABOUT OURSELVES AND--

OR IS THERE *ANOTHER* WAY...?

FOR MOMENTS, LUKE PONDERS WHAT HE MEANS TO TRY...

THEN, HIS LIGHTSABRE IS IN HAND AND HE IS MOVING WITH A FIERCE DETERMINATION!

YODA SAID IT, ARTOO: THERE *IS* NO TRY...!

ONLY *DO*... OR DO *NOT!* AND *I* MEAN TO DO!

HIS FOOTFALLS CLATTER ANGRILY ON THE CORRIDOR DECKPLATES...

...UNTIL HE REACHES THE SEALED DOOR TO THE SHIP'S *COCKPIT!* AND...

THIS CAN'T STOP ME! *NOTHING'S* GOING TO STOP ME!

VRAMMM WDAK

I'M *LUKE SKYWALKER*... DESTROYER OF THE *DEATH STAR!*

THE ONE WHO DUELED *DARTH VADER* AND LIVED TO TELL ABOUT IT!

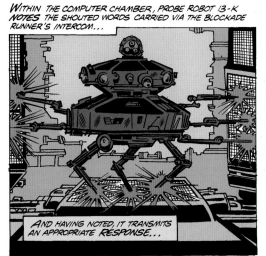

WITHIN THE COMPUTER CHAMBER, PROBE ROBOT 13-K *NOTES* THE SHOUTED WORDS CARRIED VIA THE BLOCKADE RUNNER'S INTERCOM...

AND HAVING NOTED, IT TRANSMITS AN APPROPRIATE *RESPONSE*...

FRA-KOW

...IN THE FORM OF A *POWER OVERLOAD* TO A WALL CIRCUIT CLOSE BY THE *TROUBLEMAKER!*

DOOOOOOT

ALARM SWEEPS ARTOO'S CIRCUITRY AS HIS SENSORS INDICATE LUKE'S LIFE FUNCTIONS HAVE FALLEN TO COMA LEVEL...

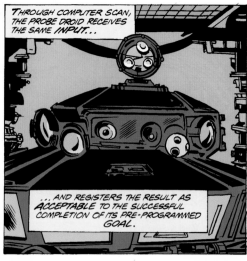

THROUGH COMPUTER SCAN, THE PROBE DROID RECEIVES THE SAME INPUT...

...AND REGISTERS THE RESULT AS ACCEPTABLE TO THE SUCCESSFUL COMPLETION OF ITS PRE-PROGRAMMED GOAL.

WHILE A HYPERSPACE JUMP AWAY, THE MAN WHO HAS BENT THIS PROBE TO HIS OWN PURPOSES PACES IMPATIENTLY...

REPORT, TRACKING OFFICER! 13-K SHOULD HAVE REACHED THE ALLIANCE FLEET! IF THAT LONE REBEL HAS TAMPERED--

NO PROBLEM, ADMIRAL KRELL! I'M GETTING SOMETHING NOW! THE FLEET'S IN SIGHT, THE INTERLOPER HAS BEEN NEUTRALIZED, AND--

AND I'M MOMENTS FROM WINNING A PERSONAL COMMENDATION FROM THE EMPEROR!

WAIT, SIR! S-SOMETHING...I-I... DON'T UNDERSTAND...

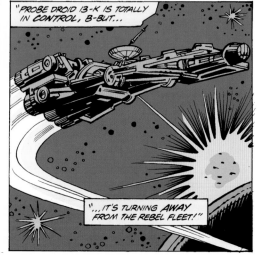

"PROBE DROID 13-K IS TOTALLY IN CONTROL, B-BUT...

"...IT'S TURNING AWAY FROM THE REBEL FLEET!"

WHAT...?! CORRECT IT...! GET IT BACK ON COURSE!

I-I'M TRYING, SIR... ONLY... IT'S REFUSING OUR COMMAND! B-BECAUSE...

"*...IT VIOLATES PRIOR PROGRAMMING FROM LORD VADER HIMSELF! 13-K CLAIMS TO HAVE FOUND LUKE SKYWALKER...! AND ALL INSTRUCTIONS WERE THAT HE WAS TO BE TAKEN ALIVE AND HELD FOR THE EMPEROR!*

"*IT CAN'T SEE THAT THAT COMMAND IS OBEYED...*

"*...AND STILL DESTROY THE REBEL FLEET!*

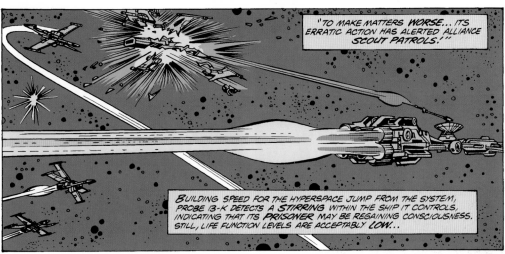

"*TO MAKE MATTERS WORSE... ITS ERRATIC ACTION HAS ALERTED ALLIANCE SCOUT PATROLS!*"

BUILDING SPEED FOR THE HYPERSPACE JUMP FROM THE SYSTEM, PROBE 13-K DETECTS A STIRRING WITHIN THE SHIP IT CONTROLS, INDICATING THAT ITS PRISONER MAY BE REGAINING CONSCIOUSNESS. STILL, LIFE FUNCTION LEVELS ARE ACCEPTABLY LOW...

...AND THE PROBE HAS A DEFENSE TO MAINTAIN.

ARTOO-DETOO'S SENSORS TELL HIM MUCH THE SAME THING...

...BUT HIS PHOTO-RECEPTORS, TRAINED WITHIN THE BLOCKADE RUNNER'S COCKPIT, OFFER CONFLICTING DATA!

JUST... A... LITTLE... LONGER...!

ARTOO! GET READY TO MOVE... FAST!

GOT TO MAINTAIN...! CONTROL MY... LIFE FUNCTIONS... THROUGH FORCE... KEEP SECRET... THAT I'M UP... MOVING... ACTING...! UNTIL...

DAMAGED ALARMS SHRILL IN THE MAIN COMPUTER CHAMBER! BANKS OF CONSOLE LIGHTS GO SUDDENLY *DARK*...

...AS THE IMPERIAL DROID FINDS COMPUTER CIRCUITRY CONTROLLING AREAS OF THE *GUIDANCE SYSTEM* HAVE BEEN *SEVERED!*

RETALIATORY ACTION IS *IMMEDIATE*...BUT AT THE COST OF EXPLODING MORE NEEDED CIRCUITS!

UNTIL 13-K REALIZES IT HAS BEEN TRICKED INTO WEAKENING CONTROL OVER A SECTION CONTAINING...

...A *LIFE POD!*

AND AS SIDE-MOUNTED LASER CANNONS TRACK TO *VAPORIZE* LUKE AND ARTOO IN MID-ESCAPE...

...HYPER-DRIVE CUTS IN!

THE CAPTURED BLOCKADE RUNNER IS APPROACHING *US*, ADMIRAL...

NATURALLY, WE LAUNCHED THE PROBE...IT WILL RETURN *HERE* WITH ITS PRISONER.

WE CAN STILL SALVAGE SOME *GLORY* FROM THAT. IN FACT, I'LL--

366

SIR--!

THE VESSEL'S *REACTOR* IS STILL PRIMED TO EXPLODE. THE PROBE WON'T ACKNOWLEDGE MY SIGNAL TO *CANCEL* DESTRUCTION!

B-BEING FORCED TO HANDLE ITS *REGULAR* PROGRAMMING ALONG WITH ALL OUR *AUGMENTATION*--

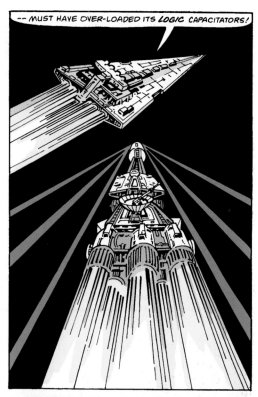

-- MUST HAVE OVER-LOADED ITS *LOGIC* CAPACITATORS!

EMERGENCY STATIONS! TAKE *IMMEDIATE* EVASIVE ACTION!

BRING ALL *GUNS* TO BEAR!

BLAST THAT THING OUT OF THE *VOID* BEFORE IT--

WITH SHOCK WAVE FORCE, PROBE DROID 13-K *ENDS* ITS MISSION...

... AND ALL OF ADMIRAL KRELL'S *DREAMS* OF SPECIAL GLORY IN SERVICE TO HIS EMPEROR.

WHILE IN THE SYSTEM IT FLED, X-WING FIGHTERS MOVE TO PICK UP A DRIFTING *LIFE POD*...

WHRRR-DIT FRA-WHEET!

I THINK I UNDERSTAND WHAT YOU MEAN, ARTOO.

WHEN I CAME OUT HERE TO CHECK HOW I'D *RECUPERATED* FROM MY DUEL WITH DARTH VADER--

--I DIDN'T KNOW IT WOULD BE *THIS MUCH* OF A TEST!

NEXT LANDO AND CHEWBACCA'S... *SEARCH* for *SOLO!*

50¢ **46**
APR
02817

STAR WARS ™

A LIVING NIGHTMARE STALKS THE UNIVERSE...

...EMPIRE AND REBEL FORCES ALIKE, HELPLESS PREY OF THE **DREADNAUGHT DEVOURER!**

Long ago in a galaxy far, far away. . .there exists a state of cosmic *civil war*. A brave alliance of *underground freedom fighters* has challenged the tyranny and oppression of the awesome *Galactic Empire*. This is their story!

LucasFilm PRESENTS: STAR WARS™ THE GREATEST SPACE FANTASY OF ALL!

| WALLY LOMBEGO WRITER | CARMINE INFANTINO ARTIST | TOM PALMER INKER | DIANA ALBERS LETTERER | GLYNIS WEIN COLORIST | L. JONES & DAN F. EDITORS | JIM SHOOTER EDITOR-IN-CHIEF |

SOMETIMES IT SEEMS HOPELESS, BUT THE SEARCH FOR HAN SOLO AND HIS CAPTOR, BOBA FETT, GOES *ON.* LANDO CALRISSIAN AND CHEWBACCA PILOT SOLO'S *MILLENNIUM FALCON* AS IT ROARS THROUGH HYPER-SPACE, WONDERING IF THEY WILL EVER SEE THEIR FRIEND AGAIN.

THIS SHIP HAS BEEN CALLED THE "FASTEST HUNK OF JUNK IN THE GALAXY"-- A HYPER-BOLIC STATEMENT, YET ONE WITH MORE THAN A GRAIN OF TRUTH.

BUT ALL THE SPEED IN THE *UNIVERSE* IS OF NO HELP WHEN A WARP-ENGINE SUDDENLY BUCKLES AND DIES!

THE DREAMS OF CODY SUNN-CHILDE!

YARRGG?!

WE'RE IN TROUBLE, CHEWIE-- *BIG* TROUBLE!

YOU'VE GOT ME, MY FURRY FRIEND-- I HAVEN'T THE FAINTEST IDEA WHERE WE ARE!

NYYORGG!

BEAUTIFUL IT IS -- LIKE HEAVEN OPENING WIDE IN WELCOME...

...ALTHOUGH I DON'T KNOW OF ANY HEAVEN THAT WOULD READILY ADMIT A PAIR LIKE *US!*

THEN THE WORDS MOMENTARILY DISSOLVE ON LANDO CALRISSIAN'S TONGUE AS HIS EYES WIDEN IN AWE...

...FOR ACROSS THIS COLOR-SOAKED VOID THERE FLOATS AN ISLAND, AND ON THE ISLAND...

A CITY?

COULD THIS BE SOME ELABORATE TRAP CONSTRUCTED BY VADER AND THE BLACK-HEARTS OF THE EMPIRE?

IT COULD BE--BUT WHAT USE ARE QUESTIONS WHEN YOUR SHIP IS PLUMMETTING RAPIDLY THROUGH AN ALL-TOO ALIEN SKY?

NO GOOD AT ALL!

SKOOM!

GROOOT?!

WHAT ARE YOU TALKING ABOUT?

I THOUGHT IT WAS A PERFECT LANDING!

THEY MAKE AN *UNLIKELY* PAIR: CALRISSIAN, FORMER CON-MAN AND SOLDIER-OF-FORTUNE, IS A NEW CONVERT TO THE REBEL CAUSE. HE'S ALSO THE MAN RESPONSIBLE FOR TURNING HAN SOLO OVER TO THE BOUNTY HUNTER BOBA FETT.

THE TOWERING WOOKIEE, BY CONTRAST, IS A SEASONED FREEDOM-FIGHTER...AND HAN SOLO'S CLOSEST FRIEND.

WITH THE SHIP INOPERABLE-- OUR ONLY HOPE IS TO GET TO THAT CITY, CHEWIE.

AND YOU NEVER KNOW--WE MAY JUST BE ABLE TO SCHEME OURSELVES INTO A FORTUNE-- PERHAPS WREST A KINGDOM OF OUR OWN OUT OF THIS MESS...

...IF THE CITY DWELLERS ARE GULLIBLE...

...ENOUGH?!

RRRRGGH!

UH... OF COURSE, CHEWBACCA--OUR *FIRST* PRIORITY IS TO FIND HAN. I'D...UH...NEVER FORGET THAT.

NOT THAT YOU'D LET ME IF I WANTED TO.

HARRUGH!

OH, COME *ON,* NOW! I SAID TH--

4

374

IT HAPPENS QUICKLY...

...THE SILENT LEAP OF A BLOOD-EYED BEAST...

...AND THE PLANGENT SHRIEK OF A CLAW-RAKED WOOKIEE!

CHEWIE!

IT IS MOST LIKELY THAT, GIVEN TIME TO PONDER, LANDO CALRISSIAN WOULD NOT HAVE JUMPED SO IM-MEDIATELY INTO THE FRAY...

WHAK!

BUT IT'S A BIT LATE FOR REGRETS NOW!

UNGGH!

GNRRRGL!

THE CREATURE'S ATTACK IS SAVAGE, UNRELENTING, AND THE TWO STUNNED STAR-WARRIORS ARE BEATEN NEAR-UNCONSCIOUS IN LESS TIME THAN IT WOULD TAKE TO SWAT A FLY.

A DISTORTED GRIN SPREADS ACROSS THE AWFUL THING'S LEATHERN FACE. IT RAISES ITS MUSCLED ARM...

...AND HOWLS!

ENOUGH. MY MONSTER-BROTHER'S VIOLENCE MUST HAVE EXPRESSION--BUT I WILL NOT ALLOW THE TAKING OF A SINGLE LIFE HERE IN MY REALM.

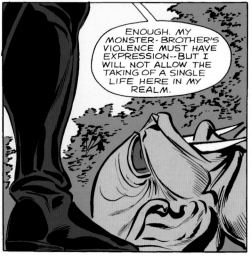

WELL--WHY DO YOU STARE, STRANGERS? I AM NOT AN ENEMY.

IN FACT, I MAY PROVE TO BE THE GREATEST FRIEND YOU WILL EVER KNOW.

6

AH, NOW YOU RISE--BUT THERE IS STILL THAT GLINT OF WARINESS IN YOUR EYES. IS IT THAT YOU DOUBT MY GOOD FAITH?

THEN WATCH NOW AS I REACH OUT AND PULL MY MONSTER BROTHER UP FROM THE GROUND-- DRAWING HIM INTO MYSELF.

"HE WILL TROUBLE YOU NO LONGER."

YOU... MISUNDERSTAND! I HESITATED BECAUSE THERE WAS SOMETHING-- FAMILIAR ABOUT YOU!

AND NOW I REMEMBER! I SAW YOU IN ACTION AGAINST THE IMPERIALS WHEN I WAS JUST A BOY.

YOU'RE CODY SUNN-CHILDE!

THE MUCH-LIONIZED HERO OF THE REBEL CAUSE?

THAT IS MY NAME, SIR--BUT NOMENCLATURE IS THE ONLY THING LINKING ME TO THE MAN OF VIOLENCE YOU RECALL.

KEEP THAT IN MIND.

ENOUGH TALK OF THE PAST! ENOUGH WASTING OF PRECIOUS MOMENTS! THESE JUNGLES ARE HAUNTED BY MANY MORE OF MY MONSTER-BROTHERS...

...LET US LEAVE THEM--AND THE PAST-- BEHIND US... AS WE ENTER THE CITY...

THE STRANGE ASSEM-BLAGE TRUDGES ON TOWARD THE GLITTERING SPIRES THAT RISE UP MAJESTICALLY BEFORE THEM... 7

...REACHING, AT LAST, THE PORTALS OF THIS CITY AMONG THE STARS.

NEVER IN HIS LIFE HAS CHEWBACCA SEEN SUCH BEAUTY--NEVER SUCH SYMMETRY, SUCH FINELY SCULPTED PERFECTION. HE CRANES HIS HAIRY NECK TO GAZE UP AT THE GOLDEN BAL- LOONS THAT DRIFT LAZILY OVERHEAD...

...AND LETS FLY AN UNBIDDEN GROWL OF DELIGHT AS A SOFT, SURREAL MUSIC WAFTS DOWN FROM THE GREAT CATHEDRAL- LIKE BUILDING AHEAD.

EVEN THE GRIM CALRISSIAN CANNOT MASK HIS ASTONISHMENT.

WHERE-- *ARE* WE?

IN ANOTHER DIMEN- SION FROM THE ONE THAT BIRTHED US. WHEN YOUR WARP ENGINE EXPLODED IT MUST HAVE SOMEHOW *PIERCED* THE WALL-BETWEEN... AND BROUGHT YOU HERE.

YOU MAY REMAIN AMONG US IF YOU CHOOSE--AND WHEN YOU SEE WHAT IT IS WE HAVE HERE, I THINK YOU *WILL* CHOOSE. BUT BE FOREWARNED--THIS IS A PLACE OF PEACE. RESPECT IT AS SUCH.

RRRR...

I DON'T GET IT, SUNN-CHILDE-- WHAT'S YOUR GAME?

8

WE PLAY NO GAMES IN OUR CITY OF DREAMS, SIR--WE HIDE BEHIND NEITHER SOPHI-STRY NOR CHICANERY!

OUR MASTER SUNN-CHILDE HAS BUILT A HAVEN FROM MADNESS. EMBRACE IT WARMLY...

...AS I SEE YOUR WOOKIEE FRIEND IS LEARNING TO DO RIGHT NOW!

VROWR.

IT HAS BEEN A LONG TIME--TOO LONG, SINCE CHEWBACCA HAS BEEN HOME.

THE SIGHT OF A FELLOW WOOKIEE MAKES HIS HEART SING.

CHE-ROOOR.

TAKE THE WORD OF *ANSIBLE BEELYARD*--HERE YOU HAVE FOUND A UNIVERSE UNTAINTED BY THE DARKNESS OF THE EMPIRE!

BEELYARD? *BEELYARD, THE HOLY TERROR?* HE WAS YOUR RIGHT-HAND MAN, SUNN-CHILDE AND--LIKE YOU--HE VANISHED NEARLY A DECADE AGO!

WHAT IS GOING *ON* HERE?!

9

EVEN AS LANDO CALRISSIAN'S QUESTION REVERBERATES IN THE HALL, A FLEET OF WELL-WORN IMPERIAL BATTLE CRUISERS SKIMS THE SPACEWAYS OF A BACKWATER STAR SECTOR.

HERE WE FIND THE FORGOTTEN FORCES, THOSE WHO SERVE THE EMPIRE CAPABLY, COMPETENTLY, WITHOUT FUSS OR FANFARE. THEY ARE THE SILENT FOUNDATION OF THE EMPEROR'S DOMINION.

BUT EVEN THE LONG-FORGOTTEN...

...CAN COURT GREAT AMBITION...

AMAZING, CAPTAIN PLIKK-- A SMALL *RENT* IN THE VERY DIMENSIONAL FABRIC! WHAT CAN IT MEAN?

IT WILL MEAN NOTHING, LIEUTENANT NIZZON--UNTIL WE HAVE LOCATED THE PRECISE AREA OF DEMARCATION.

FOR YEARS, CAPTAIN, WE HAVE PATROLLED THIS SECTOR--SEEING FEW BATTLES--GAINING FEWER GLORIES. BUT I HAVE A FEELING ABOUT *THIS*....!

YOU HEARD CAPTAIN PLIKK, DOG-- EXACTITUDE IS OF PRIME *IMPORTANCE!* THERE CAN BE NO MISTAKE!

AS DO I, NIZZON. AS THOUGH DISCOVERY OF WHAT LIES BEYOND THAT RENT WILL BRING US ALL THE GLORIES OF A *LIFETIME.*

10

IN A SUB-BASEMENT, BENEATH THE CITY OF DREAMS...

THIS EQUIPMENT IS OUR SOLE TIE TO THE OUTSIDE WORLD, MISTER CALRISSIAN. WITH IT WE MONITOR RANDOM TRANSMISSIONS FROM THE EMPIRE...

...TRANSMISSIONS THAT REMIND US HOW RAMPANT THE WAYS OF DEATH AND DESTRUCTION STILL ARE--AND HOW IMPORTANT IT IS THAT WE CONTINUE TO FORSAKE THOSE WAYS.

BUT CAN'T YOUR POWER-SOURCE EMANATIONS BE TRACED?

NO. FOR THIS MACHINE-BANK--LIKE EVERYTHING HERE IN MY CITY--IS CONSTRUCTED NOT OF COMMON MATTER BUT OF PSYCHIC ENERGY.

I...DON'T UNDERSTAND. JUST AS I DON'T UNDERSTAND WHY. A DEDICATED FREEDOM-FIGHTER LIKE CODY SUNN-CHILDE WOULD TURN HIS BACK ON THE REVOLUTION.

IT IS CLEAR THAT YOU UNDERSTAND LITTLE OF WHAT I OF WHAT I AM ABOUT, MISTER CALRISSIAN. IT IS ALSO CLEAR THAT I MUST EXPLAIN.

EVERY SCHOOLBOY HAS HEARD THE LEGEND OF CODY SUNN-CHILDE-- WHO LED THE WAR AGAINST TYRANNY BEFORE IT WAS FASHIONABLE.

"I APPEARED DEDICATED TO MY CHOSEN TASK OF ABOLISHING THE IMPERIAL DISEASE THAT HAS EATEN AWAY AT ALL THAT IS GOOD AND DECENT IN MAN-- DID I NOT?

"BUT IN FACT, I RELISHED WAR FOR ITS OWN SAKE! I LOVED THE FIGHTING, THE KILLING. FOR ME THE REVOLUTION WAS AN EXCUSE TO INDULGE IN WHOLE-SALE VIOLENCE. THOSE WHOSE REAL GOAL WAS PEACE SOON LEFT ME IN DISGUST.

11

" HOW LONG COULD A MAN FOLLOW A PATH AS IM-BALANCED AS THAT BEFORE HE HIMSELF FELL AS THE RESULT OF HIS OWN UN-BRIDLED VIOLENCE?

" MY IMBALANCE CAME DURING A TRUCULENT BATTLE ON A LITTLE-KNOWN WORLD FRESHLY CONQUERED BY THE EMPIRE. A LASER-BLAST HURLED ME THROUGH A CRAVASSE INTO THE BOWELS OF THE PLANET...

"...AND I WAS SWAL-LOWED...

" BY A MYSTERIOUS FLAME. THE M'USTS-- THE SUBTERRANEAN PRIMITIVES DWELLING IN THAT CAVERN-- COULD NOT BELIEVE THEIR EYES...

"...FOR THIS ETER-NALLY-BURNING FIRE WAS THEIR GOD, AND NO ONE HAD EVER SURVIVED IMMERSION IN IT BEFORE!

"PERHAPS IT WAS THE LATENT MYSTIC ABILITIES OF MY OWN RACE MINGLING WITH THE FLAME-GOD ITSELF OR PERHAPS IT WAS SOMETHING...GREATER.

"IN ANY CASE, I BECAME FILLED WITH A STRANGE AND UNIMAGINABLE POWER. WHILE I LEARNED TO WIELD IT, I REMAINED AMONG THE M'USTS.

"THEY TOOK ME AS THEIR HEAVEN-SENT MASTER BUT, IN TRUTH, I LEARNED FROM THEM... LEARNED OF SIM-PLICITY--AND PEACE.

"WHEN FINALLY I RE-TURNED TO THE SUR-FACE--STRODE THROUGH THAT SEA OF PUTRIFYING CORPSES-- I REALIZED THAT MY POWER HAD IN-CREASED A THOUSAND FOLD.

... AND THAT I COULD NOT FOR ANY REASON WHATEVER, ALLOW MYSELF TO LIFT MY HAND AGAINST MY FELLOW MAN WITHOUT UNLEASH-ING ALL THE SAVAGERY THAT WAS IN THE DARKEST PART OF MY SOUL.

12

"THUS, I DEDICATED MYSELF TO A QUIETER, PERSONAL REVOLUTION IN A GALAXY GONE MAD, I REACHED DOWN INTO MYSELF--TOUCHED THE UNFOLDING POWER OF THE FLAME-GOD.

"OH! THE WAVES OF AGONY AND BLISS THAT TORE THROUGH ME AS, FROM THE DEPTHS OF MY SOUL, I CALLED UP EVERY DREAM OF A BETTER UNIVERSE I'D EVER NURTURED...

"FOR WHAT THE FLAME HAD IMPARTED TO ME WAS THE ABILITY TO GIVE CORPOREAL *LIFE* TO THOSE DREAMS-- TO BREACH THE DIMENSIONS AND CON- STRUCT A KINGDOM OF DREAMS *FROM MY OWN MIND!*

"THE M'USTS REMAINED BEHIND TO TEND TO THEIR GOD AND SO I CALLED MY OLD BATTLE- BROTHERS TO MY SIDE --SHARING MY VISIONS WITH THOSE WHO COULD SEE.

" HERE WE CHOOSE TO LIVE AS SHINING EXAM- PLES OF ALL THAT MAN CAN BE ONCE HE PUTS DOWN THE SWORD."

AND THAT'S *IT!* YOU WERE GIVEN A GIFT OF SUCH INCREDIBLE POWER, SUCH MAGNITUDE -- AND YOU USED IT TO BUILD A FANTASYLAND?

EVER SINCE I SAW YOU YEARS AGO, YOU'VE BEEN A SYM- BOL OF HOPE TO ME, A SYMBOL OF THE STRENGTH OF WILL I'VE ALWAYS *LACKED...*

...BUT YOU'RE NOT STRONG, SUNN-CHILDE...

...YOU'RE JUST A TREMBLING, GOOD-FOR-NO- THING COWARD WHO COULDN'T *TAKE* IT ANYMORE!

NO! STOP! YOU DON'T KNOW WHAT YOU'RE DOING!

SMAK!

13

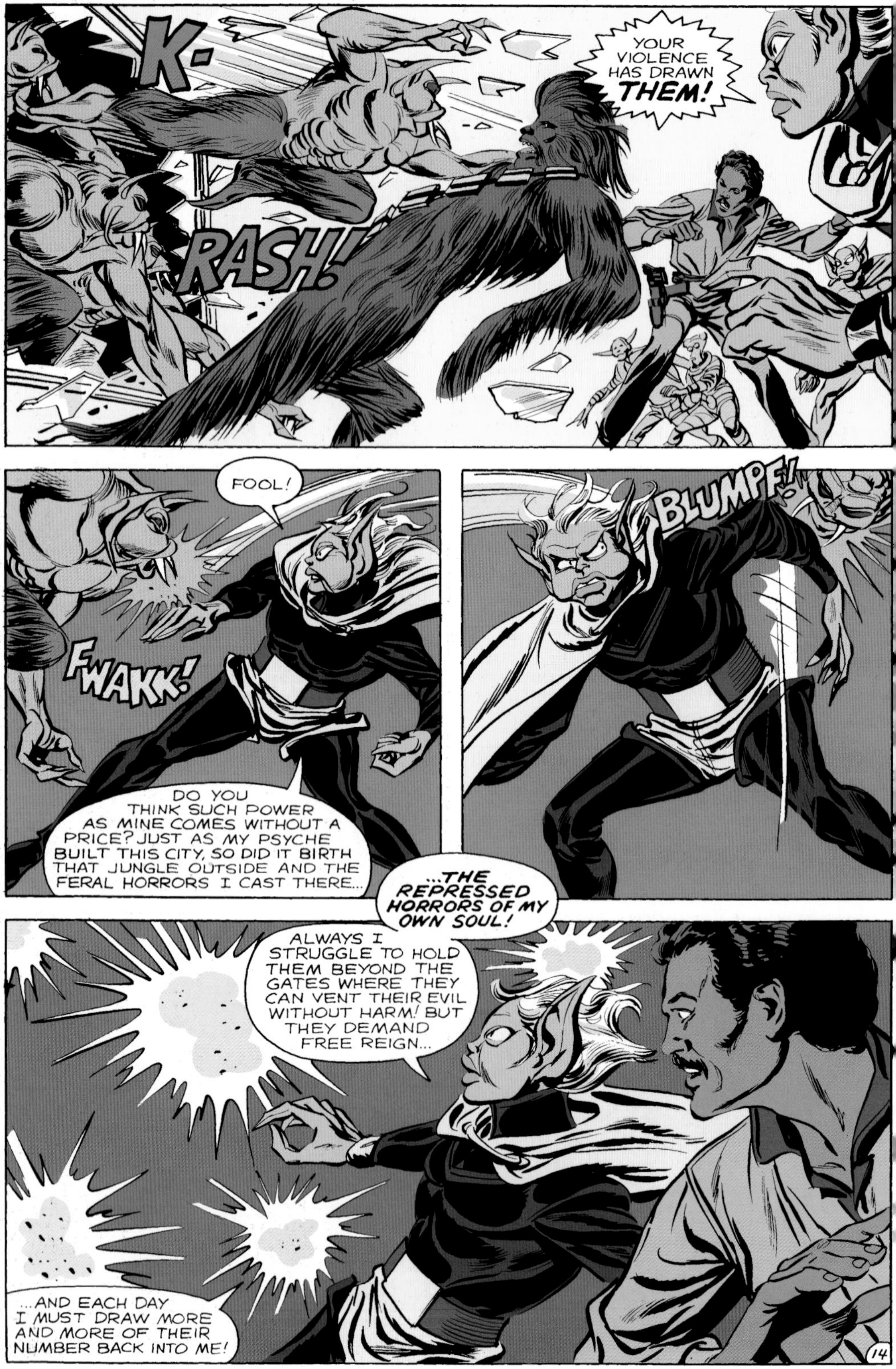
K-
RASH!
YOUR VIOLENCE HAS DRAWN THEM!
FOOL!
FWAKK!
DO YOU THINK SUCH POWER AS MINE COMES WITHOUT A PRICE? JUST AS MY PSYCHE BUILT THIS CITY, SO DID IT BIRTH THAT JUNGLE OUTSIDE AND THE FERAL HORRORS I CAST THERE...
BLUMPF!
...THE REPRESSED HORRORS OF MY OWN SOUL!
ALWAYS I STRUGGLE TO HOLD THEM BEYOND THE GATES WHERE THEY CAN VENT THEIR EVIL WITHOUT HARM! BUT THEY DEMAND FREE REIGN...
...AND EACH DAY I MUST DRAW MORE AND MORE OF THEIR NUMBER BACK INTO ME!
14

YOUR MYSTICAL THEATRICS ARE IMPRESSIVE, SUNN-CHILDE BUT-- I-- *HEY!* CHEWIE!

YOU'RE GETTING AWFULLY CHUMMY WITH THESE *PUSILLANIMOUS* DREAMERS!

CHEWIE-- I'M TALKING TO Y--

GROWWR!

I THINK WHAT HE'S TRYING TO SAY, SIR, IS THAT EVEN *WOOKIEES* CAN DREAM.

DROID... *SHUT UP!*

THAT HAIRY THUG ALMOST FLATTENED ME A WHILE AGO FOR FORGETTING ABOUT A DEAR FRIEND OF HIS! *NOW* LOOK AT HIM!

IT'S LIKE A PLAGUE.

CALRISSIAN... *LANDO!* TRY TO UNDERSTAND THE IMPORTANCE OF WHAT WE'RE DOING HERE! IF THERE ARE NO EXAMPLES OF ANOTHER PATH-- THEN NONE WILL EVER WALK IT!

WHAT *GOOD* IS YOUR PRECIOUS EXAMPLE WHEN YOU'RE SECURE HERE AND MILLIONS ARE ENSLAVED ON THE OTHER SIDE?!

CURSE YOU, CALRISSIAN-- WHO ARE YOU TO JUDGE ME?

ANSWER ME, IDIOT!

NOW THAT'S WHAT I LIKE TO HEAR-- A LITTLE HUMAN *RAGE.*

MAYBE THERE'S HOPE FOR YOU YET.

MEANWHILE, ABOARD CAPTAIN PLIKK'S IMPERIAL FLAGSHIP...

INTER-PHASE CO-ORDINATES ON SCREEN, CAPTAIN!

"THANK YOU, TECHNICIAN.

"CAPTAIN TO CREWS: AS PRE-PLANNED, WE WILL CHANNEL ALL HYPER-DRIVE ANTI-MATTER PODS DIRECTLY INTO FRONTAL LASER BANKS.

"WE MUST WIDEN THAT RENT AT ALL COSTS!"

16

LATER, BENEATH SHIFTING DIMENSIONAL SKIES...

I DON'T GET IT, SUNN-CHILDE. WE LOATHE EACH OTHER-- YET YOU AND YOUR BOYS HELPED ME TO RETRIEVE THE FALCON AND GET REPAIRS UNDER-WAY. WHY?

I FEEL NO LOATHING FOR YOU, CALRISSIAN-- ONLY PITY. I REALIZE THAT THERE IS LITTLE HOPE OF PURGING THE VIOLENCE IN YOUR HEART.

SIMULTANEOUSLY, IN STANDARD SPACE...

"DIMENSIONAL DOORWAY OPENING UP, CAPTAIN! ALL SYSTEMS FUNCTION-ING AT OPTIMUM!"

SPARE ME YOUR MESSIANIC MUMBLINGS, SUNN-CHILDE! IN CASE YOU'VE FORGOTTEN, I SAW THAT COOL EXTERIOR MELT BACK THERE. YOU'VE GOT AS MUCH VIOLENCE IN YOU AS ANY OF US. PROBABLY MORE.

YES! AND I STRIVE TO KEEP MINE AT BAY! THAT IS THE DIFFER-ENCE BETWEEN US!

CHANNELING ANTI-MATTER BACK INTO WARP ENGINES!

JUMPING INTO HYPER-SPACE.

NO--THE DIFFERENCE IS THAT YOU'VE GIVEN UP WHILE--AFTER YEARS OF SELF-SERVING--I'VE FINALLY FOUND SOMETHING WORTH FIGHTING FOR.

I SHOULD THANK YOU. IF I HADN'T COME HERE-- THAT TRUTH MIGHT NOT HAVE BECOME SO CLEAR TO ME.

WE'RE THROUGH!

"ASTONISHING, CAPTAIN! SENSORS INDICATE SOME KIND OF CITY AHEAD--HUMANOID POPULATION!"

"SLOW TO SPACE NORMAL SPEED! WE'VE EITHER STUMBLED UPON A SECRET REBEL BASE OR A POCKET OF CIVILI-ZATION UNCRUSHED BY THE EMPIRE'S HEEL! THEY MUST BE MADE TO FEAR US--ATTACK!

17

YOUR TRUTH IS NOT MY TRUTH

HMMM. I WONDER HOW LONG YOUR "TRUTH" WOULD HOLD UP IF THE WAR YOU RAN AWAY FROM CAME KNOCKING ON YOUR FRONT...

...DOOR...?!

WHOOOM!

THE DISTINCTIVE ROAR OF IMPERIAL LASERS IS UNMISTAKABLE!

THEIR IMPACT IS ENOUGH TO ROCK THE GRACEFUL TOWERS OF THE CITY OF DREAMS...

...AND ENOUGH TO ROCK TWO WOOKIES BACK TO HARSH REALITY!

SILENT, TEARFUL FAREWELLS ARE SAID...

...ALL TOO QUICKLY... ALL TOO SOON.

CHEWIE-- YOU OLD HAIRBALL! YOU'VE SNAPPED OUT OF IT! C'MON-- LET'S SHOW THOSE IMPERIAL KILLERS WHAT WE'RE MADE OF!

ZRROWWRR!

NO NEED TO GET NASTY ABOUT IT!

WELL, SUNN-CHILDE--IT LOOKS LIKE YOU'VE NO CHOICE NOW. EITHER YOU DO SOMETHING OR YOUR BELOVED CITY DIES.

MY TRUTH IS NOT YOUR TRUTH!

WE'LL SEE!

18

CODY SUNN-CHILDE CAN ONLY STAND MUTELY BY, WATCHING THE MILLENNIUM FALCON ROCKET SKYWARD TO BRUSH THE FIRMAMENT.

DEATH, HE KNOWS, INEVITABLY WAITS FOR THE TWO BRAVE SOULS WITHIN--FOR ALL OF THEM.

SOMETHING CALRISSIAN SAID EARLIER SPRINGS, UNBIDDEN, TO MIND: "WHAT IS YOUR PRECIOUS EXAMPLE WHEN YOU'RE SECURE HERE AND MILLIONS ARE ENSLAVED ON THE OTHER SIDE?"

WHA-ZANG!

NOW THERE ARE **NO** CLEAR CHOICES... AND SUNN-CHILDE IS CONFUSED.

WHERE IS THE PROPER PATH, HE WONDERS. USING VIOLENCE TO SAVE THE TWO REBELS WOULD BE A GROSS VIOLATION OF PRINCIPLE, OF THE LESSONS LEARNED IN FIRE AND BLOOD... YET **NOT** TO SAVE THEM WOULD BE THE SAME!

AND WHAT OF HIS BELOVED CITY?

AS THE HEAVENS ABOVE ARE SEARED BY DEATH-RAYS AND ALL SOUND IS SMOTHERED IN THE CLANG OF BATTER HULLS...

ZWIA- WOOM!

... A DARK AND BALEFUL HORROR, LONG REPRESSED, SWIMS UP THROUGH THE MURKY WATERS OF SUNN-CHILDE'S PSYCHE...

19

...AND DEMANDS RELEASE!

CURSE YOU--STINKING EMPIRE SCUM--FOR INFECTING MY DREAMS WITH YOUR DISEASE! I SEE NOW THERE *IS* ONLY ONE WAY TO DEAL WITH YOUR NOXIOUS KIND!

C-CODY... *NO!*

"YES!"

YA-HOOO! SEE THAT CHEWIE?

SUNN-CHILDE CAME THROUGH! HE'S SENDING HIS DEMONS TO GIVE THOSE RATS WHAT THEY DESERVE!

BY THE EMPEROR'S ROBE--WHAT HAVE WE BLUNDERED INTO HERE, NIZZON? OUR FLEET IS HELPLESS AGAINST THOSE...THINGS!

NIZZON TO CREWS-- EVASIVE MANEUVERS... IMMEDIATELY!

LOOK AT THAT-- THEY'RE TAKING OFF! I KNEW SUNN-CHILDE HAD IT IN HIM!

I KNEW HE'D REVERT TO HIS OLD WAYS ONCE THE CHIPS WERE DOWN!

UNNNGRRR...

CHEWBACCA'S TONE IS ONE OF BLEAK FOREBODING. UNLIKE CALRISSIAN, HE HAS GAINED INTIMATE FIRSTHAND KNOWLEDGE OF THIS FRAGILE CITY OF DREAMS... AND THUS CAN SENSE WHAT IS COMING.

BY THE HOLY FLAME-GOD-- WHAT AM I DOING? *WHAT AM I DOING?!*

I MUST CALL THEM BACK!

GRUNNNGG.

20

THE DEMONS, CHEWIE--THEY'RE GONE! SUNN CHILDE'S LEFT US HIGH AND DRY AGAIN!

SWAKKT!

THAT ROTTEN COWARD! WELL, I'LL SHOW HIM HOW A REAL MAN FIGHTS!

"THEN I'M GOING DOWN THERE TO SPIT IN HIS FACE!"

MY FRIENDS--LONG HAVE I PREACHED ABOUT "SHINING EXAMPLES." TODAY I LEARNED THAT--UNLESS TESTED BY ADVERSITY--AN EXAMPLE HAS NO MEANING. I MUST PROVE THE DREAM OF PEACE WORTH LIVING... BY DYING FOR IT.

IF YOU DISAGREE, I CAN STILL USE MY POWER TO SAVE YOU LOYAL DISCIPLES.

SAVE US?

WE DON'T NEED SAVING, SIR.

"YOU--?! I SEE, MY FRIENDS. THEN THE DE-CISION IS MADE."

WE'VE LITTLE POWER LEFT, LIEUTENANT--BUT THE HONOR WE BOTH CRAVE CAN YET BE OURS! IF WE RE-CHANNEL THE HYPER-DRIVE PODS BACK INTO THE LASERS--WE CAN LEVEL THAT CITY!

BUT THE STRAIN--

--WILL CRIPPLE US, I KNOW... AND THAT SHIP OUT THERE WILL DOUBTLESS DESTROY US ALL.

"BUT, THINK OF THE GLORY!"

BA-VLOOOM!

OH...

...MY...

THEY--HE--COULD HAVE STOPPED IT. B-BUT HE...JUST STOOD THERE AND DIED. ALL OF THEM...GONE. WHY?

HRRARR.

21

THROUGH A HAZE OF BEWILDERMENT AND GRIEF, CALRISSIAN ESPIES THE NOW-UNMOVING IMPERIAL SHIPS AND...

IT'S ALL THEIR FAULT! I'LL MAKE THEM PAY! I'LL WIPE THOSE MURDERERS FROM THE SKY! I'LL--

NRRROWRR.

SOME WOULD CALL CHEWBACCA'S LANGUAGE A FARRAGO OF INDECIPHERABLE, SUB-GUTTURAL GROWLS...

...YET ONE GROWL IS ELOQUENT ENOUGH TO MAKE LANDO CALRISSIAN... **UNDERSTAND.**

AND YET...

CHEWIE, I **KNOW** HE REALLY BELIEVED THAT IF HE ALLOWED HIS VIOLENT NATURE FREE REIN, HE'D BE LOST FOREVER...

...SO HE CREATED A DREAM CITY WHERE HE COULD LIVE IN PEACE. BUT HE WAS **WRONG!**

LOFTY IDEALS ALONE JUST AREN'T **ENOUGH** WHEN DEALING WITH THE EMPIRE...AS HE FOUND OUT.

THEY FOLLOWED HIM... EVEN THERE. AND RATHER THAN TURN HIS AWESOME POWER AGAINST THEM, HE LET THEM USE THE POWER FROM THEIR HYPER-DRIVE PODS TO DESTROY HIS CITY.

BUT THE WIERD PART IS THAT, BY THEIR OWN PERNICIOUS ACTIONS, THE IMPERIALS HAVE BECOME TRAPPED IN THIS DIMENSION:..

...WITHOUT THE HYPERDRIVE POWER TO ESCAPE!

I COULD TURN OUR LASERS ON THEM, CHEWIE, AND BLOW THEM ALL TO PERDI-TION.

BUT IN MEMORY OF CODY SUNN-CHILDE, I'LL JUST LET THEM **ROT** HERE PEACE-FULLY--FOREVER!

YOU MIGHT CALL IT-- SUN-CHILDE'S REVENGE!

NO! THEY'RE LEAVING!

COME **BACK!** YOU CANNOT DENY US THE GLORY OF DEATH! YOU **CANNOT!**

BUT THEY CAN.

LANDO CALRISSIAN TURNS HIS SHIP IN THE DIRECTION OF THE RAPIDLY CLOSING DIMENSIONAL DOORWAY...

...AND THE SEARCH FOR HAN SOLO GOES ON.

FINIS

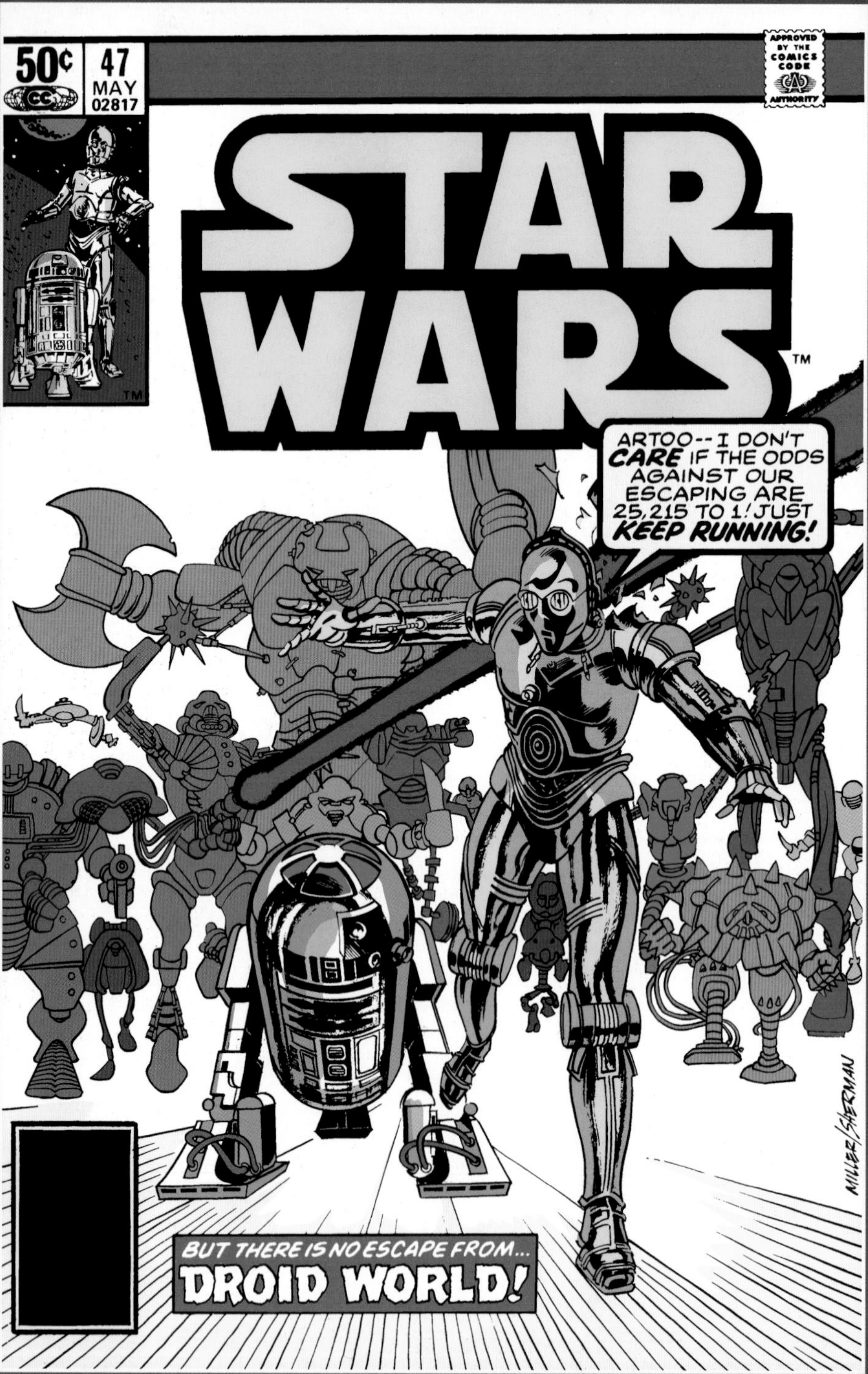

50¢
47
MAY
02817
APPROVED BY THE COMICS CODE AUTHORITY
STAR WARS™
ARTOO--I DON'T CARE IF THE ODDS AGAINST OUR ESCAPING ARE 25,215 TO 1! JUST KEEP RUNNING!
MILLER/SHERMAN
BUT THERE IS NO ESCAPE FROM...
DROID WORLD!

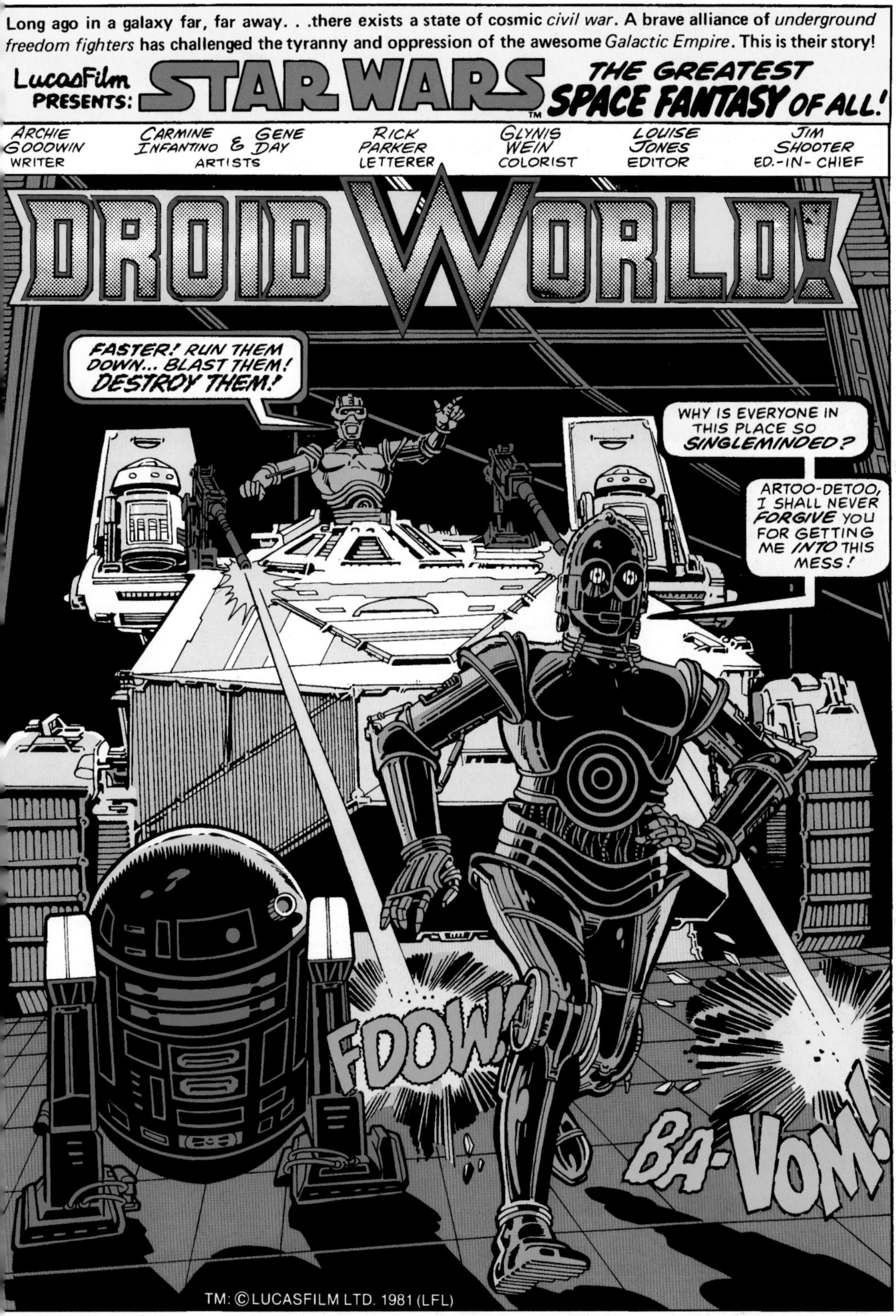
Long ago in a galaxy far, far away. . .there exists a state of cosmic civil war. A brave alliance of underground freedom fighters has challenged the tyranny and oppression of the awesome Galactic Empire. This is their story!
LucasFilm PRESENTS: STAR WARS™ THE GREATEST SPACE FANTASY OF ALL!
ARCHIE GOODWIN WRITER
CARMINE INFANTINO & GENE DAY ARTISTS
RICK PARKER LETTERER
GLYNIS WEIN COLORIST
LOUISE JONES EDITOR
JIM SHOOTER ED.-IN-CHIEF
DROID WORLD!
FASTER! RUN THEM DOWN... BLAST THEM! DESTROY THEM!
WHY IS EVERYONE IN THIS PLACE SO SINGLEMINDED?
ARTOO-DETOO, I SHALL NEVER FORGIVE YOU FOR GETTING ME INTO THIS MESS!
FDOW!
BA-VOM!
TM: ©LUCASFILM LTD. 1981 (LFL)

VRRR DOOOT WHA-DIIT *BLAAP!*

IT'S *MY* FAULT THAT WE'RE HERE...?

OF ALL THE DOME-HEADED *ARROGANCE!* HOW CAN YOU EVEN *ARGUE* THE POINT WITH *DOOM* ABOUT TO OVERTAKE US AND--

FREEET!

⁂OOOF!⁂ ARTOO! WE'LL *NEVER* ESCAPE IF YOU KEEP SCREECHING TO A *HALT* FOR NO REASON AT--

OH.

WELL, PERHAPS YOU *DO* HAVE A REASON!

THEY'RE *TRAPPED!* CONTINUE *ADVANCING*... FORCE THEM OVER THE *EDGE!*

I DON'T SUPPOSE IT TRULY MATTERS ANY LONGER *WHO* CAUSED US TO BE HERE.

I WISH *NEITHER* OF US WERE.

AND *HEAT*, WICKED AND INTENSE, PLAYS ON THE BACKS OF THE TWO REBEL DROIDS...

...HEAT THAT RISES FROM THE **WHITE HOT CORE** OF A MAN-MADE WORLD, HEAT DESIGNED TO REDUCE THE STRONGEST, FINEST ALLOYS INTO FIERY **MOLTEN SLAG.**

AND JUST AS TERRIBLE AS THE **HEAT** TO SEE-THREEPIO AND ARTOO-DETOO IS THE **SOUND** OVERWHELMING THEIR AUDIO-SENSORS...

...THE SOUND OF A **WAR DROID'S** ENGINES AS IT DRIVES THEM BACK... BACK...TO THE ULTIMATE **END**...

...AN END WHICH HAD ITS *BEGINNING* WITH THE REN-DEZVOUS OF LUKE SKYWALKER'S SCOUT CRAFT AND A LARGER REBEL SHIP OF THE LINE.

HERE'S WHAT YOU'VE BEEN SENT TO *SEE*, COMMANDER.

THE NEW MODEL *WARBOT* THE EMPIRE THREW AT YOUR GROUND TROOPS ON *XERON*...!

YEAH. THEY'RE NOT IN THE SAME CLASS AS THOSE *AT-ATs*※ YOU AND GENERAL RIEEKAN'S PEOPLE FACED ON *HOTH*... BUT IT'S NO *PICNIC* FIGHTING 'EM!

IF YOU CAN GET A *FULL SCHEMATIC* OF IT TO DISTRIBUTE TO ALL UNITS...IT'LL BE QUITE AN *EDGE* NEXT TIME THEY'RE USED.

※ALL TERRAIN ARMORED TRANS-PORT(*WALKERS*). --LOUISE.

DO YOU *HEAR* THAT, ARTOO? IT MAKES *OUR* JOB MOST IM-PORTANT...SO DO IT *RIGHT!*

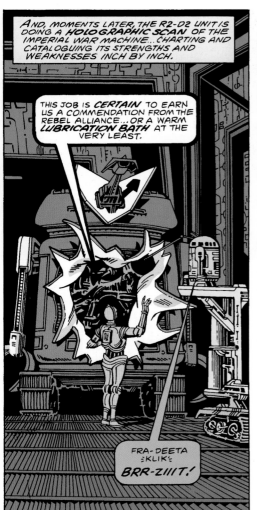

AND, MOMENTS LATER, THE R2-D2 UNIT IS DOING A *HOLOGRAPHIC SCAN* OF THE IMPERIAL WAR MACHINE...CHARTING AND CATALOGUING ITS STRENGTHS AND WEAKNESSES INCH BY INCH.

THIS JOB IS *CERTAIN* TO EARN US A COMMENDATION FROM THE REBEL ALLIANCE...OR A WARM *LUBRICATION BATH* AT THE VERY LEAST.

FRA-DEETA
=KLIK=
BRR-ZIIIT!

REALLY, ARTOO! IF THAT DAMAGED SECTION IS GIVING YOU *TROUBLE,*--

-- SIMPLY GO *HIGHER! HIGHER!*

ZDAK!

WEEET!

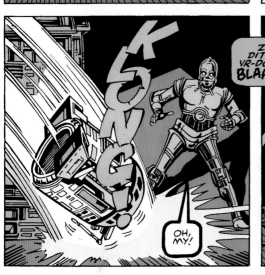

ZA-DITTA VR-DOOT, *BLAAP!*

OH, MY!

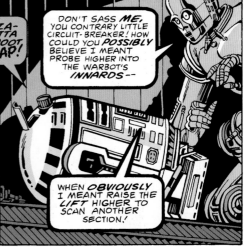

DON'T SASS *ME,* YOU CONTRARY LITTLE CIRCUIT-BREAKER! HOW COULD YOU *POSSIBLY* BELIEVE I MEANT PROBE HIGHER INTO THE WARBOT'S *INNARDS* --

WHEN *OBVIOUSLY* I MEANT RAISE THE *LIFT* HIGHER TO SCAN ANOTHER SECTION!

THREEPIO! ARTOO! WHAT WAS THAT *NOISE* WE HEARD? IT SOUNDED LIKE-- *AW, NO!*

I FEAR WE'RE EXPERIENCING A BIT OF A *PROBLEM,* MASTER LUKE.

PROBLEM? THREEPIO, THE WARBOT'S INSIDES ARE *FUSED* NOW... THERE'S *NO WAY* TO MAKE SCHEMATICS OF THAT MESS!

OH, DEAR. ARTOO AND I WOULD DO *ANYTHING* TO MAKE THIS UP, SIR.

WELL, THE ROBOT'S BEYOND OUR BEST TECHNOS' ABILITY TO SALVAGE. BUT... MAYBE THERE *IS* AN ALTERNATIVE. 'COURSE IT COULD BE *RISKY*...

ANYTHING, MAJOR... ANYTHING!

AND SOMETIME LATER, LUKE AND THE DROIDS ARE MOVING FAR FROM REBEL STAR SECTORS...

I'VE NEVER *HEARD* OF SUCH A PLACE, SIR...

THE MAJOR SAID THE PARTY WE WANT IS A *RECLUSE*... TRIES TO KEEP HIS EXISTENCE A *SECRET.*

BUT OUR SCANNERS DEFINITELY SHOW *SOMETHING* AT THE COORDINATES ALLIANCE INTELLIGENCE DUG UP FOR US.

ACCORDING TO THEM, THE PLACE WAS ONCE KNOWN AS *KLIGSON'S MOON* --

BUT BECAUSE THE MECHANICAL GENIUS WHO *BUILT* IT FROM SPACE SALVAGE INSISTS ON SURROUNDING HIMSELF STRICTLY WITH *ROBOTS* --

--THE *FEW* WHO *KNOW* ABOUT THIS SPOT HAVE COME TO CALL IT... *DROID WORLD!*

AND THE FIRST THING THE VISITORS *LEARN* ABOUT THIS MASSIVE ORBITING PHENOMENON...

...IS THAT ITS *DEFENSES* ARE ALERT AND DEADLY!

THAT IS A *WARNING SHOT,* BLOCKADE RUNNER! APPROACH NO *CLOSER* --

OUR SCANNERS HAVE DETECTED THE PRESENCE OF AN *ORGANIC* ABOARD YOUR SHIP!

ARTOO, SIGNAL THAT I'M A *FRIENDLY* ORGANIC, AND--

WE MAKE NO *EXCEPTIONS!* TURN... OR BE BLOWN OUT OF *SPACE!*

WE'RE TURNING... WE'RE *TURNING!* BUT I DON'T SEE WHY KLIGSON'S MOON HAS TO BE SO *HOSTILE!*

YOU'RE *TALKING* TO KLIGSON, REBEL! AND I SUFFERED ENOUGH IN THE *CLONE WARS* TO MAKE ME HOSTILE TO MY FELLOW ORGANICS *FOREVER!*

I'M A *CYBORG,* NOW, MORE MACHINE THAN MAN... AND *HAPPY* TO CAST MY LOT *WITH* THE MACHINES!

LEAVE *ME* AND MY DROID WORLD IN *PEACE!*

REALLY, SIR, IT'S BECAUSE OF YOUR SYMPATHY TO *DROIDS* THAT WE'RE HERE... WE'VE HEARD YOU CAN DO *ANYTHING* WITH OUR KIND.

WE'VE A DROID SO DAMAGED *NO ONE* ELSE CAN REPAIR IT! NATURALLY, IF YOU'RE NOT *UP* TO THE CHALLENGE...

I *LIKE* A CHALLENGE, BUT MY WORLD HAS *TWO RULES* THAT MUST BE OBEYED...

402

THE **FIRST** IS THAT NO **ORGANIC** SETS FOOT ON KLIGSON'S MOON. THE **SECOND**... ANYTHING I REPAIR, I **KEEP!**

A **SHUTTLE** IS BEING DISPATCHED TO YOUR CRAFT. IF YOU AGREE TO MY TERMS... PLACE THE DAMAGED ROBOT ABOARD AND SEND IT BACK.

THREEPIO, IF HE **KEEPS** THE WARBOT... HAVING IT FIXED DOES US NO **GOOD.**

ON THE SURFACE OF IT... **TRUE,** MASTER LUKE.

BUT IF **WE** ACCOMPANY IT AND A CERTAIN TRUSTY **R2-D2** UNIT **RECORDS** EVERYTHING THAT KLIGSON DOES--

-- WE'LL WIND UP WITH A COMPLETE **SCHEMATIC** ANYWAY! AND THAT'S MORE IMPORTANT THAN THE ACTUAL WARBOT, SIR.

OF COURSE, YOU AND ARTOO HAVE A KNACK FOR GETTING INTO **TROUBLE** ON YOUR OWN. STILL... WHAT COULD HAPPEN TO TWO **DROIDS** ON A **WORLD** OF DROIDS?

AND MOMENTS LATER, ARTOO AND THREEPIO ARE IN A DOCKING CHAMBER OF KLIGSON'S MOON, WATCHING TRACTOR DRONES TRANSPORT THE RUINED IMPERIAL MACHINE.

STEP **LIVELY,** YOU TWO... ON TO THE **EXAMINING CHAMBER!**

THERE, THE WARBOT IS GIVEN A REMOTE-CONTROLLED *SCAN* BY DROID WORLD'S CREATOR...

A PRODUCT OF THE *EMPIRE*...! TYPICAL CHEAPJACK CRAFTSMANSHIP!

THE DIAGRAM INDICATES *PROPER* RECONSTRUCTION--

--BUT *THIS* KIND OF PRODUCT ISN'T *WORTH* THE EFFORT. MOST IMPERIAL HANDIWORK *ISN'T*--

--*ZEE-EXTHREE* HERE IS ONE OF THE FEW EXCEPTIONS.

SHALL I HAVE THE WAR MACHINE DUMPED INTO THE *CORE*, SIR?

YES. AND WHILE YOU'RE AT IT... REMOVE THE *RESTRAINING BOLTS* FROM THIS PAIR--

-- SO THEY'LL BE FREE OF *THEIR* MASTERS TO JOIN DROID WORLD AS *YOU* DID.

TA-WEET *DLEET!*

W- WAIT... *WAIT!*

YOU DON'T *UNDERSTAND*, SIR! WE *LOVE* MASTER LUKE AND THE OTHERS WE WORK WITH. WE'RE QUITE *CONTENT* WITH THE ROLES WE PLAY IN THE REBEL ALLIANCE.

VOO *DEET* EEP!

BRING THESE TWO TO *ME*, ZEE-EXTHREE!

DROIDS WHO ARE *HAPPY* UNDER ORGANICS I WISH TO EXAMINE AT *FIRST-HAND!*

DROID WORLD IS QUITE AN *ACTIVE* PLACE TO JUDGE FROM THESE BUSTLING CORRIDORS. PERHAPS RATHER THAN *DISTURB* KLIGSON--

-- ARTOO AND I SHOULD JUST *RETURN* TO OUR SHIP.

DUBIOUS. HE WOULD NOT *REQUEST* TO SEE YOU UNLESS HE *WANTED* TO.

WELL, YOU KNOW *BEST*... I SUPPOSE. TELL ME, ZEE-EXTHREE... HOW LONG HAS THE *EMPIRE* MADE DROIDS LIKE YOU?

I AM AN *EXPERIMENTAL MODEL*, DESIGNED BY TAAGE INDUSTRIES TO WORK UNDER EXTREME PLANETARY CONDITIONS EVEN *STORMTROOPERS* COULDN'T SURVIVE.

THE IMPERIALS WERE NOT *SATISFIED*... I WAS *REJECTED*. FORTUNATELY--

-- KLIGSON *RECLAIMED* ME, AND HAS NOW GIVEN ME MANY *NEW* OPPORTUNITIES.

HIS CHAMBER LIES STRAIGHT AHEAD. I MUST TURN OFF HERE AND SEE TO THE WARBOT'S *DESTRUCTION* IN OUR *MELTING CORE*.

FOR SOMEONE WHO'S *IMPERIAL* MADE, HE SEEMS A NICE ENOUGH CHAP, ARTOO. PERHAPS THIS WON'T GO SO BADLY AFTER ALL...

BOOOOOP...

WE'VE MADE A NEW FRIEND AND YOU GOT TO *RECORD* THAT RECONSTRUCTED SCHEMATIC OF THE WARBOT KLIGSON SHOWED US.

BUT AS HIS CHATTING PARTNER STROLLS *FORWARD*, ARTOO'S SENSORS DETECT SOMETHING THAT SENDS HIM FOLLOWING *ZEE-EXTHREE*...

NOW BE ON YOUR *FINEST* BEHAVIOR, ARTOO--

WHILE WE'D *NEVER* ABANDON MASTER LUKE OR THE PRINCESS... THIS MIGHT NOT BE A BAD *SPOT* TO *RETIRE* TO SOMEDAY OR--

WHAT'S GOING *ON* HERE, TRANSLATOR DROID? I SENT FOR BOTH YOU *AND* YOUR COMPANION?

MY *COMPANION?* WHY, HE'S RIGHT *BESIDE*--

OH, DEAR! SOMETIMES IT SEEMS HIS MAIN PROGRAMMING FUNCTION IS TO *EMBARRASS* ME!

BUT THAT IS *FAR* FROM ARTOO'S LOGIC CIRCUITS AS HE *VISUALLY* CONFIRMS WHAT HIS SENSORS MADE HIM SUSPECT...

ZEE-EXTHREE'S DESTINATION COULD *HARDLY* BE THE ARTIFICIAL MOON'S *MELTING CORE*...

... IF NO *EXCESS HEAT* REGISTERED IN THE CORRIDOR DOWN WHICH KLIGSON'S DROID ASSISTANT TOOK THE DAMAGED IMPERIAL WAR MACHINE!

GET YOUR CREW OVER TO THE TRANSPORTER *IMMEDIATELY.* THOSE LUDICROUS REBEL MECHANICALS HAVE BROUGHT US *EXACTLY* WHAT WE NEED!

THEIR WARBOT IS *BEYOND* REPAIR... BUT THIS ONE WHICH WE TOOK *MONTHS* AGO FROM AN IMPERIAL DERELICT IS *NOT.*

ALL IT LACKS IS A FUNCTIONING *WEAPON-HEAD--*

-- AND THAT OTHERWISE USELESS WRECK THE REBEL DROIDS ARRIVED WITH HAS *PRECISELY* THAT!

A *VIBRATION* PASSES THROUGH ARTOO-DETOO'S CIRCUITRY...

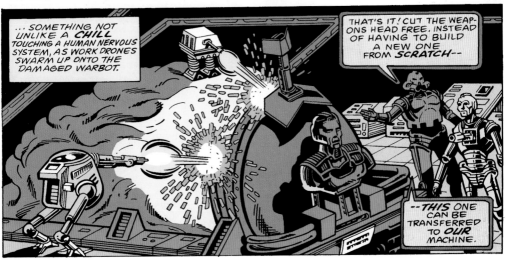

...SOMETHING NOT UNLIKE A *CHILL* TOUCHING A HUMAN NERVOUS SYSTEM, AS WORK DRONES SWARM UP ONTO THE DAMAGED WARBOT.

THAT'S IT! CUT THE WEAPONS HEAD FREE, INSTEAD OF HAVING TO BUILD A NEW ONE FROM *SCRATCH--*

--*THIS* ONE CAN BE TRANSFERRED TO *OUR* MACHINE.

EXCELLENT.

THIS PUTS US FAR *AHEAD* OF SCHEDULE AND MAKES IT UNLIKELY *KLIGSON* WILL HAVE TIME TO SUSPECT WE--

ZEE BRRRT WHRR-KLKKETTA FRRRT!

WHAT...?!

GUARD! WE HAVE AN *INTRUDER!*

THERE!!

FRAKOW!

WHRRR-BREEET!

MY DATA SYSTEM DOES NOT INDICATE THAT LABOR DROIDS MOVE SO *FAST*, ZEE-EXTHREE.

OBVIOUSLY THIS ONE'S BEEN PROGRAMMED *BEYOND* ITS ORDINARY FUNCTIONS.

FORGET *PURSUIT*--

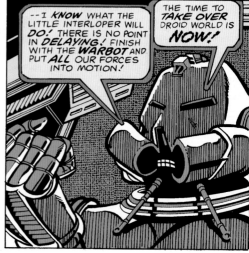

--I *KNOW* WHAT THE LITTLE INTERLOPER WILL *DO!* THERE IS NO POINT IN *DELAYING!* FINISH WITH THE *WARBOT* AND PUT *ALL* OUR FORCES INTO MOTION!

THE TIME TO *TAKE OVER* DROID WORLD IS *NOW!*

MEANWHILE, IN KLIGSON'S MAIN CHAMBERS...

DON'T YOU SEE IT DOESN'T *MATTER*, TRANSLATOR...?

REBEL OR IMPERIAL... *BOTH* SPREAD THE TAINT OF *WAR* TO LOGICAL MACHINES.

I HATE TO *ARGUE* WITH SOMEONE WHO'S GIVEN ME SUCH A DELIGHTFUL *POWER-FEED,* SIR--

-- BUT THERE'S CERTAINLY A *VAST* DIFFERENCE BETWEEN OUR MASTER LUKE AND SOME-ONE LIKE THE *EMPIRE'S* DARTH --

BA-DOOP-A WHREEEE!

ARTOO-DETOO! *WHERE* HAVE YOU --

SWIFTLY, THE LITTLE DROID TELLS THREEPIO AND DROID WORLD'S FOUNDER THAT AND MORE!

ARTOO! THIS SOUNDS LIKE--

REVOLUTION! LEAVE HANDLING IT TO *ME.* BUT I HEAR *NOISES* IN THE MAIN CORRIDOR--

-- BETTER TAKE THIS *EMERGENCY EXIT.*

NO ONE WILL ESCAPE, KLIGSON! YOUR DAY IS OVER... *MINE* IS BEGINNING!

THAT LASER-CANNON HARNESS IS *UNAUTHORIZED,* ZEE-EXTHREE! *REMOVE* IT BEFORE--

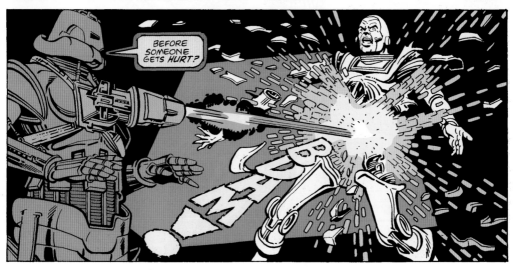

BEFORE SOMEONE GETS *HURT?*

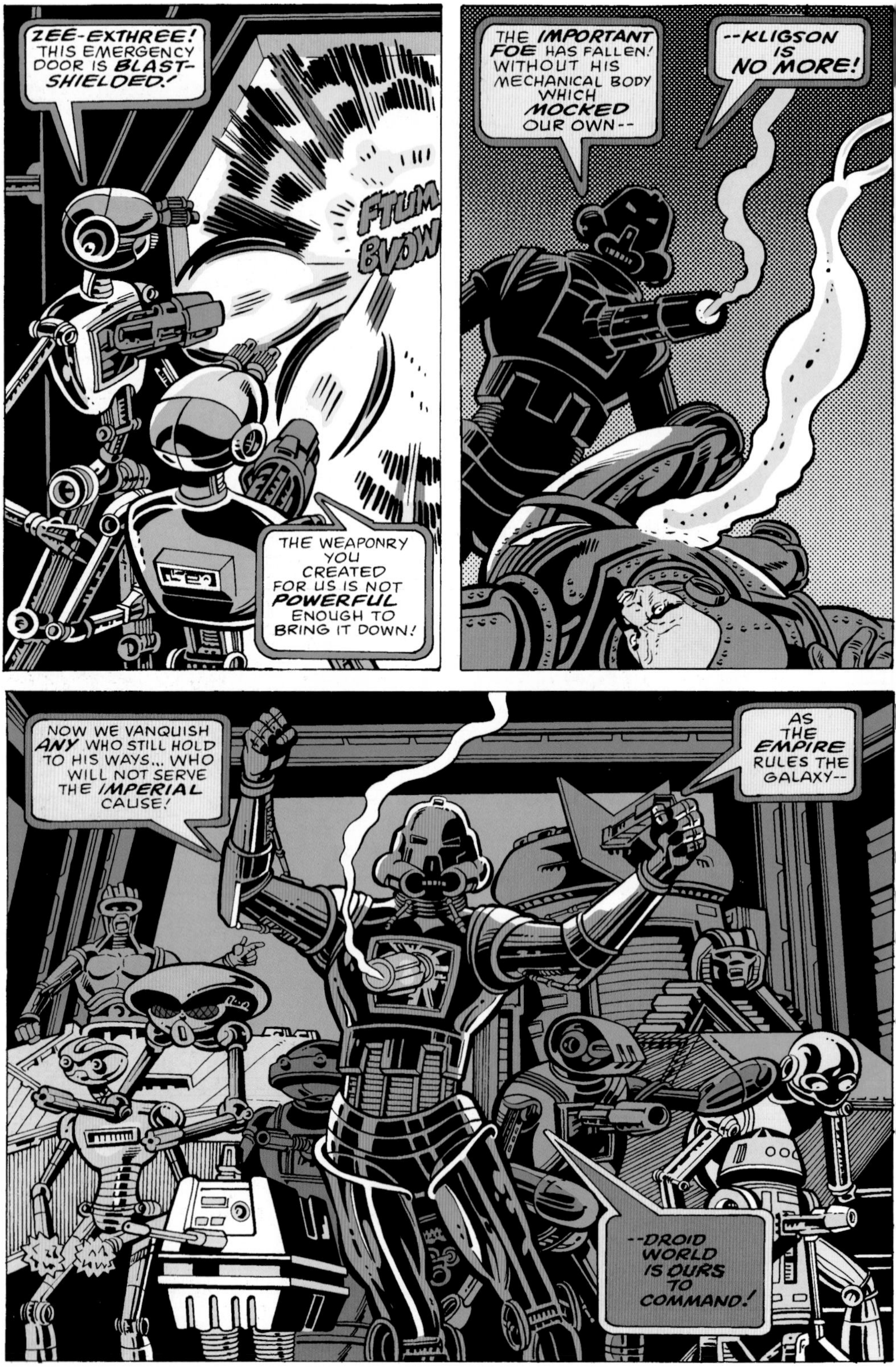
ZEE-EXTHREE! THIS EMERGENCY DOOR IS BLAST-SHIELDED!
FTUM BVOW
THE WEAPONRY YOU CREATED FOR US IS NOT POWERFUL ENOUGH TO BRING IT DOWN!
THE IMPORTANT FOE HAS FALLEN! WITHOUT HIS MECHANICAL BODY WHICH MOCKED OUR OWN--
--KLIGSON IS NO MORE!
NOW WE VANQUISH ANY WHO STILL HOLD TO HIS WAYS... WHO WILL NOT SERVE THE IMPERIAL CAUSE!
AS THE EMPIRE RULES THE GALAXY--
--DROID WORLD IS OURS TO COMMAND!

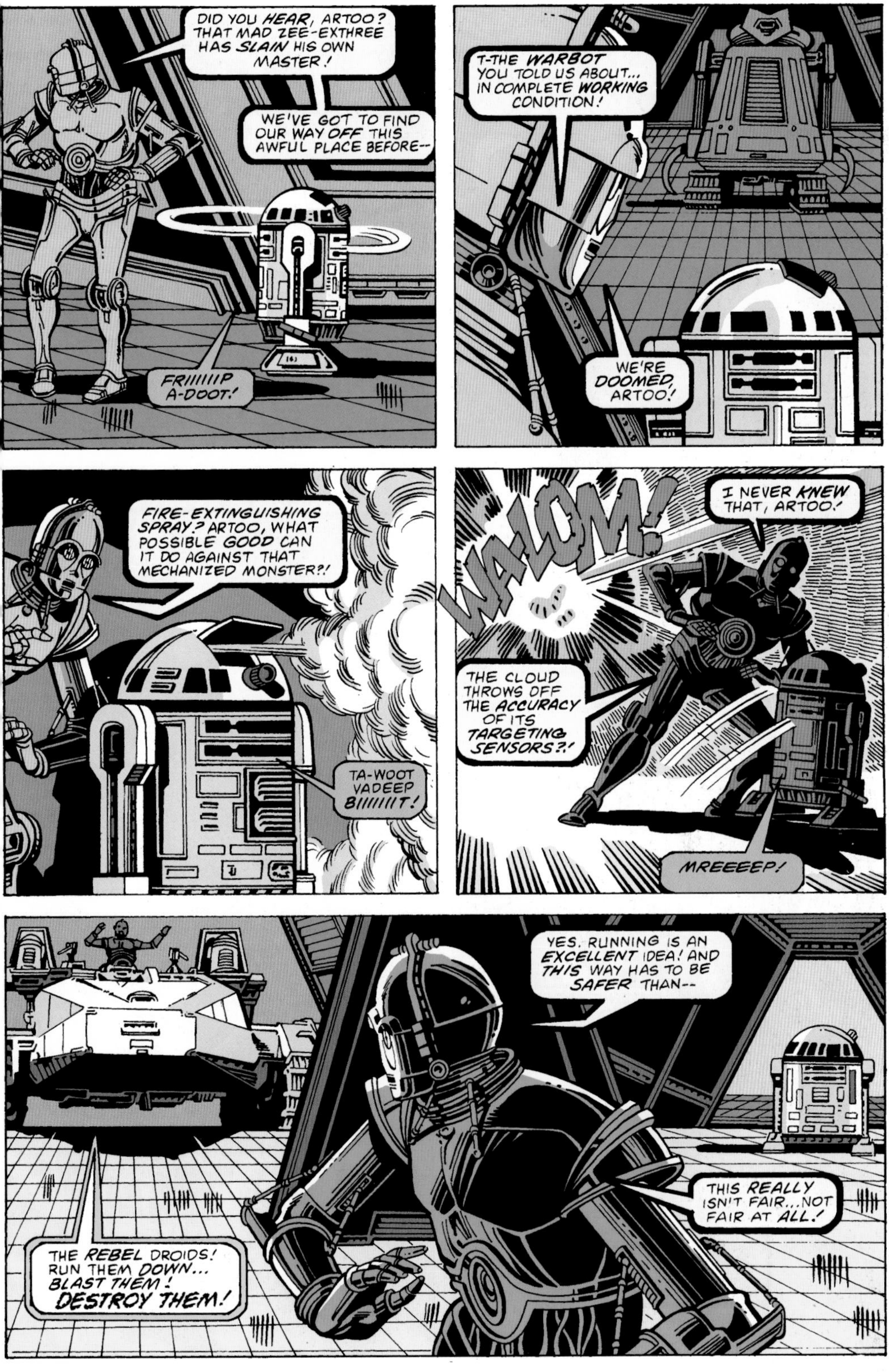
DID YOU HEAR, ARTOO? THAT MAD ZEE-EXTHREE HAS SLAIN HIS OWN MASTER!
WE'VE GOT TO FIND OUR WAY OFF THIS AWFUL PLACE BEFORE--
FRIIIIIIP A-DOOT!
T-THE WARBOT YOU TOLD US ABOUT... IN COMPLETE WORKING CONDITION!
WE'RE DOOMED, ARTOO!
FIRE-EXTINGUISHING SPRAY? ARTOO, WHAT POSSIBLE GOOD CAN IT DO AGAINST THAT MECHANIZED MONSTER?!
TA-WOOT VADEEP BIIIIIIIT!
WALOOM!
I NEVER KNEW THAT, ARTOO!
THE CLOUD THROWS OFF THE ACCURACY OF ITS TARGETING SENSORS?!
MREEEEEP!
YES. RUNNING IS AN EXCELLENT IDEA! AND THIS WAY HAS TO BE SAFER THAN--
THIS REALLY ISN'T FAIR... NOT FAIR AT ALL!
THE REBEL DROIDS! RUN THEM DOWN... BLAST THEM! DESTROY THEM!

BUT FAIR OR NOT, IT DRIVES THREEPIO AND ARTOO TO THE POINT AT WHICH WE *LEFT* THEM.

MORE *SPEED!* DRIVE THEM OVER THE EDGE... INTO THE *MELTING CORE!*

I DON'T *BELIEVE* IT, ARTOO! HOW CAN THEY BE SO ENTHUSIASTIC ABOUT *DESTROYING* FELLOW DROIDS?

TA-DOOT DITTA-BLIK!

ONLY ONE WAY *OUT?* WHAT DO YOU *MEAN* ONE WA--

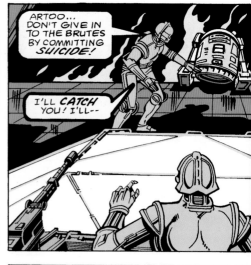

ARTOO... DON'T GIVE IN TO THE BRUTES BY COMMITTING *SUICIDE!*

I'LL *CATCH* YOU! I'LL--

YAAAAHH!

THE CORE'S INCREDIBLE *HEAT* REACHES UP FOR THE TWO PLUNGING ROBOTS LIKE A *LIVING THING!* BUT AS THEY CLUMSILY TOPPLE...

...THEY SUDDENLY *FALL UP!*

MAGNETIC GRAPPLES!

AND THEY DRAW THE PAIR HIGHER... HIGHER... EVEN AS THE ON-RUSHING *WAR MACHINE,* UNABLE TO HALT ITS SPEEDED UP DRIVE FORWARD...

...MEETS THE FATE INTENDED FOR THEM!

YOUR SENSORS DETECTED THESE BEING *ACTIVATED* DIDN'T THEY, ARTOO? B-BUT... BY *WHOM?*

THE ANSWER AWAITS THEM AT THE *ROOF OF THE CORE...*

K-KLIGSON...! IT CAN'T BE! ARTOO AND I SAW YOU--

IT WAS AN *ANDROID DUPLICATE* OF ME! MUCH AS I REGRET THE DESTRUCTION OF *ANY* MACHINE... IT WAS NECESSARY TO BUY TIME TO RALLY MY *OWN* FORCES.

I SUPPOSE I KEPT HOPING FOR TOO LONG THAT I WAS *MISTAKEN* ABOUT ZEE-EXTHREE.

WE NEVER CEASE TO BE AMAZED BY THE *DEPTHS* OF IMPERIAL COR-RUPTION, SIR.

IN THIS CASE, YOU'RE *RIGHT,* THREEPIO. IT *WAS* DEEPLY INGRAINED.... AND SUBTLY *HIDDEN.* BY THE TIME MY FOOLISH HUMAN PRIDE *ADMITTED* THE POSSIBILITY... SOMETHING *DRAMATIC* WAS NEEDED TO DRAW ZEE-EXTHREE OUT.

BRINGING TWO *REBEL* DROIDS HERE SEEMED LIKELY TO MAKE HIM *ACT.*

THEN... YOU WERE *NEVER* INTERESTED IN REPAIRING OUR WARBOT--

-- ONLY IN HAVING *US* AS... *BAIT!*

NOT *QUITE* TRUE, FRIENDS... ZEE-EX-THREE WASN'T THE *ONLY* ONE WITH A WARBOT IN NEED OF CANNABALIZED PARTS!

MY WORK DRONES DREW ON *YOUR* MACHINE *AFTER* ZEE-EXTHREE'S FINISHED!

AND THIS *NEW* WARBOT...

...BECOMES PART OF A *FINAL CONFRONTATION* THAT SHAKES THE CORRIDORS AND MAIN GALLERIES OF THE ARTIFICIAL MOON...AN *ARMAGEDDON* OF ROBOT AGAINST ROBOT.

YET, IN TIME, EVEN THE MOST *AWESOME* OF BATTLES MUST END...

OH, MY! AT... AT LEAST IT... APPEARS *YOUR* SIDE WON, KLIGSON.

YES. I'VE BEEN *THROUGH* A WAR. I WAS ABLE TO PROVIDE MORE...*PRACTICAL*... PROGRAMMING THAN ZEE-EXTHREE...

BUT AT SUCH A *PRICE*, MY FRIENDS... AND SUCH A TERRIBLE *WASTE*.

AND, SOMETIME *LATER*, ON THE REBEL BLOCKADE RUNNER...

THIS SCHMATIC ARTOO RECORDED IS EVERYTHING WE COULD *ASK*, THREEPIO... YOU DID A REALLY *FINE* JOB.

THAT MEANS A *GREAT DEAL*, MASTER LUKE, BUT I CAN'T HELP FEELING *BAD* ABOUT KLIGSON.

THE EVENTS ON DROID WORLD LEFT HIM MORE DETERMINED THAN *EVER* NOT TO BE DRAWN INTO FURTHER HUMAN CONFLICT--

BUT THE EMPIRE'S *BOUND* TO HAVE LEARNED ABOUT KLIGSON'S MOON THROUGH *ZEE-EXTHREE*--

--THEY'LL *NEVER* ALLOW HIM THE PEACE AND SOLITUDE HE WANTS FOR HIMSELF AND HIS DROIDS!

FREEDA-VOOT!

ARTOO-DETOO, W-WHAT-- OH, MY *GOODNESS!*

I... I GUESS KLIGSON *SHARED* YOUR CONCERN, THREEPIO.

HE'S OBVIOUSLY *PLANNED AHEAD* FOR IT!

AND TO THE THUNDER OF *MONSTROUS ENGINES...DROID WORLD MOVES!* AWAY FROM THE PLANET IT ORBITS...AWAY FROM THE GALACTIC WAR KLIGSON WANTS NO PART OF... AWAY WHERE THE *EMPIRE* CAN NEVER FIND IT!

NEXT: *PRINCESS LEIA* PLAYS A GAME OF DIPLOMATIC DERRING-DO AGAINST *DARTH VADER...* THE THIRD LAW!

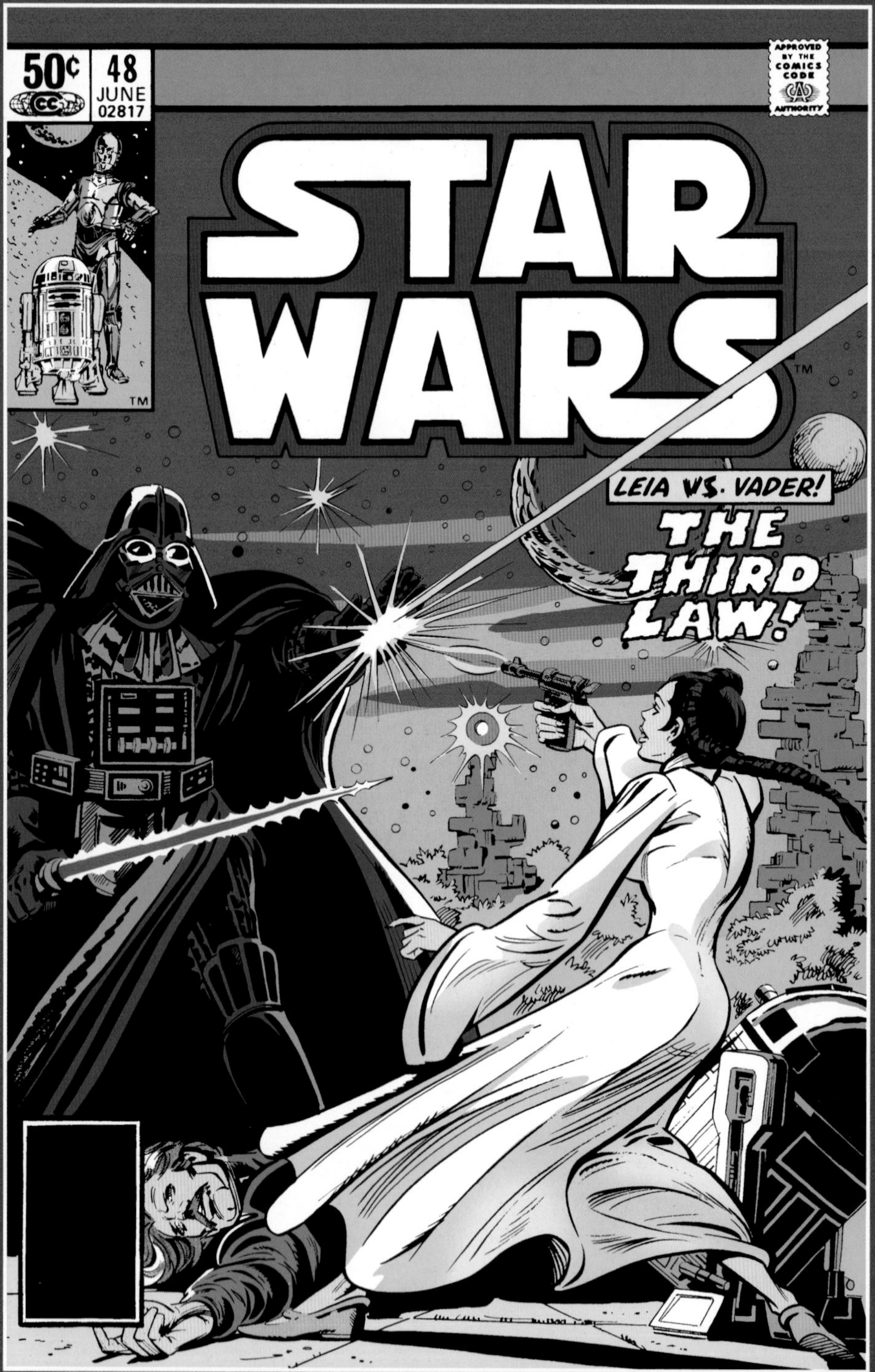
50¢
48
JUNE
02817
APPROVED BY THE COMICS CODE AUTHORITY
STAR WARS
LEIA VS. VADER!
THE THIRD LAW!

Long ago in a galaxy far, far away. . .there exists a state of cosmic *civil war*. A brave alliance of *underground freedom fighters* has challenged the tyranny and oppression of the awesome *Galactic Empire*. This is their story!

LucasFilm PRESENTS: **STAR WARS** THE GREATEST SPACE FANTASY OF ALL!

LARRY HAMA ★ CARMINE INFANTINO & CARLOS GARZON ★ RICK PARKER ★ GLYNIS WEIN ★ LOUISE JONES ★ JAMES SHOOTER
WRITER — ARTISTS — LETTERER — COLORIST — EDITOR — EDITOR-IN-CHIEF

AARGAU (är'gou), THIRD PLANET OF THE ZUG SYSTEM. THE STABILITY OF AARGAU'S CURRENCY, THE TECHNICAL SUPERIORITY OF ITS ARMED FORCES AND ITS STRICT LAWS GOVERNING WEAPONS POSSESSION AND PRECIOUS METAL EXPORTS HAVE MADE IT THE MAJOR BANKING CENTER OF THE GALAXY.

YOUR HIGHNESS, PRINCESS *LEIA ORGANA!* VISCOUNT *TARDI!* THE *BANK* AND THE *DEPOSITORS* OF *AARGAU* WELCOME YOU IN THE NAME OF THE *SACRED BALANCE!*

ALTHOUGH WE HAVE BEEN BRIEFED ON YOUR MISSION HERE, OUR REGULATIONS REQUIRE AN *IDENTI-VOICE* RECORD OF YOUR INTENTIONS... A FORMALITY--

PLEASE SPEAK CLEARLY INTO THE MIKE...

TM: © LUCASFILM LTD. 1981 (LFL)

THE THIRD LAW

419

I, PRINCESS LEIA ORGANA, AM ACTING AS ROYAL *ESCORT* TO FINANCE MINISTER VISCOUNT TARDI WHO HAS BEEN CHARGED BY THE *REBEL ALLIANCE* WITH THE TASK OF PROCURING *FINANCING* TOWARD THE PURCHASE OF A NEW SQUADRON OF X-WING FIGHTERS...

...AND I, VISCOUNT TARDI, HAVE COME TO AARGAU WITH FULL *KNOWLEDGE* OF THE COMPLEX CEREMONIAL NATURE OF YOUR BANKING PROCEDURES. *PROTOCOL* WILL BE OBSERVED. THE *LAW* WILL BE OBEYED. THE *BALANCE* WILL ENDURE.

WELL SPOKEN, VISCOUNT. ⸘AHEM⸘ IT IS *RUMORED* THAT YOU *ALONE* OF THE ENTIRE REBEL ALLIANCE POSSESS THE *STATURE* IN INTERGALACTIC FINANCE AS WELL AS THE *CEREMONIAL* SKILL THAT IS *ESSENTIAL* TO COMPLETE A MAJOR TRANSACTION WITH THE BANK OF AARGAU.

WELL...

RUMORS ARE BEST LEFT IN THE BARRACKS HALL, CAPTAIN...

IS THIS THE CUSTOMS CHECKPOINT?

YES, BUT THIS IS THE SECTION FOR PASSENGERS *DEPARTING* AARGAU.

OUR AFFLUENT ECONOMY MAKES IT UNPROFITABLE TO SMUGGLE ANYTHING *INTO* AARGAU... THEREFORE, *ENTRY* PROCEDURE IS *LAX.* ON THE *OTHER* HAND, OUR ENORMOUS RESERVES OF PRECIOUS METALS, WHICH BACK OUR CURRENCY, AND THEIR COMPARATIVE SCARCITY ELSEWHERE, CREATE A TEMPTATION MANY FIND HARD TO RESIST THEREFORE...

...EVERYTHING *LEAVING* AARGAU IS *THOROUGHLY SCANNED* WITH HIGH RESOLUTION *SENSORS!*

FORMALITIES FOR **ENTRANCE** INTO THE PORT OF AARGAU ARE SIMPLE ENOUGH. SGT. ROLEX WILL PROCESS YOU THROUGH **CUSTOMS**.

GOOD MORNING, PRINCESS-- VISCOUNT... HAVE YOU ANYTHING TO **DECLARE**?

OUR LUGGAGE HAS YET TO BE UNLOADED, SERGEANT.

ALL WE HAVE AT PRESENT--

--IS A SEALED **DIPLOMATIC POUCH**.

AH. OF COURSE A DIPLOMATIC POUCH IS **EXEMPT** FROM CUSTOMS **INSPECTIONS**. WE SHALL PROCEED WITH THE **NEXT** STEP...

...ALL PERSONS ARRIVING ON AARGAU MUST **LEARN** AND **UNDERSTAND** THE PRIMARY **LAWS**--

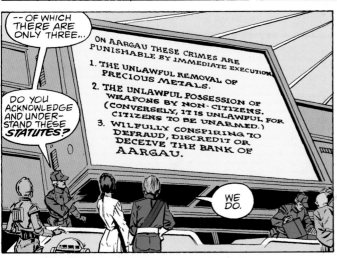

--OF WHICH THERE ARE ONLY THREE...

ON AARGAU THESE CRIMES ARE PUNISHABLE BY IMMEDIATE EXECUTION:

1. THE UNLAWFUL REMOVAL OF PRECIOUS METALS.

2. THE UNLAWFUL POSSESSION OF WEAPONS BY NON-CITIZENS. (CONVERSELY, IT IS UNLAWFUL FOR CITIZENS TO BE UNARMED.)

3. WILFULLY CONSPIRING TO DEFRAUD, DISCREDIT OR DECEIVE THE BANK OF AARGAU.

DO YOU ACKNOWLEDGE AND UNDER-STAND THESE **STATUTES**?

WE DO.

YOU ARE NOW FREE TO ENTER AARGAU. HAVE A PLEASANT AND PROFITABLE STAY AND GOOD LUCK ON...

UNFOR-TUNATELY THEIR LUCK HAS JUST SUFFERED A SEVERE **SETBACK**!

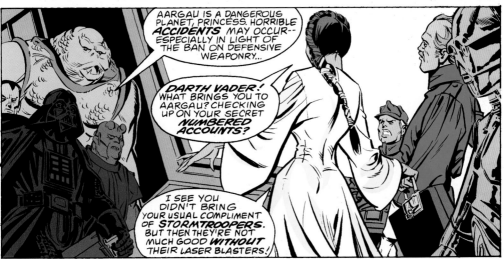

AARGAU IS A DANGEROUS PLANET, PRINCESS. HORRIBLE **ACCIDENTS** MAY OCCUR-- ESPECIALLY IN LIGHT OF THE BAN ON DEFENSIVE WEAPONRY...

DARTH VADER! WHAT BRINGS YOU TO AARGAU? CHECKING UP ON YOUR SECRET **NUMBERED ACCOUNTS**?

I SEE YOU DIDN'T BRING YOUR USUAL COMPLIMENT OF **STORMTROOPERS**. BUT THEN THEY'RE NOT MUCH GOOD **WITHOUT** THEIR LASER BLASTERS!

I WILL IGNORE YOUR PITIFUL AT-TEMPTS AT HUMOR, PRINCESS...

I COME TO AARGAU ON A *DIPLOMATIC* MISSION FOR THE EMPIRE. MY RETINUE IS *SMALL*, BUT MY NEEDS ARE SPARTAN. MAY I INTRODUCE--

--MY *PORTER*...

...MY *SECRE-TARY*...

...AND MY *VALET*...

NOW, IF YOU WILL EXCUSE ME, I WISH TO CON-TINUE THROUGH CUSTOMS...

I HAVE NOTHING TO DECLARE BUT THIS *DIPLOMATIC POUCH*.

NOTHING IN THERE BUT PAPER-WORK AND A CHANGE OF ARMOR, RIGHT?

DON'T TELL ME, IT'S A *SECRET*.

AND THIS *RETINUE* OF YOURS DOESN'T FOOL ME FOR A MICRO-SECOND!

YOUR VALET IS A *TELE-KINETIC*...

...YOUR SEC-RETARY IS A *SHAPE-SHIFTER*... ...AND YOUR PORTER IS A *HIGH-GRAVITY* CREATURE FROM RIGEL VII.

EACH IS A KNOWN MEMBER OF THE *ASSASSIN'S GUILD* AND I'LL WAGER THAT THEIR SPECIALTY IS *UNARMED KILLING!*

FURTHER-MORE...

SMUGGLER ALERT! CITIZENS STAND BY YOUR WEAPONS!

THIS MAN IS A *SMUGGLER!*

HE HAS *GOLD* IMPLANTS ON HIS *FIFTH* AND *SIXTH* RIBS!

NO! I CAN *EXPLAIN!*

KA- **ZAP!**

JUSTICE IS SWIFT ON AARGAU, PRINCESS...

JUSTICE IS A DOUBLE-EDGED SWORD, LORD VADER...

EXCEPT ON AARGAU, PRINCESS. EXCEPT ON AARGAU.

NOW, I MUST ATTEND TO THE EMPEROR'S BUSINESS. MAY THE FORCE... GIVE YOU WHAT YOU DESERVE.

NOW, THAT'S **STRANGE!** WHY WOULD THE **EMPEROR** SEND DARTH VADER OF ALL PEOPLE TO HANDLE MATTERS OF A **FINANCIAL** NATURE?

HE DIDN'T--

--THE EMPEROR SENT DARTH VADER TO STOP THE X-WING FIGHTER LOAN.

A SIMPLE TASK, REALLY...

ALL HE HAS TO DO IS DESTROY **TARDI!**

LET'S QUICKLY RUN DOWN OUR SCHEDULE FOR THE DAY--

THIS MORNING WE HAVE A RECEPTION AT THE *GARDEN* OF *BUTTERFLIES*, AT NOON WE REVIEW THE *HOME GUARD MANEUVERS*--

--THIS AFTERNOON WE HAVE THE CEREMONIAL *"PRESENTATION OF COLLATERAL."*

YES, THAT'S GOING TO BE A TRICKY ONE--*THREEPIO!* ON THAT *OVERPASS!* IT'S *DARTH VADER* AND HIS *"RETINUE"!*

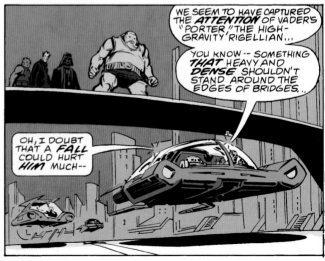

WE SEEM TO HAVE CAPTURED THE *ATTENTION* OF VADER'S *"PORTER,"* THE HIGH-GRAVITY *RIGELLIAN*...

YOU KNOW -- SOMETHING *THAT* HEAVY AND *DENSE* SHOULDN'T STAND AROUND THE EDGES OF BRIDGES...

OH, I DOUBT THAT A *FALL* COULD HURT *HIM* MUCH--

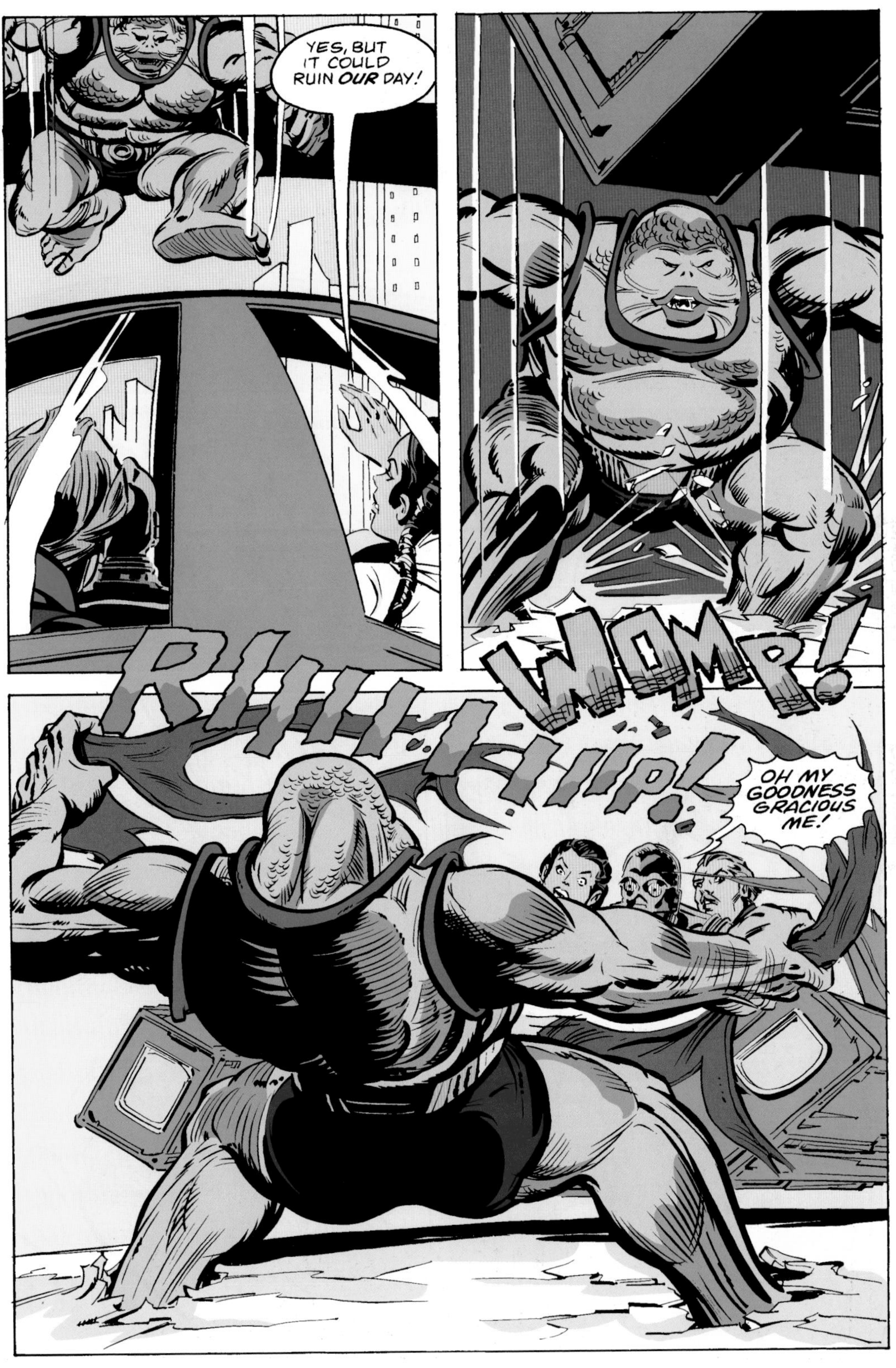
YES, BUT IT COULD RUIN OUR DAY!
WOMP!
RIIII-I-IIIP!
OH MY GOODNESS GRACIOUS ME!

THREEPIO! THE DIPLOMATIC POUCH!

THIS IS *INTOLERABLE!* WE MUST REGISTER A *COMPLAINT* THROUGH PROPER *CHANNELS--!*

NOW WHERE *IS* THAT THING?

I SAY!

HERE IT IS!

UAP!

THIS SHOULD PUT HIM IN HIS PLACE!

OFFICERS! I DEMAND THAT YOU TAKE ACTION AGAINST THESE LAWBREAKERS *IMMED-IATELY!* THIS CRIMINAL HAS *VAPORIZED* MY PORTER WITH A PROSCRIBED ENERGY *WEAPON!*

I *SAW IT!* THE POOR FELLOW *FELL*, AND SHE *MURDERED* HIM!

IS THIS *TRUE?* ARE YOU IN POSSESSION OF AN *ILLEGAL* WEAPON?

NO, OFFICERS. I WOULDN'T *THINK* OF BREAKING YOUR PRECIOUS *LAW.*

THIS IS A STANDARD MODEL GRAVITATIONAL FIELD DIS-RUPTOR, AVAILABLE IN *ANY* SPACE-PORT DUTY-FREE SHOP. YOUR PORTER *WASN'T VAPORIZED.* I MERELY INCREASED HIS *RELATIVE DENSITY*--

--TO THE *SEVENTH POWER.*

HIS ABRUPT *DEPARTURE* FOR THE PLANET'S CORE ACCOUNTS FOR THE *ILLUSION* OF VAPORIZATION.

I WOULDN'T WORRY, LORD VADER. I'M *SURE* HE'LL MAKE HIS WAY BACK TO THE SURFACE... *IN A FEW YEARS...*

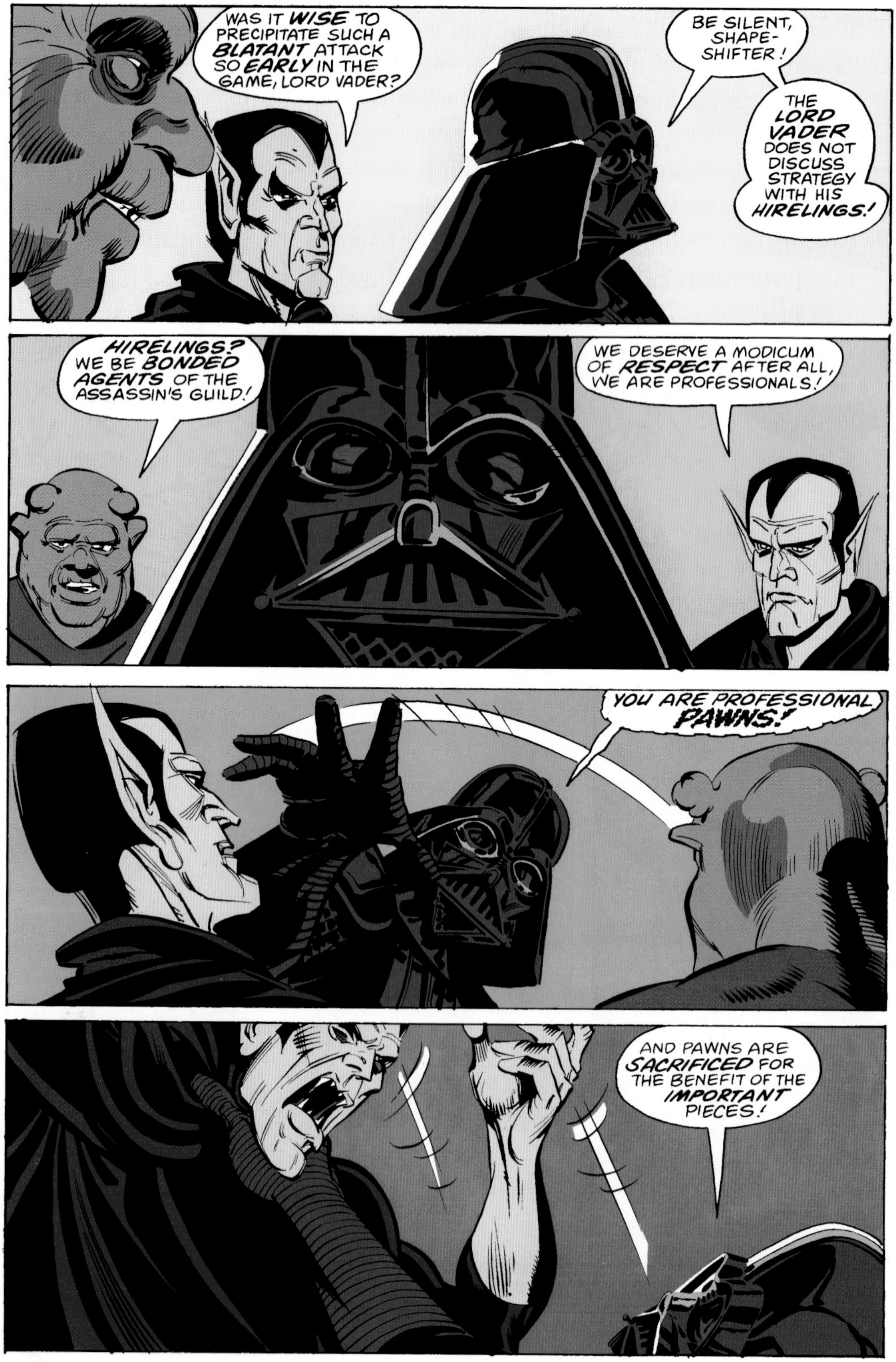

WAS IT WISE TO PRECIPITATE SUCH A BLATANT ATTACK SO EARLY IN THE GAME, LORD VADER?
BE SILENT, SHAPE-SHIFTER!
THE LORD VADER DOES NOT DISCUSS STRATEGY WITH HIS HIRELINGS!
HIRELINGS? WE BE BONDED AGENTS OF THE ASSASSIN'S GUILD!
WE DESERVE A MODICUM OF RESPECT AFTER ALL, WE ARE PROFESSIONALS!
YOU ARE PROFESSIONAL PAWNS!
AND PAWNS ARE SACRIFICED FOR THE BENEFIT OF THE IMPORTANT PIECES!

LATER THAT MORNING, IN THE GARDEN OF BUTTERFLIES...

ISN'T IT *MARVELOUS*, ARTOO? WHEN I WAS A *TRANSLATOR DROID* WITH THE DIPLOMATIC SERVICE, I ATTENDED FUNCTIONS AS GRAND AS THIS AS A MATTER OF COURSE!

BLIP?

OH, *YES!* IN FACT, ONE OF MY EMPLOYERS WAS AN AVID *COLLECTOR* OF BUTTERFLIES!

HE HAD ME *PROGRAMMED,* TO RECOGNIZE *EVERY* KNOWN SPECIES IN THIS QUADRANT!

VEEEET!

WILL YOU LOOK AT *THAT,* ARTOO? THE BANK OFFICERS SEEM QUITE *TAKEN* WITH VISCOUNT TARDI!

THAT WILL MAKE THINGS *MUCH* EASIER THIS EVENING AT THE *"PRESENTATION OF COLLATERAL."*

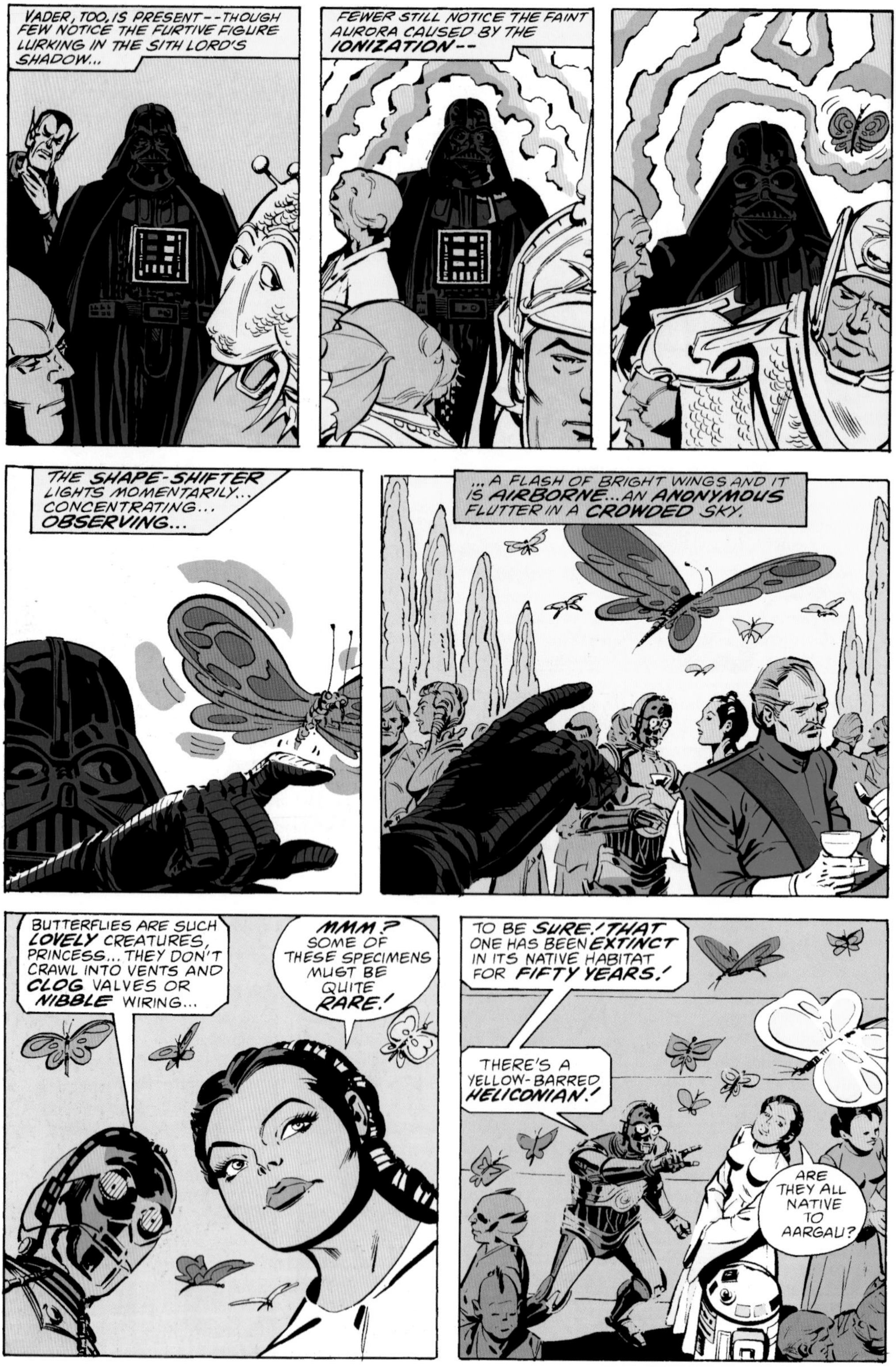
VADER, TOO, IS PRESENT--THOUGH FEW NOTICE THE FURTIVE FIGURE LURKING IN THE SITH LORD'S SHADOW...
FEWER STILL NOTICE THE FAINT AURORA CAUSED BY THE IONIZATION--
THE SHAPE-SHIFTER LIGHTS MOMENTARILY... CONCENTRATING... OBSERVING...
...A FLASH OF BRIGHT WINGS AND IT IS AIRBORNE...AN ANONYMOUS FLUTTER IN A CROWDED SKY.
BUTTERFLIES ARE SUCH LOVELY CREATURES, PRINCESS... THEY DON'T CRAWL INTO VENTS AND CLOG VALVES OR NIBBLE WIRING...
MMM? SOME OF THESE SPECIMENS MUST BE QUITE RARE!
TO BE SURE! THAT ONE HAS BEEN EXTINCT IN ITS NATIVE HABITAT FOR FIFTY YEARS!
THERE'S A YELLOW-BARRED HELICONIAN!
ARE THEY ALL NATIVE TO AARGAU?

NO. THE BRIGHT **RED** SPECIMEN BEHIND VISCOUNT TARDI IS FROM THE **ANTARES** SYSTEM--

-- ONE OF THE FEW SPECIES EQUIPPED WITH **STINGERS** AND THE ONLY ONE THAT SECRETES A **DEADLY NERVE TOXIN--!**

ARTOO! YOUR FIRE RETARDENT SPRAY!

THE VISCOUNT IS AWARE OF NO MORE THAN A SLIGHT DROP IN **TEMPERATURE** AT THE BACK OF HIS NECK...

OH, HOW DREADFULLY **CLUMSY** OF ME!

CRUNCH!

LORD VADER...

I'VE MADE **SUCH** A MESS? COULD YOU BE A **DEAR** AND--

LORD VADER?

431

LATER, AT A DIFFERENT *SORT* OF ENTERTAINMENT...

BAH! HOW DULL! THE BANKERS OF AARGAU THINK TO DETER *AGGRESSION* BY DEMONSTRATING THEIR "MILITARY MIGHT" TO VISITING GOVERNMENT OFFICIALS.

THIS DISPLAY IS *LUDICROUS* TO ONE WHO HAS DESTROYED ENTIRE *PLANETS!* AH, BUT THE PRINCESS IS QUITE AWARE OF THAT!

BY THE WAY, PRINCESS, I UNDERSTAND THAT YOUR LOAN MAY NOT BE FINALIZED UNTIL *TOMORROW...*

YOU KNOW VERY WELL THAT THE VERIFICA- TION OF COLLATERAL IS A *PAINSTAKING* PROCESS INVOLVING MULTIPLE *ASSESSORS* AND *APPRAISERS!*

VLEEP!

432

HIGH OVERHEAD, A TACTICAL FIGHTER FIRES ITS PAYLOAD...

...OF LOW YIELD ANTI-PERSONNEL MISSILES.

IN ORDER TO MOVE AN INANIMATE OBJECT-- OR IN THIS CASE, A NON-SENTIENT ANIMATED OBJECT...

...A TELEKINETIC MUST BECOME THAT OBJECT.

HE MUST FEEL THE WIND RUSHING PAST THE STREAMLINED CASING...

...HEAR THE CLICK OF RELAYS AS THE FINS ALTER THE COURSE...

...SMELL THE GYRO LUBRICANTS AS THEY STABILIZE THE AIRFRAME...

...TASTE THE ACIDIC BITE OF EXPLOSIVES IN THE WARHEAD...

...AND HE MUST SEE!

THE VISION MUST HAVE THE CLARITY OF LIFE.

IT MUST BRIDGE THE CHASM BETWEEN ILLUSION AND REALITY...

...BUT THEN, WHAT IS REALITY?

THOOM!

OH, *BLAST!* ARTOO, YOUR DISPLAY CIRCUITS ARE *MALFUNCTIONING* AGAIN?!

HOW LONG HAVE YOU BEEN PROJECTING A *HOLOGRAM* OF THE *VISCOUNT* OVER LORD VADER'S VALET?

BA-DEET!

WHAT? FOR AS LONG AS YOU'VE BEEN PROJECTING A HOLOGRAM OF THE *VALET* OVER TARDI?

SORRY...

...THEY JUST DON'T MAKE DROIDS LIKE THEY USED TO.

I'D OFFER TO LEND YOU C-3PO, BUT HE'S IN THE SHOP FOR A TUNE-UP...!

THAT NIGHT...

PRINCESS LEIA! LORD VADER HAD A *MESSAGE* DELIVERED TO MY DROID MECHANIC! HE WANTS TO *MEET* WITH US TONIGHT AT THE *OLD SPACE-PORT!*

MY, HE'S MORE *PREDICTABLE* THAN I THOUGHT! THE ABANDONED SPACE-PORT WOULD HAVE BEEN *MY* CHOICE AS WELL!

BLIT!

WE'RE NOT *GOING,* ARE WE?

÷YAWN÷ WELL, *YOU'RE* NOT!

BUT VISCOUNT TARDI, ARTOO AND I WILL BE THERE RIGHT ON SCHEDULE.

WE HAVE *OTHER* PLANS FOR *YOU...!*

MIDNIGHT AT THE OLD SPACE-PORT...

I HAVE OBEYED MY *EMPEROR'S* ORDERS. I HAVE WALKED THE RAZOR'S EDGE IN THE DIPLOMATIC SNAKEPIT.

BUT THE TIME FOR SUBTLETY IS *PAST!* MY *PRIMARY* MISSION IS TO *STOP* THE LOAN! YOU *KNOW* THAT I CAN *DESTROY* YOU AS EASILY AS I LIFT MY FINGER!

I HAVE NO WISH TO *TREAD* ON THE EMPEROR'S DELICATE DIPLOMATIC TOES, BUT IF I AM *FORCED* TO DO SO, I SHALL.

FORSAKE THE LOAN, LEAVE AARGAU AND *LIVE* TO FIGHT ME AGAIN, STAY, AND WE *BOTH* LOSE... THOUGH ONLY *YOU* SHALL LOSE YOUR *LIVES.'*

YOU INSULT MY HONOR, LORD VADER! I SWEAR, I'LL KILL YOU WITH MY OWN HANDS--!

VISCOUNT! NO--! DON'T THREATEN...

YOU DARE TO RAISE YOUR HAND TO A LORD OF THE SITH?!?

ZRAAK

HOLD IT, I HAD ONE MORE SURPRISE STASHED AWAY IN THAT DIPLOMATIC POUCH!

BLIIIIP!

I KNEW IT!

AN ILLEGAL WEAPON! THE LITTLE HYPOCRITE IS FOUND OUT!

AND WHAT DO YOU CALL THAT *LIGHT-SABER?*

ZWAAP!

WITH A MERE GESTURE, VADER DEFLECTS HER LASER FIRE.

IT MAKES NO DIFFERENCE *NOW*, PRINCESS. VISCOUNT TARDI IS *DEAD*. THERE WILL BE *NO LOAN. THERE WILL BE NO NEW X-WING FIGHTER SQUADRON!*

OF *COURSE* VISCOUNT TARDI IS DEAD. IN *FACT*, HE'S BEEN DEAD FOR OVER A *MONTH* NOW... BUT THERE *SHALL* BE A LOAN!

THE VISCOUNT'S DOCTOR, COMMANDER WILLARD, AND I WERE THE *ONLY* ONES PRIVY TO TARDI'S DEATH. WE DECIDED TO SEND A *DROID* IN HIS PLACE...

A CAREFULLY PROGRAMMED, *NON-SENTIENT* DROID, OF COURSE!

WE KNEW THAT *ENTRANCE* PROCEDURES ON AARGAU WERE *LAX* ENOUGH FOR US TO SLIP A DROID THROUGH *UNDETECTED...* BUT ONCE ON AARGAU WE NEEDED *HELP--*

--WE HAD TO FIND A WAY TO *FORCE* YOU TO *HELP* US!

FORCE ME?

WE HAD TO FORCE *YOU*, NOT ONE OF YOUR HIRELINGS, INTO "KILLING" *VISCOUNT TARDI!*

ARTOO, RUN THE *HOLOGRAM!*

BLT!

AS YOU CAN SEE, WE HAVE A CLEAR *RECORD* OF YOUR *ILLEGAL* USE OF A FORBIDDEN *WEAPON.*

I CAN *DESTROY* THE TAPE AS EASILY AS I CAN DESTROY THE *DROID!*

NOT SO EASILY, VADER. ARTOO RAN A SIMULTANEOUS TRANS-MISSION TO A *RECORDER* OPERATED BY *C-3PO...*

LET'S HAVE THAT *REMOTE* ARTOO...

THIS IS C-3PO ON *REMOTE* FROM OUTSIDE *MAIN POLICE HEADQUARTERS.* IN MY HAND I HOLD THE *TAPE...*

THIS IS *MEANINGLESS!* TARDI IS *DEAD!* THE LOAN CAN *NOT* GO THROUGH!

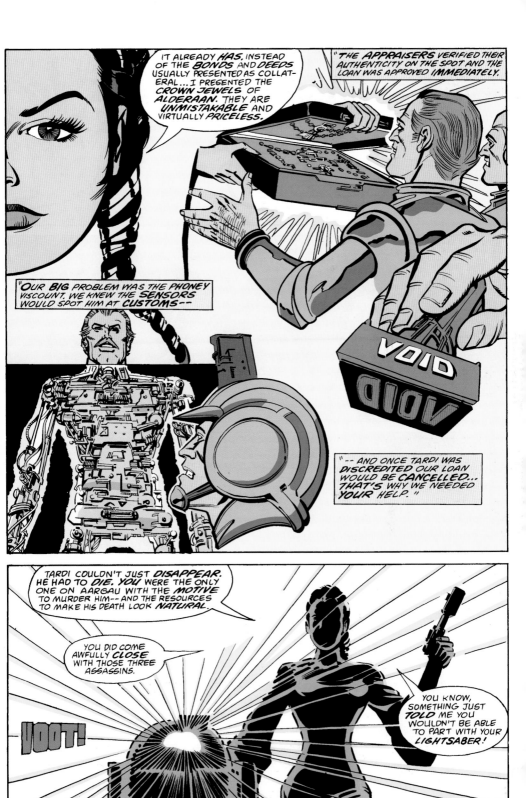

IT ALREADY *HAS*. INSTEAD OF THE *BONDS* AND *DEEDS* USUALLY PRESENTED AS COLLATERAL... I PRESENTED THE *CROWN JEWELS* OF *ALDERAAN*. THEY ARE *UNMISTAKABLE* AND VIRTUALLY *PRICELESS*.

"THE *APPRAISERS* VERIFIED THEIR AUTHENTICITY ON THE SPOT AND THE LOAN WAS APPROVED *IMMEDIATELY*.

"OUR *BIG* PROBLEM WAS THE PHONEY VISCOUNT. WE KNEW THE *SENSORS* WOULD SPOT HIM AT *CUSTOMS*--

"-- AND ONCE TARDI WAS *DISCREDITED* OUR LOAN WOULD BE *CANCELLED*... *THAT'S* WHY WE NEEDED *YOUR* HELP."

VOID
VOID

TARDI COULDN'T JUST *DISAPPEAR*. HE HAD TO *DIE*. *YOU* WERE THE ONLY ONE ON *AARGAU* WITH THE *MOTIVE* TO MURDER HIM-- AND THE RESOURCES TO MAKE HIS DEATH LOOK *NATURAL*.

YOU DID COME AWFULLY *CLOSE* WITH THOSE THREE ASSASSINS.

YOU KNOW, SOMETHING JUST *TOLD* ME YOU WOULDN'T BE ABLE TO PART WITH YOUR *LIGHTSABER!*

YOOT!

439

OH, YES, YOU'LL HAVE TO GET *RID* OF THIS LASER BLASTER FOR ME *ALSO*... WE WOULDN'T WANT ANY *NASTY* COMPLICATIONS WITH THE WEAPONS LAW, NOW *WOULD* WE?

BUT THAT SHOULDN'T BE *HALF* AS DIFFICULT AS GETTING RID OF THE *"BODY."*...

OH, I'LL JUST INCLUDE THEM IN THE *PACKAGE* WHEN I SMUGGLE OUT MY *REAL PRIMARY OBJECTIVE.*

SMUGGLE? *REAL PRIMARY OBJECTIVE?!*

YES. THE *CROWN JEWELS* OF ALDERAAN.

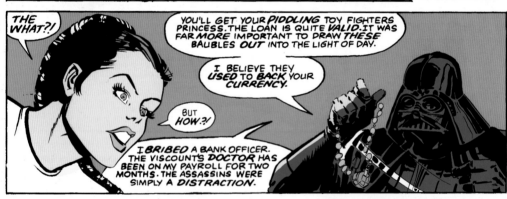

THE *WHAT?!*

YOU'LL GET YOUR *PIDDLING* TOY FIGHTERS PRINCESS. THE LOAN IS QUITE *VALID.* IT WAS FAR *MORE* IMPORTANT TO DRAW *THESE* BAUBLES *OUT* INTO THE LIGHT OF DAY.

I BELIEVE THEY *USED* TO *BACK* YOUR *CURRENCY.*

BUT *HOW?!*

I *BRIBED* A BANK OFFICER. THE VISCOUNT'S *DOCTOR* HAS BEEN ON MY PAYROLL FOR TWO MONTHS. THE ASSASSINS WERE SIMPLY A *DISTRACTION.*

YOU *HAD* THE JEWELS-- WHY *BOTHER* TO MEET ME HERE?

TO *TIDY* THINGS UP, PRINCESS. IF TARDI WERE *EXPOSED* AS A DROID, THE LOAN WOULD SURELY BE *QUESTIONED* AND THE JEWELS WOULD BE *MISSED.*

I ALSO THOUGHT TO TAKE ADVANTAGE OF THE OPPORTUNITY TO *ADVISE* YOU AGAINST MENTIONING ANY OF THIS TO THE *AARGAUUN* AUTHORITIES.

IT WOULD ONLY DO *EVIL* THINGS TO YOUR *CREDIT RATING.*

NEXT: THE *LAST JEDI!*

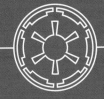

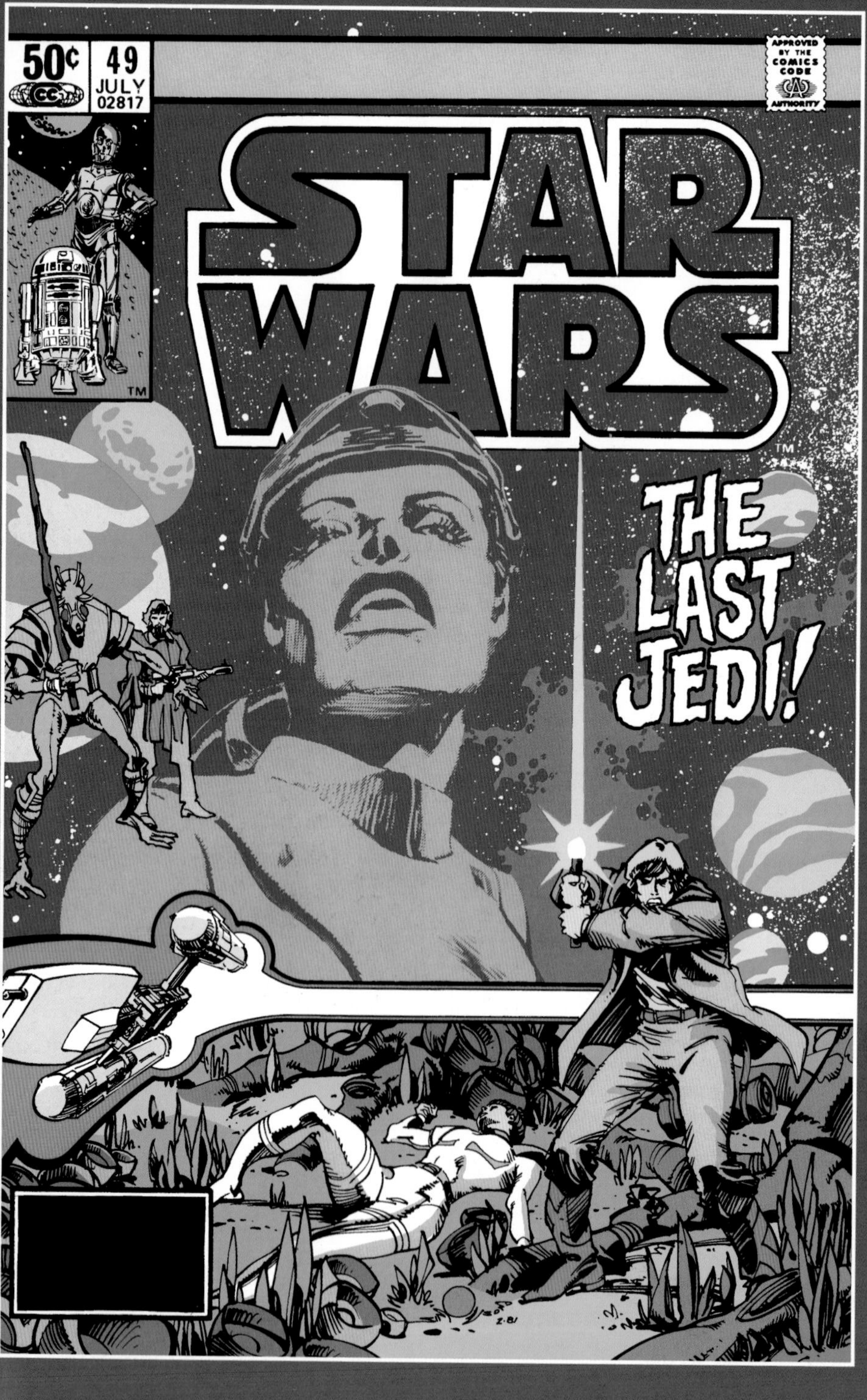
50¢
49
JULY
02817
APPROVED BY THE COMICS CODE AUTHORITY
STAR WARS
TM
THE LAST JEDI!

Long ago in a galaxy far, far away. . .there exists a state of cosmic *civil war*. A brave alliance of *underground freedom fighters* has challenged the tyranny and oppression of the awesome *Galactic Empire*. This is their story!

LucasFilm PRESENTS: **STAR WARS** THE GREATEST **SPACE FANTASY** OF ALL!

CONTINUING THE SAGA BEGUN IN THE FILMS BY GEORGE LUCAS, RELEASED BY TWENTIETH CENTURY-FOX.

| MIKE W. BARR WRITER | WALT SIMONSON & TOM PALMER ARTISTS | SHELLY LEFERMAN LETTERER | D. WARFIELD C. SCHEELE COLORISTS | LOUISE JONES EDITOR | JIM SHOOTER EMPIRE LIASON |

IT BEGINS WITH A SCREAM OF ENGINES, AS A MODIFIED Y-WING WARPS OUT OF HYPERDRIVE, INTO NORMAL SPACE...

...AND A SHOUT OF TRIUMPH FROM WITHIN THE SHIP ITSELF!

THAT'S IT! THAT OVERGROWN MUDBALL IS THE ORIGIN POINT OF THE SIGNAL WE'VE TRACED HALFWAY ACROSS THE *GALAXY*! AND IF THE *FORCE* IS WITH US...

...IT'LL GIVE US THE MEANS TO TURN AN ENTIRE SOLAR SYSTEM AGAINST THE *EMPIRE*!

The Last Jedi!

AND INSIDE...

THE RESCUE SIGNAL WAS VERY FAINT, MASTER LUKE, BUT I MANAGED TO TRACE IT, NONE-THELESS.

VA·DABLOOT WHEET

OH, ALL RIGHT, ARTOO–*YOU* TRACED THE SIGNAL...

...I WAS HERE TO HELP IF YOU NEEDED ME!

BUT THE DROIDS' FRIENDLY BICKERING IS LOST ON THE FIGURES AT THE HELM...

PRINCESS LEIA ORGANA...

...AND LUKE SKY-WALKER!

DON'T GET YOUR HOPES UP *TOO* FAR, LUKE...THOSE AUTOMATIC SIGNALS CAN FUNCTION FOR YEARS ON SOLAR POWER...

...THERE MAY NOT BE ANYONE ALIVE DOWN THERE!

THERE HAS TO BE, LEIA...

...THERE JUST HAS TO BE!

FOLLOWING COORDINATES SUPPLIED BY R2-D2, THE YOUNG PILOT FROM TATOOINE QUICKLY LOCATES THE RUST-ENCRUSTED WRECKAGE FROM WHICH THE RESCUE SIGNAL EMANATES...

...AND THEN, AS EASILY AS MANEUVERING A SHINY NEW LANDSPEEDER...

...HE LANDS, THOUGH THE ENCROACHING JUNGLE ALLOWS PRECIOUS LITTLE SPACE FOR INTRUDERS!

EVERYONE STAY PUT! I'LL TAKE A LOOK AROUND!

LUKE LEAPS TO THE ALIEN SOIL AND BEGINS A SEARCH...

...A SEARCH AS THOROUGH AS IT IS UNREWARDING!

NO SIGN OF INHABITANTS, BUT THEY COULDN'T BE SURE WE'D BE FRIENDLY! THEY MAY BE HIDING, SO --

GROORRG

UH OH...

IT STRIDES THROUGH THE THICK FOLIAGE, ITS HORNED NOSE TWITCHING, SCENTING NEW PREY... AND IF IT THINKS AT ALL, ITS RUDIMENTARY BRAIN BELIEVES THE SMALL FLESH-THING BEFORE IT TO BE HELPLESS!

GRROOORRRG

IT CANNOT KNOW THAT LUKE SKYWALKER IS NEVER HELPLESS -- NOT WHILE HE CARRIES...

...HIS LIGHT-SABER!

CRRRRR

DUMB BEAST LIKE THIS SHOULDN'T BE TOO HARD TO DISCOURAGE!

THIS WORKED ON THAT SNOW-BEAST ON HOTH... AND IT OUGHTA WORK --

--H-HERE?

MY LIGHTSABER SLICED THROUGH IT... BUT ITS FLESH SEALED INSTANTLY BEHIND THE CUT!

LEIA! TRY YOUR BLAS--!

BUT BEFORE LUKE CAN COMPLETE HIS SENTENCE...

ZZZZP

GRROOO

THE CREATURE ...IT'S DEAD!

LEIA--?

I FIRED, STRANGER--IT TAKES AN *ANTI-MAGNETIC POLARIZATION RAY* TO PUT THOSE THINGS IN THEIR PLACE!

AND UNLESS YOU TELL ME WHO YOU *ARE* ...AND WHETHER YOU'RE EMPIRE OR *FRIENDLY*--

--YOU'LL BE *NEXT!*

I'M LEIA, HE'S LUKE--WE'RE WITH THE REBEL ALLIANCE ...AND IF YOU'RE *PRINCE DENID* OF VELMOR...

...WE'VE COME A LONG WAY TO FIND YOU--AND IT WAS WORTH THE TRIP!

HUMPH!

WELL, WHAT'S THE STORY, FELLA... *ARE* YOU PRINCE DENID?

I AM.

THAT'S EASY ENOUGH TO CHECK OUT... BUT IF YOU *ARE*, THEN HOW'D YOU GET *HERE?*

"YEARS AGO," REPLIES THE PRINCE, "A MOB, BOUGHT BY EMPIRE GOLD, STORMED OUR PALACE AND SLEW MY PARENTS. MY YOUNGER BROTHER, AN IMPERIAL SYMPATHIZER, WAS NOT HARMED.

"BUT CHILD THOUGH I WAS, I WAS ANTI-IMPERIAL AND I WAS SUCCESSOR TO THE THRONE.

"MY BETROTHED AND I WERE FORCED TO *FLEE*..."

"MY LIFE WAS AS GOOD AS FORFEIT!"

...IN TOO MUCH OF A HURRY, I FEAR! OUR FUEL WAS LOW, AND WE CRASHED *HERE!*

THE CRASH TOOK THE LIFE OF MY BETROTHED, *LOREN*... HER BODY LIES 'NEATH THAT BURIAL CAIRN...

...AND THE TWO OF US HAVE LIVED HERE EVER SINCE!

THE *TWO* OF YOU? BUT IF YOUR BETROTHED DIED, THEN--

--SOMETHING'S COMING! WHAT--

CALM YOURSELF, LUKE...IT IS MERELY THE *THIRD* MEMBER OF MY PARTY--THE MAN TO WHOM I OWE MY *LIFE!*

NO! HE CAN'T BE...

-- A JEDI KNIGHT?!

LUKE SKYWALKER'S VOICE IS TINGED WITH DISBELIEF... FOR, THOUGH THE STOOPED FIGURE WHO SHAMBLES FROM THE JUNGLE IS DRESSED IN TATTERS THAT RESEMBLE THE PROUD GARB OF THE JEDIS...

...IT CARRIES ONLY A *GNARLED STAFF* IN AN OBSCENE PARODY OF THE JEDI'S PROUD LIGHTSABER...

...AND IT MUTTERS... IN AN AIMLESS VOICE UNGUIDED BY REASON OR SANITY!

PRINCE DENID *NEEDS* JEDIDIAH... JEDI WILL *PROTECT* HIM...

THE THING IS A WALKING PARODY OF LUKE SKYWALKER'S HIGHEST, MOST REVERED *GOAL*... AND IT MAKES HIS BLOOD BOIL!

JEDIDIAH ISN'T A JEDI KNIGHT, LUKE, THOUGH HE WAS ASKED TO BECOME ONE YEARS AGO. HE WANTED IT WITH ALL HIS HEART, YET HE REFUSED.

HE WAS CALLED-- AND DIDN'T *ANSWER?*

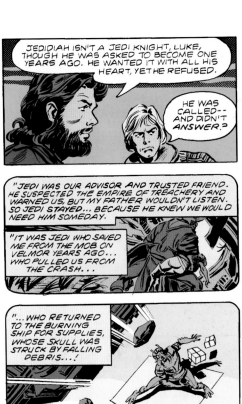

"JEDI WAS OUR ADVISOR AND TRUSTED FRIEND. HE SUSPECTED THE EMPIRE OF TREACHERY AND WARNED US, BUT MY FATHER WOULDN'T LISTEN. SO JEDI STAYED... BECAUSE HE KNEW WE WOULD NEED HIM SOMEDAY...

"IT WAS JEDI WHO SAVED ME FROM THE MOB ON VELMOR YEARS AGO... WHO PULLED US FROM THE CRASH...

"...WHO RETURNED TO THE BURNING SHIP FOR SUPPLIES, WHOSE SKULL WAS STRUCK BY FALLING DEBRIS...!

"HIS INJURIES ROBBED HIM OF HIS REASON. HE REMEMBERED ONLY HIS LOST DREAM OF BECOMING A JEDI KNIGHT...

"...AND AT THAT MOMENT, HE ENTERED A FANTASY WORLD FROM WHICH HE HAS NEVER *RETURNED!*"

A SAD TALE OF INCREDIBLE SACRIFICE, IS IT NOT, LUKE? WHAT DO YOU SAY?

YOU ARE PRETTY... JEDI WILL PROTECT YOU...

I SAY, IF WE DON'T BLAST OUT OF HERE *BEFORE* THIS EXPLOSIVE CHARGE DESTROYS YOUR SHIP AND TRANSMITTER...

...YOU'LL WISH WE'D NEVER FOUND YOU AT *ALL!*

WA-WHOOM

BUT AS THE LITTLE SHIP PREPARES TO JUMP INTO HYPERSPACE...

...THE REBELS REALIZE THE SKY HAS SUDDENLY BECOME VERY CROWDED!

LUKE! ANOTHER SHIP JUST CAME *OUT* OF HYPERDRIVE...

I SEE IT, LEIA...

...BUT AT THE SPEED IT WAS GOING, I DON'T THINK IT *SAW* US! IF IT'S FRIENDLY, THEY WON'T MIND IF WE DON'T STOP TO CHAT...

...AND IF IT'S *UN*-FRIENDLY, I'D JUST AS SOON NOT GET INVOLVED IN A FIGHT WITH OUR ROYAL *CARGO* ON BOARD!

SO WE'D BEST GET *OUT* OF HERE...

...WHILE THE GETTING'S *GOOD!*

SHA-KOOM

I MUST RETURN TO VELMOR IMMEDIATELY! SOON, THE LAWS OF SUCCESSION WILL DECLARE ME LEGALLY *DEAD*, AND MY YOUNGER BROTHER WILL ASSUME THE THRONE ...AND HIS SYMPATHIES HAVE ALWAYS BEEN WITH THE *EMPIRE!*

DON'T WORRY, DENID!

"DON'T WORRY, DENID!" BROTHER!

IN THE ENSUING DAYS, PRINCE DENID LEARN THAT THE REBELS TRACED HIS FAINT BROADCAST ON THE FAINTER HOPE THAT HE MIGHT YET LIVE...AND USE HIS INFLUENCE TO TURN HIS PLANET AGAINST THE EMPIRE!

HE TAKES GREAT PLEASURE IN THE CIVILIZED COMFORTS THE Y-WING PROVIDES AND EVEN GREATER PLEASURE FROM THE COMPANY OF PRINCESS LEIA!

OF COURSE, THE TRIP IS NOT SO ENJOYABLE FOR ALL...

JEDI STRIKES... WITH HIS LIGHT-SABER...

KLONK

SIR, REALLY...!

IF YOU THINK YOU CAN DO ANY *BETTER*, ARTOO, YOU'RE WELCOME TO *TRY!*

REEP RA-DOOT

"LET THE JEDI WIN"? VERY AMUSING, YOU OVER-GREASED SPROCKET!

BUT THE TRIP DOES PASS. FINALLY THE Y-WING LEAVES HYPERSPACE AT THE EDGE OF THE GALAXY TO FIND...

VELMOR! THERE SHE IS, YOUR HIGHNESS! AND IF THE LIFE-FORM READINGS AT THE COORDINATES YOU GAVE ME FOR THE ROYAL *PALACE* ARE ANY INDICATION...

"...THERE'S QUITE A *CROWD ASSEMBLED* DOWN THERE!"

"QUITE A CROWD", INDEED-- FOR HOW OFTEN DO THE MASSES IN ANY AGE SEE ONE OF THEIR RULERS ASCEND TO THE SEAT OF POWER?

SUCH OCCASIONS SWELL THEIR *HEARTS* AND *SPIRITS,* FOR THEY SEE ONLY OF THE *GLAMOR* AND *DRAMA* OF THE MOMENT...

...WHILE OTHERS THINK ONLY OF THE *POWER!*

...AND BY THE AUTHORITY INVESTED IN ME BY THE COUNCIL OF ELDERS, I PROCLAIM PRINCE ANOD *KING* OF ALL VELMOR, AND--

ZELOR, WHAT'S THAT *SHIP* DOING? IT MUSN'T *SPOIL* MY CORONATION!

QUIET, YOU *FOOL!*

THE MASSES OBEDIENTLY PART, FORMING A LANDING STRIP FOR THE IMPUDENT VESSEL...

...A VESSEL WHICH SOON DISCHARGES FOUR PASSENGERS...

A YOUNG PRINCESS FROM *ALDERAAN,* HER HAIRCOLOR ALTERED TO A SHIMMERING *GOLD...*

...PRINCE *DENID,* NOW WEARING GARB BEFITTING HIS ROYAL STATION...

...AND A *DISGUISED REBEL PILOT* FROM *TATOOINE,* DOING HIS BEST TO LOOK THE UNPRINCIPLED *SCOUNDREL...*

...AND, OF COURSE, *JEDI!*

NO FURTHER, CITIZEN! WOULD YOU PRESUME TO INTERRUPT THE CORONATION OF YOUR *KING?*

IF A KING IS A TRUE LEADER, THE PRESENCE OF HIS PEOPLE CANNOT *BE* A PRESUMPTION!

BUT THE POINT IS MOOT, IN *THIS* INSTANCE...

...FOR I AM PRINCE DENID, SON OF LORAC, KING OF VELMOR.

I DEMAND THAT THESE PROCEEDINGS BE HALTED-- UNTIL MY LINEAGE CAN BE ESTABLISHED!

ZELOR, WHAT CAN WE *DO?* HE IS DENID, I *KNOW!*

SHUT *UP,* ANOD! I'LL HANDLE THIS!

YOU ARE WELL WITHIN YOUR RIGHTS, CITIZEN, BUT BE *WARNED*--

--THE PEOPLE OF VELMORE HAVE BEEN LONG WITHOUT A KING! I HAVE GOVERNED THEM AS BEST I COULD AS THEIR REGENT, BUT THEY DESIRE A *MONARCH...*

...AND THEY WILL NOT BE MERCIFUL WITH ANY *PRETENDER* TO THE THRONE!

GRRRR...

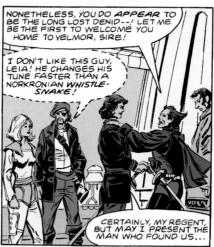

NONETHELESS, YOU DO *APPEAR* TO BE THE LONG LOST DENID--! LET ME BE THE FIRST TO WELCOME YOU HOME TO VELMOR, SIRE!

I DON'T LIKE THIS GUY, LEIA! HE CHANGES HIS TUNE FASTER THAN A NORKRONIAN *WHISTLE-SNAKE!*

CERTAINLY, MY REGENT, BUT MAY I PRESENT THE MAN WHO FOUND US...

...THE BOUNTY HUNTER, *KORL MARCUS!*

AND SHE *WHO* IS THE LIGHT OF MY SOUL, MY BE- TROTHED, *LOREN!*

WE ARE HONORED TO HAVE YOU WITH US, YOUR LADYSHIP.

THANK YOU, MY REGENT, THE HONOR IS *MINE!*

AND MAY I INTRODUCE YOU TO CAPTAIN TRAAL, OUR DIPLOMATIC ATTACHÉ FROM THE EMPIRE!

DELIGHTED.

JUST A FORMALITY, SIRE, BUT WE MUST CONFIRM YOUR *IDENTITY...*

...FOR SHOULD YOU PROVE TO BE AN *IMPOSTER...*

...WELL...

PLEASANT GUY, ISN'T HE?

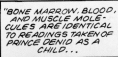

"BONE MARROW, BLOOD, AND MUSCLE MOLE-CULES ARE IDENTICAL TO READINGS TAKEN OF PRINCE DENID AS A CHILD..."

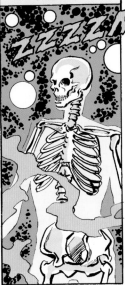

"EPIDERMIS AND RETINAL READINGS LIKEWISE CONFORM..."

NO ERROR POSSIBLE, ELDER -- THIS YOUNG MAN IS OUR PRINCE, ALL RIGHT!

-; TSK ;- I DARESAY THE REGENT ISN'T GOING TO LIKE THIS AT ALL...

MY REGENT, WE ARE -- EH -- HAPPY TO CERTIFY THAT ALL TESTS ARE POSITIVE! PRINCE DENID LIVES!

UNFORTUNATELY, THE SAME TESTS CANNOT BE MADE ON HIS BETROTHED...

AND WHY NOT PHYSICIAN?

LOREN, PERHAPS IF YOU EX-PLAINED...

CERTAINLY, BELOVED! MY REGENT, I AM FROM THE PLANET ALDERAAN, MY MEDI-READINGS WERE LOST...

...WHEN MY ENTIRE PLANET WAS DESTROYED -- BY THE EMPIRE!

HOW... CONVENIENT.

NOW, NOW, CHILDREN, NO BICKERING! PRINCE DENID'S CONFIRMATION OF HIS BETROTHED IS PROOF ENOUGH!

AND NOW, THERE MUST BE CELE-BRATION, FOR VELMOR'S BLOOD MONARCH HAS RETURNED!

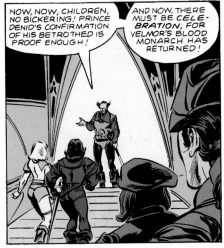

FOOD FOR VICTORIOUS JEDI AND HIS FRIENDS? GOOD...

KEEP THIS CRAZY OLD GUY AWAY FROM ME, WILL YOU, THREEPIO? I'M GONNA HAVE ENOUGH TROUBLE WITHOUT BABY-SITTING HIM!

CERTAINLY, MASTER LU-- MASTER KORL!

THE GUESTS OF HONOR ARE SEATED ON A RAISED DIAS, AND THE BANQUET BEGINS!

TO THE MAJORITY OF THE REVELERS, THE GALA EVENT IS AN AFFECTIONATE WELCOME TO THEIR NEWLY-RETURNED PRINCE...

...BUT LUKE SKYWALKER, SEATED BETWEEN A REPRESENT-ATIVE OF THE EMPIRE, AND THE MAN HE HELPED SNATCH THE CROWN OF VELMOR FROM...

...WONDERS IF HE WOULDN'T BE SAFER FACING ANOTHER DEATH STAR!

AH, FRIEND MARCUS! OUR CUSTOMS DICTATE THAT A MALE NEWCOMER TO OUR PLANET MUST PARTICIPATE IN A SIMPLE CEREMONY BEFORE BREAKING BREAD...

OH?

A TRIVIAL THING, REALLY...

IN OUR ANCIENT PAST, OUTSIDERS DUELED FOR THEIR MEALS!

OF COURSE, NOWADAYS THE CUSTOM IS PURELY CEREMONIAL! WE RARELY FIGHT TO THE DEATH ANYMORE!

LUCKY FOR ME, ZELOR!

LUCKY FOR HIM, TOO! THESE "ENERGY-SWORDS" ARE A LOT LIKE LIGHTSABERS -- I COULD PROBABLY CUT ZELOR INTO BITE-SIZE PIECES WITH THIS...

...BUT I CAN'T LET THEM EVEN SUSPECT THAT I'M REALLY LUKE SKYWALKER! I'LL LET ZELOR WIN!

READY, FRIEND MARCUS?

THEN... BEGIN!

SHHHKK

CRRKKLLL

YEOW! "I'LL LET ZELOR WIN"? THIS GUY'S AN EXPERT!

SHRAKK

STILL, I CAN'T GIVE MYSELF AWAY! GOTTA PROTECT MYSELF AS BEST I CAN...

SKOOOM

...AND HOPE THIS IS OVER...

RAKKT

...SOON? HE'S FIGHTING TO THE DEATH! DOES HE KNOW WHO I AM?

LUKE FALLS TO THE FLOOR, AWAITING THE DEATH BLOW...

...BUT THEN...

SO, FRIEND MARCUS! A FORTUNATE THING YOU DIDN'T VISIT HERE IN THE OLDEN DAYS, EH?

UH, THAT'S RIGHT, ZELOR ...HEH, HEH...

HAHA HAHA HAHAHA HAHA HAHA

NOW THAT THE CEREMONIES ARE OVER, I SHOULD LIKE TO PROPOSE A TOAST...

...TO THE PEOPLE OF VELMOR, WHOSE COUNSEL I SHALL SEEK AND CHERISH THROUGHOUT THE YEARS OF MY REIGN...

...AND ALSO TO MY BETROTHED, THE LADY LOREN...

...WHO, WHEN I ASCEND THE THRONE, I SHALL MAKE MY WIFE, AND YOUR QUEEN!

WHILE A DUMBFOUNDED LUKE TRIES TO HIDE HIS SHOCK...

LEIA CAN'T KNOW ANYTHING ABOUT THIS...

...BUT MAYBE...MAYBE SHE DOES!

AND MAYBE SHE--EH?

THIS REVELRY WILL CONTINUE FOR SOME TIME, MARCUS, MAY I SPEAK TO YOU OUTSIDE...

...ALONE?

?

IN THE MOOD FOR A LITTLE NIGHT AIR, CAPTAIN?

CAN WE DISPENSE WITH THE SMALL TALK, MARCUS? YOU SEE, I KNOW WHO YOU ARE--

--AND WHAT YOU WANT!

Y-YOU *DO*, DO YOU?

OF COURSE. I'VE RUN A CHECK ON YOUR REGISTRATION PAPERS -- AS A PRECAUTION, YOU UNDERSTAND--

--AND NO "KORL MARCUS" EXISTS! YOU'RE TRAVELLING UNDER AN ALIAS -- PROBABLY WANTED FOR A CRIME, SOMEWHERE-- PERHAPS EVEN CRIMES AGAINST THE *EMPIRE!*

I SHOULD TURN YOU IN, BUT...

BUT *WHAT?*

I WANT YOU...

HUH?

...TO *KILL* PRINCE DENID AND HIS LITTLE QUEEN AT THE CEREMONIAL GAMES TOMORROW! WHATEVER REWARD HE PROMISED YOU FOR RESCUING HIM...

...I'LL DOUBLE IT! I INTEND TO GO FAR IN THE EMPIRE, MARCUS...

...AND I'D BE GRATEFUL FOR YOUR HELP...IN ANY NUMBER OF WAYS!

YOU'VE GOT YOURSELF A *DEAL*, CAPTAIN!

I THINK WE'RE GOING TO GET ALONG *FINE*, MARCUS! SEE YOU TOMORROW...

AND TOMORROW NIGHT!

...AND WHEN LUKE HAS GONE...

YOU CAN COME OUT NOW.

DID IT WORK, TRAAL? WILL HE KILL THE PRINCE FOR US?

HE'LL DO IT, ZELOR.

MARCUS WILL KILL DENID AND THAT SIMPERING GIRL...

...THEN WE'LL KILL HIM!

EXCELLENT.

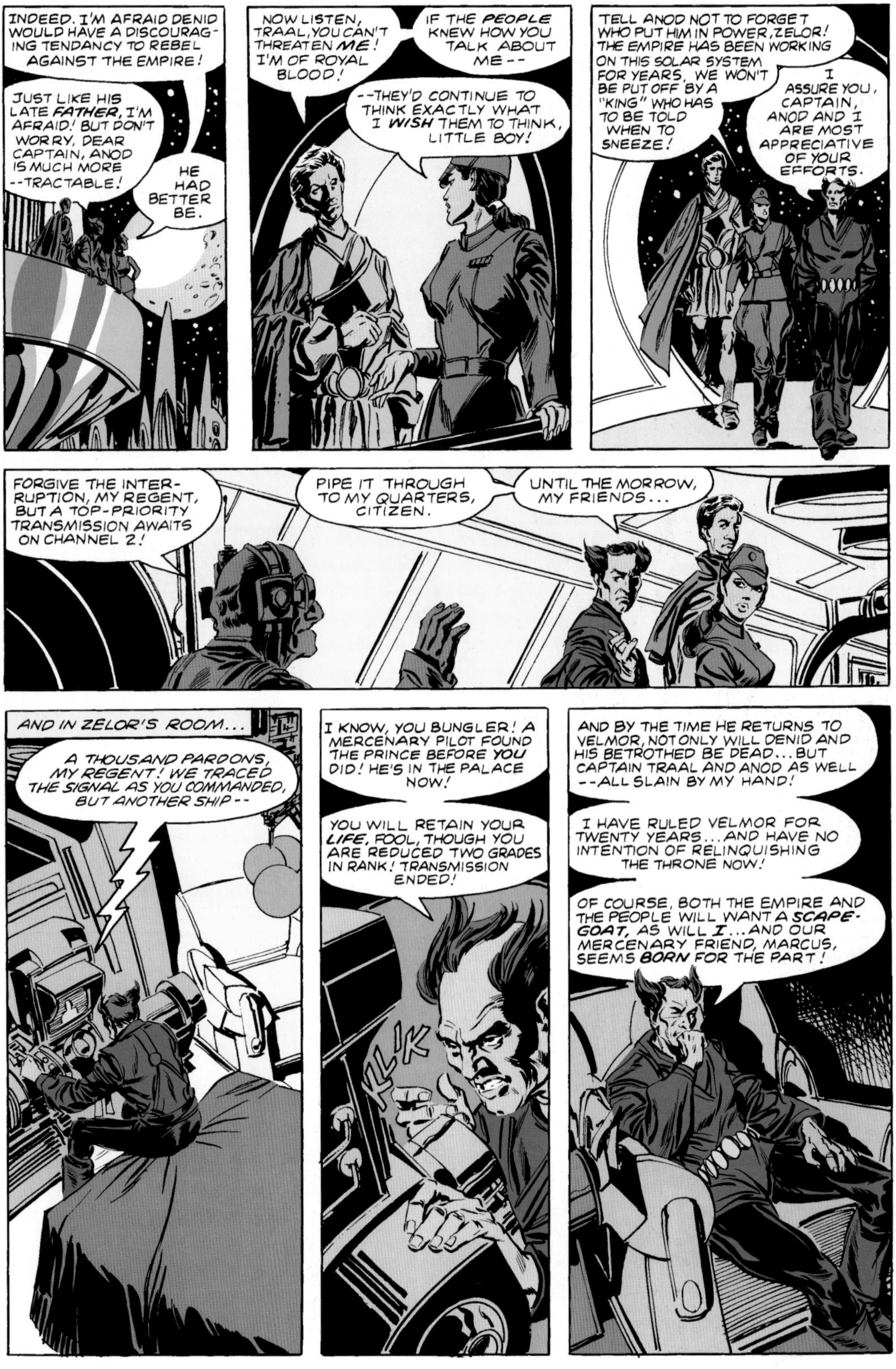
INDEED. I'M AFRAID DENID WOULD HAVE A DISCOURAGING TENDANCY TO REBEL AGAINST THE EMPIRE!
JUST LIKE HIS LATE FATHER, I'M AFRAID! BUT DON'T WORRY, DEAR CAPTAIN, ANOD IS MUCH MORE --TRACTABLE!
HE HAD BETTER BE.
NOW LISTEN, TRAAL, YOU CAN'T THREATEN ME! I'M OF ROYAL BLOOD!
IF THE PEOPLE KNEW HOW YOU TALK ABOUT ME --
--THEY'D CONTINUE TO THINK EXACTLY WHAT I WISH THEM TO THINK, LITTLE BOY!
TELL ANOD NOT TO FORGET WHO PUT HIM IN POWER, ZELOR! THE EMPIRE HAS BEEN WORKING ON THIS SOLAR SYSTEM FOR YEARS, WE WON'T BE PUT OFF BY A "KING" WHO HAS TO BE TOLD WHEN TO SNEEZE!
I ASSURE YOU, CAPTAIN, ANOD AND I ARE MOST APPRECIATIVE OF YOUR EFFORTS.
FORGIVE THE INTERRUPTION, MY REGENT, BUT A TOP-PRIORITY TRANSMISSION AWAITS ON CHANNEL 2!
PIPE IT THROUGH TO MY QUARTERS, CITIZEN.
UNTIL THE MORROW, MY FRIENDS...
AND IN ZELOR'S ROOM...
A THOUSAND PARDONS, MY REGENT! WE TRACED THE SIGNAL AS YOU COMMANDED, BUT ANOTHER SHIP --
I KNOW, YOU BUNGLER! A MERCENARY PILOT FOUND THE PRINCE BEFORE YOU DID! HE'S IN THE PALACE NOW!
YOU WILL RETAIN YOUR LIFE, FOOL, THOUGH YOU ARE REDUCED TWO GRADES IN RANK! TRANSMISSION ENDED!
KLIK
AND BY THE TIME HE RETURNS TO VELMOR, NOT ONLY WILL DENID AND HIS BETROTHED BE DEAD... BUT CAPTAIN TRAAL AND ANOD AS WELL --ALL SLAIN BY MY HAND!
I HAVE RULED VELMOR FOR TWENTY YEARS... AND HAVE NO INTENTION OF RELINQUISHING THE THRONE NOW!
OF COURSE, BOTH THE EMPIRE AND THE PEOPLE WILL WANT A SCAPEGOAT, AS WILL I... AND OUR MERCENARY FRIEND, MARCUS, SEEMS BORN FOR THE PART!

AND IF OUR YOUNG STAR-WARRIOR'S EARS AREN'T BURNING RIGHT NOW, IT MAY BE BECAUSE HE'S SOMEWHAT *DISTRACTED*...

IT'LL SERVE ME RIGHT IF I BREAK MY *NECK*, BUT IF CAPTAIN TRAAL SAW "KORL MARCUS" PAYING A MIDNIGHT VISIT TO "LADY LOREN" SHE MIGHT THINK MARCUS WAS TRYING TO *WARN* LOREN...

...AND SHE'D BE *RIGHT!*

SECURING THIS PLANET FOR THE REBEL ALLIANCE IS WORTH THE EFFORT! SINCE IT'S THE MOST INFLUENTIAL PLANET IN ITS SOLAR SYSTEM, WHICHEVER SIDE ITS LEADER SUPPORT, ALL THE OTHERS'LL FOLLOW!

WHOOPS, ALMOST TOOK THE FALL! BIONIC RIGHT HAND, I LOVE YOU!

≥UMPH≥ HERE WE ARE! WHILE I'M HERE, MAYBE I SHOULD ASK LEIA ABOUT THAT *MARRIAGE ANNOUNCEMENT* OF DENID'S, TOO!

NAH, WHY BOTHER? I'M SURE SHE'S AS MUCH IN THE DARK ABOUT IT AS I AM.

THERE'S A LIGHT ON, SHE MUST STILL BE--

OH, NO.

ANNOUNCING OUR "MARRIAGE" *WAS* IMPULSIVE, LEIA, ESPECIALLY WITHOUT YOUR KNOWLEDGE. IT JUST EXPRESSED A HEARTFELT WISH...

WHAT DO YOU *MEAN*, DENID?

I *LOVE* YOU, LEIA! MARRY ME, AND RULE WITH ME, AS MY QUEEN!

DENID, I...

HUSH, MY LOVE...

...DON'T SAY A WORD!

THE DAY DAWNS CRISP AND CLEAR, AS THE ROYAL STABLEHANDS GROOM AND SADDLE THE HUGE YCAQTS, PREPARING THEM FOR THE PRE-CORONATION GAMES! THE MASSES TURN OUT IN FORCE, EAGER TO GLIMPSE THE LIFE THAT COULD HAVE BEEN THEIRS, HAD THEY BEEN BORN TO THE PURPLE...

AND IN THE MILLING OF THE MASSES...

...A SURREPITITIOUS CONVERSATION CAN BE CONDUCTED...!

HSSST, LEIA, LOOK OUT! LAST NIGHT, TRAAL HIRED ME TO KILL YOU AND DENID, AND SHE MAY HAVE A BACK-UP!

TO KILL US....?

BUT LUKE, IF YOU KNEW ABOUT THIS LAST NIGHT, WHY DIDN'T YOU--

BECAUSE YOU WERE TOO BUSY PLAYING SPIN-THE-BOTTLE WITH DENID, THAT'S WHY!

MAY I BE THE FIRST TO CON-GRATULATE YOU?

LUKE, WAIT--!

SO LONG, "MY QUEEN"!

AND ELSEWHERE IN THE CASTLE...

YOU DO NOT REALIZE THE SEVERITY OF HIS CONDITION, C-3PO.

BUT I THOUGHT SURELY YOU COULD HELP HIM!

NOT EVEN WE MEDICAL DROIDS CAN WORK MIRACLES...THE HUMAN BRAIN CANNOT BE RE-PLACED BIONICALLY...

...AND HIS MIND IS DAMAGED BEYOND SIMPLE REPAIR!

NOW JEDI IS WITH HIS FRIENDS...

...BUT WHEN JEDI IS SURROUNDED BY EVIL, HE STRIKES...

DW-PEET WURP

NO, AN OIL CHANGE WOULDN'T HELP HIM, ARTOO! HE'S QUITE BEYOND THAT.

HE IS BEYOND ANY HELP...

...HE'LL NEVER HAVE A RATIONAL THOUGHT AGAIN.

THE MIST-SHROUDED DAWN BREAKS BLEAK AND CHILL, AS THE ROYAL PARTY PREPARES FOR THE CEREMONIAL HUNT...

CENTURIES PAST, THE *MRID HUNT* PLAYED A PART IN OUR PEOPLE'S SURVIVAL! BEFORE IMPORTANT FUNCTIONS, THE KING AND SPECIALLY CHOSEN GUESTS HUNTED THE BEASTS, IN PREPARATION FOR A ROYAL FEAST!

TODAY PRINCE DENID INVITES THE *LADY LOREN, PRINCE ARNOD, LORD ZELOR, KORL MARCUS* AND *COMMANDER TRAAL* TO JOIN THE ROYAL PARTY FOR TODAY'S PRE-CORONATION HUNT!

RELEASE THE MRIDS!

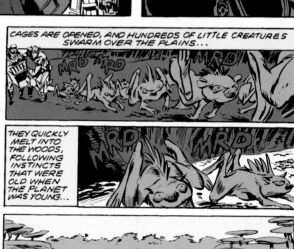

CAGES ARE OPENED, AND HUNDREDS OF LITTLE CREATURES SWARM OVER THE PLAINS...

MRD MRD MRD

THEY QUICKLY MELT INTO THE WOODS, FOLLOWING INSTINCTS THAT WERE OLD WHEN THE PLANET WAS YOUNG...

MRID MRID

...UNTIL, AT LAST, THEY ARE NO LONGER TO BE SEEN! AND AT THAT POINT...

...THE HUNT BEGINS!

TA-ROOOOO TA-ROOO

THE HUNTERS SPLIT INTO SMALL PARTIES, EACH FOLLOWING A DIFFERENT BEAST TO ITS LAIR. FOR HUNDREDS OF YEARS IT HAS BEEN SIMPLY A CEREMONIAL GAME...

...BUT THIS TIME, A HANDFUL OF PARTICIPANTS ARE PLAYING THE GAME IN DEADLY EARNEST...

SOME TIME LATER, WHEN THE ROYAL PARTY HAS STOPPED TO REST...

I'D FORGOTTEN HOW BEAUTIFUL MY PLANET CAN BE, LOREN, WITH FOG NESTING IN THE HOLLOWS AND--

DENID, LISTEN VERY CAREFULLY, BUT DON'T LOOK AROUND! WE'RE IN DANGER...

DO IT NOW, MARCUS ...FOR ME...!

ONE MOMENT, CAPTAIN--

--I'D LIKE TO TALK OVER OUR AGREEMENT A BIT MORE --AT MY CONVENIENCE!

WHAT ?!

AND THEN...

FRIEND MARCUS, ANOD AND I ARE SIMPLY ELIMINATING A FEW... OBSTACLES TO THE THRONE--

MY BLASTER! ZELOR, WHAT'S GOING ON HERE ?

--PRINCE DENID AND HIS LADY! ANOD, KILL THEM!

YES, ZELOR!

AND YOU'LL DIE NEXT, YOU FOOL!

UNNGGGH--

ZAPP!

AND NOW FOR MARCUS... OUR SCAPEGOAT!

YOU CAN'T DODGE FOREVER, MARCUS --GIVE UP!

YOU--YOU KILLED LEIA!?

DROP THAT BLASTER!

CRRRZZZ

W-WHAT KIND OF WEAPON IS THAT ?

THAT'S A LIGHT-SABER! AND-- HE CALLED THE GIRL "LEIA"!

NO, HE CAN'T BE...AND YET, HE MUST BE...!

ZELOR, DON'T KILL HIM! HE'S *LUKE SKY-WALKER!*

HE'S WORTH A SEAT ON THE EMPEROR'S COUNCIL TO ME, ALIVE!

UNFORTUNATELY, YOU'RE BOTH WORTH A PLANET TO ME--

--DEAD!

BUT CAPTAIN TRAAL MANAGES TO DODGE ZELOR'S DEADLY BLAST...

...AND SECONDS LATER HER LASER FIRE RIPS THROUGH THE TRAITOROUS ANOD...

YARRGH!

I'VE BEEN WANTING TO DO THAT EVER SINCE I LAID EYES ON THAT SLUG! NOW IF I CAN JUST FIND ZELOR AND SKYWALKER...

"...BEFORE THEY FIND ME!"

GIVE IT UP, SKYWALKER! I'LL MAKE IT PAINLESS!

"PAINLESS", HUH? THAT WOULD HAVE HURT LIKE BLAZES!

I'D BETTER GET OUT OF HERE... FIGURE OUT SOME SORT OF STRATEGY...!

LUKE FLEES INTO A WOODED HOLLOW, THICK WITH THE MORNING MIST...

...MIST IN WHICH HE MIGHT, FOR A MOMENT, HIDE... OR WHICH MIGHT CONCEAL A DEADLY ENEMY!

ZELOR AND TRAAL SEEM TO HAVE DISSOLVED THEIR "PARTNERSHIP", BUT BOTH ARE STILL AFTER ME!

AND WHAT ABOUT *LEIA?* IF SHE'S NOT DEAD, SHE NEEDS *HELP!* BUT THE INSTANT I SHOW MYSELF...

"...THEY HAVE A PERFECT TARGET!

"BESIDES BOTH TRAAL AND ZELOR KNOW THE TERRAIN--

"I DON'T.

"THEY BOTH HAVE BLASTERS--

"I DON'T."

BUT I HAVE SOMETHING GOING FOR ME *THEY* DON'T...

...THE BEST ALLY IN THE *UNIVERSE*...

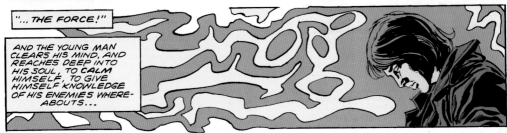

"...THE FORCE!"

AND THE YOUNG MAN CLEARS HIS MIND, AND REACHES DEEP INTO HIS SOUL, TO *CALM* HIMSELF, TO GIVE HIMSELF KNOWLEDGE OF HIS ENEMIES WHEREABOUTS...

AND AT THAT INSTANT, AT THE CASTLE, MILES AWAY...

YES, THIS PLACE *PLEASES JEDI,* IT IS FULL OF BEAUTY...

...IT--

WHAT.? THE YOUNG ONE --HE IS IN *DANGER!*

I MUST *HELP* HIM!

BUT-- MASTER JEDI... *SIR*...

YOU MUST COME *BACK!* WE'RE RESPONSIBLE FOR--

--YOU?

WHEET DA-VOOT

WHAT DO YOU MEAN, "*I'M* IN TROUBLE", ARTOO? MASTER LUKE PUT US *BOTH* IN CHARGE!

OH, HE'S GOING TO BE VERY ANGRY...VERY ANGRY *INDEED!*

461

MEANWHILE...

THERE IS SKYWALKER, AND HE DOESN'T SEEM TO *HEAR* ME!

I COULD SIMPLY BLAST HIM...

...BUT I MUCH PREFER THE IRONY OF RUNNING HIM THROUGH WITH MY ENERGY-SWORD!

GOODBYE, SKYWALKER!

THE ENERGY-SWORD BEGINS ITS DOWN-WARD KILLING STROKE...

WHEN, AT THE LAST SECOND...

NO!

IT'S IMPOSSIBLE! *NO ONE* COULD PARRY THAT BLOW!

CRRIZZ

JUST BE GLAD I'M ONLY TAKING YOUR *SWORD,* ZELOR--

--AND NOT YOUR *LIFE!*

UNNNGH!

BUT UNKNOWN TO LUKE...

I WANT SOME ANSWERS, ZELOR...

HE DOESN'T SEE ME...

...I CAN STUN HIM, KILL ZELOR...

...AND BE OFF THIS PLANET WITH SKYWALKER BEFORE THE LOCALS...

NO! YOU WILL NOT TAKE HIM!

WHO--?!

NOOO --URRRRK...

THERE IS A BURST FROM TRAAL'S BLASTER, THEN, IN A TWINKLING, IT IS OVER...

...AND SILENCE REIGNS...

J-JEDI, HE SACRIFICED HIMSELF, FOR ME--!

KEEP WATCHING HER, SKY-WALKER...

...AND I'LL--

I RARELY FIGHT TO THE DEATH EITHER, ZELOR...

...BUT IN YOUR CASE, I'D MAKE AN EXCEPTION!

CRZZ

YARRGHHH!

HE STILL DOESN'T SEE ME! IF I CAN ONLY REACH...

SORRY, CAPTAIN-- BUT IT'S OVER!

WHUD

...SOMEHOW, THIS VALIANT OLD MAN FOUND THE STRENGTH AND THE WITS TO SAVE MY LIFE... BUT LOST HIS...

...HE DID THAT FOR ME...THOUGH I SCORNED HIM AND DERIDED HIM IN MY HEART! HE LOST HIS LIFE, AND I LOST HIM!

EXCUSE ME...WE LOSERS WOULD LIKE TO BE ALONE!

D-DENID? WHAT HAPPENED?

ANOD TRIED TO KILL US, LEIA...BUT HE MUST HAVE SET HIS BLASTER ON STUN! POOR ANOD...HE WAS ALWAYS THE LOSER!

HE'S NOT THE ONLY ONE, PRINCE...

DON'T WORRY ABOUT TRAAL REVEALING YOUR WHERE-ABOUTS TO THE EMPIRE, LEIA ...WE'LL KEEP HER UNDER WRAPS UNTIL LONG AFTER YOU'VE GONE!

BUT ABOUT MY PROPOSAL...?

I'M HONORED, DENID...MORE THAN I CAN SAY...BUT MY PLACE IS WITH THE REBELLION!

I COULDN'T LOSE YOU TO A WORTHIER RIVAL! FAREWELL, LEIA!

FAREWELL, DENID!

SOON...

DON'T PUNCH US INTO HYPERDRIVE YET, ARTOO -- I'VE GOT SOMETHING TO DO.

SECONDS LATER, A SMALL, ROCKET-POWERED COFFIN ZOOMS INTO THE VOID, CARRYING THE BODY OF THE MAN WHO SAVED LUKE'S LIFE!

IT SEEMS A MEAGRE TRIBUTE, BUT IT IS THE ONLY ONE LUKE CAN GIVE...

...AND HE SPEAKS THE WORDS, THOUGH NO ONE ELSE CAN HEAR THEM:

I THOUGHT YOU WERE JUST A CRAZY OLD MAN, BUT I WAS WRONG. YOURS WAS THE SOUL OF A TRUE JEDI KNIGHT...

...THE LAST JEDI...

I PRAY THAT I MEET DEATH AS VALIANTLY AS YOU DID...

MAY THE FORCE BE WITH YOU, JEDI ...FOREVER!

NEXT

STAR WARS SPECTACULAR GIANT-SIZED FIFTIETH ISSUE!

THE CRIMSON FOREVER!